THE HOUSE THAT GEORGE BUILT

# The House That George Built

*With a Little Help from Irving,*
*Cole, and a Crew of About Fifty*

WILFRID SHEED

RANDOM HOUSE

NEW YORK

Published in the United States by Random House,
an imprint of The Random House Publishing Group,
a division of Random House, Inc., New York.

RANDOM HOUSE and colophon are registered
trademarks of Random House, Inc.

Portions of this work appeared in slightly different form
in *The Atlantic, GQ,* and *The New Yorker.*

All photographs courtesy ASCAP except for piano (page 3), iStock.com;
Richard Whiting (page 179), courtesy of Margaret Whiting; Jimmy Van Heusen
(page 225) by George Brich, courtesy of Brook Babcock/Van Heusen Music;
and Arthur Schwartz (page 301), courtesy of Jonathan Schwartz.

ISBN 978-1-4000-6105-1

LIBRARY OF CONGRESS CATALOGING-IN-PUBLICATION DATA
Sheed, Wilfrid.
The house that George built: with a little help from Irving, Cole,
and a crew of about fifty / Wilfrid Sheed.
p. cm.
Includes index.
ISBN: 978-1-4000-6105-1
1. Composers—United States.   2. Lyricists—United States.
3. Popular music—United States—History and criticism.   I. Title.
ML385.S582 2007        782.42164'0973—dc22        2006051030

Printed in the United States of America on acid-free paper

www.atrandom.com

2 4 6 8 9 7 5 3 1

FIRST EDITION

*Book design by Dana Leigh Blanchette*

*To the memory of*
*Harry Warren*

# CONTENTS

## Part Three
### The Stage—Broadway Swings

## Part Four
### Hollywood—The Sugar Daddy

## Part Five
### Survival on Broadway—
### The Curtain That Won't Stay Down

# A NOTE ON SOURCES

What follows is a labor of love, not a work of scholarship, which means that I have been researching it for most of my life without knowing it—starting at the family piano, singing and memorizing Irving Berlin's ragtime spin-offs, and ending with the last phone conversation with the last fellow addict fifteen minutes ago.

Although I've read every single word I could get my hands on, I'll spare you the list of out-of-date books, articles, and quotations that this represents in favor of a short list of people I've talked to, and in some cases sung with. The proper medium for studying the American song is, after all, neither the lecture nor the library but the sing-along and the rap session, or as it used to be called, the bull session, with its overtones of the tall story and the overconfident assertion.

In this offbeat branch of learning, the best research comes from the best bulls, and I have talked to some of the finest, including a handful who actually wrote some of the songs, one of whom tends to lead to another. In the late half of the 1960s, for instance, I lucked into the same building as the great lyricist Yip Harburg, and became, as one must with Yip, his devoted friend and fan.

Yip was never content just to leave the building and go on about his business. He invariably lingered in the lobby or in the open elevator doorway, pulling bits of paper out of his pockets, on which he'd jotted some verses about the day's news, and reading them with glee, or else telling me how his friend Harold Arlen was coping with his recent depressive breakdown. Mostly, though, he just liked to talk politics, so I was grateful that his other great pal and partner, Burton Lane, was also happy to talk about songs as long as I wanted, especially if the topic was Judy Garland, whom he discovered, or the Gershwins, who discovered him.

And it was there I also met a (recovered) Harold Arlen, quoted herein, and Arthur Schwartz, who told me how his partner Howard Dietz had greeted some life crisis or other with the repeated phrase "What is life but dancing in the dark?" "So," he said, "I dashed off the tune in twenty minutes." And I thought of the unusual soliloquy in the middle of that song ("What though love is old, what though song is old?" etc.) and I asked if *that* only took twenty minutes, and Arthur conceded that it actually took three weeks. (Songwriters' estimates of these things seem mostly designed to make a point. Irving Caesar's whole career couldn't have taken more than about an hour and a half, to hear him tell of it.)

Other great-talking writers were the lyricist-librettists Betty Comden and Adolph Green, whose work on *Singin' in the Rain* had made them both scholars of early screen musicals, and the lyricist Ed Eliscu, who had actually gone out there in the old days and lived the songwriting life.

The multiply gifted Stephen Sondheim told me over drinks what was wrong with Ira Gershwin, while Jerry Lieber, the rock poet, told me, over other drinks, what was good about him. And I agreed with both of them.

Another great source of information and atmosphere were a handful of songwriters' grown children, including Mary Ellin Barrett, whom I first knew as the excellent book reviewer at *Cosmopolitan* and only later as Irving Berlin's daughter and the author of an invaluable book about him; and Shana Alexander, the highly successful writer and daughter of Milton "Happy Days Are Here Again" Ager, who had happy memories of her various "uncles," Jerry (Kern), Harold (Arlen), and Harry (Warren). Shana also introduced me to her charming father, who told me that Ira Gershwin was upset about something I'd written (funny how he kept coming up). The singer Margaret Whiting didn't remember as much as I'd hoped about her father, Richard, but more than made up for it with her picture of Johnny Mercer, who virtually adopted her after Richard's early death. And I also met Mary Rodgers, Ellen Donaldson, and Irving Berlin's two other daughters, Linda and Elizabeth, who proved if nothing else that songwriters went in for girl children, and charming ones too. Over and against this, Hoagy Carmichael Jr. was also charming, and helpful and co-operative. But Hoagy had written two rich memoirs himself, *The Stardust Road* and *Sometimes I Wonder,* and I didn't want to make the whole book about him. So—I still owe Hoagy Jr. a phone call.

Another son I met was Dorothy Fields's only one, David Lahm, who became a first-rate cocktail pianist and gave me my jolliest evening ever by playing every song I could think of at a friend's birthday party, thus providing me the only chance I've ever had to sing some of those old lyrics that we all memorized automatically back then. And Michael Feinstein, who had served as an archivist to both the Gershwins and Harry Warren before he himself became a star, provided some great evenings too, playing and chatting and incidentally helping me to imagine Warren as if he'd been a relative of mine. Uncle Harry, indeed. Michael can also stand in for the gallant army of cabaret artists who crisscross the land like religious missionaries on a great crusade. All the ones I've talked to have doubled as scholars of the great songs and enthusiasts for their cause, spectacularly so in the case of Mary Cleere Haran.

And finally there are my two talkers-in-chief, Jonathan Schwartz and Jim Lowe, a couple of professionals who both jockeyed the classic discs for years at the legendary radio station WNEW, and have continued ever since to serve the old-time religion of great American songs every way they know how. Jonathan has compared our very first conversation (about songs, of course) to the longest baseball game ever played, a record we've broken a couple of times since, and Jim, as a neighbor, has hosted some of the best bull sessions of the twenty-first century—with himself at the piano, needing only a jug of moonshine on top of it to round out the honky-tonk scene. (In fact, I can't swear I didn't see one.)

I like to think of the book that follows as my contribution to the great bull session in the sky. So feel free to scribble in the margin in agreement or raucous disagreement.

If this great session ever settles anything, it has failed. But there's no chance of that. New verdicts are never more than just a song away. And the next song is no further away than your memory.

I must have sung a couple of hundred songs to myself in writing this book, and I hope it's contagious. And to invoke the mighty Irving Berlin for a moment, if the resulting book, or any part of it, "starts you tapping your feet, I'm happy" beyond words.

# I Could Write a Book
# if They Asked Me

The line has been stolen so often that I might as well steal it again. "This book," as somebody once said, "was not finished, it was abandoned"—and abandoned not just once in this case, but several times.

My most serious prior assault on this subject was to be a collaboration with the late Alec Wilder, who had himself just written the greatest of all books ever on the American song. Still, Alec was entirely in favor of helping a friend write another one. Our original scheme was simplicity itself, simply to assemble Johnny Mercer, and build the whole thing around him, in a series of conversations with fellow songwriters that would tell the whole story, from Irving Berlin to Burt Bacharach, and from ragtime to R & B and wherever we were that year.

Our scheming turned out to be quite Byzantine, because to begin with, Berlin no great friend of Mercer, who had probably slammed him with one boozy insult too many over the years, but he was a close phone pal of Harold Arlen, who was himself going through a reclusive phase just then, but might be smoked out by my own friend Yip Harburg. In short, Alec and I were having a high old time of it gossiping away while the clock ticked down and down and suddenly out.

"John is quite ill." I can still see Alec climbing onto our porch in the twilight to pass on this bleak bulletin. It seems that Mercer had suffered a stroke while riding a London bus, and might conceivably never be quite the same. And then, after a period of holding our breath, the call came. "John died today." In Alec's world, only two men were called by their baptismal names, John, and Francis Sinatra, which gave his voice a positively religious inflection as it spoke these last words.

And with that, Alec's heart seemed to leave the room for good. Although, theoretically, there were still lots of ways to do our damn book, Alec was not a theorist but an artist, and his vision had gone to black on the whole subject. If John could die, so could he, and he had better start work on his own testament while there was still time. And a curious testament it would turn out to be, including some imaginary letters to Francis, his other first-name friend, and a quirky account of his own personality. My friend Alec was indeed an anomaly: a proud man with a low opinion of himself.

Which left me with just the bare notion of rounding up some writers and talking to them. Big deal! And I was almost relieved to learn that someone else had just done this anyway, wonderfully well, thus supplying the only other essential book that I'm aware of on this subject. In fact, Max Wilk's *They're Playing Our Song* makes the perfect complement to Wilder's masterpiece, *American Popular Song: The Great Innovators, 1900–1950,* because it takes all the follow-up questions, such as, Who were these guys, and what precisely did they think they were doing?

This is obviously indispensable material, and when I met Mr. Wilk sometime later, I warned him with, no doubt, grating jocularity that I planned to rob him blind someday in my own book, to which he answered wistfully that I might as well do that since everybody else had. But fortunately the American song proved big enough for both of us and I haven't needed to pick on Wilk that much, except for a few priceless references to Jerome Kern and some aperçus of Johnny Mercer's, and perhaps some other bits and pieces. In the one case of Jule Styne, I felt that Wilk had done such a splendid job that there was no point in doing another one.

But was there really any point in doing another book either? And if not, what do you do with yourself next when you're all dressed up and have nothing to write? In my case, what you do first is sleep on it. In Sammy Cahn's favorite phrase, the words and music can always wait. "First comes the phone call."

And to my surprise it came, out of the blue. It seems that once upon a time some Italians had visited our apartment in New York and had later reported their surprise to find that Americans seemed to have a quaint custom of singing after dinner each night. And now their guide and translator of that evening, an old pal and editor, Alice Mayhew, was calling to talk about a possible book I might like to do on the great American songs. And I said yes, of course. I'd gotten the phone call, hadn't I? That was the hard part. So now just write the book. It will come to you as you go along.

And so it did, for years and years and years. It was as if I'd asked the Pacific Ocean over for tea one afternoon and couldn't get rid of it, and what's more didn't want to. But wasn't I getting tired of songs by now? No, I felt fresh as a daisy. Wouldn't I like to write about something else for a change? No, it's all in here, everything I want to say. How about an honest-to-God, full-court memoir while there's still time?

It dawned on me that that was exactly what I had been doing. Songs had lodged themselves in every hole and corner of my memory, reminding me of where I'd been that summer and what it felt like in the salty air or the misty light, and also what Hitler was up to just then and how far the Allied Forces had advanced in North Africa—from Tobruk to Benghazi, "From Natchez to Mobile, from Memphis to St. Joe." It was like finding a suitcase full of old letters and forgotten headlines: "Silk Stockings Disappear from Market" . . . "Nylon Needed for Parachutes" . . . "Women Take to Painting Their Legs." But "I walk alone." So who cares? So tightly are the tunes and the news intertwined that they recall each other; for example, in 1941 the baseball star Hank Greenberg was drafted prematurely to prepare the public for a war that hadn't started yet, and soon enough the hit came out that I, then aged ten, diverted to suit the occasion. "Somebody else is taking my place" went the song; "Somebody else is playing first base," I added, and still add, every time I hear it. And in fact I even remember being driven crazy by it on a hot Philadelphia night, but enough memory is enough.

Songs are circumstantial in ways that headlines can never be. I can remember perfectly things like the tree I sat in as I sang my first Latin American number, "The Breeze and I" it was called, and I can still feel the pebbles underfoot as my sister and I took turns with "I've got spurs that jingle jangle jingle" on the banks of the Delaware River, and can almost hear the piously empty streets of Wildwood, New Jersey, and hear myself muttering Porter's "Under stars chilled by the winter / Under an August moon . . ." (hey, that's a great line), and I realize that I wouldn't have remembered that tree or those pebbles and empty streets at all without the illumination of melody, which still turns on like a bedside reading lamp when I feel like remembering something.

The standards were not just about my private history, but about the whole country, concerning which they provide maybe the most trustworthy record we have. Americans are notoriously impatient with the past, and Hollywood epics used to be an international joke, so packed with anachronisms that at any moment you expected the ship's phone to ring and Columbus to say "What's buzzin', cuzzin" to his gorgeous sponsor, the queen of Spain. But then *sometimes* at the right moment, the band would strike up with a "Yankee Doodle Dandy" or "Battle Hymn of the Republic" and suddenly we were hearing the truth, as honestly as the arranger wanted to make it, but at least some kind of truth. And I still believe ardently in the "moonlight on the Wabash" and "Moonlight Bay," if not the moonshine in the scripts. In fact, if you combine a Mathew Brady photograph with, let us say, "Dixie," you are almost there, so long as you don't play it nostalgically. Once upon a time these songs were the latest thing, and that's what's so sad about them now. In this respect, the songwriter can be as crucial as the embedded photographer or reporter, and almost as precise in that, when you hear a George Gershwin tune, you are hearing not only the 1920s, exactly as they were, but the atmospheric difference between, let's say, 1924 ("Somebody Loves Me") and 1926 ("Someone to Watch over Me").

Somewhere along here, I bumped absentmindedly into my next question. "Who wrote 'Dixie,' anyway? And why don't I know?" There is surely no more atmospheric song than this one, but we've always been content to leave it there, up in the air. The whole South wrote it, that's who. But then, why do we know so much about the guy who wrote "My Old Kentucky Home" and "O, Susanna"? Probably the public didn't want to know about him either, at first. The minstrel shows that staged such songs were themselves the soul of anonymity, featuring both white actors and black ones disguised in identical blackface and singing the same allegedly black songs.

But Stephen Foster had found himself in a modern quandary that required a modern positively futuristic solution, which he only half came up with—or stumbled upon. As an upper-middle-class youth, he could hardly double as a blackface song-and-dance man. Not only was the stage the devil's playground, but there was no money in it by the Fosters' standards, and there wouldn't be so long as it stayed anonymous. So Foster's daddy became perhaps the first of many in here to say no to his son's ambitions and tell him that songwriting was a low-life waste of time. And Stephen became the first to prove his old man at least half-wrong, by making a truly huge amount of money for *someone*, if only his publishers, and a giddy, unprecedented reputation for himself out of selling his songs to the devil, and inadvertently selling his legend as well. How did a white boy from the Pittsburgh area know what it felt like to be an "old black Joe" on the plantation? The more his songs drifted loose from their minstrel ambience the more singular they seemed. The possibility that his darkies might have been just the usual stage darkies faded from mind.

Once the public has learned a new name, whether it be Stephen Foster or Sigmund Freud, we like to think of the subject as completely original, and not just as a working stiff punching a time clock. And incidentally, we also want him to have written everything, so we don't have to learn any other names.

But even the great Stephen Foster had to go through channels. Minstrel shows *were* popular music, the hot center or Motown of the horse-and-buggy era, and you either wrote for them or wrote more sedately for grown-ups and prayed that sheet-music sales would pick up.

You might almost say that Foster had to wear blackface himself to reach his maximum audience. And the role of his subject, the stage darkie, was simply to let it all hang out, to go to the furthest extreme of laughter and tears and especially of nostalgia, which goes so well with music. The audiences that laughed and cried in response were not predominantly black but white men who had brought their libidos along for an airing, before locking them up again in church the next day. And Foster's songs were so wholesome that you didn't have to confess them but could take them home to the family. His songs became so familiar to all audiences that his outline seemed to appear in them. There's a man in here! Tell me about him.

From that day to this, people have told and retold the short poignant life story of Stephen Foster in the form of books and movies and, just the other night, a TV special. Not that there is anything intrinsically interesting about a talented man drinking himself to death, but we do love to hear those songs again as much as we like to hear Christmas carols again every year.

So now if I could just find a few more Fosters, I might also find the answer to a question I'd been keeping at bay, namely, what is that interesting about *any* kind of writer? Okay, maybe if they ran with the bulls or danced in the Plaza Hotel fountain, like Papa Hemingway or Scott Fitzgerald. But if they just sat at a piano or desk with a pencil? Luckily some magazine editors, knowing of my interest in the subject, helped me out by asking me to write some review essays about the likes of Cole Porter, George Gershwin, and Hoagy Carmichael—but why? Weren't these names ancient history by now? And why not ask a trained musician about them?

Never mind. You don't ask editors such questions; they ask you these questions, usually just before hanging up. So I shut up myself and wrote the pieces and got the most mail I'd had in years. And I deduced from this small success that if you named a few familiar songs, these would form a kind of background music that would heighten the interest in everything you put in front of them. So the editors had found my Stephen Fosters for me, but there weren't that many of them, as I found when I tried out some other names on them. In this game, it seems you are either an immortal or a nobody.

And for a while after Foster, it seemed as if the nobodies had won. The nineteenth century went on about its business, attracting more and more songs out of more and more songwriters, but no more superstars, which led me to the curious conclusion, later confirmed by the movies, that the entrepreneurs were happy to exploit your fame once you had some, but were not going to raise a finger until then. Because for them the ideal audience wants Bing Crosby to create his own tunes and Bob Hope his own jokes as if they'd just that moment thought of them. Which meant, and still does, that the best road to the stars is to become one yourself and perform your own music, like George M. Cohan, or pretend it's your own, like some musicians today.

But in those days, before talkies and really good records, international entertainment was still pretty hit-or-miss, and Cohan's type of all-American songs did not come with a visa. (I'd never heard of them in England.) Foster's songs alone were contagious enough and so evocative of *something* in everybody to cross oceans and mountains, in the way that only music can, smuggled by absentminded whistlers and the kind of susceptible musicians who pick up everything lying around. As a small boy in England in the 1930s, I knew just two American songsmiths by name, Stephen Foster and Irving Berlin—who had apparently exploded some half century after Foster to write ten times as many hit songs and to live ten times as long, while creating and maintaining a more edifying kind of legend and becoming a kind of finger-snapping Benjamin Franklin for immigrants.

We surely wouldn't see anything like *that* again. And in fact we didn't quite. But we came close as, in fairly quick succession, America actually would hatch out two more names that everyone who was interested in anything had heard of at least vaguely, Berlin's occasional disciple, George Gershwin, and his most surprising one, Cole Porter, who proved that rich kids could make it too in this fabulous country; and also with a slight stretch of the rules, two more, the illustrious Jerome Kern, who'd been around a while but would assume a new kind of fame in Berlin's wake, and Irving's last rival, Richard Rodgers, although Rodgers would come in two parts, Rodgers and Hart and Rodgers and Hammerstein, one of whom you probably like much better than the other, but both of whom qualify in terms of quantity.

Which doesn't mean it had suddenly become easier. Looking more closely at the entrance requirements for this musical Mount Rushmore: Besides the quaint condition that each of them must have checked in on the public bulletin board by the end of the 1920s, with Cole Porter just making it and Berlin overlapping comfortably at both ends, there was also the nearly impossible criterion that each of them, except maybe Kern (who wrote some great, but quiet, theater songs too), had published more than fifty standards, by which I mean in this case more than fifty tunes that are still popular enough over fifty years later for most cocktail lounge pianists to have a rough idea of them, and for their copyrights still to be worth fighting for.

This is an astonishing achievement that would more than double or triple the world's total supply of singable tunes. Yet even more astonishingly, most Americans seem barely to have noticed it then or since. Although collectively it constitutes far and away our greatest contribution to the world's art supply in the so-called American Century, what the hell, they're still only songs, and this I'll admit is a limitation, because, apart from anything else, they're always over so quickly. During the time it takes to watch just one full-length stage play, you can have sung your way through the whole lifework of at least one major songwriter, and two for a Eugene O'Neill play. Elsewhere, these songs have been referred to as America's classical music, but if so, they are like a literature consisting entirely of epigrams and haiku, or at most sonnets.

So you're going to be hungry again in half an hour. And that's the limitation. Yet listening by chance to Vernon Duke's "Autumn in New York" last night, I thought, what would it *do* with more space? Oscar Wilde's one-liners are better than his plays. And what's wrong with being hungry again?

The more pressing question for the writers was, How did anyone get a chance to publish that much, and what did he live on while he was doing so? Clearly there must have been a happy moment when Murphy's Law was suspended and replaced by McGonnigle's Exception, whereby everything that can go *right* does so, beginning this time with the favoring winds and timetables that brought families called Baline and Gershowitz all the way from Russia to Ellis Island, as if in answer to some great casting call.

And then there was America's part in the Great War in 1917–18, a well-disguised blessing, which came along at just the right moment to pull the nation together and introduce us to each other, and for a giddy moment to the outside world as well.

"How you gonna keep them down on the farm after they've seen Paree," Americans sang nostalgically when they had to come home again. The farm was probably a lost cause by then anyhow, but maybe we could at least keep them in New York and make it a bit more like Paree, if only by filling it with foreigners and Midwesterners. Every great artistic movement needs a great city, and New York was more than ready, with both of its relevant thoroughfares, Tin Pan Alley and Broadway, already up and blazing, with kids like Jacob Gershowitz, aka George Gershwin, plugging songs, to kids like Frederick Austerlitz, aka Fred Astaire, of Nebraska, on the Alley. And with over five hundred theaters on the Great White Way providing all the publishing opportunities a genius could ask for, plus enough newspapers to hammer his name into the public consciousness, so that even if people didn't read the names on the sheet music, they read them in the gossip columns. And there was no better way to plug your latest hit than by showing up at the Algonquin (bringing along some funny lines by your press agent as well). Meanwhile sheet music for your latest darling might sometimes run to the same kinds of numbers as the hottest CD today, and theater, in the form of touring companies and sundry vaudeville spin-offs, circled the United States ceaselessly, distributing New York produce in bushel baskets, and naming the writers too, which counts at least a little on sheet music and a lot on playbills, but was about to count much less, as pop culture turned the next corner into the new technologies, which would be truly mixed blessings, making the writers richer than Croesus and more anonymous than the Unknown Soldier.

On the plus side, three of the hottest new developments, to wit, radio, microphoned records, and talking pictures, all addressed themselves squarely to the public's ears, and needed all the new music they could get their hands on just to strut their stuff. What they didn't need was the authors' names, unless, as noted, those names had already become famous. The phrase "Irving Berlin's latest" might actually sell a few tickets or records—not like "Bing Crosby's latest," but it was perhaps worth mentioning, while "Joe Schmo's latest" definitely wasn't. To take a sublime example among many, RKO bought Cole Porter's show *The Gay Divorce* largely on the strength of his name, then threw out all but one of his songs, the big hit "Night and Day," and actually went on to win the first songwriting Oscar with one of its own called "The Continental" by Con Conrad and Herb Magidson, whose names remain unknown even to trivia buffs who know what street Cole Porter was born on.

With the arrival of talking pictures, movie stars had quickly become, without much struggle, the only fixed celebrities in the American sky, sharing their space on a strictly temporary basis with such shooting stars as presidents, champion athletes, and the various Joey Buttafuocos of their day. Fortunately, complete cultural change never happens quite that fast, even today, and people with even the faintest interest continue to learn a few names, such as Harold Arlen, who had sort of "made it" in

New York and hence theoretically made it everywhere; and Frank Loesser, also of New York, and a few more who had had the wisdom or luck to appear on-screen themselves, such as Hoagy Carmichael, or to sing songs on radio and records, like Johnny Mercer. Duke Ellington played movie bits as a bandleader to help register his name on the national blackboard as something or other, so that his songs could move on to the next stage of recognition. In those days, the paleo-disc-jockeys just played songs without attribution until they came to one by a celebrity; then it became George Gershwin's "Soon" or Irving Berlin's "Always" or Duke Ellington's "I'm Beginning to See the Light."

What the mass media took away, or harshly rationed, in terms of fame, the songwriters of the period more than made up for in opportunity and money (thanks to their amazing union, ASCAP). Movies positively ate up new songs, not just in its deluxe Gold Diggers and Broadway Melody series but in odd items of the "Shirley Temple Goes to College" genre and nonmusicals like *Casablanca,* which needed *something* for Sam to play again, or like *Laura,* which just needed background music but wound up with a great title song as well.

Radio ate songs too, usually as provided by various big bands broadcasting from hotel ballrooms around the country, and by such shows as Bing Crosby's *Kraft Music Hall* and even by George Gershwin's own radio show, and Hoagy Carmichael's too, and who knows who else's radio shows. I can still remember a fifteen-minute slot that Dinah Shore had in the 1940s that seemed to feature a brand-new bad song every single day.

Thus, from the birth of radio circa 1922 until its death by TV and reruns in the mid-1940s, there was almost enough work for all the talent in a ballooning country, and all bets were off concerning the incidence of genius. "Who wrote that, George Gershwin or Cole Porter?" the crowd asks the piano player. But even if he's played an immortal song, the odds are that it won't be by either of them. Along with the great writers who get chapters to themselves in this book, I've dashed off a list of some fifty who have published at least two standards (see the Appendix), and I expect to hear of fifty more that I've overlooked. As with Elizabethan England and Periclean Athens, if someone will provide the stage and the cash, the genius will take care of itself.

There's musical genius and then there's verbal genius. To match the explosion in melody came a river of light verse that turned up everywhere, from the largest magazines to the smallest local papers, and it seeped into the most minor songs, guaranteeing some wonderfully literate and accomplished lyrics.

But—and here some readers and I may split—the tunes were still the big news. "Didn't they write great lyrics back then?" is a common question I've heard, to which I have two *Yes, but* . . . answers, one being *Yes, but* it's my impression that they still do. From Broadway to the Grand Ole Opry to the *Prairie Home Companion,* you still find good lyrics, and you will keep on finding them. So long as there are ears to hear, there will be tongues to wag and wit to flail.

But how long has it been since you heard a really good *new* tune—one, that is, that made your hair stand up? Compared with the dictionary, the keyboard is tiny, and a new tune is like a Sudoku puzzle that must be not only original but somehow comely. This rare achievement, however, seemed quite commonplace in the "Stardust" years.

My second answer is *Yes,* they wrote some great lyrics, *but* they also wrote some lousy ones. The standards didn't care. There have seldom been dumber words to anything than those of the young Ira Gershwin's "Lady Be Good" and "The Man I Love," while the Ellington-Strayhorn gem "Take the 'A' Train" barely *has* a lyric, only an address you wish would change from time to time.

On the other hand, there has never been a standard without a great tune—not even a great *funny* standard. Surf the Cole Porter songbook and you will undoubtedly find some great comic poems still waiting for the right tune to drive them off and make them rich and famous. But although Cole could have dashed off another two hundred choruses of "You're the Top," he couldn't have written a second tune to save his life. And without those magic tunes, his light verse was as unsalable as most poetry.

This doesn't mean the right lyric can't make all the difference. A lyricist is a musician too, one who arranges tunes for the human voice so that you can "hear" them for the first time. But once the lyrics have done that, and made you laugh or cry two or three times at most, they fade in importance. Again and again, people will request a favorite song while knowing only its tune.

To resort to a few more inches of memoir, at age eleven or so I liked the movie title song "It Could Happen to You" so much that I went right out and bought the sheet music just to have around, though I couldn't play a note of it. A few years later, I traipsed all over New York looking for a record, any record, of "There's a Small Hotel." Both songs have first-class lyrics, but I wouldn't have crossed the street just for those words. After all, I'd heard them once, hadn't I? And between songs, I'd swear I'd located the gold standard for words, though it was in a realm outside of music. Without making no-win comparisons, I felt that the poems of Keats and Byron, like the songs of Van Heusen and Rodgers, were a call to *do* something, if it was only to get out of my chair and maybe give a small whoop of delight. The world was a slightly better place now, and there was more where that came from.

Thus the tunes became for me and others of my age an entry-level art form. And with so many standards still pouring out, or being re-recorded, we became gluttons for melody and, within our limits, connoisseurs of it. When I read Alec Wilder's great book, I nearly always agreed with him, or at least I got to know in particular what he would *not* like, and why. So if I still didn't make it as an expert, I did have the makings of a snob.

Anyway, this book is no technical study. A life of Keats or Robert Frost doesn't depend on metrics. This is also a book about a time and place, America 1900–1950, in between the horse and buggy and the jet plane, and the men who wrote music that would still sound good on "Jupiter and Mars," and wherever we decide to fly to next.

Part One

The Piano Era

# The Road to Berlin

*T*here are several ways of defining and measuring an era, but an excellent place to start is by checking out the media of the day and what they could or could not do at the moment. For example, when sound recording first came along, the singers belted into it as if performing to an empty stadium. The name that springs to mind is Caruso, the world's biggest voice. But with the coming of microphones in the 1920s, singing became more personal, and the name became Bing Crosby, the world's friendliest voice. So songs became brisker and less operatic, to suit not only the mike but the piano rack and the record cabinet. In short, the familiar thirty-two-bar song, which now seems to have been fixed in the stars, was actually fixed by the practicalities of sheet-music publishing and confirmed by the limitations of ten-inch records.

Or one might define an era in terms of women's fashions and the consequent rise of impulse dancing on improvised dance floors. You can't really jitterbug in a hoopskirt or bustle. Swing follows costume, and the big news was that by the 1910s skirts had become just loose enough and short enough to liberate the wearer from the tyranny of twirling through eternal waltzes in ballrooms as big as basketball courts, and freed her to do fox-trots and anything else that could be done in short, quick steps on, if necessary, living room floors with rugs rolled up. So that's what the boys wrote for next. By the 1920s, the whole lower leg could swing out in Charlestons and other abandoned exercises. Songwriters celebrated that with a decade of fast-rhythm numbers. This has always been a dancing country, and never more so than in the Depression, when people trucked their blues away in marathons, or in seedy dance halls. "Ten Cents a Dance" was better than no income at all. And the Lindy Hop was as good as a gym class too.

And so on, through the arrival of women's slacks in the late 1930s and their increased popularity in World War II for both work and play—Rosie the Riveter could jitterbug on her lunch break without leaving the floor. All she needed was a beat. Which brings us with a final bump and a grinding halt to rock and roll and the totally free-form dancing of today, which can be done with no clothes at all to a beat in your own head while you're watching something else on television.

The huge, nonnegotiable gap between then and now is that in the past, music and dancing had always been disciplined by *something* or other. There had always been rules for doing it right, and even the wildest flights of swing and swing dancing had rested on a bed of piano lessons and dance lessons, and dress codes as well. Cab Calloway in a zoot suit was still a dressy man, a dandy; Cab Calloway in jeans or shorts over his knees would not have been dressed at all in the old sense. Going out dancing used to be an event, like going to church. Today all that remains are the rituals of prom night, which must seem weirder every year.

The era might also be measured in demographics or political cycles or even weather patterns. But the brilliant strand of music that, running through Irving Berlin and George Gershwin, has become *the* music of the standards began with a bang—with pianos being hoisted into tenements, a magnificent and noisy event, and it ended with guitars being schlepped quietly, almost parenthetically, into ranch houses and split-levels to herald the arrival of the great non-event that has been with us ever since.

But first the bang, then the whimper. There was no way of receiving such an impressive object as a piano quietly in such close quarters. Whether it bounced up the staircase or jangled its way over the fire escape and in through the window, the neighbors knew about it all right, and would be reminded again every time Junior hit the keys and shook the building. Short of a Rolls-Royce or carriage and horses, there was never such a status symbol, with the consequence that although "all the families around us were poor," said Harry Ruby, "they all had pianos." For such important matters, time-payments were born.

So the parents went into hock and found room for the damn thing someplace, and artistic Darwinism did the rest. You buy a piano for Ira Gershwin, and George is the one who plays it, although sometimes you had to live through a week of hell to learn this. As anyone knows who has ever housed a child and a piano, every tot who walks through the door will bang the bejesus out of the new toy for a few minutes, get bored, and come back, and back again, and bang some more, but then successively less and less until the dust starts to move in and claim it. . . . Unless the child finds something interesting in the magic box, a familiar tune that stammers to life under his fingers, or a promising and unfamiliar one; a chord that sounds good, and rolls out into a respectable arpeggio as well, with, saints be praised, a bass line that actually works for a bar or two— after which a gifted kid with an instrument is like a teenager with his first car and a tank full of gas. Where to, James: Charleston, Chattanooga, or Kalamazoo? Two-steps, or concertos, or parts unknown?

"Well, he'll probably settle down eventually," hoped the parents who had only bought the thing for the sake of respectability and maybe for some civilized graces around here. It speaks wonders for those parents in that era that they knew that being a famous lawyer or doctor wasn't enough in life. If you weren't a person of cultivation, you were still a bum.

But some of the kids insisted on being bums anyway, and sometimes the piano only made them worse. There were low-life uses for the instrument as well as high, and all the classical music lessons the parents could shout for weren't always enough to keep Junior out of the gutter, especially once ragtime had come along, in Frank Loesser's phrase, "to fill the gutters in gold." Talk about subversive—not even Elvis Presley rolling his hips had as many parents and preachers up and howling and sending for the exorcism unit as ragtime did. After all, not too many kids have hips like Elvis's, but anyone who could play "Chopsticks" or whistle "The Star-Spangled Banner" could syncopate, and in no time, as Irving Berlin bragged in two of his hits, "Everybody's doing it" in one form or another, from "Italian opera singers" learning to snap their fingers, to "dukes and lords and Russian czars," who settled for throwing their shoulders in the air and no doubt rolling their eyes. And there was no place to hide from it, even in an ivory tower. In fact, it would become a staple of B-movie musicals to show a professor at first frowning mightily as he hears the kids jazzing up a well-known classic, only to furtively wind up, beneath the gown or the desk, tapping his own foot too, as if the body snatchers had seized that much of him. And if the "professoriate" and the "long hairiate" couldn't stand up to it, the kid at the keyboard wasn't even going to try. Because this is where ragtime belonged, its birthplace, its office and its home, and the great Scott Joplin was still making tunes out of it, which maybe they could use in place of Czerny's finger exercises while no one was listening.

"What's that you're playing? That's not what you're supposed to be playing." Someone was always listening, and one imagines a thousand fights a day over this as George or Harold or Fats would stray once more from his scales and his Bach-made-easy and start to vamp the music of his pulse, the music of the streets.

Well, just because everybody was doing it didn't make it right. But remember: There was no other living music around except the music of the streets; there were no radios or records, or even talking pictures. Unless your parents took you to the theater, like Jerome Kern's, or to concerts, like no one I can think of, "good" music only existed in the form of hieroglyphs on a page, which meant that in effect it was a dead language, and a growing child could not survive on dead languages alone. So they listened instead to the sounds that seeped out of the vaudeville house rear

windows and under the doors of taverns, and to the riffs of the barrel or-
gans and ice cream trucks playing "Nola" and "The Whistler and His
Dog," and from the upstairs windows of the tenements themselves, where
seditious neighbors had actually acquired the latest sheet music and
couldn't wait to bang it out on their new pianos, for the rest of the community to swing to and curse.

But perhaps the most effective medium for spreading the new music
around were the average absentminded whistlers and hummers whose
names were legion in those days, and still semi-legion when I was growing up in the 1940s and '50s. In fact, I have a vague feeling I was one myself. Anyway, you had little choice about it. If you knew the music, you
whistled it, as if all the backed-up melody in your head was forcing its way
out through your mouth like steam from a kettle. And this medium was no
respecter of class or location either. As late as the 1950s, you could still
hear respectable bankers and businessmen in stark colors and homburg
hats whistling their way to work like newsboys or Walt Disney's dwarves.
The very last time I heard a recognizable tune being whistled all the way
through, it turned out to be coming from a natty distinguished senior in
the next booth of a men's room who was whistling while he whatever. By
that point in time, this man's whistling had become the only sound in a
quiet building, like a trumpet blowing "Taps" over an empty battlefield,
but imagine how that whistle sounded for the first time, back in the days
when the natty old man was still a scruffy old boy adding his two cents'
worth to the noise of the whistling businessmen and the cheerful whine
of the calliopes and the soughs of violins being scraped on street corners.

And then imagine how it all sounded to that other small boy trying to
get serious at the piano, but tempted like sin by the sounds of freedom
outside, all of which, from the barrel organ to the guy on the corner trying
to make a buck from his fiddle or harmonica, was at that moment syncopated. And it all went into Junior's ears and hands and came out again,
jumbled perhaps with Mr. Mozart's music or whoever was on the rack that
day for him to torture, and maybe with some verbal help from the wise guy
next door, the result might be a song that someday might sell like hotcakes
and cross the ocean too, until the whole world was playing and whistling
it and some of the bums whose parents had despaired of them became

very rich indeed, and the parents frowned and learned to tap their feet too, and moved uptown, where, thanks to their one very shrewd investment in a musical black box, they'd never have to work again. The piano lessons might have been wasted, but the hooky lessons were pure gold.

Or were the piano lessons really wasted? One of the proudest claims made for the American standards is that they were good music written by real musicians, however they got there, whether by studying at the best schools, like Kern and Rodgers, or by just listening, like Irving Berlin. Berlin never did learn the piano, but could spot a wrong note on the next block.

The school of "just listening" received an endorsement from the arrival of jazz in those years. The best jazz musicians created intricate harmonies without benefit of pencil or paper—disciplines that could take years to master at school. Classical lessons were still useful because they taught good from bad and what was good about good.

But playing hooky was vital—not just at the piano, playing Chopin and Brahms in ragtime, but playing hooky *from* the piano, just walking around and listening to the music of the city itself, which was experiencing a creative transformation right under these players' ears.

The same wave of good luck that had brought so many eastern European Jews to New York had also brought enough Southern blacks to mount a Harlem renaissance, and just like that, two of the principal ingredients had arrived. The standards have actually been referred to as a Jewish response to black music, but this definition is a loaded compliment that neither party has rushed to claim. With such praise, Jews never know whether to take a bow or duck. In a safe house like this book, it is the highest compliment I can think of. But in the mouth of a WASP supremacist like Henry Ford, "Jewish" meant un-American and subversive, so don't wave that compliment around or it might explode; and for blacks it just meant more of the minstrel-show syndrome. There go those darkies, making music again, haven't they got a great sense of rhythm? As outsiders, both Jews and blacks had been positively expected to entertain, but when they did so, it automatically became a second-class thing to do. Show biz in general was the ultimate club that accepted Groucho Marx and invited his scorn.

Music is not produced by whole groups, but by one genius at a time, and it may be significant that the two families that gave us Irving Berlin and George Gershwin both fled Russia on the same great wave of czarist pogroms, only to find American black people not only singing about a similar experience, but using the Hebrew Bible as their text.

Blacks too had been to heaven and back. They had found the promised land in the form of emancipation, and for a few giddy years the taste of freedom had been all the milk and honey they needed. But when they (and the white man) woke up, they realized nothing much had changed. The slaves had been moved to another part of the ledger. They would still be working for the boss, the pharaoh, but they would have to look for their own food and lodging now and pay for it out of their still-empty pockets. And somehow the boss seemed to have multiplied to include any white man who wanted a shoe shine or simply a glass of water. Just say the word "boy" to any African American, even today, and he'll remember.

Slavery had at least been a great cause that had bound them like brothers. "Let my people go," they had sung; but now they were only a people on special occasions, such as when sociologists wanted to talk about them. Otherwise, they were on their own and had to cut their own deals with the All-Mighty as well as with the Man (and the woman). So they invented the blues, which could reasonably be called spirituals with a hangover, secular spirituals to match the shabbiness and sour taste of Reconstruction. Resisting slavery had been a noble cause worthy of noble songs, but what could you sing about sharecropping except that your feet hurt and the roof leaked and your woman had just left for a cat with more bread, or your man had split for a fox with a fancy wig and a lying heart?

But was that always so bad? "I'll be glad when you're gone, you rascal you." From the first, there was as much irony as heartbreak in the blues, and by the time you got to Bessie Smith, these were funny songs. And the famous song "Basin Street Blues" is actually about losing the blues and celebrating with a blues beat.

In other words, black music was losing its specific folk content and meeting the white man halfway—or getting taken over, if you prefer. (In a lawsuit over cultural rights, the Jews could always demand their Bible back.) The five-minute promised land of emancipation would be stretched indefinitely into the fixed smile of Dixieland, which became Tin Pan Alley's image of everybody's Great Good Place where you arrived by choo-choo train, not cattle car, and the magnolias blossomed 'round *every-body's* door. The signature entertainer of the Dixieland years was a Jew wearing blackface, and there was no insult involved. It was one showman imitating another, and I've always wondered about the true color of Al Jolson's Mammy. By the time Bing Crosby began imitating Jolson, the blackface was understood and no longer had to be painted on—on Bing, or later on Elvis.

One striking bond between Berlin and Gershwin was their over-the-top love of their new country. "God Bless America," wrote Irving, with all his heart. And George, who thrived between the wars when patriotism was quieter, nevertheless said, "My place is America and my time is now" because it was clearly important to him, a statement of intent. Other new Americans, such as Italians and Irish, still sang the old songs, or new songs (like "Galway Bay") that pretended to be old songs.

But after enough pogroms, you haven't all that much to sing about. It's time to start over, as insiders this time, and in the first country that has ever asked you in. It has been suggested to me by someone who listened closely that Gershwin actually sounds more Russian than Jewish. But George wasn't familiar with either genre from his nonmusical household. He was only trying to write American as it sounded to a new arrival in a city of foreigners.

The result was American music through a distorting lens like El Greco's. To get there, George had rounded out his classical lessons by vamping regular American pop on Tin Pan Alley and finally by going to Harlem and hearing some real American music from such great jazz pianists as James P. Johnson and Willie "the Lion" Smith, whom he would later invite back to his apartment for informal concerts—a gutsy thing to do back then. But he owed them that much.

Gershwin was the last link in the chain that led to the standards, which were almost all written from 1925 to 1950. But to get to George you have to pass through Irving, who walked the streets first and founded the unofficial New York School of Song, which would eventually stretch to California without losing its accent, and would pretty much commandeer the word "standards" for its own.

And if this school had a motto and a golden rule, Duke Ellington phrased it early on: "It don't mean a thing if it ain't got that swing." All the standards harkened back to the kid kibitzing at the piano, although all those pianos were not delivered to the Lower East Side, whose reputation in fact rests largely on the one that was *not* delivered to Irving Berlin himself. And several fine standard writers, such as Victor Young and Matty Malneck, actually began swinging on violins.

But the piano remained the instrument of choice and favored home companion. Incredibly, syncopation remained the preferred means of rebellion and escape right through the Depression, which prolonged the Jazz Age by the sheer force of house-to-house inertia. People wanted at least one chance to live like Fred Astaire before they switched to something new. And then World War II gave swing, its latest name, a couple more great years, because you can't change music in midstream. After which, nostalgia held back at least some of the tide until the great writers had time to empty their trunks, leaving us the incredible body of work called the standards.

It is perhaps worth adding that even at their peak the standards never quite had the national stage to themselves. Jule Styne told Max Wilk of hearing a whole different Hit Parade as he drove west in the Golden Age, but even in New York some great Broadway songs, like "My Funny Valentine," didn't make the Hit Parade at the time, while other nondescripts, like "Three Little Fishes" and "Deep in the Heart of Texas," did.

Time, and records, and great musicians have all been kind to the standards, which live on in cabarets as sheer entertainment. Because they still have "that thing." The English critic Benny Green deplores the phrase "jazz song" on the grounds that jazz is a process, something you do *to* music, not the music itself.

True enough. But some songs are friendlier to jazz than others—as witnessed by two songs by Victor Herbert: "Ah, Sweet Mystery of Life," which just sounds silly if syncopated, and "Indian Summer," which Jimmy Dorsey and his band could swing into a national success.

Is there a word for this kind of innate swingability? The pianist Dick Hyman refers to a "built-in syncopation," which even he couldn't locate, but which even you and I can't miss. Louis Armstrong famously said of jazz, "If you have to ask what it is, you'll never know." So much for definitions. "Jazz song" is just a quick way of saying what can't be said anyway, and I've used it loosely throughout, wincing slightly on behalf of Mr. Green every single time.

To sum all this up in one sentence or so: Jazz songs were the pop music of the Jazz Age, and talented kids wrote them as naturally and spontaneously as they would later write rock songs. And when the songs lost "that thing"—or acquired a different thing—the era ended. The old piano left the building, taking its music with it.

# Irving Berlin:
# The Little Pianist Who Couldn't

IRVING BERLIN

*I*f one picture is worth a thousand words, what price a great bar of music? Or a pointed facial expression?

Fortunately, the cost of such items is not fixed. And while some pictures actually are priceless, some expressions truly are blank. Perhaps the most talkative picture I've ever come across is a small snapshot of a child that I had the good luck to glimpse one day—without a caption. Who *was* this? I had just time to ask myself, but the answer was already waiting. This picture of a young Irving Berlin was not just *worth* a thousand words, but it told you exactly what they were, to wit: Genius. Music. Russia, or one of those places. (Hungary? That was the other place.) Violin? Probably, because that's what they played around there, although a piano is possible. And, of course, his music would be classical. Just look at all that hair.

Well, that's one facet that has changed. Long-haired music is not what it used to be. But this kid is no mop-top either. That extra hair is there expressly to run one's fingers through while thinking about classical music.

But suppose, for the sake of argument, that this kid never heard any classical music and isn't about to. . . . What might become of him then? Mathematics? Perhaps, but only if it is set to music. To save him from that, one more question. What kind of music *does* this little boy hear? It turns out that he hears some synagogue chanting from his father, who is a cantor, but Papa dies when little Isidore Baline is just eight, and after that he hears nothing but street junk. Is there hope?

Since this is New York, that musical junk was at least the junk of all nations, and all corners of this one: Manhattan folk music contained a bit of everything, and all of it came with words. So could he combine this with Jewish music?

The one thing that Izzy Baline knew about music was that he'd better start making money out of it at once or move on to something else. Immigrant life was hard enough even while the breadwinner was still winning. With their father dead, the eight Balines were so broke, even by Lower East Side standards, that they couldn't even afford a piano. Indeed, they couldn't even afford Isidore, who could barely squeeze himself in at night and out again in the morning with that head of his so full of music and money—a combination that would never leave him, no matter how much it might later hurt his reputation. The critics could consider him a hack, but talk is cheap, and a "cheque" (as we say in England) is worth more than a compliment any day—it costs more and is more sincere. For Irving, honor would begin with paying his own way in life, and he never committed the basic dishonesty of claiming to write for art. He told his friend Cole Porter, "Never apologize for a song that sells a million copies." Like other children who have had to work to survive, part of his young mind became a little old man, who saw nothing at all funny about money.

So he hit the streets and began, of course, to run errands and sell newspapers—was there any famous American who didn't hawk papers back then? And he would also sing songs to anyone who would hold still for him, either in friendly cafés or on street corners while his audience waited for the cars and horses to go by. Raised on street music, he was now returning the favor, busking for a while with an old minstrel memorably called Blind Sol, who also played the city by ear and who perhaps afforded Izzy some protection in saloons, where it was probably bad luck to throw out blind people. After that, Izzy acquired his master's degree in the school of hard knocks and sweet music by working for Harry Von Tilzer, the legendary writing publisher. Plugging Harry's latest in theater balconies, Irving learned the arts of self-promotion and rights of use.

Thus, before he had written any songs at all, he knew everything about how to sell them. Soon he was old enough to work the city's fancier joints, and street-smart enough to know which ones they were. His next port of call was as a singing waiter at a fashionable Chinese place called, jarringly, Nigger Mike's, where he did what the job said, he sang and he waited, though not for long. Pretty soon the perfect fish swam into view: one Prince Louis of Battenburg, who would soon become a Mountbatten when the German image turned ugly in 1914. He gave Izzy an uninflated five-dollar tip for his combined services. This in turn gave Baline a heaven-sent chance to turn it down on the grounds that serving such a noble fellow was its own reward. Nearby, an ambitious young reporter called Herbert Bayard Swope took it all down, giving both himself and Irving a leg up with a piece in the next day's paper describing the episode—thus a new generation of hustlers was born.

All Irving needed now was some published songs of his own, preferably both words and music, because as a lyricist he would only have been a minor legend at best. Although it was obviously quite a feat for an unschooled immigrant kid to write good lyrics in what amounted to a second language, it happened so often you have to notice certain advantages as well. The syntax and vocabulary of pop songs were pretty close to those of the streets anyway, but were so far from the kind taught or even allowed in the classroom that maybe the less classroom the better. And as for Izzy's understanding of American life, he wouldn't need much of it to write his first hit lyric (the title of which is "My Wife's Gone to the Country, Hurrah, Hurrah"). Most lyrics are simply verbal clichés about emotional clichés, so once again maybe the less you know the better. And it is not surprising that several of the wittiest lyricists, such as Gus Kahn (Germany), Al Dubin (Switzerland), and Lew Brown (Odessa), were all born into foreign-speaking families in foreign-speaking lands. And purely as lyricists, each of them was, I believe, as good or even better than Irving.

As for the other point of the story, that he'd been discovered as a singing waiter in a Chinese saloon—where better? There was no "normal" way to bring on these epiphanies, but Nigger Mike's was at least close to the heart of the Lower East Side school of music. The real miracle would have been to start in a place like Peru, Indiana, like Cole Porter, or be sent to Poland on a violin scholarship at age ten like Victor "I Don't Stand a Ghost of a Chance with You" Young. And while a name like Nigger Mike's might cause a sharp intake of breath now, Irving Berlin's own song "Cohen Owes Me Ninety-Seven Dollars" would be *breathtakingly* anti-Semitic coming from someone else. (The singer is dying, but he doesn't want to let his debtors off the hook that easily.) But Irving was just proving himself a good sport, the highest accolade an immigrant could hope for. New York in the early twentieth century was not so much a melting pot as a chafing dish, and if Irving could seem abrasive in later years, it's worth remembering that he was rubbed raw himself at an impressionable age.

Berlin's first commercial hit set to his own music was called "Dorando" and was written in crass Italian dialect that consisted mostly of adding an A to everything, as in "the sonna of a gunna no runna." The news item that had inspired it concerned a quite gallant marathon runner who had recently collapsed while entering the Olympic stadium and been carried across the finish line by his fans. But in Irving's version, a sniveling Dorando comes up with a ridiculous excuse for this: He has been tricked into eating Irish stew instead of "da spaghetts." ("And dats why he no winna.") The tune is second-drawer Berlin, which is to say facile and professional and lacking any trace of genius until you put them all together. Soon he would be able to produce such songs on demand and in his sleep, which made it a useful second drawer to have.

By 1911, Irving earned his MBA in music by acquiring a publisher-cum-partner to facilitate the flow, and with that he exploded onto a new level. The triggering device was "Alexander's Ragtime Band," a song that he himself didn't appreciate immediately, but which caught on so thoroughly wherever it was played that it seemed like a standard before its time. It is called a rag because the title says it is, but it is in fact a hybrid with a syncopated verse and a marching chorus. With that in the bank, he then set out to write some regular rags. Suddenly, one hit seemed to run into another, just as they did on Henry Ford's assembly line. In his erudite book on Berlin's first songs, Charles Hamm shows how thoroughly the young man had absorbed all the pop formulas. It was like someone learning to dance with a booklet in his hand telling him where to put his feet. But this is where the miracle kicks in, for the novice suddenly begins to dance like Fred Astaire. And if everyone else has the same instructions, why is he the only one doing it? What has he added to the lesson?

Irving never really found out, but he kept on making music, better and better, while apparently becoming more and more convinced that, like some fairy-tale character with a magical gift, he might lose the knack if he asked too many questions. In this, he was fortified by his superbly well-trained contemporary Victor Herbert, who also advised him not to learn any more about music. He never did.

And in all the years since, no one else has been able to say whether he made the right decision, or even exactly what he was doing so very right on his own. After a bar-by-bar search, Alec Wilder swears that he can find no personal musical mannerisms in Berlin, and yet I'm certainly not alone in being able to spot an Irving Berlin tune every time. The same goes for his lyrics—which seem not so much brilliant as inevitable. They simply come with the notes. "Everybody's doing it," but of course they are. It says so in the tune.

At first, observers may have supposed that Irving's genius was entirely wrapped up in the latest thing, ragtime, in which case he would probably grow out of it. At his most introspective, he would never call his gift anything but a knack, and knacks never know what they can do next until they've already done it.

Irving himself may have wondered too. But before time could tell anything, Berlin's life took another turn that launched him willy-nilly into a second legend. Later on, Irving would acquire a reputation for fierce publicity-seeking, and no doubt he always knew the value of the stuff. But at this stage, he began to demonstrate another law of American life, which says that just as money makes more money in a capitalist society, so do legends beget legends.

In fact, Irving decidedly did not want the next bit of attention he got. In 1913, he had married a young lady called Dorothy Goetz, who promptly died after contracting typhoid fever right after their Cuban honeymoon. Irving was heartbroken and wrote his first successful ballad in mourning, which would indicate a life beginning after ragtime. But because legend calls for a *great* ballad, posterity has conspired to overrate this particular song. In the cold air of the morning after, "When I Lost You" has the ring of a barroom tearjerker yanked from Irving's second drawer. Few if any great songs have ever been written on demand or for an occasion. The muses prefer your undivided attention. And when they've got it, they'll probably send you a funny song, as they did several times that year to Irving. Save the sad stuff until you feel better.

Which was fine so long as the funny songs sold enough copies. Irving's actual response to grief was maybe the sanest possible one, which was to work harder than ever, on every aspect of the business, from his own publicity to the publishing of others, which kept him right in the middle of the swim as his rivals mailed him their distillations of the latest sounds. As Irving Berlin, Inc. (he shed the partner), he promoted the whole profession, not just one writer at a time—but in the form of a new craft union that protected last year's songs as well as the very latest, thus making a real, full-time profession possible. So even colleagues who found him outrageously self-centered owed him something for his crucial support of ASCAP at the creation.

But Berlin himself certainly didn't get overlooked either. And I was startled to realize that less than a year after his wife's death he went barnstorming through England as the King of Ragtime—a title that seemed easier to claim over there, but wasn't. The British public might not have known much about ragtime, but they were sufficiently weaned on the minstrel tradition to know that whoever the king was, the beat itself was black. The joke went into permanent circulation that Irving kept a little black boy in his trunk to help him out with it.

In fact, Irving kept his black friend closer than that, never went anywhere without him. Whatever he'd heard as a boy in Harlem was part of him now, although he used it more on some days than others.

Even more then than now, triumphs on either side of the Atlantic automatically reverberated to the other, so that by the time Irving came home to write his first Broadway show, called *Watch Your Step,* he was an "international star," and not just in the sense that an airport with one flight to Canada becomes international. The name Irving Berlin seemed to have translated catchily into French and German as well, and his geopolitical timing was perfect: The world was about to enter the first of its great wars, and wars, the bigger the better, have a tendency to freeze the music of the moment and give it abnormal weight and duration. (How long would "Tipperary" have lasted in peacetime, or "When Johnny Comes Marching Home"?) "Alexander" seemed like a natural anthem, "so natural that you want to go to war" all dressed up and ready to go. But it wasn't just a matter of hits. By sheer dint of fertility, Irving Berlin had done more than anyone by then to secure the beachheads of the dance floor and the music rack for his own kind of lightly syncopated, semi-black, and faintly Jewish melodies, which may seem like nothing but housebroken jazz nowadays but constituted the light at the end of Gatsby's dock for all the fresh young geniuses waiting in the postwar world.

And what the Great War, as it was called, did for his songs it double-did for his legend. By chance, a rival sharpshooter called George M. Cohan had virtually cornered the corn market on patriotism with "You're a Grand Old Flag," and on team spirit with "Over There." So Irving went around to the back with a song about the little guy in the trench and about the particular blahs of reveille, the trumpet call that jerks you out of bed just as you are falling asleep every night.

Later on, insomnia would actually prove to be Irving's defining nightmare and his downfall, so it's nice to know that he got not only a bestselling hit out of it ("Oh, How I Hate to Get Up in the Morning"), but a touchstone song for two wonderful wars. Personally, it dawned on Irving with his first bugle call that the only way to get away from this noise was to blow his own horn even louder, and he let the army know immediately that the famous Private Berlin was available to do a benefit show for this very army that would put it on the map and raise recruitments to infinity.

"Operation Chutzpah" one is tempted to call it. But who knows how much purebred government-inspected ham lurks in the hearts of generals? Irving would get his way completely in both wars and en route become what he wanted most in the world to be: a great American citizen-songwriter who had paid his dues and would reap untold rewards, in the form of a national Irving Berlin Day in 1919. He'd won so much glory by the end of World War II that there was suddenly nowhere to go but down, and plenty of time to get there.

But that truly is another story. Not the least legendary of Irving's feats was to live to be one hundred, by which time all guarantees can be assumed to have expired, but running the tape back to, let's say, his thirty-first birthday in 1919, one finds what should be by all rights a happy, completed man. *Yip Yip Yaphank* had just brought off the ultimate triumph in street smarts, and in the course of it Irving had quietly made the army over in his own image, by turning his whole base into a wing of Broadway, where several postwar theatrical careers would get their start and Irving would get at least one first-class client for his publishing house, namely, Harry "Three Little Words" Ruby.

Berlin had, in short, passed through World War I like a rattlesnake through a cobra, emerging intact and ready for its next adventure. Which would come, of course, immediately, when Irving was offered part ownership of a Broadway theater called the Music Box, to do what he liked with. By now it seemed that the very name "Irving Berlin" that he'd plucked from the air one day to replace Izzy Baline had become his greatest creation and was already worth its weight in old-world titles. It was plastered all over postwar New York and London: words by, music published, produced, and staged by, and even in a pinch sung by Irving Berlin. He could do everything for a song except play it properly on the piano, and even this had become a story; the kid who couldn't even afford a piano to learn the white notes on could now afford one that played only black ones.

At a later date the word for all this might have been megalomania, and he'd have been advised to drop at least a few of his stars and ribbons. But success stories were steaming hot, and since he was being compared to the likes of J. P. Morgan and the ghost of John Jacob Astor, he offered a welcome change. Speaking as a willfully unsuccessful schoolkid of the period, I can personally report the relief of finding a rich songwriter among all the steel magnates and money managers. "I'd rather lead a band," said Irving, and every time I heard it, my own prefrontal lobes and cerebral cortex would break into spontaneous applause.

A cynic might interject here that Irving had gotten over his broken heart pretty thoroughly by this time, but the fact is that he hadn't really.

So far as anybody knows, he lived a completely celibate life for over a decade, abstaining from even the showgirls who were considered virtually part of a songwriter's salary. (Like heads of state, the writers were deemed to be just dispensing favors to the little dears.) His love songs during those years tended to be anything but sexy. "A Pretty Girl Is Like a Melody" sounds wistful at best, while "All Alone" and "What'll I Do" sound downright desperate.

But then a young woman at a dinner party told him one night that she loved his song "What *Shall* I Do," and the spell was broken. Ellin Mackay's gentrification of his song title defined in one word what a different world she came from and what a perfect romantic-comedy couple they would make together. And she was drawn to him like a moth to a flame, a fan to a movie star, or a reporter to a good story, while attracting him right back insofar as convention permitted. "A man chases a girl until she catches him," he would later write, describing and obviously approving of this process that had somehow freed him from the bonds of his own past, making him again a young lover capable perhaps of writing real love songs.

The first thing to be said about Ellin Mackay and the family Mackay is that they were not an old New York family themselves or even a famous new one, but just anonymous new money from the Midwest, which made them outsiders too. And as a sometime writer for the new "in" magazine, *The New Yorker,* Ellin knew where the real balance of social power lay those days. "I was the one who was marrying up," she would say succinctly, and as far as the headlines were concerned, she was embarrassingly right. "Irving Berlin Pursues [Weds, Elopes with, whatever] Heiress." Not the Vanderbilt heiress or the Rockefeller heiress, just "the heiress," which in the new café-society aristocracy meant "the nobody," "the extra," "the pawn."

What she could not have known, because it was unprecedented, was the sheer size and force of the wave of curiosity that was about to hit her because of Irving, or how little control either of them would have over the public story.

One could define the twenties and thirties as the start of the information era, overlapping the last days of King Print. In other words, everything was out there now, but the only way to immediately hook into it was through a primitive device called the stop press, which teletyped scraps of breaking news onto a corner of the front page. So while people might dream about wristwatch radios and such, what they still actually did was buy newspapers all day long, to follow the stock reports and the latest from Flamingo Park and Ebbets Field and to keep up with whatever stories the press had goosed up and strung out into national dramas. "Jury Is Out in Scopes Trial," "Jury Is Still Out, Foreman Sneezes" snaps the stop press while the rest of the paper struggles to come up with fresh angles and aperçus that made it all worth reading.

"Stop the presses! Get me rewrite!" Newsrooms in the movies always seemed like outpatient clinics in mental hospitals. And what in the world could be so important? Well, it was a question of whether *The Sun* could beat *The Star* by an hour to the latest fragment of trivia from today's hot news story. Like much else in the twenties—marathon dancing, flagpole sitting, and so on—journalism was both redeemingly silly and casually cruel.

"Names make news," as Henry Luce decreed when he founded the first newsmagazine in 1925. And if you happen to have a famous name like Irving Berlin, you could become a hunted man or woman overnight as reporters from all over the country lined the docks and train platforms like so many bloggers scavenging for stories, after Clarence Mackay gave them a perfect lead by refusing to give his consent to his daughter's marriage. Irving and Ellin did the rest by eloping anyway, bringing into play those great 1920s stage sets, namely, ocean liners and first-class hotels.

In fact, Clarence's opposition to a wedding between his Catholic daughter and a Jewish show business legend fifteen years older was inevitable and so reasonable that Irving himself would claim to understand it. At that point, Lutherans thought twice about marrying Methodists, while Jews and Catholics viewed even their own members with squinty-eyed suspicion (Orthodox or Reform? Rich or poor?). And since Irving had no wish to put on a public show, or an uptown version of *Abie's Irish Rose*, the press itself had to do most of the hard work.

They had plenty of clichés at the ready to help them out. The moment after Clarence unwittingly unleashed the hounds of publicity, like Buster Keaton tripping over a loose wire, the world knew everything it wanted to about him. He became the eternal fuddy-duddy and snob that every generation needs, the cartoon character with "Old Fool" practically printed on his back. The role of an American upper class has never been that clear to most people anyway, but one of its functions has always been to be laughed at, and when the joke wears thin, to be sneered at too, in this case for anti-Semitism, which doesn't seem to have been a real issue. Anti-Semitism has always made so little sense in this nation of outsiders that it loses almost all its spice when mixed in with our real religion, Celebrity.

Anyhow, the story ended delightfully for the public when the self-made Jewish songwriter had to bail out the huffy millionaire in the Depression. ("Poor Clarence is down to his last four million," as my father overheard someone say.) And it ended well enough for Clarence too, who would cut a benign, slightly fuzzy figure as Grandpa, a role he was born to play. Ellin's scorecard was more mixed.

She had won her battle of wills with her father, but how could anyone tell when he or she had won around here? Irving took her to the Algonquin Round Table, where she found herself a nobody, Irving's *shiksa*, a gold trophy wife. And back in her world, some doors (dull ones, but still) were now closed to her. The Mackays had not advanced on any fronts at all.

But here was the press anyway, still hanging about and still hounding Irving and the wife of Irving, the unknown millionairess. And one day, while undergoing the ups and downs of early pregnancy—which hadn't much improved since the Garden of Eden—she snapped. These same implacable "just doing my job" journalists would soon turn Charles Lindbergh from a bright young man into a premature sourpuss and near traitor who loved Nazi Germany because it didn't have a free press. In a smaller way, the press broke Ellin too, removing much of her fun and youthfulness, and for the rest of her days subjecting her to a series of what she called "walking breakdowns."

And I think some of the fun went out of it for Irving too, or at least it began a slow leak, although he still cultivated lapdogs like Alexander Woollcott to write Mother Goose stories about him and his princess. But the dark side of the press had turned even darker, and the least he could do now was protect his young wife and oncoming children from any more of it. So he built a metaphysical fortress of silence around them all, a sort of Castle Irving from which he would venture forth alone within strictly controlled parameters, and in which he would eventually entomb himself in his old age, after the glare of the American dream had worn him out.

But to begin with, his uptown captivity had been anything but tomb-like. Irving was simply doing what "everybody" (who was anybody) was doing now, and the upper class was part of America too and part of his subject. So his Central Park apartment served not just as a first-class work-shop but also as a spy-hole on the rich at play. "Let's go slumming," as he wrote, "on Park Avenue." Some doors might be closed to the Berlins, but they weren't the ones he needed and there were more than enough tal-ented arrivistes behind other ones to make up the difference. Musical theater did not expect you to write about the very top people, the Cabots and the Biddles, but only about imitation top people like Fred and Ginger and occasionally Bing Crosby, two hoofers and a groaner dressed up in evening clothes to constitute a kind of take-out aristocracy of make-believe.

And not the least of Irving's studies and research tools was his own wife. The one thing that had *not* suffered from the recent unpleasantness was the marriage itself, which could probably have endured on their joint determination alone if necessary—failure was unthinkable—but their union had a couple of other good things going for it besides.

For openers, they passed the first and most crucial test of a happy mar-riage by simply enjoying each other's company, and not just in its hard-breathing aspects. They both liked to talk, and as a professional lyricist, Irving was a scavenger of talk, forever on the prowl for fresh turns of phrase and untrodden byways to get from here to there. And Ellin enjoyed the sheer game of it too. Their daughter Mary Ellin remembers growing up to a crackle of smart-chat and literal word games, some of which would undoubtedly metamorphose into song lyrics at the other end of the as-sembly line. A likely suspect pops into my mind right now, along with a matching clue to go with it. "I'm going around in circles, getting nowhere." Clue: Express futility in seven words or less. Where else but in games and songs could one hear such phrases? Ira Gershwin's " 'S Wonderful," for in-stance: Don't ever try using it in the real world.

The game is contagious, even when just describing it, and I can imag-ine Alan Jay Lerner popping his head in right here with "Why can't the Ba-lines teach the Mackays how to speak?" Later, Cole Porter would talk ironically of envying Irving's advantages, so it's nice to think of Berlin in-structing his young bride in the niceties of Lower East Side English. Mar-rying up might be called the very highest form of slumming, but it hadn't been the couple's only wedding present to each other, because Ellin also gave him whatever it took to write real love songs, which is to say a muse, a model, and a sense of potential excitement, and real love. (By which I don't mean the famous one, "Always," that he had ostentatiously given to Ellin as a lifelong wedding gift, royalties and all, but that he had apparently written a bit earlier to help out a friend, who had a girlfriend named Amy, which has the same cadence as "always.") And this raises some instructive questions. Does "I'll be loving you, Amy" still sound like a great song, and can you simply transfer the whole *schlamozzel* to somebody else and still keep it a love song? The unmusical George S. Kaufman would point out the basic difficulty when he called it "I'll be loving you, Tuesday" instead. "Always" is a song of generalities, a kind of hymn to whatever you feel like today, almost a rental, which would happily come into its own as background music, expressing nostalgia for a fallen hero in *The Pride of the Yankees*. A somewhat more real song written around then is "You Forgot to Remember," but this also plunges us back into wistfulness and paper-thin heartbreak, and we've done that. By contrast, "How Deep Is the Ocean" seems to me his first full-throated love song written by one real person to another. It pulls out all the stops on the organ at once and plugs the air with genuine feeling. "And if I ever lost you/how much would I cry?" There is nothing paper-thin about that. The man really means it.

Doesn't he? Once again, it seems as if the muses were just having their little joke. Irving did not write "How Deep" on a great tide of emotion, but on a widening ripple of aspiration, as he strove to claw or con his way out of a composing slump, a "dry spell" that nobody else was aware of. And as far as he could judge, this particular attempt had failed as much as any of the others, and went into his trunk for an even rainier day.

So his slump went on, and on, and on, until it seemed, in Mary Ellin's account of it, to fill up the whole house, as if song creation were a palpable form of combustion that required endless tinkering with the boiler. "I'm breaking my neck, trying to find a new sound" was how he put it, and since even the best-trained writers can sound like piano tuners while creating, one boggles at the thought of the untrained Irving "breaking his neck," humming and whistling like a teakettle and batting out strange chords. Park Avenue had probably never heard the like. But seriously— what *had* gone wrong? And what did he *think* had gone wrong?

Somewhere in the vague area of 1931, Irving found himself at major war with his own self-confidence—a battle that seems all the more gripping by its invisibility and by the sheer number of songs that nevertheless kept appearing. His own typically puritan explanation of what he called his inferiority complex was that he just hadn't been working hard enough, that is, around the clock. But breast-beating aside, there was an awful lot for anyone to feel inferior about just then. From the moment George Gershwin walked into his office looking for work, Irving must have felt subject to occasional second thoughts about his own willful ignorance of music as well as his blind faith in simplicity. Should a boss really know that much less than the help, and be that much simpler? By 1925, he had pronounced that all of America was now a listening nation, rather than a performing one, which was grounds for another small twinge. After all, simplicity might be good enough to sing, whistle, and dance to, but listening might want a little something to think about as well, and to sink its teeth into, and in that same short period Richard Rodgers and Cole Porter and Harold Arlen came blazing out, flashing new ideas with trained musicianship to burn.

What made Berlin's new sound so particularly elusive was that he neither knew exactly what it was he was looking for, nor could be sure of knowing when he found it. Like most of his colleagues, only a little more so, Irving always needed someone else to tell him when he was good. Witness the famous instance when he almost discarded that most palpable of hits "There's No Business Like Show Business" because his secretary didn't like it, and perhaps more seriously, because Richard Rodgers didn't light up when he first heard it. A more confident man might have realized that Richard Rodgers never lit up over anything and that he was hearing this new song under the worst possible conditions: Irving was playing it himself. And Irving's pianism was so primitive that Hoagy Carmichael once said that it had given him the heart to go on, on the grounds that "If the best in the business is that bad, there's hope for all of us." Because Irving's variety of ineptitude was not just manifestly self-taught, but badly self-taught, as if by a deaf person, he couldn't trust it himself until he had heard one of his famous musical secretaries play it to him and show him how good the latest Berlin tune sounded outside his own head.

Luckily, the rest of humanity had less trouble knowing it when Irving was good. His dry spell abruptly ended when someone in his office went behind his back and offered one of his rejects, called "Say It Isn't So," to Rudy Vallee with results so spectacular that Irving agreed to reconsider an adjoining lemon, "How Deep Is the Ocean." These were no ordinary songs but A-list standards, and once all the second opinions were in, Berlin himself considered "How Deep" among his greatest ever.

Possibly it even contained that new sound he was looking for, now that someone else had heard it too. And with that taken care of, he would return to Broadway in triumph, as if he had actually been away someplace. He then fired off a volley of brand-new hits such as the haunting "Soft Lights and Sweet Music" and his nod to the Depression, "Let's Have Another Cup of Coffee," that must have been gestating in his trunk during his dry spell, which, when you throw in a couple of fine movie songs, "Puttin' On the Ritz" and "Let Me Sing and I'm Happy," must have made this either the richest or the shortest dry spell in the history of droughts. His Broadway spectacular after that took an equally long stride in the way of all-around sophistication. *As Thousands Cheer* was a revue arranged like a newspaper, with songs and sketches to illustrate the various sections, for example, "Heat Wave" for the weather page and "Easter Parade" for fashion. Thus, the institution of journalism that had so plagued the Berlins lately was reduced to a series of harmless entertainments with Irving getting the last word and the last laugh each time.

However, the high point of the show gets no laughs, or even applause, but takes its chances on stunned silence. The subject of it actually did not appear in the papers, or not often enough. "Suppertime" must be the first pop song ever written about a lynching, and the tone is just right, without one false note or melodramatic word. A member of the family will not be coming home this evening, or tomorrow, or in fact ever again so we'd better just get on with life. And the tune says the same thing. The song is written in that rarest of forms, an understated blues, and it sounds just African American enough to show that Irving "gets it" as much as Gershwin or any other white man can. Like his clumsily titled "How About Me," "Suppertime" shows that Irving digs the blue sound but isn't planning to horn in on it or take over à la the white man. There's a long distance between "Dorando" and "Cohen Owes Me Ninety-Seven Dollars" and the political correctness of today, but Irving Berlin's brand of irony and respectfulness in "Suppertime" seems like a felicitous way station and a good place for a white songwriter to stop. Berlin had made his statement and would not be making it again.

It was a high point. Yet if Irving Berlin's career had ended right there, he would no doubt be enshrined today as an incomparable pioneer, or missing link, though not quite as a colleague, of George Gershwin or Duke Ellington in the field of the jazz song. But something radical would still happen to the know-it-alls who make these estimates, or at least to me. During my wartime layover in the United States, there had been virtually no such thing as movie revivals: Either you caught a film on its first whip-round ("Tues. to Thurs." or, if you were lucky, "Fri. to Mon.") or you caught the next one. But when I finally escaped from England in the fall of 1947, I found that New York had changed delightfully in this respect. Presumably Hollywood had begun to gird itself for its last stand against TV, and simultaneously for its new role after that as a supplier of TV, by releasing lots of its old movies for general distribution and exposure. And I spent that whole fall catching up with the Marx Brothers, and spent Christmas day itself alone in an empty movie house, catching up with Fred Astaire and Ginger Rogers, who until that year I had seen over and over in just one (excellent) movie, *Shall We Dance*. This time the film was *Top Hat* and I haven't recovered yet.

"Isn't this a lovely day to be caught in the rain"—incredible. Who wrote this again? Where has he been all my life? And what on earth is he doing with the beat now? "I just got an invitation in the mail." This couldn't be Irving Berlin because it wasn't simple enough. Before leaving London I'd already been inundated with the score of *Annie Get Your Gun* and had found it amiably regressive and a touch simpleminded. Okay, it was also perfect. That was the least you could expect from America in those days, but except for one lonely song called "Moonshine Lullaby," it completely and ominously lacked the sound that I was going back to America for.

But now here it was, that sound in all its glory, and not just a good copy of the sound but in some sense the original that all the other guys had been copying. At least a part of Irving Berlin was an intuitive jazzman who had once heard the sounds of Harlem as clearly as those of Hester Street and had, so to speak, finally hatched out the embryonic sounds of his early rags into the swinging majesty of "Cheek to Cheek." "Heaven," as he puts it perfectly, "I'm in heaven."

You can say that again. Also, "I'm fancy free and free for anything fancy." The fact that it was Christmas might just be a coincidence, but I had just received an incomparable present anyway that has kept on giving from that day to this. What Norman Mailer has called the little capillaries of bonhomie began to go off everywhere like firecrackers.

Broadway itself smiled on the way out, and now every year I think the same ritual words, "I'm dreaming of a white Christmas," but with any luck I won't get it. And I'll have to settle for Fred and Ginger in the rain again, or perhaps just Fred solo celebrating Easter, Washington's birthday, and July the Fourth.

Fred Astaire was of course a phenomenon unto himself. Every writer did his best work for Fred, because, among other reasons, he asked for it. But *Top Hat* is somehow always the first that comes to mind, the proto-type. It's as if Astaire's sense of the sounds he wanted and Berlin's sense of Fred's essence, his image, added up to a third personality, a city boy harnessed to a country boy in the cause of that magnificent anomaly, American sophistication. And wonderfully, inexplicably, their songs still sounded simple, although they were anything but. For instance, the bridge of "I'm Putting All My Eggs in One Basket" seems to drop into an abyss when you try singing it, and you'd better know where he put the branch that you'll have to hang on to; and the second B section of "Let's Face the Music and Dance" makes a small move that can leave egg on your face time after time. And so on. "I Used to Be Color Blind" actually goes on what the Australian aborigines call walkabout. It's as if the singer were deciding where to put his feet down next.

Under cover of Astaire's dancing and his flexible, throwaway singing, Irving didn't need to rush to any conclusions, but could, as he said, "write anything" without fear of commercial reprisal—Astaire's feet would turn it to gold, whatever it was. And the result is the only tunes in this whole book that I've ever had trouble memorizing, most particularly the one called "You're Easy to Dance With."

On second thought, Irving had always liked to play games with the beat, and I have almost as much trouble learning his song "Everybody

Step," vintage 1921, but that one is clearly a rhythm number as opposed to a "felt" one, written for the feet and not the heart. With Astaire, everything is a rhythm number, love songs and all, so you get the whole Irving writing at once, the jester and the troubadour moving like quicksilver but in no special hurry, and with the added bonus that Fred was always in fashion. As a Broadway veteran, Astaire had worked out his own West Coast compromise so that everything he touched became the latest thing, and now Irving did likewise, whipping out a trunk song and a retread, "You're Laughing at Me" and "I've Got My Love to Keep Me Warm," and transforming them into the toast of 1937 for *On the Avenue* with Dick Powell and Alice Faye. And then there's the Astaire-type nonsense song, "My Walking Stick," sung in basic Broadway style by the other side of Berlin's brain, Ethel Merman, in the film *Alexander's Ragtime Band*.

But now it was time for another war and for another burst of two-fisted patriotism, although Irving would actually begin this one by taking a huge step backward in hepcat esteem. Even when he had first written "God Bless America" in 1919, Harry Ruby had talked him out of using it then, on the grounds that the country was already drowning in patriotism and didn't need another bucket of it from its greatest songwriter. But that's when Berlin should have published it anyway, because that's when it still sounded right. By 1939, "God Bless America" seemed strictly from squaresville and Berlin himself seemed to have gone backward in time to where perhaps he belonged, a grand old man singing grand old songs.

It suited World War II just fine, as it happened, and thus suited Irving too. The U.S. home front was in a retro frame of mind throughout, as it would prove by falling in love with the defiantly corny *Oklahoma!* (which actually uses the word "corn" in its very first song), and as homesick GIs had already proved by laughing nostalgically as Irving himself sang "Oh, How I Hate to Get Up in the Morning" for his show *This Is the Army* in a quavering voice that sounded as old as their collective grandfathers. *This Is the Army* remains, note for note, a splendid historic artifact, beginning with its title song and running on through a twinkling trove of second-drawer tunes that have all been scrupulously updated. "How About a Cheer for the Navy" actually names the current secretaries of the army and the navy while Berlin's politically dubious "That's What the Well-

Dressed Man in Harlem Will Wear" features the "Brown Bomber," Joe Louis himself dressed up in ODs (olive drabs) "with a tin hat for overseas." Irving might not walk the streets in person anymore, but he was still a singing journalist and those were exactly the sounds I remember from *my* streets.

Afterward, a war commonly grants its heroes a few years of momentum and grace on the house, so that an Audie Murphy can capsize gently from a great soldier to a third-class actor, and an Irving Berlin can evolve from a great American into a great *old* one. In fact, the saga of his first postwar show, *Annie Get Your Gun,* could almost be called a ceremony of grand old men, because Jerome Kern had agreed to write it first with his grand old partner Dorothy Fields, but had died just before he could, and grand old producers Rodgers and Hammerstein were producing it, but couldn't very well write it themselves because Ms. Fields had already agreed to combine with her brother Herbert on the book and lyrics, and Dick hadn't been married to Oscar long enough to cheat on him with Dorothy.

But Irving by himself took precedence over everyone, and besides, he suited Rodgers's retro game plan by even being the right age. The original "Alexander's Ragtime Band" had actually been written around the same year that the original Oklahoma had become a state. And Rodgers and Hammerstein's show of that name had established a style that might also appeal to the fogy in Irving, the part of him that wrote "God Bless America," that is, no sophistication or street smarts. (Try a little country-lane smarts—stop "Puttin' On the Ritz" and try "Doin' What Comes Natur'lly.") And try to avoid syncopation, if possible—that stuff's fer city folk.

And best of all, Irving really needed no advice at all as to which way the wind was blowing. The growing popularity of country music was in itself a welcome invitation to come home to simplicity, and fill out his musical portrait of America. So he proceeded to build *Annie's* love story, which is to say the heart of the matter, on a simple waltz, "The Girl That I Marry." He surrounded it with such a simple, down-home score that he out-Hammersteined Oscar himself, as he had once tried to out–Porter Cole himself with Fred Astaire. The results haven't come down yet, but still circle the globe eternally alongside *Oklahoma!* and *Kiss Me, Kate* and the other classic postwar musicals. It had been one more stupendous triumph of the will for Irving's mantelpiece, and can only have left the cranky Richard Rodgers with the most exquisitely mixed feelings in history.

Berlin had once unforgivably upstaged Rodgers by writing a song of his own for Flo Ziegfeld to insert into an early Rodgers and Hart show. It had been insurance for Flo's investment, and to please his star singer, one Belle Baker, who had worked well with Irving before. The song turned out to be the immortal "Blue Skies," which stole the show and the reviews, leaving a nasty cold sore on Rodgers's wintry soul that probably still cried out for some balm of vengeance.

As good luck would have it, though, Rodgers was also a snob, a practicing gentleman, who understood the uses of sportsmanship, if not the point of it, and being the producer of a major musical must have provided its own kind of balm as well. In his bland memoir, *Musical Stages,* he would get a chance to pay his superficial respects to Irving and sound like a hell of an all-around good chap in doing so. So there were no losers. Irving had played right into Richard's hand by giving him such a great score. So hooray for all of us! A hit show heals all wounds, at least, as I say, superficially.

For a moment, the total triumph of *Annie* shot Irving back to the top. But at his age, no one expected him to stay there long. So he bent his talent to at least one more surprise, and with the help of good old reliable Ethel Merman, he came up with another only slightly smaller smash Broadway hit, *Call Me Madam,* which, with its contrapuntal hit song, "You're Just in Love," forms, in my mind anyway, a memorable bookend around the primest part of his prime with "Play a Simple Melody," written more than thirty years earlier. Outside of Gershwin's elegant "Mine," I can't think of another song by anyone that accomplishes this tricky piece of musical calisthenics. So perhaps the old boy was just trying to show he could still do it. After that, he wrote another great movie with his other prewar alter ego, Fred Astaire, called *Easter Parade,* featuring one of his most passionate, most exuberant, no-holds-barred songs, "It Only Happens When I Dance with You." "A Couple of Swells" featured Irving slumming again, and getting Fred and Judy to slum with him, under a gross of greasepaint and some slept-in evening clothes. It only goes to show, as Irving's own career had, that class will always tell.

So okay, the guy was immortal, and you don't bet against the gods. As long as postwar America stayed mostly in the past, Irving seemed safe. But rock and roll could not be kept at bay forever, after which a case can be made for him, as for the others included in this book, that the music began to leave him and not the other way around. At least I have heard a couple of unpublished songs of Berlin's that might have gone somewhere, if anyone else had been going that way too anymore. And conceivably, if he'd been younger, he might have learned to play a guitar at this point, at least as well as he played the piano, and dashed off some rock and roll to top things off—the kid in that early photograph I was talking about seemed capable of anything short of hip-hop. But so few creative musicians have lived as long as this that there were no precedents to guide either him or us. How much can you or he ask of an eighty-year-old man, anyway? And then what about when he turns ninety?

All we can say for sure is that he died not long after his 101st birthday, before the question could come around again. But long before that, he had retired all the way into his own castle on the Upper East Side, just a couple of hard-earned miles away from where it had all begun, but with enough space now to house, with a little notice, all the Balines in Russia and most of the tea in China. And here, in a just world, he should have been free to cash his last chips and live happily ever after. But in the doleful phrase of the great Satchel Paige, something had "been gaining on him" for a while now and perhaps it was just an inherent melancholia (a sister committed suicide in the 1920s) or perhaps it was not having enough work to do, or, most likely, it was mainly the sleeping pills he'd been popping for years to keep his own personal buglers out of range. As a mythical character, Irving was inevitably promoted to drug addict, but this is much too melodramatic; lots of respectable folk took the same pills, including a couple of others in this book. So maybe the rule should be that if the doctor prescribes it, he's the one with the problem.

Meanwhile, Irving seems to have kept up a telephone friendship with one of his fellow pill poppers, Harold Arlen, during several years of mutual distress. By the late 1960s, the songwriters of their era no longer needed Nembutal to feel sorry for themselves. It was now official that musical fashion had turned its back on them for good, and they all needed someone to cry with as their collective lifeworks inched toward the brink of extinction.

Although Berlin and Arlen might seem like two basically different breeds of cat, Berlin tended to regard all kinds of other songwriters as family, and in return they tended to see him as a father or uncle. After all, these songwriters had each grown up with Berlin and knew where he belonged in their own development. And I believe most would have agreed that if there had been no Irving Berlin, there would have been nothing, for instance, quite like Harold Arlen either, or Jimmy Van Heusen, or even Cole Porter in quite the same form. So in those latter days, at the very least they owed him a phone call. And of course, he'd already written a song about his end of the deal. "All Alone (by the Telephone)" had been written in his mother's last years, but it remains the last word on old age and loneliness and perhaps on his own fears as well.

But if so, he needn't have worried. For a famous recluse, he stayed surprisingly talkative. If only telephones could talk, Berlin's telephone would have become his best, last biographer. At least one phone call has survived in full that tells as much about his last days as that old snapshot does of his beginnings. Irving had just read Alec Wilder's great book on songwriters. Naturally, he was calling to complain. Typically it seems that he had either missed the purple profusion of compliments that Wilder had heaped on him or else had read them but wasn't interested. Instead he had fastened on one extra-mild demurral of Wilder's where he said the song " 'Always' is frankly not a favorite of mine." At this, Irving went wild. What does he mean "not a favorite"? Who the hell did Wilder think he was?

Luckily for us, the phone was answered not by Alec himself but by his literary partner, James T. Maher, who captured the whole thing, including the growls. And it leaves us with a core question. Allowing that "Always" was certainly a burningly sensitive subject, because it was an official part of his love story, who exactly did Irving *want* Alec Wilder to be? Whose authority would he have accepted? One senses how fragile the whole edifice had become. Irving had always had a chip on his shoulder about critics. Songs were written for people, damn it, not experts. The man in the street and the woman in the kitchen—these were his people, his judges. And also, a check representing a million copies sold was the only prize worth having.

But now, if he so much as opened the window or turned on the radio, there were his judges, the real people, all dancing to "baby, baby, baby," or words to that effect, and the prizewinners with the gold platters knew even less about music than he had. It wasn't a listening nation anymore, but a shaking, rattling, and rolling one, and frankly, who cared what the man in the street thought anymore? Public taste was not, as he supposed, the last word, but is only as good in each generation as the music it gets to feed on. And the current diet was enough to drive a man into the arms of the nitpicking connoisseurs. But not if they were going to dump on "Always" and "God Bless America" and "A Pretty Girl Is Like a Melody." Good songs are forever and he didn't care to trade his old ones in for the new models.

Boy wonders may be obliged to pay a steep price for growing older. As Irving Berlin's songs had become more sophisticated, as the 1930s went on, so had his audiences, so that when he seemed to change his mind about this in the 1940s, the whippersnappers who sneered at him actually had to stand on his shoulders to do so. He had taught the whole world too well.

But were we ever right to sneer, even from the vantage point of his shoulders? Right after the terrorists struck at the very heart of Irving's own city on the 9/11 that lives in infamy, nobody's words or tunes rang the bell more resonantly or accurately than good old "God Bless America." So if you allow for ups and downs, perhaps Berlin's songs *are* forever.

Opinions remain mixed about Irving, though—more so for him than for just about anyone else—partly because he was so mixed himself, with a bright side and a dark one almost agreeing to take turns. It is hard to read the mind of a hermit, but especially when he seems to expect both the worst and the best at the same time. For instance, he had thought when it came along that this new gizmo, radio, would ruin the song business by overexposure, and that the movies would ruin it too, by moving the publishing business to Hollywood. And yet toward the end of his life, when Steven Spielberg asked permission to build his next movie around "Always," Irving said that he had "other plans" for it, which suggests that his boyish optimism was still giddier than ever.

So Spielberg used Jerome Kern's "Smoke Gets in Your Eyes" instead, which means that Irving's decision likely altered the balance of power and popularity slightly for a moment, as would other decisions he made restricting the use of his tunes. For instance, I can't remember hearing a single Berlin tune in a commercial, for what that's worth, or—except for "Always" in *The Pride of the Yankees*—as background music in a movie. In general, it would seem to me that for any of these men or their estates to play hard to get was futile verging on crazy. But having scrambled for pennies once in his life, and having ended up in a palace, Irving Berlin was not in the market for professional advice. Since he'd practically invented the business, there was no point telling him about it now. You didn't lecture this man—you took notes.

Perhaps the darkest sequence in Irving's telephone life came when his long conversation with Fred Astaire finally ended. It is impossible, but tantalizing, to imagine how such a great musical friendship might have translated into chitchat. But so long as the conversation lasted, one could still imagine Irving writing another completely original song for Fred at a moment's request, and another and another.

In such a relationship, it seemed almost a dirty trick for either man to die first. But everyone in the music game had died before Irving, leaving him a bit lonelier each time, to the point of infinity, and the death of Astaire must have seemed like a final amputation. "It's over," as he'd once written in an achingly sad song. "All over . . . but how about me?"

It doesn't answer his question, but perhaps it serves poetic justice to note that at least Irving Berlin's reputation seems to be doing nicely again, after its own dry spell. He himself might never be able to get quite past those early death struggles with money, but he had raised three generous-minded daughters, who could now do so for him, and they, plus whoever else the estate consists of these days, have made his songs more available than they've ever been—and now there's not a damn thing Irving can do to stop them.

Also, I'm afraid that his ghost may have to settle for a connoisseur audience now, which seems, incidentally, to be getting younger every year. In such bull sessions as I've had lately, he goes straight into the top five before the argument even starts, along with Gershwin, Kern, Rodgers, and Porter, plus usually one more per player—Harold Arlen in Wilder's book and Arlen's best friend Harry Warren in mine, and of course whoever you like in yours.

One always feels one needs to add one more word about Berlin. Something to sum up his sheer scale and importance. Cornerstone? Fountain-head? His colleagues seemed to use the word "genius" about him more than about anyone else except George Gershwin—and perhaps more significantly, Igor Stravinsky also used that word to describe Berlin. Stravinsky was a great musical theorist with a special curiosity about the nature of melody, which after all Igor's theorizing still seems so elusive that maybe Irving was right after all—it actually helps if you don't know what you're doing.

What matters most to this particular story is that perhaps our most gifted original musician gave his whole life and whole gift entirely to popular songs, and that he overlapped so closely with another genius, who could add classical training to the mix. Many other types of song have been written in America, and there are many varieties within this type too. But parts one and two of the standard jazz song trace back to the man who wrote "I can do anything better than you" and to the man (or men, if Ira Gershwin counts) who answered "It Ain't Necessarily So."

# Of Thee I Sing, Gershwin

GEORGE GERSHWIN

$L$ike many artistic happenings in this hurry-up land of ours, the jazz song boom seems in retrospect like a movement that didn't know it was a movement. Harold Arlen, that most introspective of second-wave writers, did know that he and his buddies were doing something special all right, and even that they were in some sense all in it together. But if so, they were in it like a jazz band, not a chorus line, which is to say that they wanted the other guys to be good so that they could be better. The greatest solos come from the greatest ensembles, and the biggest sales occur when the whole market is bullish. So the lore of the trade is amazingly full of encouraging words and deeds, from Berlin to Porter, and Kern to Arlen, and from Gershwin to everybody—a level of uncomplicated niceness unique among the arts.

But a movement? Come on—they didn't like each other *that* much. And besides, "movement" was just the kind of word that these refugees from piano lessons and respectability had signed on to get away from. The whole essence and point of syncopation is to kid formal music and kick the stuffing out of it. If the maestro says the tempo should go thus and so, let's surprise him with this and that. And let's do it with a gorgeous new chord that has never seen pen nor paper—a chord straight from heaven itself. You don't find such in movements.

But even if they didn't know they were a movement, there was no doubt who their leader was. Evidence suggests that every writer of the time who met George Gershwin (and nearly all did) was mightily proud of his friendship. Those who missed him looked up to him anyway, as the closest thing to a role model that this happy-go-lucky profession would allow itself.

George even passed the most acid of tests for great leadership by remaining a presence to his followers even after he'd left the planet. Ann "Willow Weep for Me" Ronell told me some half century after his death that she still "saw" Gershwin regularly in the crowds of the Upper West Side, looking as if he'd just walked out the door. And on that same day, Burton "How About You" Lane testified to an even more precise epiphany. Lane had recently been to a concert of Gershwin's newly refurbished piano rolls being played on a baby grand pianola in a pool of spotlight. And as the notes began to go mechanically down and up, "There was George for a moment," he exclaimed, "playing away. I almost passed out."

Both Ronell and Lane had good reason for their memories. And since their memories were all about the excitement of meeting George Gershwin and getting to know him, they might as well serve the same purpose here. Because George the man, the phenomenon, is at least as important to our story as George the writer, which is to say absolutely central.

Ms. Ronell, a cheerful, pocket-size individual, was particularly cheerful the day I met her, because Clint Eastwood had just played her song, her lifework, "Willow Weep for Me," in his latest movie. And with minimal coaxing, she proceeded to hand me a list of the ninety-some recordings that had been made of "Willow," featuring everybody you could ever want to have record you: a Hall of Fame and who's who of great bands and soloists.

So I jumped into the conversation with a go-fish type of question about this. Why had she dedicated her masterpiece to George Gershwin? And at this, she lit up as if I'd accidentally turned on all the lights of the Rockefeller Center Christmas tree. Although Ms. Ronell had obviously told her tale many times before, she hadn't lost an ounce of her delight in it. Imagine a little girl from the Midwest meeting a great man like George Gershwin! And this is how it happened.

Way back when, Ms. Ronell, née Rosenblatt, had gone from Omaha to Radcliffe with her eye on a career in music, which she decided could be advanced by interviewing as many musical eminencies as she could for the Radcliffe student paper.

But it turned out she wouldn't need more than one, because after maneuvering her way past Ira, who tried to keep his brother's bulging guest list within reason, she found that "in five minutes, George was interviewing *me*," and auditioning her too, to see if she could dance or sing or anything else he might be able to help her with. And when he learned about her writing dreams, George didn't just give her the usual vague advice, and the usual list of names to call ("Who the hell are you?" is what they say if you make those calls), but followed up by personally introducing her to the names himself, as if he were an agent and she his star client. So not only was Ronell spared the usual hours of waiting in a publisher's office, vainly hoping to catch a glimpse of the back of the boss's head as he went out to lunch, but she had also been represented by the most distinguished and irresistible salesman in the business. "Your songs don't have verses," snapped the great Max Dreyfus. "They don't need verses," snapped back Gershwin. And that settled it, at least as long as George was around. Later, she would find herself waiting in offices again, but she did get her classic song published, thanks to George.

Nor was this just an isolated case involving a pretty girl who'd caught his eye. George might have done the same, or something like it, for anyone who got past Ira and walked through his door, as witness the very next person whose door I walked through that day, namely, my old friend the aforementioned Burton Lane, who, like Ronell, continued to live on the Upper West Side in the heart of the Gershwin country.

Since I already knew Burton's basic Gershwin story, I didn't ask him to repeat it, just to embellish it a little if he felt like it. But I'll repeat it here in the short form. Young Burton, né Burton Levy, age sixteen, had been dutifully practicing the piano and hoping to find a song in there at a New Jersey resort that his Realtor father favored, when he heard a booming Russian-sounding voice that could only be coming from someone as important as Catherine the Great. "You play just like my son George," said the woman's voice, and before he knew what hit him, Burton, like Ronell, found himself swept into the Gershwin family circle for what amounted to the next two years. Under Mama's formidable wing, he would, of course, have no trouble getting past Ira, but he did sometimes have a little difficulty getting past the court jester, Oscar Levant, who used to intercept him and insist on a game of Ping-Pong before letting him in.

It was a small, amusing price to pay for entering the enchanted Kingdom of George. Half of New York always seemed to be there—the exciting half, the young artists and writers who were going places—and at the center sat the king on his throne, his piano bench, with a different consort at his side each time, dispensing magic music from his enchanted piano.

Or so it seemed to a teenager. And no doubt a squinty-eyed psychobiographer would fit this into the standard legend of George, the sublime egomaniac, who obviously recruited acolytes like Ronell and Lane just so they could join the crowd at his feet. "There was nothing small about George Gershwin," said Jerome Kern, but the same cannot be said for some of the people who have written about him. What would be missing from their picture this time would be that no matter how well Gershwin played, (1) some of the worshippers apparently never stopped talking themselves, which didn't seem to bother the king at all: George could have composed music on the floor of the New York Stock Exchange at high noon, and (2) what Lane and Ronell talked to me about was not George's spectacular playing, which soon became part of the background, but his attentiveness between times to them and their particularities, to the things that made them different. Burton recalled with particular wonderment how George had personally set up an appointment for him with Walter Damrosch, the panjandrum of the New York Philharmonic, in case Lane had classical possibilities like his own. If Lane just wanted to join him downtown in the Alley, great! But if Lane had uptown potential as well, okay, he'd help with that too. For an egomaniac, George Gershwin took an astonishing interest in other people.

The third thing wrong with the picture of George as an egomaniac is that, of course, he didn't have to send out for acolytes; he had only to leave the door open. Perhaps the longest and strangest pilgrimage to Gershwin's court was made by one Vladimir Dukelsky, a White Russian on the run not from the czars, like Gershwin's other friends, but from the czar's enemies, Lenin, Trotsky, and the whole unwashed revolutionary rabble, as seen from the top of the ivory tower where families like the Dukelskys lived.

Any generalizations about Gershwin's benefactions must surely pause at this one because Dukelsky was not only *not* a pretty girl, but he was not helpless or, by God, inferior to anyone on the planet. Born into the Cossack class, Vladimir had been trained as a music prodigy from the age of four, and had predictably grown up to be, at least at first and by most accounts, a fairly insufferable adult, whose basic relationship unit with the outside world seems to have been the feud. Perhaps if one splits the difference between Dukelsky's fellow White Russians George Sanders and Vladimir Nabokov one can at least imagine the capacity to annoy, and be annoyed, of such a creature.

At that, Dukelsky's hauteur might have passed unnoticed if he had simply proceeded on his appointed way to classical music, where snobbish wunderkinds disappear in the crowd. But meanwhile, a funny thing happened to Vladimir on the way out of Russia. During a stopover in Istanbul, where he supported his family playing the piano (no doubt with his nose in the air) in cafés, he heard a record of Gershwin's "Swanee" and was transfixed. Suddenly he too wanted to write like that, and began on the spot dashing off Gershwin and Irving Berlin imitations, made in Istanbul, with lyrics painfully winnowed out of an English dictionary. And unlike most classicists slumming on Tin Pan Alley, Vladimir kept doing it for the rest of his life, even when his pop songs decisively flopped at first and his classical compositions showed signs of taking off, with Diaghilev signing him up to write some ballets. It isn't often that you find pop music lined up on the side of art versus commerce. But for a while it seems as if Dukelsky actually wrote ballets for money and jazz songs for love.

So obviously the next step was to meet George Gershwin himself, and the next act finds him in a setting where he was really out of place, the Gershwin apartment on Riverside Drive, where he got hooked in earnest, this time by George's piano playing and the man's endless, breathtaking improvisations. (He noted with surprise that George never varied his tempo—a holdover from his job of making piano rolls, perhaps.) Dukelsky also got hooked on George himself, with his bubbling curiosity and the sense he gave of infinite possibility. So his visitor wrote songs too? Great! Gershwin liked a couple of "Duky's" art songs and the one-man Gershwin promotion machine rumbled into gear. How about changing the name Dukelsky to, say, Vernon Duke? And how about meeting my publisher? And when that didn't work out right away, George lent him some money, and some more after that, without ever making it seem like a big deal or a wall between them.

What followed is as much a history of the new-born Vernon Duke, who deserves one for himself anyway, as it was a history of Gershwin, because Duke became one of our best, most distinctive songwriters and more gradually turned, according to Bobby Short, into a genuinely nice and helpful guy, easily outstripping his classical twin Vladimir the Oaf in both respects.

So perhaps Gershwin's generosity was as contagious as his music, and maybe that was part of his service. At any rate, the Vernon Duke saga makes such a picture-book example of George in action and of the ripple effect of his influence that it's worth dwelling on just one moment longer. To repeat, Duke was not some hard-luck case with a small talent, the kind great men love to patronize, but a major potential rival with extraordinary musical gifts and self-confidence that needed bolstering from no one. Never mind. Gershwin would later lend moral support to Harold Arlen, too, who would eventually threaten almost to eclipse him. It was as if George wanted all those great songs to be written by *somebody,* preferably by himself, of course, but not exclusively. And in this cause, he studied other people's music so closely and empathetically that Duke was startled one day to hear Gershwin break off from his usual piano soliloquy to imitate Duke's own piano playing perfectly.

Since George listened so closely, he must also have noted that Duke actually played the piano better than he did, which a lesser man might have considered another good reason to get rid of him. But George, as usual, was fascinated and Duke became part of the set at Riverside Drive, whatever the rest of the set may have made of him. (Oscar Levant once said, "Since you're destined for oblivion anyway, why do you need two names?" which shows what *he* thought of Vladimir, anyway, but Duke found Levant to be a nerve-racking neurotic, so they were even.)

Joining Gershwin's set was like hooking into a powerhouse that consisted of more than just George. Within a few years, Duke found himself writing songs with Ira's old classmate Yip Harburg, who would never have worked with a guy like Duke in any other circumstances. As the most dedicated left-winger in the business, Harburg disapproved on principle of Duke's foppish, foreign-sounding harmonies, and after each of their first two standards together, "April in Paris" and "I Like the Likes of You," failed to take off right away, Yip really yapped and hollered nasty words like "European" and "decadent" and "Never again!" But perhaps what had happened was that Duke had brought out Harburg's own inner fop, and Yip never wrote better. Then later when Duke found himself stuck with a tune that literally couldn't get started in the marketplace, Ira himself would chime in with a title and lyric based on that very phrase. "I Can't Get Started" became Duke's biggest hit.

So knowing George could be a total experience, and Duke's decision to drop in on him that first day would produce, in effect, a whole great songwriter that might not have happened otherwise. And as a truly far-out bonus, a most charming and surprising memoir from Duke called *Passport to Paris* brings Gershwin back to life as well as anything we have.

Beyond the creative windfall, it was quite an extraordinary case of what might be called social lion-taming. The stiff-necked Duke must have seemed like quite hopeless disciple material, but he responded to George with a total loyalty to both the man and his music, happily putting his own reputation on the line by defending both against his highbrow buddies like Prokofiev and Diaghilev, and even taking the trouble to complete his old friend's unfinished songs and arrangements for Gershwin's posthumous movie, *The Goldwyn Follies,* of 1938. And for good measure, he would defend both Ira and his prickly wife, Leonore, against charges of callousness toward George in his last days.

This is to introduce yet another large aspect of the Gershwin phenomenon. To love George was at least to try to love his relatives. George became famous for ostentatiously not getting married, but he was also a great family man who made sure no one ever got left behind; not Ira, whose lyrics he began to use perhaps before they were strictly ready (some of Ira's early attempts are plain awful); nor his sister, Frances, whose singing career he watched over as vigilantly as he watched over her honor (like other lotharios, he was terrified that she might run into someone like him); nor even his parents, who were just the kind of rough-edged immigrants that arrivistes commonly try to hide but whom George seemed to relish and expect other people to relish too. Gershwin obviously saw the world not just through rose-colored glasses but through magnifying ones, so that Papa Gershwin became, in his son's versions, one of the great characters of all time, while Momma Gershwin got promoted to the equivalent in mothers. So who wouldn't want to meet such giants? Anyway, there was no question of leaving them behind. So anyone coming to see Gershwin, however grand, might find himself desperately trying to decipher one Russian accent or the other from the parent in residence that day instead.

George would probably have laughed. Perhaps he could afford to feel so detached about his family because he actually owed them so little. In fact, since both senior Gershwins were completely unmusical, and George had been making his own living since age twelve or so, his debt was about as small as a child's can be. But he probably did owe them something, and was all too happy to acknowledge and exaggerate it. From his mother, George may possibly have inherited his powerful drive to "be somebody," although her own version of how you did this was as crude as any peasant's. All that young Rose Gershowitz had learned about the great ladies of Russia was that they glittered and shone: So one imagines many quixotic trips to the beauty parlor and the dressmaker. Females new to America have always been easy to make fun of for their optimistic do's and dyes and their death-or-glory stabs at makeup. But Rose also raised some very functional children in an alien world who would, partly thanks to her, have plenty of time and money to get those things right, and it's entirely possible that George appreciated that.

A couple of other clues to the Gershwins can perhaps be deduced from two disconnected remarks of Levant's, one being that they were an "even more undemonstrative" family than his own. Back in Russia, Rose had probably also observed that great ladies tend to act standoffish, or, as the word then was, hoity-toity, toward the outside world. Both Lane and Ronell would testify that Rose actually treated them quite warmly once they were safely inside the circle, but she did believe in style, as she understood it, and she presumably passed this on to George, leaving it up to him to translate the concept into American.

Most immigrant parents could only transmit the vague yet powerful ambition that brought them here; the children usually had to do most of their own steering. But Momma did do George one favor that would make up for any mistakes. Although she could see (it's hard to miss it) that money was the one indispensable component of Being Someone in this country, she also knew, or sensed, that classiness mattered too. So while all she basically wanted was for her gifted son to write a lot of hits like Mr. Berlin and make the family rich, some impulse (of snobbery? ancestral memory?) also told her to make sure that he got the best classical training that the Gershwin treasury could spring for. Which makes her one of the great unconscious benefactors of all time, a patron of the American arts second to none.

Levant's second comment was that George seemed to have a "natural aristocracy" about him, which sounds like the same thing Kern was talking about, but doesn't sound like Rose at all. Whatever her virtues, Rose was anything but a "natural" at anything, and when she got what she wanted, namely, a successful and classy son, her instincts told her absolutely nothing about how to handle it. So George's fame went to Momma's head a lot more than it went to his, and it ultimately rendered her, from all accounts, rather pointlessly aloof and difficult and not particularly happy about it. If, as his music suggests, George had his own streak of melancholy beneath all the bubbles, this at least may be due to Momma, who at any rate makes a better suspect for the blues than Papa the clown.

But it's hard to tell about Papa. As in many bios of the period, the father seems to be almost missing from George's formative years. And maybe Morris was—sister Frances says he was missing from hers. But even a remote father can leave traces, if only sometimes in his observed style. "The way he wears his hat," as Ira would say, "the way he sips his

tea." These are the kinds of things you remember, especially about someone who doesn't talk much.

So, since Morris undoubtedly wore his share of hats in that hat-
wearing age, and probably sipped a barrel of tea as well, during his
beloved pinochle games, it is probably among these small touches that
something as elusive and hard to pin down as "natural aristocracy" is to be
found. At any rate, it may be worth nothing here that, George's own opinion to the contrary, Morris Gershwin was the parent George reminded
people of, not Rose. In fact, Papa Gershwin's response to fame seemed to
have mirrored his son's precisely in that he was pleased as punch about it
("I'm *Judge* Gershwin's father," as it sounded like to the traffic cop, a misunderstanding that caused the cop to promptly wave him through--was
this a great country or what?), but oddly bemused and detached. Morris
knew more than most people about the ups and downs of life. And though
he is mostly remembered now, when he is, for his malapropisms and off-
the-wall observations, it should be noted that he passed the sternest of all
Lower East Side tests with flying colors: He always had some money.

"The Gershwins were not poor," confirmed Yip Harburg. But why
weren't they? Rose and Morris had no natural advantages over here, no
grubstake or rich relatives, and Morris's only professional training was in
a trade (shoe-cutting) that apparently bored him, so instead he plunged,
broken vowels and all, into the restaurant business and the Turkish bath
business and any other business he could take by the scruff and manage
for. And this did his son George the unwitting favor of introducing him to
the whole city, as the family moved from one address to another, picking
up new sights, sounds, and neighbors, and giving him the day-to-day
panorama that would make the "Rhapsody in Blue" such a unique evocation of a modern city. Yet even regarding this particular masterpiece, Morris affected only boredom. "Again? The 'Rhapsody'?" he would say each
time it was played.

But that's about all the hard news we're going to get about Papa Gershwin. One of the sturdiest barriers between that era and this is the hedge
of wisecracks and funny anecdotes that automatically brewed up around
celebrities and near celebrities, sometimes hiding their true selves completely. For instance, the young Gershwins used to bandy the name of one
"cousin Botkin the painter" around so facetiously that I was surprised to

find years later that there really was such a person and that he was a most distinguished painter.

And at a second glance, one wonders further whether George and Ira might not have invented Morris altogether, along with Cousin Botkin, for their own professional purposes as counters in the endless game of Can You Top This? played at the Algonquin Round Table and in the gossip columns. Never has the humor of broken English been quite so over-worked, and Papa Gershwin could have been inserted into Georgie Jessel's menagerie of goofy relatives without anyone noticing.

So too Morris, who must in real life have worked very hard and una-musingly to support his family, comes down to us now entirely in the form of a few funny stories. All his real work has gone the way of Rose's washing and ironing and floor-mopping, to be replaced by a kind of lordly insou-ciance. Viz, one day, when George was showing off his art deco apartment to some upscale visitors, Papa Gershwin tiptoed up and, in his most win-ning manner, said, "Tell me, ladies, whatever became of 'oh fudge'?"

With a slight change in circumstance, one can easily imagine some daffy peer of the realm or lord of the manor saying this, but one can't imagine Rose doing so. She would have boasted; Morris had reached the next stage in evolution, where you don't need to boast—you know it. In his book, the ladies wouldn't have come to the apartment at all if the Gershwins hadn't been very important people, so that was taken care of, and he could concentrate on being a perfect host. Most of the jobs he'd taken had required certain PR qualities and some natural charm, so it's safe to assume that George got some version of these from his old man. But did Morris even know that he was funny? Well, he knew that people laughed and that they came back for more, and we know that the Gersh-wins always had some money. So it is safe to guess that much of his charm had a commercial basis, and that, when he wasn't promoting ei-ther his son or his business, he became again one of the "undemonstra-tive" Gershwins.

But that really is it for both Papa and Momma, because George didn't hang around the house like Ira, absorbing influences, but was out the door every chance he got, absorbing something his own size, namely, the city itself.

Juggle the chromosomes as one will, and squeeze every nuance out of the anecdotes, and one can still find nothing in Gershwin's immediate background to account either for his musical genius or the extraordinary aura and the magnanimity that seemed almost to flow out of the music, in the direction of other songwriters. "He was very warm and very encouraging," said Arthur Schwartz, who as an unknown youth had just brazened his way into George's apartment and been asked immediately to play some of his tunes. "And he gave me the feeling that perhaps I did have some talent and to persevere." Or, as George said to young Harold Arlen, "Hey, kid, that new song of yours is a pip."

"I had the thrilling feeling he meant it," added Arlen, who, like Schwartz, would go on to give Gershwin some of his stiffest competition, without ever losing his friendship.

Gershwin's extended family of songwriters was never just some private club consisting of fellow New Yorkers and/or fellow Jews. One day, the Boston Irishman Jimmy "Don't Blame Me" McHugh ran into George on the street and confessed under friendly questioning that as a matter of fact he had just been wiped out by the stock market crash and could use a new piano. So naturally he found that very thing waiting for him when he got back to his apartment, courtesy of George.

Once again, one is struck, as Lane and Ronell would be, by the particularity of George's thoughtfulness. All a celebrity strictly needs to do to be considered a great guy is to strew a little money around vaguely or, if that's too painful for him, to dispense smiles, warm handshakes, and unspecific words of encouragement. But George took the trouble to find out precisely what was needed, even if it took time as well as money—or even if all it took was thoughtfulness. For instance, when the young Anglo-Scots Midwesterner Hoagy Carmichael decided to get married in New York, it was George who coaxed Hoagy's mother to play the piano at the wedding. Although Mrs. Carmichael had once played ragtime at a local movie house, no one else had apparently learned this or thought to ask her. But she jumped at the request and played up a storm that day—"much better than that Gershwin fellow," according to her dour husband.

Gershwin's embrace of other songwriters was, in short, universal, reaching back into the past and forward into the future. Someone who once made the mistake of questioning Irving Berlin's musicianship in George's presence was met with an answering volley of felicitous exam-

ples that the junior of the two geniuses had obviously memorized. And
even after serious people had begun asking George serious questions about
his own concert works, he'd passed up the invitation to show off with lists
of impressive classical influences and would continue to cite Berlin and
Kern instead, not out of coyness, but out of loyalty and his usual discon-
certing honesty. He had been influenced by the older songwriters and was
still being influenced by younger ones and wanted the world to know it.
Mozart didn't need his help now. Ronell and others did.

"He listened to all of us," Arlen told me—after, of course, they'd listened to his latest first, an agreeable condition that they would probably
have set themselves if the roles had been reversed. And again, "We were
always together in one bunch trying to help each other," as Arlen added
another time. Curiously, I found this second quote cited in a book that
otherwise tends to slight Gershwin's songs in favor of his concert work, as
most of the writing about George has tended to do, even if it has to fly in
the teeth of its own evidence.

But suppose we follow George's own lead for once, and think of him
first and last as a songwriter instead—how did even that happen? There
was no music of any kind in the Gershwins' various houses, even if he'd
stuck around to listen, and the chief sound he heard outside was the nonstop clatter of his own roller skates. He didn't even know he liked music
until age eleven or so, at which point it must have hit him all in a body—
classical and pop alike. Where Berlin had grown up with and assimilated
the melody of the streets, Gershwin found his ears flooded simultaneously with both Berlin and Beethoven, the latest and the oldest. And no
sooner had he started serious tutoring under the esteemed Charles Ham-
bitzer than he went to work plugging songs and making piano rolls and
steeping himself in that as well. So, theoretically, he had a choice of directions. But when his adventurous piano playing began to wander into composition, there was no contest. Songs were the currency around there.
Even young Mozart would have had to start with pop if he'd been born on
the Lower East Side. And if pop music wasn't ready for Gershwin yet, he'd
have to make it ready.

If he could, that is. Even Gershwin's preternatural optimism seems to
have paused at this. The songs he must have been plugging and piano-
rolling circa 1910 were catchy but trite beyond measure and could all be

vamped on exactly the same chords, like some of the rock hits of the 1960s. And who was to say that the folks who bought the sheet music and sang it round the piano could ever be wooed into wanting anything better? None of the places George's fingers chose to roam seemed to lead in the direction of sing-alongs. So what was a teenage prodigy to do?

In the lingo of Horatio Alger, it was Ragged Dick's darkest hour, and it is in this context that Gershwin's reverence for Berlin and Kern should be viewed. Their timing in his life was perfect, as if they'd been waiting in the next room. Although both men had been writing quietly for several years, Berlin didn't really find his voice (or his copyrights) until about 1911, when George was twelve or so, at which point Irving rolled out a sufficient sample of ragtime songs to show how much room there was for more. Where earlier songs in this mode seem mostly to call attention to their own syncopation, practically tapping your foot for you, Berlin syncopates or not as it suits him, burying it in the verse of "Alexander's Ragtime Band" and sliding it in and out of songs like "I Love a Piano." "Over the keys/the ivories" is like a miniature sleigh ride placed in the middle to reward you for getting this far. Irving is at play in the fields of ragtime, and Gershwin never needed two invitations to a party like that.

And then while he was still playing around with that, along came part two of the course, Jerome Kern's show tunes and especially "They Didn't Believe Me" (1914), to show how the new jaunty, loose-gaited American style could be transferred to truly distinguished music and could be marched right up the hill to the most distinguished addresses on Broadway, which must have towered like Mount Fuji above George's various workshops.

Now if only George could write like that himself . . . but of course he could, magically soon, and so well that both his idols welcomed him to the fraternity as an equal while he was still young enough to savor just meeting them. In fact, no songwriter ever wasted less time reaching his prime and coming into his own. For once, it happened almost the way it did in the movie. Al Jolson, the hottest entertainer of the day, comes around to George's place of business, looking for new material, and falls in love with "Swanee," the selfsame song that would captivate Vladimir Dukelsky a little later, presumably in Jolson's very own version. "How I love ya, how I love ya." Thus Gershwin had answered the main question about himself with his very first hit. He would not need to write two different kinds of music to win two different kinds of audience. Jolson, the blackface minstrel, and Duke, the White Russian fussbudget, were brothers under the skin. Of course, in the normal course of events, Gershwin's lowbrow career had come first, in the form of regular assignments on the tits-and-ass end of Broadway, where the follies and scandals, the gags and the gals, labored to divert the tired businessmen. No matter how crummy the milieu, Gershwin's music turned it just as classy, and before he knew it, he'd caught the approving attention of Kern and Berlin.

After that, nothing could harm or deflect him. There are no idols like your first ones, and although Gershwin would soon have other targets and more highbrow models, he would never forget that it was by aiming at Berlin and Kern that he had arrived at wherever he was now. And besides, his heroes hadn't precisely handed the baton over to him, but clung teasingly to it themselves, and kept right on running. "You're pretty good, son. Now try to catch me," and the three of them were still chasing each other's tails, unofficially of course, as they disappeared one by one over the horizon.

So, in this book anyhow, Gershwin is first and last a songwriter—which doesn't mean we have to throw a drop cloth over his classical work. The two sides of George were exquisitely mixed and played into each other constantly. But classically minded writers on the subject have tended to assume that their kind of music in some sense "won" because they consider it better music and more worthy of George's ambitions, but this was never true. Every great concert work of his would be followed by a volley of new and better songs, clearly based on the same inspiration that gave him the longer work. The year before George died, he went to Hollywood, not just to make up for the money he'd lost while working on *Porgy and Bess,* but, by Levant's firsthand account, to catch up with Cole Porter and Richard Rodgers, who'd sneaked past him as songwriters while he was plodding through his masterpiece.

Guesses as to what he would have done had he lived longer outnumber our conjectures about Jack Kennedy—who, like George, said different things to different people, depending on the arc of his enthusiasms—but what Gershwin did do was write songs, right up to the final day, when half of his brain was occupied with a tumor.

So songs literally did come first and they came last, and in between he brought out a book of his best ones that spells out what they meant to him. In contrast to most sheet music, which was always as simple as the publisher could make it, Gershwin's arrangements look like Jackson Pollock paintings and can only be played properly by expert pianists. And in his introduction, he makes the illuminating argument that it is precisely the improvement in the nation's piano playing that had made possible the great leap forward in American songs in the 1920s. And if this leap can, by any stretch, be called a movement, this one-page introduction was surely its manifesto, because unlike the Gershwin of legend, he wasn't just talking about himself or his songs. Gershwin's vanity was never small enough to settle for mere preeminence in his field; he wanted the field itself to be preeminent, and he watched the competition like a hawk for signs of excellence, noting, for instance, that the musical phrase in the first measure of Arlen's "Stormy Weather" is never repeated, and expressing envy over the bridge of Ellington's "Sophisticated Lady." He needed these men to be good if only for the sake of his own place in music, which, as he may have sensed, depended squarely on the "genus of the American song" and its final stock price. If Jerome Kern sank without a trace, Gershwin might wind up clinging to a footnote himself.

At any rate, the highbrow critics of his own day had no trouble remembering that he was a songwriter, and never missed a chance to hold it against him. To them, Tin Pan Alley was a critical disability, a chain around his leg, and every time they seemed on the verge of saying something nice about him, they would remember the magic phrase and hit him over the head with it instead. And despite the changes along that street, the name Tin Pan Alley never sounded any better to the critics, but remained the same old dead-end street between Skid Row and Featherbed Lane that could always be used to put George back in his place, perhaps even after one had grudgingly admitted his God-given, thoroughly wasted gift.

On these terms, the serious reviewers were predictably kinder to Gershwin's early work than they would be to his later, because it made no uppity claims. According to George, they actually overpraised *Blue Monday,* which was a fragment of opera, or song-plus. George was a surprisingly cool self-critic. And "Rhapsody in Blue" got off lightly too, perhaps because it was part of a pseudo-jazz concert in which, if nothing else, it outshone the competition. (Elsewhere in the program, there was even something by Victor Herbert, and the mere phrase "Jazz by Victor Herbert" is enough to put anyone in a good mood, so the critics felt free to throw out the rulebook, praise the composer's vitality, and in one or two cases even to enjoy themselves, on the understanding that tapping one's foot is not what music is really about.)

One critic mysteriously found "Rhapsody" "lifeless [and] derivative"—of what he didn't say—but the derivative charge would be leveled again, more plausibly, some years later, from George's own side of the tracks, by his friend and fellow songwriter Hoagy Carmichael, who thought "Rhapsody" was made up mostly of familiar bits and pieces of jazz, and that George "was not a real jazzman" anyway, but merely a "Tin Pan Alley genius," concerning which type Hoagy had interestingly mixed feelings.

With this we're back where we belong. Inasmuch as Carmichael was a jazzman himself, he was predisposed to despise commercial music as much as any highbrow, and the above criticism shows him defending his turf every bit as stubbornly as his counterparts on the musical right. Jazz didn't want to let George in at first any more than Carnegie Hall did, though both sides were quite happy to concede him Tin Pan Alley. But the catch for Carmichael was that he had just written the most commercial song in history himself, and hoped to write some more, and there was no denying that the success of his "Stardust" owed at least something to George's enlargement of the form.

So if George wasn't precisely a jazzman, he'd opened the door to jazzmen, and was someone you could talk to on the Alley. (Hoagy's two memoirs reveal no other friends in the songwriting business at all, except his collaborators.) Better yet, Gershwin was someone you could play tennis with as well.

It's symbolic of the great Gershwin misunderstanding that everyone seems to know about his tennis games with the famous atonalist Arnold Schoenberg, but no one seems to know that he also played it with the likes of Hoagy Carmichael, an equally piquant pairing in its own world—or indeed, that he would play it with anyone who'd give him a match. The *thunk* of tennis balls and *plink* of Ping-Pong balls, and whatever the sound is that golf balls make, followed George everywhere, like background music that's too insistent to ignore. How a man spends half his waking hours surely belongs in the text, not the footnotes, of his life. It seems that whenever George wasn't playing the piano, he was playing something else (he has even been called a sexual athlete), and at the piano itself, he was playing as much as working, in the compulsive style of America in the 1920s, when you played until you dropped. No one ever got more sheer physical exercise out of a keyboard, so perhaps it isn't too Hollywood-fanciful to flash back again to the beginning, to our hyperactive hero's boyhood, at the point where he has just gotten hooked by Dvořák's "Humoresque" and Rubinstein's "Melody in F" and can put off music no longer. And one pictures him hitting the piano with the force he usually devoted to hitting balls or occasional faces, and deciding on the spot that this is a great game too, because, like a character in a dream, he could play it superbly almost on sight and could have this same dream anytime he wanted.

Everyone talks about the childlike awe with which Gershwin discussed his own music, and about his famous sprints to the piano at other people's parties, as if to show off this new trick he's just learned. But seldom has a vice been easier to understand. Imagine a great, somewhat tongue-tied athlete who is actually encouraged to play his sport in the living room and who, by doing so, is guaranteed to outshine the brightest company in London, Paris, and New York. Who could ask for anything more?

It really was a new trick too, every single time, and not just a worn-out party piece. "What comes out of that piano frightens me," he's alleged to have said, and it was this sheer unpredictability as much as his technique that drew people. Who knew what great song might be born tonight and merely live forever? George seemed as excited to find out as anyone.

"George at the piano was George happy," said Rouben Mamoulian, which means that he must have been happy an awful lot of the time, although witnesses report bursts of operatic gloom when George was at rest—all the more reason to keep playing. Relief was never more than a keyboard away. (Speaking of gloom, though, Joan Peyser passes on the important news that George first smelled burning rubber as early as 1934, which means his fatal tumor might have set up shop three years before his death, which would explain the gloomy episodes I've heard of.)

"He was the only man I knew who could make a piano laugh," said

Abram Chasins, and numerous photographs show the piano apparently returning the favor, with George fiendishly grinning over the instrument's latest joke. Also, he had a cheerful way of attracting pretty girls to come sit next to him at the piano bench, a knack Vernon Duke says he was never able to master himself, although he too was a handsome fellow and a dazzling pianist.

Yet Gershwin's hyperactivity was too laid-back and self-possessed to be mistaken for simple nervousness, or escapism, or the other pop-psychology staples that his less physical critics might be tempted to reach for. But it wasn't all hyperactivity; he also enjoyed goofing off and kidding around. Levant records the two of them actually lolling about, talking football and girls like college roommates. And Carmichael reports that one day after he and George had wrapped up their business on the court, they swore a mighty oath never to write a piece of music set for the ukulele. One picks up the immortal sounds of the locker room and of athletes winding down with wisecracks and jocose rituals of friendship. This side of George is missing from the conventional biography—George the jock, the sports-man, a type so alien to writers on the arts that they've tended to circle this robust figure cautiously, as if it were a Hottentot or noble savage, reading whatever they like into him. (One analyst has even suggested Gershwin had low self-esteem, a diagnosis that would have had his friends roaring for days.)

Expeditions to Gershwin's dark side have a way of foundering on his boisterous physicality, which seems to call for a different kind of analysis. This was not some introvert discovering his body aesthetically, but a macho little street brawler hitting the arts like a cyclone and realizing they're not just for sissies after all, but can fit perfectly into his daily round of ball bashing as it ascends from roller-skate hockey to tennis to the top of the hill—golf, which he found kind of slow, and played occasionally at the speed of Charlie Chaplin, but played expertly too; and in the same spirit, he would, as time went on, add such indoor sports as oil painting, interior decorating, and ballroom dancing (at which he was a whiz) to his frantic schedule.

When George hit upon anything new, be it art deco or Joseph Schil-linger's mathematical theory of composition, he was, says Vernon Duke, like a kid with a new toy, as if mental activity were to be prized for its gamelike quality. (Gershwin's interest in Schillinger was picked up by Oscar Levant, who studied with him to no avail. The one positive result I know of from Schillinger's theories was, of all things, Glenn Miller's theme song, "Moonlight Serenade." Go figure.) Luckily for all concerned, Gershwin was no superstar at his various games (his tennis was only fair), so he brought his athletic temperament to bear on music instead, where it seemed as strange as an artistic temperament would seem in a baseball dugout.

One doesn't want to exaggerate this. George might have seemed a little strange in a dugout too. Yet a sportswriter might note that at least some of Gershwin's puzzling quirks are commonplace in the sports world, including his slightly comical "I am the greatest" swagger, his stoicism under fire—criticism rolled off him like jabs off Muhammad Ali—and the curious blend of generosity and competitiveness that characterized his dealings with colleagues. Only in sports can people be such wholehearted enemies and friends at the same time, and only in sports does a man actually feel let down if the opposition isn't good enough and he wins too easily. Thus, when George declared his envy of "Sophisticated Lady," it is not far-fetched to picture a tennis player jumping over the net to congratulate an opponent. "Well played—I'll get you next time."

Ellington had just raised the stakes, and forced George to play better too. Yet perhaps only a man who also gets to play both music and tennis with the likes of Arnold Schoenberg could manage to be quite as sporty and breezily good-humored as George. Gershwin's classical alter ego may have had a bumpy ride at times, but at least Gershwin had an alter ego, to absorb life's shocks: Most songwriters had no alter egos at all. And tellingly, one of the few who did, our old friend Vladimir Dukelsky, actually received worse reviews for his classical work than George ever did, but behaved as if he came from a superior species anyhow, just for having written it.

Gershwin was certainly pleased with himself too, but his sporting impulse was to share the wealth, and his magnanimity undoubtedly helped usher in an era of goodwill along Tin Pan Alley, which a battle-scarred veteran like Kern might have particularly appreciated. Earlier in the century, a songwriter "with nothing small about" him would have been as lost as Gulliver. Veterans like George M. Cohan and Irving Berlin had to fight so many small fights with small people—over copyrights, royalties, credits, survival—that they remained slightly crouched and suspicious for the rest of their days. But by the twenties, ASCAP was in place and the new technology of radio and records was about to open up a musical superhighway like unto a yellow brick road for composers to stroll down arm in arm. So it was high time for a large free spirit like Gershwin to come bouncing along, and his name went up on the national marquee almost immediately and stays there still alongside Babe Ruth's and Scott Fitzgerald's as a symbol of that Roman candle of an era.

With all this established and certified in neon by the midtwenties, it may not have required all that much stoicism for George to shrug off the scattering of sneers that greeted his concert works. If Schoenberg fortified one for Ellington, he also equally fortified one for Virgil Thomson and the other highbrows. Still, it must have taken the detachment of Morris Gershwin himself to withstand the gale force advice that blew in from all sides after his Concerto in F in 1925. It seemed that everyone was telling George how to use his, unfortunately undeniable, talent. Since, among other things, he would eventually write a perfect pastiche of Wozzeck for "Of Thee I Sing" and an authentic madrigal for *A Damsel in Distress,* it seems odd that Gershwin couldn't have taken the few simple steps it required to placate the New York critics—whose own brilliance should not be exaggerated—and remove the curse of Tin Pan Alley forever.

If he'd wanted to. This was the heart of the matter: George did not consider Tin Pan Alley a curse at all, but a gold mine into which one could probably invest all one's time and talent, including one's classical talent, in hopes of finding a genuine new American art. So he went his serene way, alternately writing songs and concert pieces that ran together into a single sound that could be played in a pinch by a jazz band or a symphony orchestra, or by some fusion of both that didn't yet exist.

But while everyone noticed, and mostly deplored, the effect of this process on classical music, only a few initiates like Arlen and the envious Vincent Youmans seemed to take in the simultaneous effect it was having on songs. While the critics were guarding all the entrances to make sure Gershwin didn't smuggle any of his dirty Tin Pan Alley tricks into the classical shrine, George was busy smuggling the sophistication and resourcefulness of "good music" out the exits and into Broadway musicals, and thence onto the street. Alec Wilder, who was oddly allergic to Gershwin, blurs the importance of this development by comparing George's 1920s songs with other people's more evolved 1930s ones that had built on them. But if you go back to the very beginning, to the piano piece "Rialto Ripples" (1917) or the song "Some Wonderful Sort of Someone" (1918), you can already hear something completely fresh and different, something not quite jazz and not quite classical, but a newborn sound that would influence American songs for the next and best quarter century.

Fortunately, a book has been written that illustrates roughly how the traffic worked. Although Deena Rosenberg's *Fascinating Rhythm* doesn't undertake to trace Gershwin's influence through the whole American songbook, her X-rays of a few of his songs are enough to establish a continuum between his classical work and his popular, and to suggest another continuum between his songs and other people's. Clearly, one of the games he most liked to play at the piano was to see how many songs he could winkle out of a single musical phrase, the most spectacular examples being the three he got from simply reciting his beloved pentatonic scale— the reflective "Maybe," the noisy "Clap Yo' Hands," and the comic "They All Laughed"—and three others he "found," with a little help from Ira's words and a few grace notes of his own, lurking in the "Good Evening Friends" sequence in "Rhapsody in Blue." And I have no doubt Rosenberg could have discovered as many in the Concerto in F if she'd gotten around to it: the song "Soon," for instance, which illustrates beautifully how a song runs one way and an orchestral piece another. Gershwin never stopped shuffling his themes until, or after, he'd found the perfect setting of rhythm and emphasis. "Maybe" is a gorgeous song, "Clap Yo' Hands" sounds too busy, and while that theme from the "Rhapsody" may have sounded cliché to Carmichael, it seemed breathtakingly original to everyone else once George had disguised it lightly as "The Man I Love."

In fact, Rosenberg considers that particular song such a breakthrough that it cleared the way not only to George's own best, but to other people's best too, like "My Funny Valentine" and "Night and Day"—in short, to the best of Rodgers and Porter as well—thus locating a single pipeline between Carnegie Hall and Broadway. And whether it was one song that did the trick or many, "The Man I Love" makes a plausible landmark because in 1925, the year after George wrote it and started putting it into shows and taking it out again (it holds some kind of record for this), three break-out songs by other writers appeared among the usual welter of "Yes Sir, That's My Baby." Rodgers's first hit, "Manhattan," Carmichael's first, "Riverboat Shuffle," and Kern's far and away hippest to date, "Who," which signified respectively that a classical music student, a "jazz baby" (as Carmichael described himself), and a master of American operetta had all found homes on the new Tin Pan Alley, as at least partly redesigned by Gershwin.

After which, the deluge. Over the next five years, Youmans went from "I Want to Be Happy" to "More Than You Know." Berlin, following his brief ego-shaking crisis of confidence, would go from "Always" to "How Deep Is the Ocean," and Donaldson from, indeed, "Yes Sir, That's My Baby" to "Little White Lies" . . . and so on all along the street. Gershwin had proved with one song or several that sophistication sells, and had shown his comrades at least one way to write it, and the bell curve, the boom within the boom, began to rise sharply, with Gershwin sitting on top of it all the way until his death a decade later.

And it was in that same epic year of 1925 that the serious New York critics began seriously to give up on George, like philanthropists who've tried everything for some child of the streets and found the kid just hope-less. His most ambitious work, the Concerto in F, orchestrated after some laborious self-instruction, had debuted, and all it proved to them was that you can't take the Alley out of the boy, especially when the Alley has turned into a boulevard. To Gershwin's ear, the kind of American music that the critics themselves thought they wanted *had* to contain elements of pop (as they didn't yet call it), partly because Berlin and Kern happened to be the most interesting composers in the country just then, and partly because in his brief, kaleidoscopic apprenticeship, the two kinds of music had, as we've seen, arrived simultaneously and virtually intertwined. There was no stage at which George could have organically evolved from one to the other, because he was too busy evolving back and forth be-tween the two of them in a dizzy dialectic, studying the classics at one moment with a teacher who was already urging him to higher things, just like a critic, and at the next making his ragtime piano rolls and plugging schlock. But perhaps the most annoying thing about the Concerto was that Gershwin hadn't even needed to get pushy about it—a vandal crashing the temple and writing graffiti—but was in the concert hall by invitation again and always would be. The grim fact was that the serious people needed him there to attract their own customers, their own highbrow fans. It was humiliating, so the least they could do was insult him for it.

If the critics were not going to like his concert stuff any way that he did it, maybe he should skip all that for now and try doing it all with songs, which, incidentally, had recently become a family business—always a factor with George. In fact, the late 1920s might be called the years of apprenticeship for Ira as well, as he edged his way up from the simpleminded *Lady, Be Good* (1924) to his own sound in " 'S Wonderful" (1927), and then the Pulitzer-winning lyrics of the political satire *Of Thee I Sing.* "All the sexes from Maine to Texas" is more than confident: It also hits the notes just right, and makes the whole song work better. "Who cares what banks fail in Yonkers?" The brothers could do their own banking now.

A trip abroad that same epic year of 1925 might also have been an occasion for Gershwin to concentrate just on his songs. Europeans had their own kind of snobbery, and it was almost the opposite of ours. For at least two centuries, they had been sneering at pale American imitations of their own forms, but they could be awestruck, and reluctantly impressed, by our vulgarity. Americans could study their hearts out in Paris, but our grand master was Walt Disney, our Mona Lisa was Donald Duck. And what the Europeans liked about our music was that they couldn't do it themselves.

To American critics, Gershwin sounded exactly like what they wanted to get away from. It was the essence of their own time and place represented musically, just as James Joyce had verbally rendered Dublin in *Ulysses.* This kind of rendering absolutely had to include the time and place's vulgarity, its flash and its hustle, and what can only be called its gorgeous ugliness. Two years earlier, G. K. Chesterton had pointed out how beautiful Times Square must look to someone who couldn't read, and here was that same thought set to music. If Gershwin's music had been any purer or more correct, it wouldn't have been New York.

And the rest of the world probably wouldn't have liked it so much either. After all, Europeans couldn't read Times Square themselves, and the phrase "Tin Pan Alley" probably sounded both Dada and wonderfully American.

If the Old World wanted anything from us at all it was modernity, and Gershwin was as modern as a skyscraper. And, as it so often is, the curse of commercialism and cheap popularity was softened in translation. Call a song an aria, or a show an opera, and it steps up in class. Call Gershwin's music "le jazz hot" and it takes on artistic pretensions. Thus every popular musician—from Chopin to the Beatles—needs to be heard by fresh ears against a fresh background. At home, it usually takes forever for pop music to become folk music, let alone classical music, but foreigners don't have to wait that long, and Gershwin's reception in Europe in that same overflowing year of 1925 was less grudging and embarrassed than it was here. He would thenceforth return from each of his few trips abroad fortified and bubbling with ideas and optimism. Levant says that Gershwin was particularly taken to learn that the last movement of his Concerto in F had been reprised by audience demand at the Venice International Festival of Contemporary Music, something that had happened only once before in history, "In 1894," as he told people reverently.

With this in his pocket, or about to be, the American critics probably looked as small to him as he did to them. After all, they had their own troubles in the twenties, trying to lay down the law in the world of the New and post-New, and they must have been relieved to find someone they could condescend to so confidently. If Stravinsky wrote something in jazz, he could make up his own rules. But if Gershwin did the same, he was judged by the strictest European standards. Gershwin was a kid from the neighborhood, trying to improve himself. And not trying hard enough.

Because no matter how serious he tried to be he wouldn't stop writing songs, as if concert music couldn't scratch his itch by using up enough of the tunes in his head. Thus it came to pass that even while he was studiously orchestrating the last movement of his make-or-break Concerto, he was dashing off songs for his next musical, *Tip-Toes*. And by the time he had brought the finished concerto to New York (a phrase that sounds show-bizzy itself), he was actually shepherding two musicals through rehearsal. He was like a man cheating on his wedding night. No wonder some critics—not all—railed at him like schoolmasters. They knew impertinence when they saw it. Gershwin was in effect saying that Broadway songs were just as important as what they did, and this was intolerable.

Anyhow, there's no need to caricature Gershwin's critics here or anywhere else. George could be maddeningly cavalier about his musical ABC's, and you didn't have to be a provincial American to construe this in terms of his haste to make lots of money doing something else.

The Europeans probably assumed the same thing (he was an American, wasn't he?), but were less annoyed and more impressed. In a wonderfully useful anecdote, Vernon Duke describes taking his expatriate pals Prokofiev and Diaghilev to hear an execrable French translation of the concerto played in Paris, and all three were variously disappointed; Duke by the French musicians; Diaghilev because it was "good jazz and bad Liszt" (if you wrote rhapsodies, you had to sound like Liszt); and Prokofiev by the same thing that bothered the American critics, Gershwin's failure to build adequate bridges between his themes.

The big difference was that Prokofiev, being less familiar with the cheap American materials in Gershwin's work, was better able to hear the completely new thing he'd made of them; and whatever he heard was enough to make him immediately want to meet Gershwin. Accordingly, George showed up the next morning at Sergey's hotel and proceeded to "play his head off," after which the Russian was pleased to pronounce that his guest would go far "if he left dollars and dinners alone."

Like everyone else, Prokofiev assumed that Gershwin wrote songs only for dollars and had to drop his real work to do them. Yet the chances are that for at least some of the morning, he'd been listening to George's songs and enjoying them just as much as the "serious" parts. But if he'd known the songs better, he might have realized, as Duke did, that Gershwin just wrote Gershwin, and the dollars he made only helped him to write more Gershwin. And the same went for "dinners" in his honor and other attentions, all of which he seems to have regarded as so many more invitations to play the piano and impress new people with new ideas. American geniuses as a breed are known to have notoriously weak hearts for flattery— one compliment wipes out some of them—but George could take any amount of it because it played to his strength, and he emerged like a giant refreshed from an orgy of recognition in Paris and elsewhere, recognition much noisier and more palpable than the amount that so poleaxed Ernest Hemingway. The curious detachment that George had inherited from his father must have told him that some of the attention was chic and silly— Gershwin's blue notes were "in" this year like Papa's fractured sentences—

but he loved the attention anyhow; and at least some of it was the real thing. After all, Prokofiev *had* wanted to meet him, and so would Alban Berg in Vienna, and other serious musicians everywhere he went. There seems to have been a consensus, as firm as it was vague, that Gershwin was on to something and that he mattered, whether or not any particular pieces of his music did. And there the matter rests to this day, with Arnold Schoenberg's heartfelt eulogy summing up the unresolved consensus at the time of Gershwin's death. "George Gershwin was one of this rare kind of musician to whom music is not a matter of more or less ability. Music to him was the air he breathed, the food that nourished him, [etc.]. There is no doubt that he was a great composer." But was he a good one also? Never mind. Gershwin was of this rare breed that doesn't have to be.

Primed with such ambiguous approval ("Why be a second-rate Ravel when you can be a first-rate Gershwin?" as another prospective teacher told him), Gershwin returned from Europe apparently less anxious to prove himself in the traditional forms of serious music—why be a second-rate Mozart? And right then "being a Gershwin" could be satisfied by immediately writing some new songs. However important his concert music had ever been to him (and you couldn't be a great composer without it, could you?), he could wait for the critical acclaim. In the meantime, one particular song, "I Got Rhythm," sounded as much like "being Gershwin" as anything else he ever did.

His mad sprints to the piano were prompted not just by vanity, but by deadlines, as he hustled to finish his new show and the one after. Musicals were perfect because they required new songs immediately, never mind polishing the old ones. It is often overlooked that for all of their harmonic brilliance, some of his early songs had the same slapdash quality as his concert pieces. Just as Vernon Duke notes how unadventurous Gershwin could be in matters of tempo, relying on the same old beat that had seen him through his piano-roll days, Alec Wilder comments on the conventionality of Gershwin's song forms, even when he was writing for the theater, where you could use any form you liked. Thirty-two bars divided four ways, A A B A—who had time for anything more? Although he could chop up the beat with the best of them, as in "Fascinating Rhythm," and would write his last great song, "Our Love Is Here to Stay," in the slightly more demanding (and I think rewarding) A B A B + form, in general he stuck to the fastest kind of delivery he knew.

In other respects, his songs began to sound markedly better and more thoughtful as the twenties went on, and his orchestral pieces more slap-dash, as if they were now the thing that was being done to meet his contractual obligations while the songs were his real self. "He Loves and She Loves," "Someone to Watch over Me," "Embraceable You"—the additional warmth of these songs hark back to that second trip to Europe in 1928, which may have prompted him not just to write like Gershwin but to find out what a Gershwin was.

With this in mind, he even allowed his disciple-cum-girlfriend Kay Swift to talk him into a fling with the latest rage, psychoanalysis, but without his magic piano he seemed to have found himself not particularly interesting. What came out of the piano might frighten him, but what came off the couch probably just bored him and made him want to go out and play something, either a game or a piano.

Without his instrument, he wasn't really George Gershwin anyway, so he took to exploring himself in ever more varied musical settings instead. Each of his next, and last, three orchestral works could have been a journal entry chronicling his response to some new experience. *An American in Paris* starts with a tourist's description of the city he's just arrived in (with a tip of his cap to one of his early heroes, Debussy), then switches to the visitor's sense that he doesn't really belong there and wants to go home, before proceeding to a joyous reconciliation as the American hears a way to have it all, his own city and this one, a richer version of himself. What Gershwin couldn't know was that he had also contributed to a form that didn't exist yet, that might be called a travelogue-ballet, complete with animated postcards from the Louvre. "They did right by George," I said to my father when the eponymous movie ended. "Yes," he thoughtfully answered, "they did right by George."

After that, the second "Rhapsody," which was originally called "Rhapsody in Rivets," returns the American to New York with a bang and with a slight sense of alienation—what's happening to this place? By the late twenties, Manhattan was right in the middle of the frantic building boom that would give it most of its famous skyline, with scaffolding indeed seeming to scrape the sky, and hammers pounding down from there like thunder, and this is what it sounded like to George—the aural equivalent of Fritz Lang's jarring film *Metropolis*. Fittingly, though, George's piece was originally written as a species of special effects for the movies, yet already one feels he'd rather say it in a song or two, and perhaps he finally did in the sunny number "Slap That Bass," which shows the American no longer in awe of technology, but airily familiar with it as he dances along with the ship's pistons. And the "Cuban Overture" would probably have worked itself out as songs too, had Gershwin lived a few months longer. By the midthirties, Latin rhythms had insinuated their way into Tin Pan Alley and Hollywood, and his Broadway rival Youmans had already written a samba and a tango for the film *Flying Down to Rio* in acknowledgment. But as it stands, Gershwin's "What I Did on My Vacation" homage to the Caribbean sounds perfunctory, like a bread-and-butter letter, as if he hadn't really started to think in this form yet, and perhaps never would. "Just be yourself" was mischievous advice to give to this man of a thousand whims living in the land of perpetual change, but Broadway musicals had recently become coherent and more hospitable to the kind of social and political satire that the times suddenly seemed to call for, so he had to try one or two of those. *Strike Up the Band. Let 'Em Eat Cake.* Gershwin didn't do politics, he did moods. And as usual, he was up-to-the-minute.

Surely no American has ever done so much work so well *after* being the toast of Paris. But now as Broadway itself began to slow down in the early 1930s, Gershwin too decided to settle down with his true love, a little novel he'd read sometime before called *Porgy,* which really was worth taking his time over, and losing some chances to make money over. He had always been fascinated by black music and must have brought just about every black pianist in Harlem home to his apartment at one time or another, and to hell with the landlord's opinion. But this would give him a chance to go back a step further to the beginning and write black choral music as well, which is where it all began.

He'd often had to work hard, but in the Broadway sense of blitzkrieging projects through marathon sessions (he'd even scored his concerto that way). But now he had to slow down and work *really* hard, like a bank clerk or intricate craftsman, laboriously cranking out pages and pages by hand of the kind of music that gets you unbrilliantly from here to there, the equivalent of Yeats's "numb" lines of poetry. Unfortunately, Gershwin's vision did not reach all the way into production. And by the time *Porgy*, with "Bess" added to the name, opened for the first time on Broadway, his hard work had disappeared, leaving behind the usual malcontents in the press box and a dysfunctional hybrid on the stage: a Broadway musical slowed down by gobbits of opera, but not by enough of them to attract *that* audience either. The show dribbled along for one hundred-odd performances and died—to everyone's dissatisfaction. Later, other souls learned to get *Porgy and Bess* just right, and some brilliant words have been written about this.

So George wouldn't live to see it and at this point in time he didn't even have time for a broken heart. "I'd be very upset by this if I wasn't so busy right now," he's reported to have said after a busted romance— although really the words could have applied to any of his life's tragedies up to and almost including death itself.

Levant's book suggests a mood of enormous postpartum buoyancy after *Porgy*, marked by much stepped-up portrait painting and interior design and rumors of marriage. Gershwin had just written a masterpiece and knew it, and he had also had a ball with the black actors in *Porgy*. He now had a blank slate and a head full of melodies, so where to next? Certainly not to Broadway, where so many theaters had turned into movie houses that even a Gershwin had to line up for the next one, and where his songs would be expected to make some kind of sense in terms of a play that he hadn't even seen yet. In contrast you could go to Hollywood in a boom year like 1936 with a suitcase full of hits and dump them anywhere, regardless of subject matter. Love could "Walk Right In" absolutely any place it wanted and land on any singer of either sex who happened to be on the set that day, and anyone from Mickey Mouse to Zasu Pitts could remember the way anyone else "sipped his (or her) tea" or "danced till three."

So Gershwin signed on with Fred Astaire at RKO, the closest thing to a safe house for Broadway writers in Hollywood. But even Astaire couldn't guarantee his old friend the basic Broadway privilege of seeing his own songs through production—or even prevent Ginger Rogers from singing a couple of them. Actually, George didn't think that highly of Fred's singing either, perhaps wanting a bigger, richer instrument. Still, Fred would turn out to be not just his most effective interpreter then, but has remained so ever since, as he continues to audition Gershwin's last great songs for one generation after another. Astaire had already gone from being the least likely suspect as a movie star to the closest thing to a guaranteed immortal in film musical history.

Also, as Irving would say, Fred could sing just about anything you gave him, including whatever you had in your trunk. And George undoubtedly gave him at least one from there, "They Can't Take That Away from Me." But in general George never used an old song when a brand-new one would do, and he seemed to be in a particularly hyperactive phase at the moment, painting some great portraits, conducting some major concerts in L.A., chasing Paulette Goddard and Simone Simon around the backs of limousines, and playing golf and tennis at the same time, as if he didn't have a moment to lose.

In the circumstances, and with his fatal brain tumor pounding in, Gershwin's last days in Hollywood and on earth seemed downright epic, but also a bit confusing because the tumor seems to have struck so erratically. At one moment, we find George cast into deep gloom by Sam Goldwyn's command (for his next and last film assignment) to "write me some hits like Irving Berlin," which is where he'd come in some twenty years earlier. But at another, he's chuckling, perhaps for his last time, at hearing Sam and George Balanchine hotly arguing in broken Russian, the language of his youth. To judge from Levant's resolutely sunny—and indispensable—account in A Smattering of Ignorance, George barely seems to have had time for a tumor. So one deduces that its jabs remained intermittent, though increasingly ferocious, till very near the end, and it seems certain that George stayed at his post as long as he humanly could. If trouble really was coming, where better to be than at the piano?

Besides, there was work to be done. The competition had caught up with him amazingly fast, and what Rosenberg says about Gershwin's late songs applies equally to everyone else's as well, circa 1936, "George's music . . . is on the whole less given to the repetition of melodic fragments against shifting harmonies" (as in, to take a quintessential non-Gershwin example, Donaldson's "Carolina in the Morning"). Now he (and everyone else) preferred to use "a style of longer melodic lines and phrases . . . the harmonies, while still complex, sound even smoother and more fluid" and they contain what she quotes Dick Hyman as calling the "built-in syncopation," which was by now their defining ingredient of the whole jazz song movement. His Astaire movies gave him a chance to fool around with a form of music specific to film, which might be called the background cartoon or illustration. In *Shall We Dance,* Astaire and Rogers get into a unique love-hate walking-the-dog contest that you just have to see for yourself, and Gershwin's sublime music for it just has to be heard as well: It goes perfectly with Gershwin's two great preludes as a sublime concert substitute. In this case I am also reminded of a *New Yorker* one-liner set to jazz. Then the whole score of *A Damsel in Distress* seems to help the movie in telling its story, as if he has thrown away his trunk and is actually thinking of music for Joan Fontaine to sort of dance to, and for George Burns and Gracie Allen to be funny to. He even writes a madrigal to fit the English castle in the background.

It's too bad George didn't keep a diary—although its entries would probably have surprised *him* every day as much as anyone. What's missing in that last year or so is his next big plan. The problem was that modernist music took him away from his people, his audience. He'd managed to get away with a brilliant pastiche of Wozzeck in "Of Thee I Sing," and maybe he could score a whole movie in the style of "Walking the Dog," but ominously the "Second Rhapsody" and the "Cuban Overture" were the only things he ever wrote that you couldn't whistle on your way out of the concert hall.

It might be unfair to blame this on the modernism he'd picked up abroad. Still, for now, Porter and Rodgers were more stimulating targets than Shostakovich or Sibelius. The game seemed to be to see how much he could say in songs—from the laid-back country style of "I'm Biding My Time" to the wisecracking buoyancy of "Let's Call the Whole Thing Off" ("you say either, I say either"—what kind of song is that?), to the somber satisfaction of "A Foggy Day," which could be called "An American in London" to complete the trilogy and incidentally show how far he had come himself. Since "A Foggy Day" also comes so near the end of his life, it provides an elegiac moment to pause and consider George's own evolution from wide-eyed young genius to grand master.

Just as Gershwin had previously captured the screaming clangor of New York and the good-natured squeaks of Paris, he and his brother now set to work on the defining sounds of London, which they apparently (and quite correctly) took to be a compound of bells, and of people talking about the weather. Anyone lucky enough to have heard the carillon at Riverside Church in one of its exuberant flights of fancy toward the end of World War II will recognize how brilliantly "A Foggy Day" plays with the possibility of bells, from the verse's stentorian opening, on through the American's jazzy interjections, to the mock-solemn chimes that greet the final dispersal of the fog, like a winking Te Deum. The Age of Miracles hasn't passed. The sun has come out in London!

The other notable thing about "A Foggy Day" is that for once the lyrics make a real difference to the effect, so that George can now say almost as much in a song as he ever had in his concert works. Unlike George's ear-lier tunes, which had seemed like moving targets for Ira to throw lyrics at if he could ("I got rhythm . . . music . . . my man" . . . time's up), the long lines of his last songs finally gave his lyricist some room to breathe and work in, and the brothers began to click as never before.

It may come as a shock at this point to realize that George and Ira were still a shade younger when George died than Harpo and Chico were be-fore the *first* Marx Brothers movie. Both were still in the middle of matur-ing. Already it's hard to imagine any of George's last batch of tunes (all of which even the Gershwin-phobic Alec Wilder praises to the utmost, ex-cept for "Slap That Bass") being composed in his early rattly-bang, race-you-to-the-barn piano style, and equally hard to imagine the author of "He'll be big and strong, the man I love" being up to matching them. But as far as the team was concerned, this was just the beginning.

George's death at that excruciating moment would give all his last songs a weight of association that is for once altogether worthy of them. Songwriters regularly used to put more power into musical comedy songs than the settings strictly justified, in the hopes that some great singer or band would come along later and yank them out of the boy-meets-girl context and drive them at full speed. But in this case the mere passage of time has done the trick. The throwaway title song of the film *Shall We Dance,* for instance, now echoes across the years like music over water, conveying the jaunty, sad sound of a whole society that won't let the band go to bed, because tomorrow is going to be so awful: "The Long Weekend" between the wars was almost over, Gershwin music and all. And the brothers' last song together, "Our Love Is Here to Stay," has since been rescued from the trackless waste of *The Goldwyn Follies* of 1938 to become an anthem to friendship—a final hand-clasp of the Gershwins as the ship goes down, an ode to immortality in four-quarter time.

"The Rockies may crumble, Gibraltar may tumble" said the song, which George had just written with the half of his brain that hadn't been eaten yet by his tumor, and which he was still working on the day before he died. It was like a man planting a flag in the future, and giving rivals and partners in the Great American Jam Session something else to shoot for after he'd gone. In fact, like all his work in that dazzling Indian summer of creation, the song could have been expressly designed to stay here itself, and when I heard it again a decade later in Vincente Minnelli's gorgeous production of *An American in Paris,* I found myself thinking that this song simply gets better every year.

His dramatic death right after that would ensure not only that all his songs were here to stay but that everything about Gershwin was here to stay as well, including questions about the nature and inevitability of his death, which scientists have been arguing about ever since, but not in here they don't. Here, the big story is the shuddering impact of his death on his own gang, particularly on the two great rivals who had been most obsessed by him.

"I'm so upset at the moment I can hardly think," wrote the usually phlegmatic Richard Rodgers to his wife. "I just can't believe he's gone. . . . The whole town [Hollywood] is in a daze and nobody talks about anything but George's death." And Rodgers's fellow Gershwin-envier Vincent Youmans showed comparable shock in his own particular way by grabbing a bottle of scotch and playing Gershwin tunes on the piano till dawn the next day. An obsessive needs his subject (what would Ahab have done with himself the next day if he had ever actually killed his whale?), and trying to keep up with George had given not only the disheveled Youmans but the whole fraternity a target to aim at for the next quarter century or so, when this kind of music began to peter out on its own.

But perhaps the strongest evidence we have of George's sheer charisma is the annihilating effect of its absence on his brother. For the

next two years or so, Ira seemed simply paralyzed with regret, as if his spirit
had been unplugged. By nightmarish chance, just weeks before he died,
George had actually received something like a clean bill of health from
the Cedars of Lebanon Hospital, which had ruled out a tumor but had
suggested he might have psychological problems (though George's former
shrink knew better and had actually advised him to see a regular doctor).
Ira's fussy wife, Leonore, had suggested that George take his erratic,
tumor-related behavior elsewhere for a little while until he got over it.

So Ira's ruefulness was apparently compounded with guilt and he had
no inner fire to fight it with, or strength of his own. He needed help, so
naturally he eventually got some from his brother in the form of the sublime record that Astaire would make with Johnny Green of the brothers'
last songs together. Ira listened and suddenly felt as if George were "back
in the room" and power had been restored. Soon after that, his friend Kurt
Weill suggested that the two of them do a show together, and Ira batted
out some surprisingly high-spirited numbers for *Lady in the Dark,* and a
few after that for *Cover Girl* for Jerome Kern, until he'd run through a
quite satisfactory second minicareer, using all the skills he'd just begun to
master when George died. So Ira had become half a songwriter and a very
good one after all, fully worthy of his own place in here. But he was not a
natural, and one pictures him in the ASCAP group picture squirming and
tugging at his collar like the late Rodney Dangerfield. Tunesmiths could
be shy because their talent talked for itself, but lyricists had to make
themselves heard like gag writers over the noise of their talented rivals, so
an heir to the throne like Ira never quite fit. The equally shy Burton Lane
had once confessed to taking a sedative before he could face a business
lunch with Ira, and Ira had confessed right back that he had to take one
too. And perhaps the strain of going it alone began to tell, and he let out a
desolate howl of a song called "The Man That Got Away," with Harold
Arlen, and quit soon afterward. "The road gets rougher, it's lonelier and
tougher." Ira wasn't really writing about himself, but coming from the author of "Do, Do, Do" and " 'S Wonderful," the voice is unrecognizable and
would not be heard again in a musical score.

As if to keep an eye on George and make sure he never left the room
again, Ira retired in earnest this time, to become the full-time keeper of

the flame, reviving unpublished songs, giving countless interviews, and in general living the kind of scholarly, word-playing, arm-chair-dwelling life that nature had probably designed him for in the first place. If there had been no George, the odds seem good that Ira would have become an English teacher with a sideline in light verse and an unassuming wife to match.

What he got, unfortunately for both of them, was the stage-villainous but somewhat maligned Leonore, who may have been the worst victim of George's absence of anyone, and with whom you don't have to be a feminist to sympathize a little. As a bright young woman from a brilliant family, Leonore Strunsky had once had every reason to look forward to an exciting lifetime spent within Gershwin's glamorous, unpredictable ambience. And now she was stuck with this placid lump, living out his and her endless days on their own personal Sunset Boulevard, scarcely able to move, it seems. A friend of mine once called Ira and was startled to hear the old boy wheezing heavily into the phone. Had Ira's house caught fire? Had someone, by some miracle, persuaded the chap to jog or something? "No," panted Ira, "I'm just breaking in a new pair of shoes." So a trip to Europe was probably out.

By the time young Michael Feinstein moved in to lend Ira a hand with his archives, he found himself obliged willy-nilly to play kindergarten mind games with his hostess as well, who would treat him some days like her best friend on earth, and on others like a trespasser with bad breath. In a word, it seems safe to guess that the lady had become bored out of her mind. On one of her friendly days, she told Feinstein that she'd really wanted to marry George all along, but one suspects she told a lot of people this. It didn't really matter. None of the several other accounts I've read of other people's visits to Ira's even bothered to mention her.

A glum household indeed. But people's old selves shouldn't be held against their young ones. And even as Feinstein describes them, one has only to imagine, as Ira probably did again and again, young George bounding into the room and perching at the piano, for the whole scene to be transformed. George was the whole point of these people, and one pictures them coming to life like waxworks in a dream, and the lights going on all over the house to greet him.

Having myself witnessed old Burton Lane and Ann Ronnell lighting up at the mere mention of his name—and having also heard his own light, quicksilver voice on tape—I have no doubt about George's electricity, or about how far it reached or how long it lasted. "Oh, yes, my father really loved George Gershwin"—I have heard some variant of this from the daughters of Richard Whiting, Walter Donaldson, Milton Ager, and Irving Berlin, and I'm sure I'd have heard it from more daughters if I'd known any more.

If Gershwin's contributions had stopped at cheerleading, they would still have been major, because his judgment was so sure both musically and professionally. His song playing had been a crucial part of his education, teaching him not just about songs but also about public taste as it was that very afternoon at four P.M., and his own songs can still be used as a diary of the twentieth century: "Swanee," "Do It Again," "Somebody Loves Me," the latest song was great, but get a load of this next one! George was never content with last year's revolution, so no one else was allowed to rest either. Irving Berlin's epic late-1920s malaise and his sense that he was "losing it" spoke for a whole profession. After hearing a particularly snazzy new arrangement of something or other, Vincent Youmans groaned apocryphally, "It's no use. I can't keep up with these new guys," only to be told, "But, Vincent, you wrote that yourself."

And it wasn't just the writers now who had to keep moving at the speed of Gershwin, but the audience. While Irving had called this "a listening nation," George was teaching it how to listen better and more adventurously, to the benefit of all the writers, but of two general types in particular: those raised mostly on the classics, like Vernon Duke and Johnny Green and Jule Styne, and those who had grown up with jazz, like the three who come next, each of whom collided with George one way or another, without necessarily being influenced directly.

And here I must resist a show-bizzy temptation to exaggerate Gershwin's legacy. By no means did he invent the jazz song by himself, or any of its aspects. In the end, nobody else wrote quite like George, but perhaps a few of them wrote better because of George; in particular, the brilliant cohort of stage writers who followed in his wake—Rodgers, Porter, and Arthur Schwartz, and by degrees a couple of holdouts, the aforementioned Youmans and, kicking and screaming, the great Jerome Kern himself, who started the ball rolling with the proto-jazz number "They Didn't Believe Me," but then left the game until Gershwin and the others had made it worthy of him.

So I'll limit George's claim to this: You can subtract any other great name from the story, and it would be basically the same story. Without Gershwin, or his godfather, Irving Berlin, it would be unrecognizably different. And you probably wouldn't be reading books about it, and people like me wouldn't be writing them.

*Part Two*

# Consequences—The Great Jazz Songwriters

# Harold Arlen:
# The Songwriter's Songwriter

HAROLD ARLEN

While working on—or maybe the phrase should be "wallowing in"—this book, a remark I heard again and again was, "Do you know who my real favorite is?" Well, yes, after a while I did, because it was always Harold Arlen. Whatever the essence of this music is, Harold Arlen had the most of it.

And perhaps it's a coincidence—but perhaps not—that unlike Gershwin and the rest, Arlen really knew Jewish music, and unlike the other white writers, he had actually worked professionally with some of the best black musicians from quite an early age. His father, Samuel Arluck, was an active cantor with a good ear who had also picked up some other sounds in his own travels from Louisville to Buffalo and incorporated them into his own work, so that when he first heard Louis Armstrong, he could honestly say in effect that "he's doing some of the same things I do." Which means that his son Hyman must have heard them too.

Thus began what seems like one of the most important father and son partnerships in music, at least since the Bach family. To be sure, Papa Arluck did eventually try to talk his son out of becoming a professional jazz musician once he saw what was happening, but by that time he had already filled Hyman's head with enough music, both sacred and profane (opera mostly), and worse still had allowed the devil's latest instrument, a Victrola, into the house, that it was too late. And when he did try to dissuade his son, his spokesman was Jack Yellen, an Orthodox Jew, but also a successful songwriter himself, who a few years later would wind up asking Harold to do a show with him. So it's hard to believe that Arluck Senior wasn't just going through the motions and was, at least subconsciously, pleased to have a son who could chaperone him in this strange, sinfully attractive pagan world.

If this story, or legend, were entirely about music, it would have been a relatively happy one, beginning with young Hyman jazzing up some of his father's holy music on the family piano, and ending with Cantor Arluck introducing bits of his son's hits such as "Stormy Weather" and "Blues in the Night" into his temple singing. But Cantor Arluck couldn't really be all that happy about his son's tendency to swing absolutely everything he touched. And any hipness the two shared would end sharply at the piano's edge. The cantor's ears might be Liberal, but his heart was Orthodox, and Harold would have to pick up the other elements he needed, Americanness and black-American-ness, by rebelling at least a little bit and striking out into a world diametrically different from his old man's.

Nature had never intended him to be a rebel; it was a triumph of vocation. When I met Harold Arlen in person years later, I could only wonder, as many people must have, how such a mild, unimposing little man could have produced such powerful and turbulent music. Since appearances are seldom completely deceptive and all witnesses agree that Arlen really was mild in most respects—a man who would go to great lengths to *not* talk things out—the force of his vocation must indeed have been nuclear, and might be enough to account for the power of the music itself, as well as for the unhappiness which would blight his later years.

Then again, his father also tended to be an evasive and nonconfrontational man. Perhaps it didn't take that much chutzpah for Harold just to walk out the door and find someone else to play with. He certainly didn't have to go far. World War I had done its appointed work of stirring the music and excitement about the music around, and Arlen's biographer, Edward Jablonski, reports an estimated number of sixty thousand dance bands at large in the land, playing everything from the sweetest sweet to the hottest hot. And by the time Harold accidentally found himself writing songs in his early twenties, this sheltered youth had lived the life of a minor league ball player or a vaudeville hustler, banging around the Northeast in buses and picking up the usual dents and scratches along the way, along with a sense of middle America that Gershwin and the New Yorkers were not yet privy to.

"Hear that lonesome whistle blowing/'cross the trestle" John Mercer would write to Arlen's music, and suddenly Tin Pan Alley seemed to contain railway yards and bus depots that hadn't been there before. "It's quarter to three/there's no one in the place except you and me," writes Mercer also, and Arlen's music conveys all the solitude of a roadhouse in the outback, as far from Johnny's Savannah social register as it is from the Arluck parlor. Both Mercer and Arlen saw this other America as clearly as the half-British Raymond Chandler saw Los Angeles, with the freshness and sharpness of outsiders, and their songs constitute priceless social documents. "I've been in some big towns/and heard me some big talk." But the most important place either of them had visited was the black section, where Harold had apprenticed with, among others, the incomparable black pianist, bandleader, and composer Fletcher Henderson, whose arrangements would go on to make Benny Goodman the alleged "King of Swing"; and Arlen would come of age by writing some of his greatest songs for the famous Cotton Club in Harlem while the Duke Ellington and later the Cab Calloway bands were in residence.

Perhaps there really was a natural affinity between black and Jewish sensibilities across the board, or perhaps it was specific to certain east European musicians. (There's no trace of it in the west European Kern and not much in the part-Alsatian Richard Rodgers.) But insofar as black subject matter is contained in the blues, Arlen not only wrote it but sang it more authentically than any white person, Jewish or otherwise, has a right to. Like Hoagy Carmichael, Arlen was a singing pianist, but in his case, it is the voice that seems like the primary instrument, the mirror of his soul. Unlike Hoagy, whose singing can be extremely artful and sly, Arlen's is shatteringly direct, and what it sounds like is something close to clinical depression warring with a stoical vitality and at times a curious impishness. "Can't go on" say the words. "Everything I have is gone." But the tune seems to add, like Samuel Beckett himself, "I'll go on."

Arlen's sad songs bend to the wind, but they don't break. Yet Arlen could never quite get out of the wind either. Even when he swings into a snappy number like "Happy As the Day Is Long," he still sounds, at best, like a melancholic trying to look on the bright side, while his version of "Accentuate the Positive" is as far from the gleeful cackle of Johnny Mercer's recording of it as you can get. As sung by Arlen "Accentuate the Positive" could almost be funeral music.

Still, it is a funny song, and Arlen himself could be a funny man at times. The bass line of gloom that runs through his art and his life couldn't keep him from being a great laugher as well, and an occasional practical joker. An artist doesn't need to feel the emotions he's expressing at the moment he's expressing them, only to have them somewhere in his system. "Stormy Weather" was, as he told me, a throwaway. He wrote it first, and found out why years later.

In retrospect, Arlen's manic side may have been almost as necessary to his compositions as his gloomy one, simply because it gave him the heart to write in the first place. In other words, he had to feel that good to tell you how bad he felt; if he felt any worse, he couldn't have written at all, even sadly. And when, for reasons beyond his control, he couldn't write any more anyway, the depression that had been waiting to happen became quite suicidal. As described earlier, another old partner of Arlen's, Yip Harburg, happened to be my upstairs neighbor for several of Harold's worst years, and he described his friend as living in catatonic gloom and solitude as if the lousy weather he'd been reporting on for thirty years had all landed on him at once.

But just because I entered Arlen's life at the end is no reason to do so now. In fact, Arlen's first major hit song was a happy one that he wrote without even knowing he was doing it. Arlen had recently signed on as a rehearsal pianist for Vincent Youmans's *Hit the Deck* and was just fooling around with some chords he liked for the dancers to rehearse to. Someone else heard a song in these chords, and the composer Harry Warren not only heard the song but found a lyricist for it and a publisher. Just like that, the young singing pianist learned that he was a songwriter as well.

By a curious chance, Arlen's boss of the moment, Youmans, was also a manic-depressive, the occupational disease of songwriters, who was famous for his get-happy-damn-you music. So Arlen's lyricist gave the song a Youmanizing title, namely, "Get Happy," which neatly suits its role in history. Youmans had blazed brilliantly in the early 1920s, but was already looking back to see where the next fire was coming from, and when I asked Arlen in the early 1970s if any of the great songwriters had been jealous of one another, he said, "Yes, Vincent Youmans. Every time he heard a new Gershwin song, he said, 'So the son of the bitch thought of it.' " And here, in his very own employ, was another son of a bitch in the making, thinking of things that would carry this kind of music even further beyond his reach.

Certainly young Arlen had begun writing very close to the top, so much so that even his contemporary and fellow boy wonder Richard Rodgers wasn't sure he could keep up with his intricate harmonies. Rodgers probably had better formal training than Arlen, but like Carmichael, what Harold had was the extra training you get from improvising jazz and hearing it improvised all night every night for a few years. Later on, the fussbudget Alec Wilder would be enthralled by Arlen's pure musicianship, but the rough-and-ready give-and-take of the bandstand had been his finishing school, and the Cotton Club was the name on his diploma, not the Juilliard or the Sorbonne.

To top off this brief run of luck, the lyricist his friend Warren had chosen for him proved to be just right too. Ted Koehler was one of the many word-men who might still be famous if they'd just made a little more noise about themselves. Then again, he was the man who also wrote about ill winds and stormy days, and he seems to have understood his partner's moods so well that when Harold finally wanted to work with somebody else, but, typically, didn't want to tell Koehler—he understood that as well. (Koehler's response seems to have been, "You'd be a fool not to try it.")

Of Arlen's three principal partners, one might sweepingly say that Yip Harburg was the most literary, Mercer was the flashiest and most "with it," but Koehler wrote closest to the gut, to the essence of Arlen.

And on the scoreboard now, a few of the early songs Koehler wrote with Arlen have stood the test of time, better than Harburg's and almost as well as Mercer's: "Stormy Weather," of course, but also the exuberant "I've Got the World on a String," "Between the Devil and the Deep Blue Sea," and perhaps the sweetest of all Arlen melodies, "Let's Fall in Love," which, if not quite his and Koehler's swan song together, was part of their swan medley. And Arlen had been inspired to write it on their first and last train ride together to that most sundering of places, Hollywood, the home of divorce, where business partners break up even quicker than married ones and where even Siamese twins are likely to wind up just good friends.

To carry the image one sentence further, Arlen had actually begun to play around before leaving New York, and the primary agent of change in his life had been not the movies but that other mighty institution, the Gershwins. As far as I can tell, no song ever got written in New York without George hearing and judging it immediately, and "Get Happy" was no exception. So before he knew it, Harold found himself another Gershwin acolyte at large, receiving visits and verdicts from the master in a manner that sounds more French than American. If Arlen didn't appreciate "Stormy Weather," Papa Gershwin would tell him exactly what was so good about it. And if he needed professional connections, "My empire is your empire." Meeting the Gershwins was a total experience somewhere between a social debut and a Baptist baptism. And it usually meant meeting Broadway too, which must have seemed like practically an extension of the Gershwins, part of the family estate. So to put it all together, Arlen soon found himself writing a Broadway show with virtually a member of the family, Ira's old schoolmate Yip Harburg, and another with both Yip and Ira himself as lyricists.

In fact, Harold would soon have needed to make a move anyhow, because with the end of Prohibition in sight, glorified speakeasies like the Cotton Club would soon be closing their doors, and their employees would find themselves mingling on the street with refugees from vaudeville, almost all of whom would end up in Hollywood but who right now did not know what to do with themselves. So an invitation to Broadway inscribed by the Gershwins was a handy thing to have, and Harold would make the most of it. In the end, his stage work would occupy a comparatively small place in his catalogue, but a vital one, because it is just different enough to show how different he could be. Counterintuitively, songs like "Down with Love" and "Let's Take a Walk Around the Block" were lighter and frothier than his nightclub work and would place him at the moment in a middle class of one in the musical celebrity register, which is to say just below the big five and Arthur Schwartz and just above Vernon Duke and all the Broadway writers you've never heard of. And it gave him a useful credential to wave at the moguls when he inevitably went to Hollywood next.

Writing with Harburg had solved one problem but would create another. Like Oscar Hammerstein, Yip was first and last a Broadway man who had helped Arlen pick up a Broadway sound, but what Arlen needed right then was a Hollywood sound, with cash registers thrumming softly in the background. And he was not going to get much of this from Yip, who loathed every inch of Hollywood and seems to have spent his spare time out there becoming even more radical than when he started.

The Harburg years would be characterized by some of Arlen's most interesting and entertaining songs, for example, Groucho's "Lydia the Tattooed Lady," but a rather modest list of standards or radio songs. In New York, the two of them had written "It's Only a Paper Moon," which still flourishes, but in Hollywood—besides "Over the Rainbow"—they wrote only the gorgeous but difficult "Last Night When We Were Young," which is sort of a standard after the fact and against the odds. In fact it was based on an old tune of Arlen's that even Gershwin had advised him to forget about because it couldn't possibly be a hit. No doubt George hadn't reckoned on the coming of Frank Sinatra and his capacity for making a hit out of any song he loved so much, and his record of this one is so beautiful that it virtually forces its way into your heart. But even if George had reckoned on it, so what, these guys were not writing for posterity. A hit song in twenty years' time would have seemed cold comfort on the brink of World War II.

But if Arlen wanted a hit any sooner than that, he'd better find himself another partner, because Yip Harburg was simply not lotus land material.

First, though, in a burst of inspiration, luck, and homesickness, the two friends had returned to New York for one goodbye show that still shines brightly in both of their dossiers. Timing is everything with Method plays, and a show about a young woman who insists on wearing bloomers instead of hoopskirts turned out to be just right for 1944, when the issue was skirts versus slacks in the workplace and when independent women were about to be let off the leash for the next few years. And the setting of *Bloomer Girl* in the middle of the American nineteenth century would give Arlen a great chance to widen his own vocabulary with, among other things, the nostalgically choral "Evelina" and the faux primitive "The Eagle and Me," a sound that he would return to a couple of times after the war.

In the post–Pearl Harbor era, morale became the magic word—morale for everybody: for soldiers, workers, mothers, and infants, and Harold and Yip reported back to Hollywood to align themselves as entertainingly as possible for the duration. And Harold at least would have the time of his life. For one thing, he was one of the few songwriters on record who actually liked Hollywood. And unlike his old friend Harry Warren, Arlen had never really spent enough time there to feel trapped or seriously bored. On his first trip out he had been caught up in the gaiety and sadness of Gershwin's last month, and can still be seen smiling shyly and happily in George's home-away-from-home-movies. So they returned to Broadway— and got their major-motion-picture break and ticket back from there.

MGM had been casting around for a Broadway-like score to go with its latest hot property, *The Wizard of Oz*. This meant thinking not in terms of hit songs that would turn up over and over again on radio, but of total scores specific to that one story and meaningless outside it. Unsurprisingly, Harburg actually argued against using the one out-and-out standard in *Oz*. "Over the Rainbow" is emphatically not a Broadway song, but one of those rich, heavy, and vague numbers that radio loved and Harburg hated. And yet he wrote a great lyric for it anyway. That was a paradox about Yip: He neither cared nor possibly even realized that having your songs on the Hit Parade sold tickets and was good for your movie regardless of whether it belonged there. And yet he wrote some wonderful Hit Parade songs in spite of himself.

As if by magic, they had been whisked from the black-and-white breadline city to the Technicolor of MGM Studios to take the white-hot

*Wizard of Oz* assignment. And the magic didn't end there. It was implicit in Harold's unwritten contract with life itself that if the music ever stopped, he would go back to black and white immediately, like Dorothy translated back to Kansas. But out here in Oz, everything looked good. "They brought us money on bicycles," Arlen explained at our meeting: And the image of a kid tossing a check onto your porch as casually as an evening newspaper must have packed a positively Norman Rockwell enchantment to eyes used to Depression New York.

Before those West Coast bicycle messengers had lost their charm, Arlen joined forces with a new West Coast partner, Johnny Mercer, who in some ways perfectly combined the best of both coasts. In New York, Johnny had sung with Harold's brother, Jerry, as members of Paul Whiteman's Rhythm Boys, part two. But since then he had been in Hollywood long enough to learn movies the way Harburg knew plays, and particularly what he could get away with in movies. A song like "Blues in the Night," for instance, was much too long for sheet music and just a little too abstract for Broadway: It tells no story and illuminates no character. It doesn't go with anything, except with a bunch of images that you could easily render for yourself if the camera didn't feel like it. And Arlen loved it on sight. "Did you ever write a song that you knew was good before anyone else said so?" I asked him. "Yes, thank God," he answered. " 'Blues in the Night,' because Harry Warren saw it lying around the house and said, 'That middle section has to go. It'll never work.' "

Warren was hearing it as a songwriter, with a songwriter's sense of limits. But Mercer and Arlen had already heard it as fellow jazzmen under the skin who knew that a riff has to run its course and to hell with the sheet-music publishers and their three skimpy pages or the record companies with their piddly ten inches of wax, or even the film producers with their tiny attention spans.

So Arlen not only got to keep his middle section but succeeded so well with it that he felt free to launch into another rambling masterpiece called "That Old Black Magic," which had been granted some extra slack anyway to accommodate a ballet of sorts for George Balanchine's special friend, Vera Zorina. Playing this for the umpteenth time in my head one day, I realized that these extra-long riffs are most likely to occur when Mercer is the lyricist, and when he is, he is most likely addressing himself to the space requirements of jazz licks, to wit: Ziggy Elman's great trumpet solo that became "And the Angels Sing," Rube Bloom's "Day In, Day Out," and the super suspension bridge of Hoagy Carmichael's "Skylark." At a first, superficial listen (to "Magic" in particular), it sounds as if it's the words that are taking their time, and that the melodist is just supplying notes to accommodate Mercer's long-winded poem. But if you separate the elements, you'll see that Johnny is the one who's vamping, virtually ad-libbing extra lines, and the tunesmith is the one writing the poem and providing the continuity and momentum. Meanwhile, Mercer really puts the imaginary narrator through his paces, at one moment as a man in an elevator and at the next as a leaf caught in the tide, right after which, so help me, he seems to be on fire and needs help putting himself out.

Stop the elevator. I feel like flying for a while.

But meanwhile you realize that the melodist has told his own story in all its complexity and that Mercer's words have helped at every turn. "Darling, down and down I go/Round and round I go"—I defy anyone to forget these lines of music any more than one can forget "From Natchez to Mobile, from Memphis to St. Joe." (You may forget the order the towns come in, but the general idea is embedded deeper than forgetfulness.)

Probably the best-known and defining moment in the partnership came when Arlen looked at Mercer's notes for "Blues in the Night" and moved a line—"My mama done told me"—from the bottom of the page to the top. He never presumed to write lyrics himself but he knew what he wanted them to do, and Mercer was delighted to oblige. As two gentlemen of two old schools, the rabbi's son and the son of the South seemed to have accommodated each other at every turn. Indeed, in that sublime little hitch in the tune of "My Shining Hour" ("Like the lights of home before me/Or an angel watching o'er me"), which made the hair stand up on the back of Alec Wilder's neck, the words and music actually seemed to be holding the door open for each other. It doesn't get any better than that.

In the five years of 1941 to 1946, between, let's say, "This Time the Dream's on Me" (which I can't even mention without humming the whole thing through) and, let's say, "Out of This World," the names Arlen and Mercer seemed to be fixed in the stars like Roosevelt the president and Joe Louis the champ. But then the whistle blew, after which it proved to be just another wartime marriage, intense, doomed, and slightly puzzling.

In the bonus year of 1946, which combined the best of the wartime boom and the safety of peace, the team extended its holdings from the West Coast to Broadway with the show *St. Louis Woman,* and once more they did what they did so well—they produced a great album of songs that played wonderfully well on its own, and one powerful standard, "Come Rain or Come Shine." But the show itself closed quickly, and suddenly everything about it seemed wrong. In the orgy of finger-pointing that followed, there is no conclusive reason to single out Mercer's lyrics, which still sound swell on records. According to witnesses, Pearl Bailey's unremitting orneriness might have sunk any show ever devised. But Mercer was just starting on a lifelong losing streak in theater, which would make him a more likely suspect with each failure. And Broadway doesn't give you much time to prove your innocence. A bum rap is usually forever, and our two fixed stars would only try one other musical together, and that only when Harold was desperate.

Okay, no big deal. *Louis* was just a flop, not a portent. Before the war, Harold had learned his lesson about Harburg and movies, and now he had learned it about Mercer and plays. But Broadway was still booming, and there was always Hollywood, wasn't there? In 1946, everything seemed possible, and it is almost tempting to end the story right here. But the air went out of Harold's dreams so quickly that it is possible to tell quickly too. In the short version, Arlen did get to do some more films, but only one innocuous one with Mercer. And there would be a few more Broadway shows, but only two with Harburg. All in all, the high points in postwar Hollywood boiled down to no more than about two. First, a silly movie with a great score called *Casbah* (1948), which Arlen wrote with the chronically underrated Leo Robin, and which contained the standards "Hooray for Love" and the near-standards "Written in the Stars" and "What's Good About Goodbye." And, second, his last filmed hoorah, if not quite his last film, *A Star Is Born* (1954), which includes "The Man That Got Away." This Judy Garland weepie features a strong lyric by Ira Gershwin and, to my ear, an unsurprising tune that fits the story almost too perfectly. (Every critic has his deaf spots, and this is one of mine.) It seems poignant to the point of corny to find this fading song, getting older and colder in the midst of this age-old tale of rising and falling stars. But that was the Hollywood studios just then, cashing in their old assets, selling their old feature films to TV and immortalizing them as quickly as possible, all the while canceling contracts and keeping wonderful songs around purely for background music.

So Broadway was suddenly the only place to be, but this time preferably with an old pro like Harburg, who knew the stage and who knew the street. Yip had already had a huge postwar success there with their mutual friend Burton Lane. What Harold needed now was for Yip to respect this and do another *Finian's Rainbow,* but with him this time.

But something had gone wrong here too, it seemed. Besides its great songs, *Finian's Rainbow* had contained some quite clumsy analogies to American politics, which had been okay in 1946–47, but were highly suspect in 1948–55 or so. In no time, Yip would find himself on the omnivorous blacklist, which of course Broadway was free to ignore if it wanted to, but only if it wanted to very much. Harburg was on the wrong side of the divide. In the harsh 1930s, his left-wing radicalism had seemed close enough to the mainstream to get pretty much lost in the crowd, but by the fat 1950s, he stood alone—a menace to conservatives and a bore to liberals, who had heard that song before. In fact, even his fellow West Side Democrat, Lane, eventually got tired of old Yip's insistence on message musicals and even more tired of having them turned down, while his other old partner, Arlen, wasn't a liberal to begin with.

So by the time Harold and Yip finally got around to doing another show together, ten years had passed and the national mood had changed completely in the subtle but imperious way of these things. McCarthyism had largely faded away, not for any specific reason, but because it didn't interest people anymore, and Yip could now send all the messages he wanted, so long as they were entertaining. And Arlen, for his part, found himself faced with sounds that wouldn't have been possible in his prime, such as steel bands and bongos and calypsos, which he found melodically dreary. (Fortunately, perhaps, he didn't live to hear rap.)

It was enough to make a man feel his age. The show, called *Jamaica,* was a success anyway, because David Merrick insisted on it, but it was Merrick's show more than Arlen's or Yip's. By the time I talked with Harold, it was clear that the last musical he had really enjoyed and was still proud of had come three years earlier. *House of Flowers,* as it was called, represents his last sustained attempt to "keep up," and give the world one more new Arlen. And perhaps if he'd done it with Merrick, it might have worked. As it was, *House of Flowers* flopped, and in a small way, this broke Harold's heart. The end had begun.

Thanks to the one incontrovertibly good invention of modern times, namely, sound-recording, one can at least hear the remains of this last good moment. To get to *House of Flowers*, Arlen agreed to the most improbable partnership in this, or any other, book. Truman Capote at that stage was entirely famous for his self-promotion and for flaunting his teeth-grinding cuteness and his Southern childhood to any audience that would have him. And now he and Arlen were about to undertake a show in an idiom completely new to both of them, West Indian folk.

Fortunately, Capote turned out to be a serious and very good writer under the act, to whom Arlen responded both artistically and personally. And Capote returned the compliment by understanding Harold and his demons as well as anyone had. On the one hand, Truman felt that Arlen was "obsessed with a tragic view of life," but on the other, Arlen also genuinely loved to laugh, and did a lot of it, with a signature laugh you could spot anywhere. And somewhere between the laughter, which Capote induced even more by passing on outrageous gossip, and the tears in both of their hearts, they found a remarkable score, unlike anything else in Arlen's repertory, and unlike anything else a mass audience could assimilate. So Arlen now showed wonderful promise as an avant-garde, serious composer, but none at all as a commercial one. And he might have had trouble even with the avant-garde. *House* flopped off-Broadway too, and the end came a little closer.

To sum it all up, Arlen could do no wrong in the 1930s and nothing right in the 1950s, even when he took no chances. The one card he still held that was money in the bank was the score of *St. Louis Woman*, which people kept on praising right through the disasters, so he and Mercer put it together once again in the form of an opera and threw in "Blues in the Night" and "That Old Black Magic" just for good measure, and sent it on a world tour that was meant to eventually culminate on Broadway. But it fell sick in Amsterdam, and died in Paris. And this time, that was really that. One last show with Mercer, called *Saratoga,* was hailed as "another *Show-Boat,*" which has always been the kiss of death. Arlen's Broadway career was over.

With work petering out, Arlen's defenses against depression had gradually begun to come down too. Up to now, his rule of thumb toward real life had been to ignore it and hope it would iron itself out. Thus he knew he had been courting his parents' rage when he first lived with and then married a beautiful gentile girl—but maybe they would get used to her, especially if he kept her out of sight; and maybe this girl, a model-cum-showgirl named Anya Iaranda of Russian Orthodox origin, was lonely herself in his long absences. But maybe she could make some friends on her own and perhaps acquire some hobbies or something; and even when he knew for sure that this wasn't working and that Anya was becoming tense to the point of insanity, he thought that maybe she would still be okay if she lived in a nice sanitarium for a while. By all accounts, he really did love her, but apparently in the manner of a love song, and not in the more workable manner of a long-running soap opera.

And meanwhile, he tended to see a bit of Marlene Dietrich when she was in New York—and why not? She was, after all, a musical soul mate and inspiration. One always assumes sex with Dietrich—it was her version of a handshake. The gossip columns never tell you what people actually do when they "see" each other; presumably Harold and Marlene did whatever people do. But as creative artists go, Harold Arlen was not at all the monster that the above makes him sound. Even nice artists have to do what it takes to keep their work flowing. And Arlen's work depended on his not slipping below a certain level of euphoria and unreality. "Forget your troubles, come on get happy" was no whim with Arlen, but an order: Ignore your troubles and keep on working.

But as every manic-depressive artist (and is there any other kind?) knows, the whole machine has to operate together. The work has to deliver its share of euphoria too, or else one has to find some substitute for it. And the most popular one is that ultimate depressive, tranquilizers, which, of course, make things worse. These now entered Harold's life, and soon those troubles he'd been forgetting came pounding back like Hieronymus Bosch goblins. His parents' disapproval, for instance, had never really gone away at all, but had become a habit that would last until they died reproachfully, or so it must have seemed to their son. So long as the music kept coming, he had never needed to grow up at all and face things head-on. But now he found himself transferred back to adult black and white, and shipwrecked on the blank reefs of real life, which he'd hitherto written about but sailed safely around. And to his infinite credit, he did his best with it, living with Anya full-time in New York, and right through the 1960s working grimly on individual songs with younger partners who just might lead him back to the promised land. And because, by his own admission, he was almost terminally depressed, these songs had to serve as his shrink and his confessor.

But a song that nobody else listens to can't bear that much freight, and meanwhile Anya was getting worse and worse, twitching, making faces, and throwing tantrums until a brain tumor similar to George Gershwin's was finally discovered behind it all—too late to be removed completely. She died, leaving Harold to feel like a bad son, a failed husband, and a burned-out songwriter all in one go.

According to Harburg, the truly suicidal depression that rounded out the sixties was caused by Harold's relief that Anya had died, combined with his guilt over this relief. By Yip's no doubt accurate account, I picture Arlen locking himself in his room like a teenager until he'd figured things out. But from Jablonski's biography, I would also learn that there were enough pills in there with him to account for his depression all by themselves.

Whatever the cause, by the time I met him in 1972, two years after Anya's death, Harold seemed more or less himself again, guardedly cheerful and even willing to be interviewed at some later date. (Max Wilk finally got the interview, and it was amazingly loquacious.) Perhaps the most surprising thing he said to me was that "Stormy Weather" was "a song I could have mailed Monday or Tuesday. It wasn't anything special." After that, of course, real life walked him through it again, slowly and painfully, the shrink to end all shrinks. "Keeps raining all the time." Yes, indeed.

But he was out on the other side of that too, and if it wasn't exactly the other end of the rainbow, it would do. Instructively enough, the last time he and Anya had been happy together had been on a trip to Europe with Harry Warren and his wife in the early fifties. Harry was a down-to-earth, non-show-bizzy kind of guy, and Anya felt comfortable and blessedly sane around him. And the secret of Warren's equilibrium was his nonstop grumbling, beginning with his own anonymity—which was a dirty, rotten shame—but branching out in all directions. And now that all the old songwriters were slipping out of the spotlight in a body, Warrenism, or grumble-therapy, began to catch on throughout this particular retirement community, and it's my confident guess that Arlen's lengthy phone calls to Irving Berlin must have been in the Warren vein: What's happened to the damn music, anyway? And will the public ever return to its senses? Or will we, like Bertolt Brecht's dictator, simply have to order up a new public?

Misery loves company, and this company was of the finest, even though these two men had actually been forgotten a lot less than most of their colleagues. Berlin was still a monument, although not so many people went to that part of the park anymore, and Arlen, who hadn't been all that well known in his prime, seems to be at least as well known now. Tributes are still paid to him on TV just often enough to keep his name in play, and his fans still seem to find one another like Maltese dog owners. No composer has a better ratio of recognition-to-adulation. And there's always just enough Arlen music in the air to keep the converts trickling in, and the reservoir remains at the same medium level. Arlen may not be our best songwriter, whatever that means, but in one sense he is our most necessary one, because he is the one you have to hear if you want to know exactly what the vague but necessary phrase "jazz song" meant, and where the Gershwin wing of it went next, and where it wound up.

# Hoagy Carmichael:
# The Jazz Song Goes West

HOAGY CARMICHAEL

If Harold Arlen is the special favorite of jazz song connoisseurs, Hoagy Carmichael probably comes first with just about everyone else, regardless of time, place, or musical persuasion—partly because of his early-American image at the piano and his collector's item of a voice, but even more so because of at least two songs he wrote that still speak to Americans all over. The first is "Stardust," with which he first announced his presence and which went on to become the most recorded song in its era, and the second is "Georgia on My Mind," which on my occasional travels seems to take turns with "Route 66" as our real national anthem. And what makes these numbers central to our story is that they both *are* and *are not* New York jazz songs, and because of this they give the category a much-needed infusion of outside, all-American blood.

If jazz songs hoped to maintain their sway over the ever-widening country, they had to start recruiting a bit farther out than Buffalo. This was easier said than done.

Once upon a time, a guy I knew from Pittsburgh tried to sell some songs and found in effect that you simply couldn't do it from there because (1) you couldn't mail your stuff without receiving it back immediately unopened, and (2) you couldn't call up anyone in the business unless you already knew someone in the business, and how were you going to do that in Pittsburgh? Songs were harder to fence than diamonds. And in both cases, the other guy wouldn't even look you in the eye as he said no.

So my friend did the only other thing he could think of. He marched onto a local stage and demanded an audition with a well-known band that was passing through. By that point, all he *thought* he wanted was a hearing and a verdict, and in a sense he got both, plus a lesson as to why all those precautions were necessary. In fact, the bandleader liked his best tune so much that the next time he came to town, he was still playing it as part of his own repertory, and my friend found that there wasn't a damn thing he could do about it.

There was of course one more option that might have given said friend at least a chance in hell of making it, and that was to take his songs in person to the cold heart of the city, New York, or the frigid one of Chicago, and try to massage himself into the system as a song-plugger or rehearsal pianist—which by the 1940s must have been like trying to get your kid into Harvard or West Point, though sometimes it happened. Tommy Dorsey held some talent hunts and came up with a striving young singer from the West Coast named Matt "Angel Eyes" Dennis. And before that a coal miner from Ohio named Isham "It Had to Be You" Jones had parlayed his own band into a songwriting career.

But as radios and phonographs fanned out farther across the country, it was easy to imagine that a lot of local talent just couldn't be bothered with the old cultural center. Moving house was a big deal in those days, and besides, Horace Greeley hadn't said, "Go west, young man—and then come back again." The current ran the other way, if it ran anywhere, and the natural thing was to work with local stations and under local labels to produce increasingly local music. As Jule Styne told Max Wilk, there was a whole different Hit Parade in the Southwest on the cusp of the 1940s, but the one man he might have heard on either program was Hoagy— a geographical anomaly who just seemed to write generic American that sounded just right regardless of where you were—even in New York.

Hoagy Carmichael was, like many Americans, a divided soul, part nomad and part homebody, who seemed a little bit at home everywhere, but was probably more so someplace else, if he could just find it. In fact, you'll still see him on Greyhound buses, either hoping to change his luck in the next county or heading back after failing to.

What had dislocated him the most was the arrival of jazz, which had sneaked into rock-ribbed Indiana by way of the great music river, the Mississippi, and which would hit young Hoagland with the force of a religious conversion. When he came to his senses the next day, he was puzzled to see that the lawns and the houses hadn't actually changed. Life went on. But there was a force at large now that could take him a million miles away anytime it wanted to, while—and this was the curious part—leaving him back home when it was done.

Thus, in his early teens, Hoagy became one of the first "jazz babies" (his phrase) in the land of Square; but part of him would stubbornly remain a square in the world of Hip, and some thirty years later, we would find him actually squaring off, in the other sense, with Humphrey Bogart over a matter of politics, an Indiana Republican versus a Hollywood liberal, "Put up your dukes." (Fortunately, their womenfolk easily restrained the two bantamweights.)

Even in the matter of deciding whether to become a professional musician, Carmichael stayed in two minds as long as he decently could, solemnly studying the law and working a cement mixer for a living by day, and bopping the piano by night, alongside Bix Beiderbecke and other nonacademic specimens; also, recording his first song, "Riverboat Shuffle," with Paul Whiteman in 1926 (aged twenty-seven by now) and being called to the bar as an attorney that same year.

How long he could have kept going in opposite directions like this as a jazz lawyer was suddenly resolved for him by a deus ex machina, aka a check in the mail, or the promise of one. On the strength of that one Whiteman record, Irving Mills, the new apostle to the outback, offered Hoagy a contract to write more songs; and just like that, the Great Divide or man-made chasm that kept New York safe from outside talent had been cleared and all Hoagy had to do now was write the songs.

This turned out to be the easy part. As Sammy Cahn would famously say, every song begins with a phone call, and no sooner did Hoagy have his contract in hand than he also received a private epiphany which would confirm his gift once and for all, at least in his own mind. Rolling home drunk and early one Sunday morning from an all-night jam session, he "found" a tune in his own head that resolved every last doubt—if he could just find a piano to play it on. There followed a minidrama as he began searching the Indiana campus for an open door with a piano behind it before the tune could escape and turn him back into a lawyer for good.

Fortunately for him and posterity, the door of the college lab opened in time and Hoagy's masterpiece somehow survived the night. That one tune told that he was a songwriter for a life, but he had to wait another few years before he was able to convince anyone else. This bought him precious time to polish his art and find his voice before the outside world caught sight of him and began asking him to repeat himself. That one incredible song was like an insurance policy that only he knew about. After a brief, disdainful look at Hollywood, where absolutely everyone told him he was uncommercial ("We'll just see about that!"), he hitched a ride to New York, where, among other things, he would join and jam with some other out-of-towners, such as his old friend Bix Beiderbecke and such other names as Dorsey, Goodman, and Crosby, who were also trying to insert as much jazz as they could into their commercial work. As America continued to homogenize itself into one Great Picture Show, it seemed that the old distinction between hot bands and sweet bands was about to melt away, and that whatever they wound up doing would be a compromise. But sometimes the public surprises you. And one famous night when Goodman was playing California's Palomar Ballroom, the audience made it clear that it would rather listen than dance. This was the best news that the jazz babies could have hoped for, and it would make the jazz song the official sound of America right through World War II—after which, fashion would blow these same men off center stage with unexpected violence.

As for Hoagy, he arrived in New York certain that the jazz he had worshipped as a kid was already dead. But then one night he heard Duke Ellington play, among other things, "Mood Indigo" at the Cotton Club, and he realized that he might barely have to compromise at all. Because "Mood Indigo" was the real thing and all that Duke had actually done to it was remove the sense of danger, and replace what Hoagy calls the "switchblade" from jazz with something more peaceful. He had changed a nightmare into a beautiful dream—but wasn't this exactly what would happen to the tune in his pocket, which he had named provisionally "Stardust"?

By then "Stardust" had already failed fair and square as a hard-driving jazz song, but now it was in the same hands that had guided "Mood Indigo," and Irving Mills was about to make the same suggestion to Hoagy as to Duke, that they slow their tunes down and get Irving's house lyricist, Mitchell Parish, to write some dreamy lucrative words. And just like that "Stardust" would prove that Hoagy could actually make money being himself, keep his integrity, and eat his cake too. With one song, Hoagy became both our most and least commercial composer. And meanwhile, he had become too set in his ways to sell out, even if he'd wanted to. Before he had a hit, he had a style.

Which doesn't mean that success had done the impossible and put Hoagy completely together. One moment, he was still a Hoosier poet on Tin Pan Alley, dealing in such down-home matters as washboards and rocking chairs, lazy rivers, and little old ladies passing by; the next he was a licensed lawyer and snappy dresser whose best friends were still his clever college chums and whose favorite nonmusical pastimes were new acquisitions like golf and tennis, neither of which was played much on the Alley, at least below the level of George Gershwin.

In the circumstances, it probably struck him as the most logical thing in the world to dash off a heartbreaking hymn to a completely different place, where he'd never been at all. In his second memoir, *Sometimes I Wonder*, Hoagy describes how his father would get a faraway look in his eye, and then the family would light out hopefully for parts unknown—

only to find that this wasn't the right place either, and return to Indiana puzzled. So when Hoagy got that look, he didn't bother going anywhere. He stayed home and wrote a song instead—in this case about Georgia, which was on his mind if not his itinerary, and later about New Orleans, Memphis in June, old Hong Kong, and even Indiana. Few writers have ever traveled less than Hoagy in ratio to the number of miles he logged in his dreams.

So naturally, his next real-life port of call had to be Hollywood, the dream capital, where *everybody* was a misfit. Yet even there, Hoagy managed to seem like an odd man out. "He wasn't one of the (songwriting) gang," said Shana Alexander. This may have been because he felt, deep down, that the real composers were the guys who played and improvised the music in the first place, the pipers, strummers, and troubadours of jazz. And these would always be his musical gang of choice as they blew in and out of town, and he would not so much hang out with them as sit in, a lonely prospector eternally prospecting for gold at the piano while his companions let the gold dust slip through their fingers.

Then as now, the one way to be truly different in Hollywood was genuine, off-camera domesticity, and Hoagy now flung himself into this with enough thoroughness and intelligence to help raise two loving and flourishing sons (not adopted) who are still around at this writing to sing his praises when called upon. And he also invested enough imagination into family life to extract some of the few first-rate songs that we have relating to this condition, including "Small Fry" ("My my, put down that cigarette/You ain't a grown-up high and mighty yet"), "Two Sleepy People" ("Do you remember the reason/why we married in the fall?/to rent this little nest and get a bit of rest"), and "We're the Couple of the Castle," a little-known title that speaks for itself. All three were written with a fellow bourgeois named Frank Loesser, who, like Hoagy's other lyricists, managed to sound exactly like him so long as they worked together. (Carmichael wrote some lyrics entirely by himself, but obviously had a voice in all of them, which may be why he wrote so disappointingly little with Mercer. Two stubborn men with a taste for strong waters might have trouble agreeing, and I believe there was at least one actual fistfight with no wives to break it up.)

Thus, following his own eccentric star, Hoagy picked up enough bits and pieces to become eventually "the great American songwriter"—if there is such a creature. To my mind, he clinched that mythical title once and for all (in peaceable cahoots with Mercer) in the epic "The Cool, Cool, Cool of the Evening" ("In the shank of the night/When the doings are right/you can tell them I'll be there"). Different words may be used to describe different details now, but the whole laid-back essence of this country can still be found in the multiple cool of this song.

Hoagy didn't just write the nation's songs, but unusually for his day, he sang them himself in a voice that sounded as if it had actually been grown in American soil and aged in a cracker barrel or a keg of hard cider. And this voice would be the tiebreaker between the two faces of Hoagy—the one he preferred himself, that of a dandy who looked so good in a dinner jacket that Ian Fleming originally described James Bond as looking just like him, and the face of the roustabout at the piano with his hat tilted back and features that looked like a road map of the United States. The great director Howard Hawks captured that look one day when Hoagy came in from the yard dressed, for once, in old work clothes and looking comparatively disheveled. "That's it," piped Hawks, or words to that effect. He'd been casting around for some birds of passage to populate a saloon in the film *To Have and Have Not,* and he'd just hit his fourth home run in a row, Bogart, Lauren Bacall, Walter Brennan, and now the man who would, for many of us, steal the movie out from all of them.

So that, like it or not, was the official Hoagy Carmichael from then on, the one we all know so well and that he would proceed to embed in the world's consciousness with several similar screen and TV appearances, with songs to match. "Baltimore Oriole" in particular takes lonely barfly songs to a new level. This guy has been there—as well as everywhere else, of course.

So was this the real Hoagy Carmichael? Probably yes and no, as usual. San Francisco's beatniks would make him a mascot in the late 1950s. He liked the way the beats were trying to keep jazz alive, and was amused by the rest. Unlike most of the old-timers, he was interested in the twists and turns of modern jazz and did not feel displaced by it. And nobody who had hung out with Beiderbecke and the others was likely to be shocked by anything the beats could come up with in the way of bad behavior. After all, he had once been a wild young man himself—half the time. You can't pin the whole of a dreamer like Hoagy down at one moment. In the gorgeous song

"Skylark," his alter ego jogs down some of the territory Carmichael's music and Mercer's words fly over, including "a meadow in the mist . . . a valley green with spring . . . [and] a blossom-covered lane." And that was just one trip.

So he finally settled in Palm Springs, which is somewhere you go when you don't know where to go, and he did his damnedest to write some more songs. Failing that, he would play a bunch of golf and drink a bunch of booze. And one hopes that some of his dreams were still beautiful, even if they didn't come with tunes anymore. But there was undoubtedly some sadness too because that was part of his greatness. Listen to "Memphis in June," with the clock a-ticking in the kitchen and the chairs a-rocking on the verandah, and it's gorgeous all right, but unbearably sad.

Anyway, whatever the mixture of joy and sadness, the only regret he ever voiced was his wish that he'd "tried harder" when the tunes were still coming. Well, then, there might have been *more* songs, but it's hard to believe they would have been *better* ones. Songs don't get any better.

In fact, Hoagy's best songs are literally incomparable. The moment you move into, say, "I Get Along Without You Very Well," you realize that no one has ever been down this road before, or anywhere near it. And I can imagine a lesser man than Hoagy saying, "So what the hell am I doing here?" And perhaps after the next bar adding, "Hey, this isn't a song at all. I'm getting out of here."

But Hoagy had lived through the epic night of the "found song" and still had the "Stardust" memory to prove it. So he trusted his stars all the way, as he would again when he came to the respective bridges of "Skylark" and "How Little We Know" (not to be confused with a later namesake, which simply isn't as good). Once again, our imaginary hack would see at once that both these bridges are way too long, and would probably desert halfway across, but Hoagy keeps on marching like Alec Guinness, crossing the River Kwai, trusting the song itself to tell him when it is finished. Meantime, he allows his number-two themes full equality to grow to their natural limits, and to hell with the rules. Let the bird sing his whole song if it takes all day.

Thus with these two adventures at least, as well as with the verse that was later added to "Stardust," you feel as if you've escaped completely from the drawing board and the music paper, with all its lines and boxes, and into the open air, and the result can be almost dizzying. Once upon a time, a friend of mine was driving out West when he came, without warning, upon a choir, arrayed up the side of a hill, singing Hoagy's gorgeous song "One Morning in May."

Naturally, my friend thought he'd died and gone to heaven. But as it doesn't quite say in the movie, it wasn't really heaven, it was only Indiana, which, in one of my own dreams, Hoagy never really left at all but where part of him still sits on the porch flirting like Tom Sawyer with his Aunt Polly, or he's off down the river, like Huck Finn and his black companion, looking for the one thing that Mr. Twain had failed to report on, the music of the river.

But with one major difference. The black man is not a slave in this version, or even a former slave, but, so long as they are on this mission, a master and a model. Although the square side of Carmichael would never completely quit but would continue to think that even so modest a step as interracial dancing was in bad taste, the swinging side of Hoagy had known the score from the start, and immediately after his teenage rebirth, had gone straight to a local black musician for instruction in his new religion. Later he would find no better or more simpatico interpreters of his work than Ray Charles for "Georgia" or Louis Armstrong for "Old Rockin' Chair's Got Me" and everything else.

It seems at least arguable that what had happened here was that he, like his pal Mercer, had been wantonly and fatally seduced by black music and was fighting for his honor, his identity, in other ways. Their first great song together, "Lazy Bones," seems to make fun of the laid-back black boy "sleeping in the sun," but they had to be that boy themselves to do their best work and be their best selves. So Hoagy had lost his all-white musical identity, and everyone is the richer for it. The excitement that greeted him in London after World War II tells the story. If Mark Twain was the first completely original American sound to reach foreign ears, and ragtime was the second, Hoagy added a vibrant variation to both: laid-back at one moment but moving with the speed and sureness of a cat in his fast-patter songs like "Billy-a-Dick" and "No More Toujours L'Amour." A few years later, Norman Mailer would foresee the arrival of a white Negro, but here we already had one—up to a point. This least likely suspect had, to my ears anyway, combined white and black perfectly.

# Duke Ellington: Royalty

DUKE ELLINGTON

$\mathcal{D}$uke Ellington undoubtedly wrote some of our greatest songs, if, that is, they really were songs and if he actually did write them. Alec Wilder couldn't decide whether Ellington strictly belonged in a book of American songs at all—but there was no question of leaving him out either.

And there is no question of *not* talking about him, perhaps more than any other American composer of any kind, because he did first-rate work in several fields at once, from classical to spiritual to pure jazz, stretching each of their boundaries while challenging the genre itself. Many younger Americans now believe that categories don't count, and the Duke surely had a hand in this.

For instance, what exactly is a song, anyway? Is it just a bunch of words and music timed to go off together, or are there fixed rules—and why? And to what extent can anyone be said to create one as opposed to the recurrent phenomenon of finding it? The air is so full of sounds (and clichés to go with them), and yet the tonal range is so small that the problem is not just that the sounds get stolen, but that even the most original writers keep bumping into one another in their pursuit. Richard Rodgers's "This Can't Be Love," for instance, swipes a couple of crucial bars from Bach's "Peasant Cantata" while Berlin's "Cheek to Cheek" seems to recall some riffs from Chopin. "We only steal from the best," George Gershwin said to Milton Ager optimistically, and in the same vein Arthur Schwartz would deliver the last word on the subject when someone asked him whether an agreement he'd just made to write a song a week for radio wouldn't "take a lot out of" him, and he said, "Not as much as it will take out of Bach, Beethoven, and Brahms."

That's who he would poach from on his good days, anyhow. On others, you might catch him stealing even more from Tom, Dick, and Harry without even knowing it. Since you need so few notes to establish a tune, anybody from one to a hundred can do that part, and the composer is simply the guy who can see the possibilities and know what to do next. For instance, suppose for the hell of it some little kid at a piano decides to drive everyone crazy by playing D and B over and over, until he finally bores even himself and moves on to a repetition of E and C: He will by then have written over half of "Carolina in the Morning," which might seem like grounds for a lawsuit. (But could the babysitter claim the rights to it, under the ancient right of finders keepers?)

Far-fetched, no doubt, but far-fetched in the right direction. If Duke Ellington was not exactly a babysitter, he was the next best thing, a jazz bandleader (which sounds like a contradiction in terms: Jazz cannot be led). As such, he was immersed day and night in the unpredictable sounds of jam sessions, all begging to be noticed and turned into songs, and we'll never know how many were. Frankie Carle's "Sunrise Serenade" and Glenn Miller's "Moonlight Serenade" were just two bandleaders' songs that might have been arrived at by just following the logic of someone else's catchy phrase; or if the leader was also part of the band, like Duke at the piano, he might introduce an idea of his own into the mêlée and let them fight it out. Whatever Ellington's methods, the results sound as if they all came from the same man, but who was that? To be on the safe side, Duke signed everything "By Duke Ellington and His Band," allowing for an enormous spread and endless questions. Was the band being a full partner today or just a brilliant instrument?

Either way, it was not unheard of for the leader of a jazz band to slap his own name on the final product, on the Walt Disney principle that people weren't going to remember more than one name anyway and it might as well belong to the guy who signed the contracts and paychecks, Mister Big, Il Duce, the Leader himself. And this system must have had an enormous appeal to minority geniuses. In the 1920s, there weren't that many distinguished careers open to African Americans, and Edward Kennedy Ellington was born and raised to be distinguished, by a father who exuded style and a mother who got down to brass tacks and made sure he learned not just to play music, but to speak and think like a gentleman. Indeed, a snobbish boyhood friend christened him Duke simply because he wanted him to be one. And Ellington was definitely duke material, if he could just find the right duchy.

So it was his lifelong good luck to be a genius in the one field where blackness did not count against you, but might even be made to serve. A decade earlier, before World War I had done its extremely modest bit to bring Americans together, Irving Berlin's famous black alter ego would not have needed to stay in a closet. In the same way that women had been conceded to be quite good novelists long before they were allowed to vote, so too African Americans were understood to be pretty good at this kind of music, inferior though this kind of music might be, and besides, whoever knew who actually wrote the songs? The minstrel show tradition of anonymity behind painted faces had left the matter conveniently vague. Stephen Foster wrote some of them, and "I Don't Know" wrote the rest. And now they were either by another white man, Irving Berlin (with a black one in the closet), or by no one in particular.

Since nobody cared, nobody had to hide, and it's not surprising that maybe the first of the really great jazz songs, "Some of These Days," was both written and performed loud and clear by a black vaudeville pianist called Shelton Brooks, an aristocratic-looking Canadian who would follow it up later with the politically incorrect classic "Darktown Strutters' Ball." Singing and playing one's own material would remain far and away the surest way for blacks to get their stuff known and paid for, and it's possible that they actually possessed a small advantage along this route. The central irony of the entertainment wing of segregation was that an African American who tried to buy a theater ticket would likely find himself sent right up to the stage.

Obviously, he'd come to the right place, he belonged here, but the closest thing to a servants' quarters was the dressing rooms, and in 1917 the great piano man Eubie Blake would take full advantage of this dispensation by filling all the dressing rooms with fellow blacks and writing the music for an all-black show, that is, a minstrel show called *Shuffle Along* that used real black faces. It also included Blake's first standard, "(I'm Just) Wild About Harry." And some fourteen years later his signature song, "Memories of You," would turn up in another such show. There was a limit to how many all-black shows the traffic would bear, and waiting for the next one was no way to build a full-time Irving Berlin–type career.

A better bet for that would still be to lead one's own band and wait for the right white entrepreneur or agent to come along and do the introductions and paperwork. Ellington didn't have long to wait. Irving Mills, the unsung songwriters' helper of the early twenties, who had spotted Carmichael as well, snatched Ellington up at once, not specifically for songwriting, which might or might not come along, but for the sheer sound of his band, which Mills could start selling right away to the two color-blind young media, radio and records, which were just then hitting their full strides and were reaching out blindly for any kind of music that could be squeezed into three minutes or so, the exact length of a song.

Ellington ruled the music, while Mills did the paperwork. Napoléon meets Napoléon. Fortunately, Mills thought big too, and long, and not just in terms of immediate hits. And he knew that the first thing to do for his client was to make sure he had the best possible band to work with, his very own Stradivarius of a band, primarily just to play on, but also to compose on if he could. So he bankrolled Ellington a couple more members to dispose of as he saw fit. Probably not even the Duke could have put into words exactly what he wanted, because it was a complete impossibility; namely, the best of both worlds, a band that could improvise like a jazz band but also follow his instructions perfectly. In other words, he wanted a musical instrument made up entirely of human beings, who could practice free will and obedience at the same time. It was a godlike wish that, to put it temperately, would take a little time, as he handpicked the players and broke them in to their unique chores. And I was not surprised to learn that Frank Sinatra some twenty years later would find the latest edition of Ellington's band exasperating to sing with, because, unlike Count Basie's disciplined outfit, they consisted entirely of prima donnas. And their mandate apparently did not include accompanying singers, or possibly even playing songs as such. In their ideal world, you just played music and saw what happened.

So, presto, Mills would provide them with a place where they could do just that, the perfect lab in which to learn what they were doing. In other words, Mills signed Ellington up for a gig at the Cotton Club in the booming community of Harlem, which was already witnessing an artistic renaissance of which Ellington was about to become a crucial part. The Cotton Club was at that stage a distillation of America's zany racial patterns and might sardonically be called an example of segregation at its finest. The cast and the neighborhood looked and was black through and through, but the audience was equally white. And while the music sounded black, whatever that meant, some of it was written by white men like Harold Arlen and Jimmy McHugh, who immediately became honorary blacks, if honorary is the right word, while the rest of the music was by blacks like Cab Calloway or Ellington, who could, in this ambiguous setting, be completely himself and incidentally produce his greatest songs—not jazz songs, but jazz compositions, which, if time had stood still, is what they would have remained.

There are some things that publishers know quicker than anyone, and what Irving Mills knew best was that by the time Ellington had begun to unpack his melodic gift, jazz as such had already lost its novelty for the larger public, so he might as well start chopping up his music into songs right now. By 1925, the human voice had finally started to sound like itself on records, under the unofficial leadership of Bing Crosby, who was a great jazz singer capable of keeping things going in the right direction for a while. (If Bing ever stopped swinging, it would all be over.) Anyway, so long as you gave your music some words and called it a song, maybe you could just go on doing your own thing.

So what kind of lyrics went best with Ellington? Obviously, you wanted lots and lots of mood. Establish, for instance, the dark, dark blue of the singer's mind right now. This is indigo, man. You could never go back to mere blue after this. Or mere "Solitude" after you've heard that one. "I sit and I stare" de-dum-de-dum-dum. The song text has already been riveted into the melody, and people will just think you're saying something.

A few key words are quite enough if the listeners only want to have a particular mood reinforced while they drive their car or try to sleep or fall in love. Later on, they'll think that the words were perfectly swell too. But real singers want a little more than that: not just words that make sense occasionally, but some connection with the melody. The great saxophone player Lester Young used to talk about "playing the lyrics," as if this was the best way to read the composer's mind. But this is to assume a real connection between the elements. At some point the tunesmith looks at a bunch of words and says, "By George, you've got it! I couldn't have put it better myself." After which, all he needs is for the right performer to come along to dig them both, and you have magic à la Astaire and Berlin or Ethel Merman and Cole Porter.

Since both Berlin and Porter wrote their own songs all the way, coordination could go no further. These are our two best pure songwriters, and singers still love them both. Contrariwise, for the furthest you can go in the other direction, I can't think of a less inviting lyric to step up to than that of "Sophisticated Lady," for which Mills had allowed his hayseed hit man Mitchell Parish to apply a country boy's reading of the word "sophisticated," thereby turning an enigmatic *chanson* about a city at night into a cautionary tale about what happens to nice girls when they leave home. This is not "down in the depths on the ninetieth floor," as in Cole Porter, but down in the depths in the diner, with the mascara running and the roots showing and the lipstick smears piling up in the ashtray. It seems that this poor lamb not only drinks but smokes and (the line that always brings down the house) dines "with some man in a restaurant." Gasp!

It sounds more like an army training film ("one minute with Venus can mean a lifetime with Mercury") than a great ballad, and for once Ellington was heard to murmur that it wasn't quite what he'd had in mind. So why had he let it happen? Well, Parish wrote the hits around here, and he seemed to have a good thing going with the American outback. And clever lyrics can be quite distracting.

More seriously, the Duke had already delivered his own version, all he had to say, with his band. Jazz was not in its heart a singing medium, and if the public insisted on words anyway, Louis Armstrong's response was instinctively right—to sing nonsense, sing scat. Use the human voice purely as an instrument, and make clear that that's what you're doing. Jazz tells its own stories. It doesn't need words, and scat is simply jazz's way of saying, "Get lost."

Yet Ellington's music doesn't seem to scat all that well either. In his own arrangements of numbers like "Mood Indigo" and "Prelude to a Kiss," there don't seem to be any parts for singers at all that wouldn't sound better played on something else. And singers can take a hint. Once the master has spoken, you'd feel like a fool answering back with your own interpretation, so his songs just don't seem to get sung as much as other people's. "Prelude to a Kiss" carries a serviceable lyric, but unlike most such, I've never found myself memorizing it automatically the way my generation used to, or even been fully aware of it. The bare chords as played on the piano are so gorgeous that for once I can imagine why bobby-soxers used to squeal over Frank Sinatra and tribes used to beat their tom-toms: Some music demands a response, if it's only a low growl, and I would instantly vote this the most beautiful song ever written, except for this one problem of the words. By contrast "All the Things You Are," its nearest rival, is a singer's song in the most fundamental sense; you want to start singing it immediately. And although it's a great piece of music in its own right, I've never heard a purely instrumental version of it. Although the words boil down to the usual grandiose piffle, you are quite likely to find yourself singing them with real feeling.

"Prelude" came out in 1938, and one senses that Ellington, or whatever constitutes Ellington, was thinking a bit more about songs as such by then. The two matching tunes "I Let a Song Go Out of My Heart" and "Don't Get Around Much Anymore" go perfectly together, as if they were written that way, but they also break down into most singable songs, while "I Got It Bad (and That Ain't Good)" is so songlike that it's even got a humpty-dumpty bridge that is manifestly just there to carry singers across. Perhaps Ellington's most successful and least debatable song in the 1940s was "I'm Beginning to See the Light," but "Do Nothin' Till You Hear from Me" also passes the automatic memorization test and the compulsive sing-along test too, as does "Satin Doll," with some help from Johnny Mercer's lyrics. And finally there are several others, like "Jump for Joy" and that pleasant surprise "Just A-Sittin' and A-Rockin'," that may not be conventional songs but that still require singing if you're going to do them at all.

The list goes on. Out of the huge mixed bag that the Duke has left us, you can certainly extract at least one genuine songwriter—but possibly one with another black man or two in his closet. This time, the gossip can't be avoided altogether, because for Ellington's great early instrumentals the suspects were usually Barney Bigard and Johnny Hodges, while for the songwriter years, the tragic young Billy Strayhorn appeared in the picture, and his name has since replaced the boss's in first place on Ellington's jazzy lead-in "Take the 'A' Train" and probably should at least share full credit on "Satin Doll" and others.

Yet one hears no sharp breaks or strange voices in the music. It is still the same Duke Ellington talking—not three different men taking turns at it, but one man in different moods and phases trying different things. As my son, Frank, pointed out when George Harrison died, each of the Beatles wrote his best only as a Beatle, as a member of a band. The Duke was a master not just of music but of human interaction.

Just from reading about him, one senses that the man was a presence, a focal point, the producer and director of his own scenes. His father, James, had been at various times a butler and chauffeur to the Washington, D.C., elite, both positions that could teach one an awful lot about irony and the way the world works, and perhaps James imparted some of this outlook to his son. Indeed, by the end of just one meal or one week's driving, a servant would probably know more about most kinds of people, white and black, than they would ever know about him.

Wherever he got it, Ellington always entered the room with enormous confidence in the cards he was holding for today's game. Photos from the late 1930s show him jamming happily with white musicians like Tommy Dorsey and Eddie Condon and joshing with politicians as if he was born to do so. Like Joe Louis, Ellington didn't "beat down doors," he walked through them. And if some people didn't like it, well, this might be a white world, but the music was black right now and he was royalty.

Irving Mills knew it. Usually, when a white name and a black one are linked like theirs were, it is automatically assumed that the white one must have exploited the black one. But no one ever exploited Ellington unless there was something in it for him; a fair exchange of exploitations. And both he and Mills profited enormously from their association.

As an aristocrat of the servant class, his daddy must have learned the one profound secret, namely, how much more his employers needed him than he needed them. Rich people tend to be disproportionately helpless, and never more so than in their endless, wistful search for good servants. William Ellington knew that he could always get another boss, but where were they going to find a great butler? He was a luxury item, like a yacht or an extra house, by virtue of his style and smarts and whatever mysterious quality makes a man seem like officer material and makes Fred Astaire's clothes look better than anyone else's. Whatever indeed it was, father William seems to have passed it on to his son by precept, example, and simple inheritance.

Now Ellington was a boss himself, an aristocrat in his own right, and as such he knew how much he now depended on other people, and how to get what he needed from them, not by confrontation, which would have cut him off from half the country—including the half that jazz came from—but by an instinct for the possible. For instance, when he *did* take his band down South, he didn't fight the railroad, he simply acquired his own railway carriage so that his men could travel first-class.

This kind of thing would come to seem far too roundabout for the radicals of the 1960s, who considered Duke inauthentic and irrelevant. For them, black experience had to be harsh and bitter, or else it didn't count, and black power was supposed to come from the barrel of a gun, not from a smile or a handshake. The Pullman porter image of the grinning darkie with the natural sense of rhythm had put a curse on simple politeness, and even Martin Luther King Jr. was considered a borderline Uncle Tom. Yet even by then, such totally hip geniuses as Charlie Parker and Miles Davis had once again demonstrated that artistic originality and authentic black style have an awkward way of coming from the middle class, and indeed that there *was* a black middle class. In fact, there was a chapter missing from the Black Panther cosmology, and it would take Bill Cosby several years to help publish it.

Meanwhile, though, Ellington was quite insistent about his own black heritage, considering it intrinsic to his music, and virtually his subject matter. The distinction was that, to him, black did not mean primitive but referred to something like a great lost civilization that was right now in the vibrant process of rediscovery. And he was happy in the best black American tradition to accept that great African book, the Bible, as his guide to the promised land.

Not altogether surprisingly, his theology seems to have caused him to take a sharp turn against his friend Gershwin's *Porgy and Bess*. At first I assumed that his problem with it was the usual possessiveness all groups feel when their idioms are commandeered. Foreigners writing American slang usually get it wrong, but how dare they anyhow?

Ellington's chief grievance, though, concerned just the one song "It Ain't Necessarily So," which, in the voice of a scapegrace character, pokes fun at the Good Book. Ellington felt that Gershwin was risking hellfire with this one, and that maybe his surprise brain tumor was retribution for it.

It must have come as a jolt back then to find a sophisticated man like Ellington throwing the Book at a sinner like this. The reading public had been sufficiently conditioned by H. L. Mencken's sneers at fundamentalism to sneer at it themselves, but obviously the Duke lived in a different world part of the time, and at least there can be no more question about his authenticity in it.

Sometimes the best part of a story doesn't come at the end, and for a true believer death isn't the end anyhow, and within a year of George's fatal tumor Ellington had authorized his "Prelude to a Kiss" to carry a friendly reference to him. There were no hard feelings. A much more typical story is the one about the new band member who nervously asked Ellington what he should start out with. "Just play 'I Got Rhythm,'" said the great man, "and we'll think of something."

It was one thing for white musicians to accept their own "inner blacks," quite another for African American musicians to accept *them* as brothers. To some extent, Duke's attitudes were dictated by the practicalities of band leading. During their most creative years, Ellington and his men still had to double as a regular band playing other people's songs, including the early proto-black ones of such great white contemporaries as

Arlen and Jimmy McHugh written for the Cotton Club. Resentment would have thrown a spoke in his own wheels. And pray, who did Edward Kennedy Ellington have reason to envy?

Perhaps, though, there was a little something else at work between him and Gershwin. If jazz songs really were a Jewish meditation on black music, these two would be the prototypes, the best black musician and the most brilliant and thoroughly converted Jew. Fortunately, George's admiration for Ellington was not only profound but irresistible, and the friendship held. But perhaps when George took the logical last step into *Porgy and Bess,* the Duke let out a yelp. "What the hell are you doing *here?*" One man's homage is another man's encroachment. But there was something almost biologically inevitable about this. Gershwin had needed to work this closely to the black ethos in order to produce the baby, but you probably can't get this close without falling in love.

George's love was not, I believe, unrequited. *Porgy* may not be Ellington's version of black life, or anyone else's, but it has acquired by now a kind of artistic validity, and the proof is that only black actors can play it. *Guys and Dolls, Kiss Me, Kate,* even *Oklahoma!* could be performed by anybody, but "Bess, You Is My Woman Now" just doesn't sound white and never will. Gershwin had been there and sung with the choir, even taking part in the famous shouts.

After an awkward pause, Gershwin's homage, his gift, was accepted and adopted, and something had changed. Although whites had been imitating blacks from the moment they'd clapped eyes on them a century earlier, they had always done so in quotation marks and disguise. But *Porgy* is as real as it gets on a stage, and Catfish Row is his real address too, the first Southern one we've ever really visited in a song, and a triumphant landmark on one of our most satisfactory national journeys.

After World War II, foreigners would likely have voted popular music to be both the best and the most American thing about us. A good reason for this was that it fed from both our major streams at once. Everything else about us might be segregated, and even this was as segregated as we could make it; for example, as late as 1938, Benny Goodman would make the headlines scream when he took Lionel Hampton onstage with his white band. And that was in Chicago, not down South in Little Rock. But the essential truth here is that Lionel Hampton fit in perfectly from the first note, and with their eyes shut, the audience wouldn't have noticed a thing.

Music is, of course, incorrigibly promiscuous, and its devotees are constantly fraternizing. But it forms its own mainstreams anyhow in response to time and circumstance. In our own technically unsegregated, if not totally integrated, world, a white kid may, if he likes, sing rap, or even soul, but at first it will sound like a pure imitation and his "street" and "hood" will seem as phony and made-up as the tin pan land of Dixie: But maybe, after a while, it will be called white rap.

So why didn't it happen that way with jazz? The hardest part may have been to find enough white musicians who could keep up with the black ones, and to this day there are snobs of both races who insist that we never did find them. (This argument flares up and subsides on a regular basis, and probably nothing can be done about it except to apply the famous Roy Eldridge test on a case-by-case basis, that is, play some obscure jazz passages, and ask the listener to name the race of the musicians. Be warned: This test may cause nervous breakdowns.) As one who spent some formative years ricocheting around Fifty-second Street between the white School of Chicago Jazz and the black Sons of New Orleans, I have my own opinions. But whatever the final answer as regards live performance, performance at the composing desk is another matter, and there is no serious doubt on either side that certain geniuses like Gershwin and Arlen truly were able to *think* in jazz and make immortal music with black virtuosos like Louis Armstrong and Billy Eckstine and Sarah Vaughan.

But if the white folk could do it at all, the odds were that they would soon take it over completely, not through racism but through the inevitable arrival of an old-boy network, and they would wind up bleaching it out and making way for things like rock and roll and rhythm and blues and other things they could bleach out too—all of which did happen, but not quickly, and not before we'd had enough time for a good long Golden Age. And this is where Ellington becomes one of the two or three essential figures, the one who kept the music honest, and ensured that the proper jazz levels were maintained, even if he had to overdo it at times. By writing some songs that really weren't quite songs and others that were, he defined the concept of jazz songs as well as it could be defined, and I am willing to rest my own case right here.

*Part Three*

# The Stage—Broadway Swings

# Jerome Kern:
# Jazz Comes to Broadway . . . Slowly

JEROME KERN

*I*n any bull session on the general subject of songs, everyone inevitably praises Harold Arlen, but it's also foreseeable that at some point someone leans forward with eyes glittery and says, "Of course, Jerome Kern was the best." In fact, it's almost a part of his definition, that his music makes you want to say something nice about him and immediately declare your allegiance. Even that professional crab and Gershwin-champion, Oscar Levant, proposed that a taste for Kern's music should actually be made a requirement for citizenship, as if it were a test of moral character and simple decency.

Like George Gershwin, Jerome Kern projected an aura, but one made entirely of music. Gershwin at least had a face; Kern was pure sound. If Gershwin was Times Square at midnight, and skyscrapers and jackhammers by day, Kern was more like a cathedral at high noon for worshippers to gaze at and dream about. Kern's music leaves one feeling not just good but noble. The world must be a superior place to produce such music and such peace (and such a good building too, because simply as music, his songs are sturdy as well as beautiful, and you can move right in).

Not surprisingly, Kern's real self, insofar as one can find it now, did not entirely live up to this. Anecdotal history gives the impression that the words heard most often to describe him at his funeral, officially and otherwise, were alternately "pixieish" and "overbearing," which not only don't seem to fit his songs, but don't even fit each other. P. G. Wodehouse, who met Kern early in both their lives, skips both images and describes "Jerry" as something else again, a ball of energy who looked on sight as if he could get things done, a look I find it difficult to conjure. But Wodehouse also makes a useful distinction between a young Kern, who sounds like fun to work with if you could keep up with him, and an older one, slightly overwhelmed by his own magnificence.

Or so Wodehouse had heard. And that's the problem. There has always been more hearsay than fact about the private Kern. When I asked Harold Arlen why there were so few anecdotes, he said, "Maybe because he was such a son of a bitch that nobody wants to talk about him." Whether or not Kern himself was impressed by his magnificence, other people certainly were. Nobody, it seems, who had ever heard "Smoke Gets in Your Eyes" or the music from *Show Boat* could ever view him as just another human. So all it took was an occasional growl from him to terrorize practically everybody, including such potential new lyricists as Leo Robin and Johnny Mercer and the incorrigibly underconfident Ira Gershwin. And Kern wasn't above giving the legend a nudge by browbeating waiters and such in the manner of a bratty European maestro, or by imposing his favorite party games on visitors and playing them pedantically and indigestibly.

Yet while poring over Kern lore in all its vagueness and unreliability, one notes another sentence recurring its way into a pattern. "He was much nicer than I expected." So perhaps there really can be such a thing as an overbearing pixie. Shana Alexander, who had a child's-eye view of Kern, considered "Uncle Jerry" the most fun and the kindliest of any grown-ups she knew, an opinion pretty much endorsed by another song-writer's daughter, Margaret Whiting. Like his disciple, Richard Rodgers, Kern got his best reviews from women of all ages, including the one he worked with the most, Dorothy Fields, the lyricist. But unlike Rodgers, he also got occasional raves from men too, most notably from the cantankerous Harry Warren, who found Kern's lordliness funny—a word seldom used about Rodgers. The truth seems to be that Kern liked to keep people guessing.

But who was he? Ancestrally, the Kerns had the cachet of having arrived in this country before the Civil War. But they were also some distance from the "Our Crowd" of great Jewish families. Jerry's mother, Fannie Kakeles, might conceivably have made the very outside edges of that world, courtesy of her father, who was a popular sexton at a fashionable temple, but Henry Kern remains such a shadowy figure that one might almost suspect a con man. Even after Jerry spent some time in Germany himself, neither he nor his brothers could ever name a single relative or ancestor over there, or even state for sure whereabouts the old man came from in that country. And to top it off, his biographer Gerald Bordman couldn't even find a record of his marriage to Fannie over here either.

Shadowy or no, Henry did manage to succeed almost immediately, first as a stabler of horses in Manhattan when that was hot, and later as a merchant in neighboring Newark. Maybe it was his mobility that made him so untraceable, but the main thing was that, while Henry Kern was obviously not too keen on supporting a songwriter, Jerry always had some kind of money in back of him, which in itself raised him several tiers above his colleagues in song.

To reinforce his status as a rich kid, he had most likely also been spoiled fairly rotten, which can be as good as a title in terms of self-confidence. The clue here is that of Fannie Kern's seven sons, four died in infancy, a monstrous toll by the late 1800s. But then, toward the tail of this woe, along came number six, a fragile little genius who seemed to have blessedly inherited all her own musical tastes and gifts, only more so, and who seemed to be almost ready to use them at birth, as born musicians so often are. So just like that, she had someone else to play with and a stake in the future, a child who might make the Kerns a truly great family someday. And to complete *her* happiness anyway, he even looked like Fannie. So what was not to spoil?

Unfortunately, Fannie is a bit shadowy too—maybe it went with the Henry Kern territory—so we don't know how she acquired her own musical education, only that the results suggest a terrific one, and we do know that she enjoyed playing eight-handed concerts with her three surviving boys while Jerry was still a tot. Since he was far and away the youngest, he must, as he unwrapped his own gifts, have practically begun his life feeling giddy with accomplishment and ready to take on the world—so long as the game was music.

His strong suit was indeed strong, maybe the best one that a kid can have outside of a gift for humor or football. Unlike baby physicists or mathematicians, musical prodigies can usually entertain their way out of trouble. And all the scant records and memories of Kern's school days show him perched at the piano, playing songs and writing them for his life. From now on, music would be his shield and his sword and his calling card; to be on the safe side, it would be show music. For his tenth birthday, his mother took Jerry to the theater, and whether or not it was lifelong love at first sound, as it would be with Richard Rodgers, this kind of music was obviously a game he could play at school as well. Classical music wars with community life, by yanking away the kid for hours at a time of solitary practice, but show music fits right in. In fact, songwriters and comedians may be the only kinds of artists who learn anything really useful in school, and Kern is not the only subject in this book to have taken full advantage of this.

By the time Kern graduated from high school, his vocation had become not just obvious but imperious. And after botching his first business assignment (by famously ordering up two hundred pianos instead of two), his doting parents left him to pursue his own musical apprenticeship in his own way, studying here and making a buck there. A certified genius now, both at home and at school, he hit the ground purring, with a coating of self-satisfaction that nothing could dent, and the aristocratic gift of not needing to be liked or understood, just a bow or a curtsy would do. So he has probably been misunderstood a lot, not least by me.

Kern could take care of himself in anybody's world, with charm and with iron and workable dialogue, and perhaps a touch of guile too, inherited from who-knows-exactly-where. What we do know is that in the course of a too-short life he had a way of getting involved in high-profile lawsuits, and would be accused of plagiarism a suspicious number of times, even for this coincidence-plagued profession ("We only had twelve notes between us," as Arthur Sullivan explained), all of which suggests the type of guy who, despite his almost sacred-sounding music, definitely bore watching—which may have suited the role-playing Kern just fine.

Now back to business. Since Kern seemed to be locked into some kind of theater music, by both fate and inclination, the question now was, what kind? French or Austrian? Strauss or Offenbach? Perhaps Sir Arthur Sullivan? As the twentieth century loomed, what was then called the civilized world, and now just the Western one, was seized with a millennial frenzy. Art was about to be stood on its head by Picasso, ditto the novel, by Joyce and Proust, and music by Stravinsky, and ditto everything else by someone or other. So maybe we could actually try an American musical? Well, it was just a thought.

There have been three generally acknowledged (though seldom by the same people at the same time) revolutions in the American musical theater, but since two of these involved Oscar Hammerstein, one might expect those ones anyway to have rolled backward. Oscar loved the past like a trendy taxidermist who is happy to use the latest techniques to bring it back to life. And since two of these revolutionary moments also involved Kern, you can bet that the music was beautiful but not radical.

Uprising number one is sometimes named after the Princess Theater, a cozy off-Broadway-size house where the trio of Kern, Guy Bolton, and P. G. Wodehouse undertook to sabotage the two reigning styles of American musical. The first of those was the Transylvanian operetta, in which the queen of Ruritania, disguised as a chambermaid, is wooed by the crowned prince of Bratislava, disguised as a busboy, to the strains in both senses of imported music, or quasi-imported music. The other would be the revue, aka follies, scandals, and so on, made up of bits of business—here a comedian, there a tenor, everywhere a chorus girl—in short, vaudeville to the nth degree, dazzling at times, but innately frustrating because it is in the nature of audiences to want to know what happens next to these people, to the tenor and his victims, and what kind of songs they will all wind up singing about it.

So the game plan of revolution one (and incidentally of revolutions two and three as well) was simply to integrate the songs with the dialogue and the dialogue with the songs in order to combine the best (or worst) of opera with the ditto of theater. It was a great but obvious idea, and the only wonder was that no one had thought of it sooner—if indeed no one had.

The one element nobody else could have thought up sooner was Kern's music, which, if not yet precisely 100 percent American was at least Anglo-American, which means several pounds lighter. Kern has sometimes been called the greatest Austrian composer ever born in the United States. But despite a year spent studying in the Heidelberg vicinity, Kern's overseas training was overwhelmingly pursued in English theaters and music halls, and his very first hit—"How'd You Like to Spoon with Me?"— shows just how much of London's street sounds he had absorbed into his style. Kern's personal haughtiness, combined with the aristocratic distinction of his music, has persistently led people to assume that he was basically a highbrow slumming with musicals. But, as noted, his affair with stage musicals went back to childhood, particularly his affair with English ones, and much of his professional apprenticeship was spent running musical- or vaudeville-level songs back and forth between the two countries. "How'd You Like to Spoon with Me?" was precisely that— an "English-type" song interpolated into the American production of an English show, with nothing Viennese or semiclassical about it.

So when World War I came along, making England our friend and Transylvania our enemy, Jerome Kern was sitting particularly pretty. Although the war was officially being fought to avenge the death of an Austrian archduke, which sounds like our kind of cause, a mind-blowing maze of alliances left us on the side of the Serbian assassin and his friends instead, and thus fighting for English humor and French pastry and against German and Austrian heaviness and turgidity, and by extension against the Chocolate Soldier himself.

Jerome Kern may have seen it coming. At any rate, he had begun by then to pool his talents with those of the young Englishman Guy Bolton in the creation of some genuine transatlantic musicals, in which Vienna and the Wilhelmstrasse might magically emerge as Mayfair and Park Avenue, and in which the busboys really were busboys and the chambermaids generally turned out to be the daughters of self-made millionaires from Kansas, who, when they appeared in the last scene, sounded suspiciously like Englishmen with dictionaries of Yankee slang in their pockets. A further Englishing would occur a couple of shows later when the team of Bolton and Kern became a trio with the piping on board of Wodehouse, soon to be the great humorist and right now about to be the best lyricist on Broadway.

But since Kern and Wodehouse had already worked together successfully in London back in 1905, it's possible to say that the first great American musicals were actually born in England—but they were never quite English, because just as Kern was less highbrow than people thought, he was also considerably more American. Before he had gone to England as a young man, and shortly after Irving Berlin and the boys had popularized the ragtime song, Jerry worked as a song-plugger at Wanamaker's department store in New York. And Kern wrote at least one rag too, as if to prove he could. But in the best circles, ragtime was still considered a vulgar, low-life-and-rent fad, and it would be another twenty years or so before Fred Astaire induced the great Kern to topple off his throne and really swing. In the meantime, he forged ahead with his own sound of a well-brought-up American who had lived abroad a bit and missed the jazz epidemic altogether except to write, as if with his left hand, one song in the "new" American mode, which would prove to be perhaps the most influential song in this book.

"They Didn't Believe Me" shines out brilliantly and eccentrically in the history of American musical theater. In the year it was written, circa 1914, syncopated songs could usually still be identified by a certain facetious jocularity, and frequently by the word "rag" in the title as well. No one had begun writing real songs in this style yet—until suddenly here it was: a perfect loosey-goosey, syncopate-me-if-you-care, a relaxed and smiling American asterisk-jazz song.

But by the time most people were aware of it, Kern had gone on about his regular business, leaving the next step to a couple of other and younger geniuses who would hear it and decide on the strength of it precisely what they wanted to do for the rest of their lives. George Gershwin, who was already plugging rags on the Alley and studying for Carnegie Hall on the side, found in "They Didn't" the answer to a prayer: distinguished theater music that actually swung—or could be made to ("And when I told them [syncopate? It's up to you] how beautiful you are [ditto], they didn't believe me," and so on). It was sassy but high-class, commercial but not cheap; and young Richard Rodgers coming the other way, from uptown to down, felt the same. "They Didn't Believe Me" was a gentleman's rag, without paw prints or coffee stains. As Alec Wilder would say, it didn't smell of cheap-cigar smoke.

After Kern fired the starting pistol, he seems to have lost interest in the chase, and would later have to run to catch up with his own disciples. The Princess show scores were not particularly syncopated or emphatically American. In fact, for the U.S. upper class and its camp followers, who included Kern, Rodgers, and haute Broadway in general, British was probably as close as they wanted to get, because anything more American might contain the dreaded jazz virus.

If you had an ounce of the snob in you, or the smallest stake in the system, jazz was the enemy, and perhaps it seemed even more frightening because so many other parts of the sky were falling at that same time. Modern art had gone crazy and turned ugly, the buildings didn't know when to stop and neither did the flappers, and jazz was just the music to make it all sound dangerous and uncontrollable. Also, it was terribly rude. As civilization strove to pull itself together from the recent bloodbath in France, denouncing jazz provided a field day for fogies.

In the wake of World War I, Kern now *was* the establishment, but outside of avoiding any jazzy arrangements (or indeed any arrangements other than his own) of his songs, Kern doesn't seem to have had any fixed ideas about librettos. He stuck with his English partners until the inevitable rift (over money), after which he seems to have looked around for the least jazzy American collaborators he could find, which would bring him straight to that reactionary revolutionary, Oscar Hammerstein.

Whether Kern knew it or not, he was now on course for revolution number two, an even more integrated musical, telling a *real* story about *real* people. Wodehouse once wrote a funny piece about starting on a script for a singer who couldn't dance and winding it up with a dancer who couldn't sing. It was hard to create real characters out of such a fluid labor pool. But for Kern, there was now no turning back from integrated musicals, if only because they made the composer a much bigger player than revues ever had, virtually the author in fact; revues could use a dozen songs by as many different writers, who would all remain equally anonymous. But in a book musical, the composer's voice had the chance to sound off in all its various modes, and perhaps more crucially, his name had a chance to dominate the Broadway playbill, the famous poop-sheet that stares up from your lap during intermissions, and it was a hundred times more likely to make you famous than five times as many movie screenplays. "A musical by Jerome Kern" became as plausible a description of a whole evening as "An opera by Richard Wagner."

But what story would Kern tell? There is no reason to suppose that he had anything particularly striking in mind as the roaring twenties began. Formally speaking, his partnering with Hammerstein would suggest that for now he was willing to go backward into the fusty world of operettas and to heck with revolutions. Hammerstein, along with his mentor and partner Otto Harbach, was already on record as wanting to bring operettas back to New York even before they had completely left. So undertaking anything new with either of them would be like driving with the brakes on.

However, their effort together yielded *Sunny,* an old-world type of American show that included the great bridge song between the old Kern and the new, "Who?" (which for some reason sounds like a French café song to me—that is, it swings, but not quite Americanly).

Any revolution with this cast of characters would only go so far and no further. If all they wanted to do was move Viennese shows to various parts of the globe, why not go back to England again? The country would continue to tempt Kern, partly because of his mastery of both musical languages, and partly because of whatever it was that also persuaded him to marry and stay married to an English wife. But while *Sunny* was technically transatlantic, anyone really keen on writing English dialect would probably not turn to Hammerstein for it.

Hammerstein's role in two of these so-called revolutions was never more than what the AA people would call an enabler. In the case of the great *Show Boat,* it was Kern who first read the book and insisted on its musical possibilities. And with the groundbreaking *Oklahoma!* the equally strong-willed Richard Rodgers not only found it but had also tried the story on his old partner, Larry Hart, before springing it on Hammerstein. So it looks as if both men chose Oscar Hammerstein partly because he was so obliging and adaptable.

With such authors, it is not surprising that *Show Boat* now seems a lot more like, yes, an operetta set in America than like the totally new kind of musical that has been advertised ever since. By later standards of authenticity, the plot and dialogue now seem as stagy and artificial as if they had been set in a German beer hall. The novelist Edna Ferber of the Algonquin had only just heard about showboats herself when she wrote the book, and yet both Jerry and Oscar were quite content to take her word for them and for the Old Man River they sailed on, and did not bother to go out and see or hear for themselves whether any of it rang true. And indeed most of its incomparable songs are not particularly any kind of American, except in the sense that everything Kern wrote sounded a little American. "Make Believe" had an unspecific kind of beauty—American? Okay, if you say so. And the same goes for "Why Do I Love You?" While "You Are Love" could almost pass for downright Viennese with just the slightest trace of Kern's Yankee accent. Only the stylized "Can't Help Lovin' Dat Man" makes any concession to the new American sound either in lyrics or tune. But then as the authors might answer, why should it? You could probably hear all kinds of sounds on the old riverboats, who really knew for sure?

The point about *Show Boat,* as it would be about *Oklahoma!,* is that the writers were both at least temporarily on the run from jazz and had found properties dealing with a couple of imaginary Americas—imaginary to them, anyway—that predated the Jazz Age, or lived outside it, or both. And they used these Americas as canvases on which to paint their own feelings and impressions, using Hammerstein's all-purpose slang and universal emotions. And each is handsomely justified by the work of the composer, the actual dreamer who dreamed the dream and wrote the tunes. Kern's score in particular is so good and indeed noble that *Show Boat* has been overrated ever since. *Show Boat* without music would be laughed off the stage, not to mention jeered off.

Yet nobody seems to have doubted *Show Boat*'s absolute greatness the night it came out, or its nobility of heart. The only question might be whether the public was quite ready for it or worthy of it. Although the critics agreed unanimously that on this night of nights the American musical had finally come of age, impresarios like Flo Ziegfeld and the Shuberts could not necessarily see what was supposed to be so hot about this. (Call me when the audience comes of age too.) From where they sat, the tired businessman and the buyer from out of town were still the demographic that counted for long-running musicals, and these simple fellows didn't really care where the girls came from or why, or what kind of folk costume the comic was making fun of. So for all *Show Boat*'s acclaim, it would be almost a decade before a writer with equal clout to Kern's would be able to get even a streamlined version of *Porgy* into a Broadway theater (where, as we've read, by Gershwin's standards it flopped badly the first time).

Revolution two would in fact have to wait for revolution three for its final ratification. By the time *Oklahoma!* came along in 1943, Americana had become a thousand points of pride as well as curiosity; as the choral stunts and special effects became ever more expert, it became clear that what was winning the war was all those clambakes and cattle drives. As a youngster myself, perched in the back of the theater, watching *Oklahoma!*, I can still feel the surge and glow that rose through the house with the title song. Yessir! If we could tame this great crazy bronco of a country, I reckon we can patch up this funny old world any time we put our minds to it. And the simple fact that I was there should have told me something too, namely, that all the grown-ups were missing, of the male persuasion that is, except for the very occasional serviceman and for the odd businessman, who really did look tired by now and didn't care if the showgirls wore bloomers and didn't kick, anyway. However, all over the place were the ladies from Scarsdale, probably calling the new tunes as much as anyone.

Whoever we were, we were worlds away from the audiences that Kern had first written for—not only a world of war and depression, of course, but also the world of Busby Berkeley and Walt Disney and of technological hijinks that had left Broadway flickering in last year's gaslight. No sooner had *Show Boat* advanced the stage musical a couple of daring moves on the old checkerboard than talking pictures transferred the whole game to another dimension and began to co-opt the very word "entertainment" for itself. Was there anything that the stage could still do better? As if to settle the question, Hollywood quickly purchased Broadway's crown jewel, *Show Boat* itself, and reached a whole continent with its own excellent version.

*Show Boat* was not so much the start of something as the summation of everything, like a gorgeous firecracker on display celebrating the grand climax of the Jazz Age, when the stage was still king and could, for one last breathless minute, still do anything better than you could. And there was Jerome Kern perched by acclamation on top of the old ship *Showbiz,* virtually an institution himself now, and just the tiniest bit stuck up there.

At any rate, even he could never do *Show Boat* again, although he was constantly expected to. Because, with the coming of hard times in the 1930s, it seemed like just what the doctor ordered, but it wasn't. And Broadway instinctively began to specialize in the things that it *could* do better than Hollywood, notably sophistication, the in-humor of the small audience that could still afford an evening out, as opposed to the large audience that just grabbed a movie and some budget-busting popcorn.

The next surprise would be that sophistication would be what moviegoers wanted as well. But that's a joke for another chapter. The headline for now is that Cole Porter and the young team of Rodgers and Hart were and remain the names that best conjure up the Depression in Manhattan, while Kern spent much of the decade in Hollywood, like a king in exile. His partner in revolution, Hammerstein, went into a bicoastal slump on both stage and screen, one that could only be snapped by the war and the rather special atmosphere of the postwar, with its curious blend of piety and optimism.

As if history wanted to draw a diagram, any chance that Kern's prestige and musical charm might have been able to hold their own against both the talkies and the gals an' gags preferences of the butter-and-egg men was scotched once and for all by the market crash of October 1929. Up to that very day, Kern and Hammerstein's follow-up show, another integrated slice of Americana called *Sweet Adeline,* had been doing a brisk business. But upon hearing the grim news, the box office immediately plunged alongside the millionaires. Maybe it was bad luck at this particular moment to have a hit song called "Why Was I Born?" Not that most people foresaw a whole Depression, but Broadway was always primarily about what do we want to do tonight. And so with the first sign of discouragement, the great American musical went on indefinite hold, while Harbach and Hammerstein took advantage of the confusion to return the American musical to Europe and to opera and operetta-land, taking Kern, at least temporarily, with them.

Kern's next two shows—*The Cat and the Fiddle* with Harbach and *Music in the Air* with Hammerstein—were not really operettas but light comedies about operetta. While World War I had been harsh on Transylvania, it had been kind to England and France, and the years that followed would be even more so as ships began to cross the Atlantic faster and faster until every man, woman, and child who wanted to had "seen Paris," and probably taken in a Broadway show before leaving. By then the transatlantic musical did not need any actual foreigners in the cast, but simply reasonable facsimiles who could play either Englishmen or Americans and in a pinch do French or Italian accents convincingly enough to fool Anglo-American audiences with a will to believe. Theatrically speaking, London and New York had become twin cities, connected by an unbroken stream of ocean liners that took turns exchanging road companies. So the faster you could get your show over there or here and reassembled without fuss or undue expense, the better.

Thus Gershwin's *Oh, Kay!* is set in a Long Island mansion that could easily pass for an English mansion and starred Gertrude Lawrence (English, but it doesn't matter), while Cole Porter's *Gay Divorce* requires one hotel room, one ballroom, and Fred Astaire.

At this name, one pauses, because with Astaire the form had found its archetype, its ideal expression, and it is tempting to say that all that any transatlantic musical needed was this man, in one of his familiar settings, to wit, somewhere between a first-class stateroom and a hotel lobby, because by then the ships themselves had become standard locations, and hotels were where you went when you got off.

Kern's next Broadway show was based on a book called *Gowns by Roberta,* which was made to measure, featuring Americans in Paris singing costume-music without the old starch or upholstery. All the same, under Kern's personal direction, *Roberta* played so heavy that the legendary Max Gordon removed the starch in Philadelphia, and insisted on adding a slice of pungent vaudeville ham—young Bob Hope—to modernize and Americanize the show. And when *Roberta* went to Hollywood, it still creaked a little, because the movies didn't yet trust Fred Astaire to carry the show. In a prestige match against Kern, Astaire was still number two and he was consigned to a variant of the Bob Hope role as the kibitzer from the world of swing, crashing the old-world garden party. So all Fred could do was commence the two-stage reconstruction of Jerry. By amazingly good chance, Fred himself had already heard just the song he needed in a Kern show that had never made it out of London.

It could be said without too much exaggeration that this song, "I Won't Dance," deftly inserted into *Roberta,* would do as much as any one thing to drag Kern, kicking and screaming, out of the old realm of Prince Rudolph of What's-His-Name and into the modern world as then constituted. By the time Astaire was through with this song, it had introduced the public, and perhaps Jerry himself, to a new flavor of Kern, of which it would soon be wanting more. And incidentally, it would introduce Kern to the perfect lyrical partner to lead him around in this new language.

Dorothy Fields had already written (with Jimmy McHugh) such swingaroos as "Diga Diga Doo" and "Doin' the New Low-Down." You could get no hipper or hepper than that. Despite her credentials, Ms. Fields was as terrified of the ferocious Kern legend as anybody. For the film *Roberta,* she'd written some lyrics for a brand-new Kern tune called "Lovely to Look At," which had gone into production before he'd had a chance to hear them, so she thought she had plenty to be afraid of. She needn't have worried. Kern loved her lyrics, and loved her, and they were up and running together, hand in hand through the lower depths, or as close to them as Kern ever allowed himself to get.

So "Lovely to Look At" is pivotal too, and like *Roberta* is itself something of a hybrid, halfway between the grandeur of the old Kern and the friskiness of the new; at a stretch, it might have been at home back in *Show Boat,* but it also sounds like a Fred Astaire song. Either way, I have always found this song absolutely hypnotic and it was the first Kern number to jerk those time-honored words out of me. "He's the best, you know, the very best."

The bar was so high by the early 1930s that *Roberta*'s score had to be great to be good, so Kern responded with a marvelous one that included perhaps his best song yet, although he may not have known he had written it.

The origins of "Smoke Gets in Your Eyes" are sublime evidence of just how subtly the music in the air goes about the work of getting itself written, and of how subconscious and sneaky the pressure of the New could be. Because the tune of this classic had actually begun its majestic life as virtually a throwaway, a piece of "material" for the dancers to tap to while the scenery was being changed, and although Kern himself always denied this, that's all it might have remained if someone else hadn't spotted its potential. "Try playing it slowly," said the director. And voilà, the same angel dust that had turned Carmichael's "Stardust" to gold a couple of years earlier sprinkled itself on Kern's jingle, immortalizing it on the spot and renewing Kern's lease on the crown too, for another millennium or so.

To admit that perhaps his greatest song ever was partly an accident was too much to ask of a control freak, or perhaps of anyone. "I may not have thought of it," as Hoagy famously said of "Stardust," "but I'm the one who found it." But Kern hadn't even precisely done that. Finding music where others have failed was and is just as good as finding it in your head, and Kern had gladly shared credit for "I've Told Every Little Star" with a bird who had obligingly whistled the bridge for him outside his window. But all he could honestly have said about this one was what he said elsewhere about songs in general, that you may feel twenty tugs on your line and only one of them will turn out to be a fish worth keeping, and it might sometimes take a while to know which one.

Kern had by no means converted to the new music full-time, and his decision to go to Hollywood and stay there might actually have been made in a reactionary mood, because if there was any place left where he could still write the old songs the old way and get anyone to listen, it was Hollywood, where Jeanette MacDonald and Nelson Eddy might have been warming up expressly for him. And then there was the money, which he intermittently seemed to need very badly indeed. Benny Green has written disdainfully of Kern's apparently insatiable avarice, but he leaves out the crucial fact that Kern was also a lifelong gambler of a kind that is sometimes called degenerate, with an insatiable need for quick fixes of cash. In his biography of Alexander Woollcott, Samuel Hopkins Adams says that Kern was one of the high rollers who ultimately drove the Algonquin Round Table's poker playing branch out of business by raising the stakes too high.

Hollywood was where the big money was now, and Kern's decision to camp out there was presumably sweetened by the prospect of finding someone to play with again. But first of all, he needed a grubstake himself. Shortly before the Crash, Kern had sold a huge rare book collection that he'd been quietly compiling for years for an impressive sum of ready cash, but instead of betting the proceeds, like a sensible man, on a horse or a greyhound, he bet it all on the stock market in its last few minutes of life. And overnight, he found himself as broke as a Whitney.

Far be it from Kern to complain, or indeed to acknowledge the Depression in any way at all; but not far be it to think about money as he wrote his Hollywood songs. "Stay uncommercial," as he once advised a young disciple, "there's a lot of money in it."

Or so he hoped, at any rate. The first film he agreed to make with MGM was to be an original operetta so uncommercial that it should have made a fortune. But this would be Kern's introduction to the caprices of the industry and its apparent compulsion in those days to give its new arrivals their comeuppance. Because, despite his status as a living classic, Kern's first musical was simply dumped, after he'd already written three songs for it, and was replaced in toto by Rudolf Friml's clanking *Rose-Marie.* Baptism by insult.

Kern prided himself on being a good businessman, and after that he began to stick to one film contract at a time with smaller studios like RKO, over which he might hope to exert some shadow of his old Broadway mastery in exchange for slightly less expensive-looking movies.

Once again, as in the early twenties, Kern began to get his own way right and left without quite knowing what his own way was. He made all of two movies about the humanizing of opera singers, Lily Pons and Grace Moore, respectively, and the one you still see occasionally, *I Dream Too Much* with Pons, is truly charming, especially the title song, and a number called "The Jockey on the Carousel." But there is something small and "niche-y" about the film—Jerome Kern under glass.

He was still royalty, and advertised as such, but there was a lot of minor royalty in Hollywood—crowned heads of obsolete powers known for their postage stamps. If he was a master, he was an old one now, vintage Victor Herbert, and spelled in smaller type (this year) than Cole Porter and (next year) who knows?

The problem was, Hollywood tended to make two kinds of movies in the midthirties, big bad ones and good small ones, and the big musicals tended to be overstuffed turkeys like *Rosalie,* for which MGM would pay Cole Porter zillions of dollars.

Fortunately, though, a school of good small movies emerged that would rescue Kern and three more of the Big Five writers (all but Richard Rodgers). In one sense, Fred Astaire movies, with their goofy, airheaded plots and their cornball sophistication, must have struck Kern as a step backward to the frothy musicals he had cooked up with P. G. Wodehouse way back when. Whatever he did with Astaire would not only be a far cry from *Show Boat* but, worse still, an ominous stride toward the jazz he abominated.

Or did he still abominate it? Like Rodgers and Youmans and everyone else in here, he had heard the music in the air, and like the professor in the movies, he was unconsciously beginning to tap his foot. And if he wanted to be a headline-size master again, perhaps he shouldn't resist too much this time.

*Swing Time* was an interesting site for a baptism because for once Fred was not playing an American dancer in the Old World, but a small-town gambler very much at home in America. Frederick Austerlitz of Nebraska would be touching base at last in a thoroughly relaxed and finger-snapping ambience. And the professor could start tapping his foot for real.

Unlike *Roberta,* which is Kern's creation all the way, *Swing Time* is Astaire's turf. Fred had uniquely mastered the art of swinging tastefully, without entirely tipping over into the down and dirty. He could be hot and cool at the same time. So if Kern was ever going to get hot himself, clearly this was the man to do it with. Whether anyone else could ever have persuaded Kern to make the crossing into jazz songs, we'll never know, because the fact is that nobody else ever did, until world politics turned the screws once again and assigned him to write some songs for *someone* in uniform, preferably not a four-star general, as the name "Kern" might suggest. In wartime, even national monuments were expected to take a cream pie in the chops occasionally to show solidarity. So Kern would swing one more time with Gene Kelly in *Cover Girl,* to which, incidentally, the awed Kelly contributed a quite classy performance himself, to go with Kern's quietly swinging score.

But it was Astaire who really gave us the best of the new Kern, including the songs that people ask the cocktail pianists to play most often, particularly "The Way You Look Tonight," but also "I'm Old-Fashioned" and "A Fine Romance." And it was Astaire alone who really got Kern to swing all the way to the outer limits in "Bojangles of Harlem."

The story of how this number came about provides one of the epic moments in pop history. Fred had seen Kern's original score and pronounced it undanceable. "No syncopation at all." So he and Dorothy Fields went up to the master's suite at the Beverly Wilshire and undertook his education, which Astaire apparently tapped out for him all over the furniture in what must have been one of his most inspired routines. By the end of it, Kern had learned, if nothing else, how to "let himself go" with the kind of classy abandon that was Fred's stock-in-trade.

What is easily missed in the blinding light of Kern's conversion to swing is how far *Jerry* took *Fred* out to where *he* wanted to go. "Bojangles" and Kern's other great dance number, "Never Gonna Dance," were as close to gutbucket as anything written for Fred so far. And he responded with some of his most intense dancing yet. He had challenged Jerry, and Jerry had answered in kind, in a dignified version of the old "call and response" of black music. And what makes *Swing Time* so curiously happy a movie is the sense of not one but three kids let out of school and chasing one another around the playground, as Fred and Ginger enjoy the American air and freedom from hotel rooms and ship decks, and in the unlikely company of our greatest European songwriter.

But that was as far as Kern could go in that direction without vandalizing his image, and he certainly wasn't planning to go there again with anyone else. The next few years would find his libido safely back on its throne. After the humanizing of his second opera singer, Kern continued to march backward by working with his old partner, Oscar Hammerstein, who was so out of it himself at this point that he could scarcely get work on either coast. (An act of kindness on Kern's part? It's not the sort of legend that suited him, but Oscar was at Jerry's bedside when he died and gave him the most moving funeral oration he could have gotten from anyone.)

Kern's health had actually become part of the story as early as 1937, when he received a killer warning shot in the form of a heart attack, combined with a mild stroke. In those days, as I've often been reminded in my recent reading, the first heart attack usually meant "you're out," unless you were lucky indeed. So any sense Kern had while growing up of living a charmed but precarious life must have been reinforced in spades by this episode, and one imagines his remaining years being passed in its shadow.

Nevertheless, he emerged smiling, and for his next movie he wrote a positively bouncy song called "You Couldn't Be Cuter," smacking of his English music hall days, and dedicated it to the baby in Dorothy Fields's womb, or so the story goes. Actually, the baby himself, who is now named David Lahm and is a terrific café pianist, tells me that he would have to have been in utero for about five years for that to be the case. But with legends, it's the thought that counts.

Actually, this story fits in well with other people's Kern memories, as if he truly were a European prima donna, heckling writers and making bad puns in English. In fact, Jerry kept a little bust of that most unlikely role model, Richard Wagner, which he turned to the wall when he was having a bad morning. "Mr. Wagner is not pleased today."

But would Wagner have been pleased with "You Couldn't Be Cuter"? There were two Kerns by then, numbered after his two revolutions, and after he'd made his Wodehouse-type movie with Astaire, he wrote a song in his number-two mode with Hammerstein. "The Folks Who Live on the Hill" is a warm ball of fluff about reg'lar folk doin' a heap of livin'. Oscar had found his rich vein of calendar poetry, and was back at war for Jerry's soul. One could only wonder what Wagner would have thought about that one.

But it would take an ugly war to make Oscar's version look like good sense to Americans. And meanwhile, the rhythms of show business and of regular history suggested another film with Astaire—this time set in Cuba, now that Europe had pulled down its shutters so sharply. And once again, Jerry's ghost owes a debt to Fred's ghost, if only for the title song, "You Were Never Lovelier," which does honor to the word "lovely," as well as to the lilt in Fred's voice. And Jerry's ghost also owes for the great song "I'm Old-Fashioned," which is one of Kern's finest cathedrals, a regal song that sounds wonderful even as sung by Rita Hayworth's voice-over.

As if to prove that composers don't know best, Kern's own favorite in the film, "Dearly Beloved," sounds more like a suburban wedding with too many flowers on the altar, while his other song, "The Shorty George," is a war-effort song that performs its function. It's the kind of song that proves Kern was a good sport, while the hit from his next film, *Cover Girl,* "Long Ago and Far Away," for all its majesty, has a cut-rate sound to it that could have come from a pool of World War II songwriters. It's the only Kern song (good or bad) that doesn't bear his signature.

About that same midwar time, another signal went out. The smashing success of *Oklahoma!* proved that it was already time for Hammerstein— time for regular Americans to start boasting in an unpretentious sort of way about our own sheer variety and colorful ordinariness.

As the other author of *Show Boat,* Jerome Kern saw his destiny and jumped to it, with two America-the-wonderful movies. *Can't Help Singing,* which is Hollywood's answer to *Oklahoma!,* and a ponderous clunker called *Centennial Summer,* which belonged more in the Smithsonian than the Roxy. Kern couldn't have enjoyed the latter much, to judge from the way he's said to have growled at his word-man, Leo Robin, who was paralyzed with awe, and who consequently wrote slowly and indifferently. Presumably, neither was in the mood for Philadelphia in 1876, and like everyone else, wanted to get it all over with and find out what the postwar world would be like.

The first order of business would be, of course, a revival of *Show Boat,* which had just reached its prime as an American monument. Every second review of *Oklahoma!* had said something like "not since *Show Boat,*" and Jerry was already primed and cocked to give them the real thing. In fact, Kern's absorption in this work during his last years almost suggests a man making out his last will. And as his clock struck sixty, it must have sounded quite deafening.

So he went to New York on *Show Boat* business and also to discuss a project suggested by the new production team of Rodgers and Hammerstein to musicalize the story of Annie Oakley, the great sharpshooter. It's a tantalizing note to end on; but one show can only answer so many questions. And *Annie Get Your Gun* is such a thorough progress report on Irving Berlin that it couldn't have done that much more for Kern as well.

"Whom the gods love die young." By the time Kern collapsed definitively on a New York sidewalk in 1945, he was not that young by the standards of his time, but he was still young enough to leave the world wondering what he might have written next, whether more jazz songs in his own refined sense of the form, or more operettas. There are hints both ways.

Although almost all his jazz-worthy songs so far had been written for movies, *Annie Oakley* had been written by Herbert Fields, who worked as a team with his sister Dorothy as lyricist. She was an expert swinger and starch remover onstage as well as on-screen, as she would prove a few years later with the toe-tapping *Up in Central Park* with the ponderous Sigmund Romberg, who was a much stodgier proposition than Kern.

Also, it's possible that Kern may have noticed that every time he got down from his high horse, he wrote hits, and when he got up again, as in "The Longest Hour" and those folks on the hill, he sounded like a second-drawer Richard Rodgers. So it was a choice between stage and film, and between Oscar and Dorothy. Uptown or downtown?

Meanwhile, in a riveting parenthesis, Kern had left Hollywood briefly in 1939 to write his greatest song in this swinging mode, and everybody else's greatest as well, for the Broadway flop *Very Warm for May*. And he wrote it with Oscar Hammerstein. The only hitch was that the song, "All the Things You Are," was almost too good and is so musically sophisticated that Kern almost yanked it from the show because the public wouldn't get it. And speaking strictly as a failed pianist and lifelong beginner (the word "amateur" is much too pretentious), I can testify that its sheet music is the most formidable I've seen so far, outside of Gershwin's own arrangements. Listening to it, I can only marvel at how it gets from here to there.

The closest parallel I can think of to its uncanny progressions is a mountain-climbing fable called "Mallory's Pipe." It seems that after a hard day's workout on a rock face, the greatest of all climbers, George Mallory, said, "Whoops" [or "Damn" or "Egad"], I seem to have left my "damned [dashed, bloody]" pipe behind. And with that, took off in the deep twilight up what must have been the wrong side of the rock, the one without the footholds, returning a few minutes later serenely puffing on the still-warm pipe.

Just so, "All the Things You Are" finds footholds no one else had ever noticed before, or anyone has used again, and in no time it went straight onto the Hit Parade. This was surely a great moment in our history and perhaps the public's finest hour. Kern, who swung one foot on the stage with "They Didn't Believe Me," finally swung out the other with this greatest of American songs. And the rich kid wound up part of the gang anyway, second only to the *really* rich kids in the next chapter.

# Cole Porter:
# From Peru to Paree to Broadway

COLE PORTER

Of all the friendships in this business, the one between Cole Porter and Irving Berlin seems the most superficially improbable. Respectively rich and poor, WASP and Jew, Yale and sidewalk—maybe it was one of those rare cases when opposites actually do attract; or maybe they were not quite as different as they seemed. At a minimum, they were both self-generated legends with outrageously enlarged glands of showmanship and a love of it. And in Cole's case, the show he put on himself is still running, a reassuring fixture on the American scene like *42nd Street* or *The Nut-cracker.*

New celebrities whiz by so quickly these days that even the real ones seem to last only fifteen minutes. Yet all the while, Cole Porter still sits up there high and dry on the ninetieth floor, untouched by time or fashion, like a cast-iron statue of a basic joke. Whatever else the culture may be up to this year, there always seems to be room for Cole at the top. His wit still clicks, his tunes lilt, and the mere mention of his name makes people smile in both anticipation and memory.

Most surprising of all, sociobiologically speaking, Cole's love songs still work. Evolution doesn't know much about music, and still less about interior rhymes, but it does like to keep those babies coming, and a Porter song can still jump-start the process as well as anyone's—from Jerome Kern to Elton John to whatever is hot this minute. Whether you're in the market for a "let's get married" song or a "let's not wait to get married" one, you can't do better than a Cole tape playing in the back of the canoe, the limousine, or even the pickup truck.

Yet the other curious thing about Cole Porter is that when people talk about him, they often leave out the music altogether, concentrating instead on the funny lyrics or the funny fellow who wrote them, who sounds as if he wouldn't have been caught dead in the back of a pickup truck, let alone endangering his crease with a mad embrace. In short, a cool chap who free-associates roughly as follows: Adjectives—dry; brittle; serve slightly chilled. Setting—parties (pause) great big parties; fancy dress preferred. Working clothes—smoking jacket, velvet. Principal product—wit. Hobbies—writing songs. Real occupation—giving parties, and so forth; also traveling abroad; first-class all the way, with an option to pose in grass skirts, war paint, and so on. Phobias—boredom; fresh air; Behaving himself. Orientation—well, not the kind to keep those babies coming.

The logo "Cole Porter" represents a brand image so imperious that it gets stamped on certain songs whether he wrote them or not, for example, "You Go to My Head" by J. Fred Coots and Haven Gillespie *must* be by Cole, because who else writes about champagne? But think of "You've Got That Thing," "Let's Do It," and "Most Gentlemen Don't Like Love." You can't miss a real Porter song. It must have been lonely at the top of Cole's skyscraper.

In each of his scores, though, you will find at least one song, secreted among the singing commercials for penthouses on the Lido, that seems to come from somewhere else completely, if not several places. For practical purposes, Cole Porter can be boiled down to at least three different song-writers: one, a smarty-pants like for those songs above; two, a passionate writer of jazz songs; and three, a sentimental country boy who can tug on your heartstrings without any tricks at all.

Turning next to the Hot and Bothered file in search of missing pieces, one finds something even less like the mannequin with the cigarette holder—to wit, a devastating lack of coolness and protective irony. Cole's noble little masterpiece "After You, Who?" (catch it any way you can) must be, words and music, one of the most naked songs ever written, a wild cry from the heart, and it sounds a note that recurs again and again.

"For without you there, what could I do?" Note that nothing has even happened yet in the song, but the singer can't wait to be abandoned: He's heartbroken by the mere possibility. Anyone as vulnerable as that obviously needs a good carapace, be it a smoking jacket or a clown's costume, just to hide his hide from the world's laughter and curiosity—not to mention its rejection of his songs at the ticket window. To this day, many people have trouble swallowing love songs from gays, but fortunately, in Cole's own day the general public didn't know a homosexual from the Father of the Bride, and he was able to hide his gay self inside an even gayer persona, and wrap it all up in an acceptable marriage and pass the whole rigamarole off as a facsimile of Cary Grant, who played him in the hilarious movie *Night and Day* (and there couldn't be anything odd about Cary, could there?).

Insofar as Cole's brand image had PR value, Cole's third kind of song-writer was a real menace, and word leaked down from the Porter camp that songs like "Don't Fence Me In" and "Rosalie" were not the real Cole at all, but were written purely for money—as if, for the right price, our hero was even willing to be corny.

Concealment by exaggeration—well, it worked at the time. But now that everyone knows everything, and can explain it too, there's no place left to hide the fact that those love songs were indeed written by not just a gay man, but by an off-the-wall, over-the-top gay man. His latest biographer, William McBrien, documented this exhaustively, almost Kenneth Starr-ly, listing enough names and dates to suggest that Cole could be serially monogamous and serially polygamous at the same time, depending on which kind of song he needed.

It was the monogamous streak that put him over the top. Cole was never just an itchy man writing for itchy people. Great ballads also have to prove themselves on quiet, shadowy porches, and it is here that Cole actually scored best, partly because, like Cyrano de Bergerac and other odd-looking lovers, he was a great seducer by other means. He had the formula down cold for alchemizing lust into romance, and for selling the customer on a lifetime of bliss in exchange for a few trifling minutes of hoop-di-do; but mainly because, like the greatest seducers, he meant what he was saying. More than anyone, he craved the happy ending he was selling, and was even more heartbroken when he didn't get it. For the time being, anyway.

Even at its most agitated, as in "I've Got You Under My Skin," Cole's fever typically wars with, and finally gives way to, something quite thrillingly tranquil, if only in the form of eggs and bacon or a seat by the fire. And even when the words don't find this kind of peace, as in "Get Out of Town," the melody goes ahead and makes a separate one anyhow. "The thrill when we meet is so bittersweet that, darling, it's getting me down." The words solve nothing, but the notes could be wedding bells. And it is these musical phrases, just as much as his lyrics, that most clearly identify a song as Cole Porter's. All his tunes at least have happy endings: The mood they arouse is satisfied and everyone drives, or rows, home happy, regardless of gender.

It is these same chronically undervalued tunes that make it perfectly safe to ask the man at the piano to "play some Cole Porter," knowing that whether he picks a funny one or a sad one, and whether he sings the words or not, it will do. And it will do not just for you, but for most of the barflies in most of the bars in the English-speaking world, obliging one to wonder whether gay love might be closer to straight than either team cares to recognize. Whatever the answer to that, Cole's gay lifestyle seems to have given him an awful lot of practice at falling in love, and he kept on doing it as assiduously as a research student and as ardently as a teenager long after most married men have finally conquered the habit, and after even his famous electric eels and moths in rugs had packed it in. And each new lover seems to have been an occasion of song, as he "concentrated" on this one, and kept "his eye on" that, and experienced yet again the torment of breaking up and the joy of starting over almost with the speed of a swinging door. In fact, it seems that Cole sometimes wrote his lyrics and love letters in the same giddy, boozy rush, which is why the love in the songs seems so real. And if his lyrics couldn't name who he loved, or even precisely what, they certainly could show how much, and he doubled up on this part, expressing his passion with a gusto that simply blows away such pantywaist contemporaries as Ira Gershwin and Oscar Hammerstein. "Only make believe" coos Oscar, and "Come to papa, come to papa do," twitters Ira, and a couple of powerful tunes are slightly weakened, but "the look in your eyes when you surrender" writes Cole, and the tune picks up enough steam to drive home triumphantly.

But where is the fop in the smoking jacket amid this blur of activity? Probably hanging in the closet next to Fred Astaire's top hat and tails. Neither of these Midwestern masters of sophistication was born that way—and in fact Fred could only play the part onstage and on-screen. Between gigs, he remained a lifelong hayseed, as did an important part of Cole.

Geniuses don't let anything go, they just add stuff. As a mythical neighbor from Peru (pronounced Pea-ru), Indiana, might put it, different folks have different ways of coping with the Big City. Cole's fellow Hoosier, Hoagland Carmichael, for instance, was a university man, a licensed lawyer, and a snappy dresser, but elected to go the good-old-boy route, becoming more down-home than he'd ever been back in Bloomington. Cole preferred to beat the slickers at their own game, literally outwitting them by being more Yalie than Dink Stover, more New York than Eustace Tilly, and more Parisian than Ernest Hemingway and Gertrude Stein rolled into one.

Talk about different strokes . . . but both boys loved their mothers and wrote good American music and kept their own tough kind of integrity. When Cole died, it seemed perfectly fitting for him and his globe-trotting wife, Linda, to be buried together, torment over at last, in Peru, Indiana; and when Hoosiers still get together to celebrate Cole as a native son, that probably rings true too, hauntingly so, in fact.

"Don't Fence Me In" was absolutely genuine.


ROLLING IT ALL BACK to the beginning, one finds a suspiciously typical gay childhood, with an overpowering mother force-feeding her son the arts, and a shadowy, withdrawn father. But the wrinkle in this case is that it was actually Cole's father, Sam, who had the real artistic interests, including a passion for romantic poetry and an indeterminate skill at the guitar, and his withdrawal seems to have been as much social and economic as personal. For instance, the affable Sam left the matter of his son's education entirely up to his wife, Kate, not necessarily from indifference but because it was really a question of deciding what schools his rich, cantankerous father-in-law, J. O. Cole, could be talked into paying for. Sam had no say in this, or in anything else that mattered. So although the genes that he'd already passed on to Cole would eventually prove infinitely more valuable than J.O.'s provincial real estate fortune, this was not clear at the time and Sam had to content himself with his local pharmacy, which he grittily expanded, and the consolations of poetry.

Kate's bequest, on the other hand, became clear immediately. Like her father, Mrs. Porter had nothing much to offer genetically save a blind drive to succeed, and if music was the way for Cole to get there, she would see to it that the kid had music coming out of his ears, with piano and violin lessons and practice sessions scheduled round the clock—which she expected Sam to enforce with the approved growls and spankings of the pre-Spock era. So Daddy was pain and Mommy was encouragement, and the war for the boy's love was presumably over if it had ever begun.

The exhibitionism he seems to have provided himself. By the age of eight, Cole had already bounced onto a real stage at the local (silent) theater, played the wrong music on the piano, and been bounced off again. And not long after that, we find him being chased off one of the lake boats and into the water for sitting at the steamboat's piano, this time in a wet bathing suit, and pounding away as the boat set off.

A gift like his is a great liberator, and by the time Cole left Peru for school at the age of twelve, he was a welcome regular at both the movie house and the steamboat, with a lifetime visa stamped on his brain entitling him to go anywhere in the world he liked that contained a piano and an audience.

In view of which, Kate's eagerness to have Cole's first song published by age eleven seems less pushy and more like an attempt to catch a ride on a whirlwind. "Take me with you," she started saying early, and sometimes he would and sometimes he wouldn't.

Away from the piano, Cole seems to have been a spasmodically shy but immensely curious and sociable little boy, just as interested in words as he was in music. His curiosity led him repeatedly to the local circus, where he learned all about clowns and their strategies, and possibly of the mating habits of "chimpanzees" and "bears in pits," among other things. His sociability introduced him to friendship, which he would swiftly make into an art form, a beautiful alternative to life. Before he'd left knee pants, his prototypes were in place: a boy and a girl, and himself in the middle as best friend of both.

Desdemona Bearss was the girl he would have fallen in love with if he possibly could have, and thus in a sense she was his true love, the one his heart could go "all the way" with without fear of being hurt. Since friendships with women were guaranteed never to become too hot not to cool down, he could indulge in the pleasures of constancy, and when Desdemona died unseasonably young, Cole was as shattered as he later would be by the deaths of his mother and his wife, Linda. When male lovers left, he presumably died a little, but when women checked out for good, it was like a crack in the universe. Even permanence let one down eventually.

At what exact point Porter also discovered that men were fickle and began to "kick it around" himself, is a secret he proceeded now to bury in the best of all possible hiding places, a couple of all-male establishments, Worcester Academy and Yale University (both in the sinful Northeast—Kate won that fight with J.O.). Through these places, a certain number of inmates perennially pass through under a question mark—it's no big deal. In stag societies, all the parts have to be played by males anyway, and Cole's natural roles of mascot and court jester, Puck and Yorick, are traditionally ambiguous—all sexes and none—and often musical too. (See Michael Jackson.)

In later years, Cole would allegedly say that he wished he'd had his friend Irving Berlin's "advantages," which is funny because, in his own odd way, he kind of did. As a rule, the old prep schools produced few artistic geniuses, because the well-rounded curricula they favored were no match for the monomania and total immersion available to dropouts like Berlin, who was off plugging songs for Harry Von Tilzer, or ad-libbing his own lyrics as a singing waiter, at an age when Cole was still supposed to be bounding over playing fields, parsing Greek verbs, and taking in sermons about clean minds and clean bodies.

Fortunately, though, Cole's own monomania was already full-blown and now asked only the basics of life, and once he'd gotten a piano installed (immediately) in his room, the second basic took care of itself: A whole school was out there waiting to be wooed and amused to the best of his adolescent ability, and it's fair to deduce that he used, as usual, everything he had in the cause, from his father's love of poetry to the classics he was devouring at school to the slight hypochondria instilled by his mother, which kept him indoors and added a welcome lick to his new persona. Cole might not be plugging songs for a living like Irving, but he had just as much riding on them, because he was putting his whole self over, and creating that self as he went, while in general making the world a safe and hilarious place for a Cole Porter to be.

His songs had to be, above all, likeable, or he would have instantly reverted to a noxious young outsider from the boondocks. And maybe he still felt like that anyway. At any rate, his best friend at Worcester seems to have been the headmaster, and teenage boys don't dig teacher's pets, so the art of friendship would be put on hold until Yale, which he would love with the grateful devotion of someone who hasn't really cared for school that much but has used it well and is ready.

Yale must have seemed like the big leagues of schoolboy entertainment. All the envious little creeps and the slow-witted ones who don't get the joke magically disappear into the gully between the twelfth and thirteenth grades, and he could be precocious now forever. And better still, Yale was close to New York and had a "special" relationship with Broadway. Age for age, Cole had probably matched young Irving song for song, and the only advantage he even half-seriously envied was Berlin's setting. New York's Lower East Side happened at that moment to be the Vienna of the American song, and you had only to keep your ears open there to advance your education daily. Cole, meanwhile, was stuck with the quaint sounds of young WASPs at play, which had in no time entered his own throat for good, driving out any trace of the Midwest and forever cementing him into the role of urban dandy.

On the surviving recordings of his own singing, Porter's voice comes across as not merely campy but so preppy that Henry Higgins could probably identify the exact schools and the years attended. Funny travel photos notwithstanding, Cole would never really be just a dilettante passing through places, but a natural enthusiast who sucked up the air and steeped himself in the sound and style of wherever he happened to be. So, probably nobody ever got more out of either Worcester Academy or Yale than he did, or wound up sounding, vowel for vowel, less like a Broadway songwriter.

Yet he used Yale as a professional school, a songwriting school where work and play were the same things. In those happy-go-lucky pre–World War I days, the game at most Ivy League colleges was still to see who could have the most fun this year, this term, this second, and since Cole's talent fit this agenda perfectly, it was child's play to string the clubs and private parties together into a species of upscale borscht belt where Porter could work nonstop at making up doggerel about the guests and about Yale and Shakespeare and bulldogs and whatever anyone hollered for. Just how far he still was from nearby New York he would later learn when he took a batch of his material to the equally unreal world of Broadway and got clobbered, or worse, ignored: His collegiate-style comedy *See America First* sank without a trace and Cole either had to start work devising a bridge between the two cultures or content himself with playing the prep school circuit forever.

But any conjectures about Cole's professional plans and dreams run onto a blank tape at this point, because Old Ivy had placed yet another layer of reticence upon his bubbling soul. A gentleman, it seems, should never appear to want anything very much, unless it's something quite trivial—a rare stamp, a perfect boiled egg—let alone be seen working at it. And one wasn't even allowed to send messages from this prison of style, because letters to friends had to be kept light, shallow, and slightly off the point.

So to the naked eye, Cole's only care at this time, no deeper than a Wodehouse plot, was to flimflam his grandfather into thinking that he was a solid citizen who thoroughly deserved every penny of the old boy's fortune, and this basically boiled down to not getting thrown out of Yale, which from his grandfather's distance presumably looked like a serious place. And even after he had graduated, then gotten thrown, or nudged, out of Harvard Law School in the direction of the music school, all he had to do was pretend it hadn't happened and the charade could continue.

Or so he may have supposed. In fact, J. O. Cole dispossessed him anyway, perhaps because he was watching more closely than supposed, or because that was simply what Coles did to Porters, and left all the money to his daughter—who split it with Cole, thus becoming a fuller partner in his life than perhaps either had planned. Grandfather Cole departed the planet totally oblivious to what he'd wrought or to the kind of story he'd just taken part in. Too bad: If he'd lived long enough—say another fifty years or so—he might have realized that his grandson was basically a chip off the old block in gorgeous disguise, a J. O. Cole with talent. "Frankly," as Alec Wilder would put it in his book *American Popular Song,* "I find it extraordinary any time a wealthy person manages to create anything besides more wealth," let alone such a huge body of painstaking work as Porter's. Yet so much heavy labor also went into Cole's pretense of *not working* that for most of the 1920s he was able to pass for the worst kind of rich brat, succumbing to every temptation that a well-heeled young Yale man at large in the world's great cities could find to succumb to.

College lifestyles of Cole's particular type did not necessarily end with graduation in those days, but were known to gather hurricane strength as the Whiffenpoofs and Old Crimsons, lions and tigers, transferred their frat house shenanigans to a larger stage with more opportunities and fewer rules. And Cole would stay their troubadour, their living legend, paying dues to both the jolly side of that life by tomcatting around town with his old pal Monty Woolley until he was almost too old to walk, and to the dull parts, by leaving his door open to Yalies of all kinds, bores included. Because Yalies never bored him, and neither did Peruvians, with whom he kept in touch too, in the spare time of his spare time by going home every chance he got to talk local talk to local people, as if his art commanded him to keep in touch with ordinary citizens just as much as clever ones.

Although Cole's horror of boredom was a running gag in his usual set, the word actually seems to have meant something more like depression, a blankness and coldness that startled visitors who caught him between laughs and shows. So long as he was "up," Cole was interested in just about everything, as one might guess from his lyrics. So his life may be viewed as an endless campaign to stay up, unbored and undepressed.

The difference between Cole and such musical fellow-depressives as Berlin, Rodgers, and Harold Arlen was that most of the time he was able to chase the blues with sheer hyperactivity, starting with a bang in World

War I, which he seems to have treated as his private fancy-dress and coming-out party. Monty Woolley claimed that Cole showed up at the fashionable cafés in a different uniform every night, as he bounded from group to group, looking for ones that would keep him in Paris a bit longer. He had found a subject and he had found a style in this incomparable city, and was not about to budge.

And if he could change his uniform, why not his whole identity? It was there, amid the forged passports and phony résumés of war that Cole hit his stride as a fabulist and self-creator. If he could pretend to be straight, why not fake the French Foreign Legion as well? And would a Croix de Guerre be going too far?

Porter's actual war record is, in fact, so impenetrable that some of his less playful commentators have dismissed the whole farrago as a neurotic evasion, but the subject was having much too much fun for that, trying on different faces for the real party that was to follow. Paris was filling up with brilliant refugees from the Russian Revolution, and these would soon be joined by their Western counterparts on the run from Prohibition. Cole would be there waiting, like a maestro watching a new audience, the perfect audience, file into the hall.

Although it's hard to date the actual writing of some of Porter's early songs, one can almost hear the hum of the party in the funny ones and picture Cole smiling at the keyboard, as he knocks the smart set dead, night after night. The eternal preppie has seen Paree now, and knows all about gigolos and cocottes, and serenades them in a cosmopolitan style closer to Noël Coward's than Irving Berlin's.

Surely at this pinnacle, a million miles from Peru and with the laughter of princes real and imaginary braying in his ears, a less driven man would have come to rest and wallowed. For the average American genius in Paris, the big news would be simply that he hadn't cracked up yet, because Porter seemed to drink enough to crack up anyone, and his love life constantly threatened to spin out of control as well. Paris had also filled up with brilliant homosexuals. Cole experienced a grand passion with one of Diaghilev's dancers and was very probably tempted by the whole troupe.

Yet in a surprising but wise move, he kicked off the twenties by marrying a woman with an equal genius for appearances. Bernard Berenson claimed that Linda Porter had perfect taste in absolutely everything, and in his memoir, *Musical Stages,* Richard Rodgers suggests that she was somehow perfect in herself too, both to look at and to talk to, an art object worth collecting in her own right.

Cole proceeded to use his wife as a safety brake on his wantonness by insisting on the Jane Austen–like condition that all his lovers must first make friends with her before proceeding. But it would be a mistake to assume the cliché that Linda was his mother all over again, because the evidence suggests that Cole preferred to worship his real mother, an unreconstructed hick, at a slight distance, while he relished Linda's company.

So the truer parallel would surely be with Desdemona Bearss, his inseparable pal and dream girl, who had magically returned to him all grown up now, as if to specifications, to play the part of Zelda Fitzgerald better than the original ever could and to pose for happy endings as needed. Regally cool and lovely, Linda could henceforth serve as Cole's indispensable muse of eggs and bacon and everything else that might be nice for his songs and himself to "come home to" and cool off with after the fiery tortures of love. He, for his part, would be true to her "in his fashion."

After having fled from her own previous brutal marriage, Linda could now easily play the lighter role of providing a beard, not just for her new husband's sexuality, but for his ferocious work habit. By the time Cole's songs had made him unmistakably famous, legend had already decided that it must be his wife who was dragging him home from the party and making him do it—as if a Cole needed help getting to work. In fact, what Linda wanted was for Cole to become a serious composer, not a famous one, and he cheerfully went along with this detour by studying advanced composition and harmony at the elite Schola Cantorum and even scoring a ballet that earned respectful notices in Paris.

But no matter how hard he pretended to look the other way, Cole apparently never for a moment took his eye off Broadway. Both his ear and his curiosity must have told him that his natural rivals there, men like George Gershwin and Jerome Kern, were classically trained musicians too and that the harmony he was learning at the Schola Cantorum might be jazzed up à la Gershwin into the Broadway sound he was looking for.

Thus, under cover of the high life, Cole patiently polished his songs to the familiar gleam, and quietly sent them off to New York and London, where they began to catch on a bit, then suddenly a lot. By the end of the decade, Cole Porter had been most thoroughly discovered overnight as a mysteriously accomplished Broadway professional, who also happened to be a well-known around-the-clock playboy in exile.

During his long apprenticeship, Cole also worked so hard at the self-promotion end of the business that his famous image had actually arrived in New York and London several years before his songs. By cultivating such dedicated exhibitionists as Elsa Maxwell, the fabulous society-hostess-cum-reporter, and Elsie de Wolfe (later Lady Mendl), the far-out decorator, Cole saw to it that his name got into the papers before he'd done anything at all, except make the Riviera the place to be in winter, and Venice the place to throw parties. (You mean he writes songs too? Wow!)

Later, of course, he immortalized his promoters in song, as round and round the publicity machine went: café society between the wars consisted largely of people like Cole and the Elsa girls, all hard at work in the cause of play, and scratching one another's backs to beat the band, in a daisy chain that stretched from the Algonquin Hotel to the Lido, or wherever the Porters happened to be at that moment.

In 1926, Cole's worlds of work and play collided with a small bang when Noël Coward, who epitomized the whole arrangement, introduced him to his future rival, Richard Rodgers. Since these two men would later be contesting or sharing the title of King of Broadway for over two decades, it seemed only right that Cole would take the occasion to announce his wish to write "Jewish songs" from now on, which was the next best thing to throwing his hat into the ring. The year before, George Gershwin had blown through Paris, playing pianos everywhere he went, and had either told Cole in so many words or shown him by example the element Cole had been missing in the Broadway sound. Later, Rodgers acknowledged that Porter wound up writing "the most enduring Jewish music" of anyone.

"I want to write little Jewish songs" became Cole's mantra. There was absolutely nothing condescending about it because the more "Jewish" he got, the better his music. By adding the mystery ingredients of jazzness and bluesness, he reached a new depth in himself that hadn't been previously accessible to the public. It was a turning point for both him and his art, and if this book were a musical, the chorus would burst into a shout-song here, like "Oklahoma!" or "Happy Days Are Here Again." The movement that wasn't quite a movement had made its most important convert, and Cole really meant it too. As just another "American Gilbert and Sullivan," he probably could have gone just so far and no further; there are limits built into the very phrase. Instead, Porter stayed in Paris another three years, looking for the sound he wanted among the minor keys and innate melancholy of so-called Jewish music.

He had probably known all along that the tunes would be the hard part, but they were also the part he wanted most. In a defining anecdote, Michael Feinstein reports that Cole and George were once asked at a party to write a song together, and Cole retorted that he preferred the hard labor of devising his own melodies. Writing lyrics was by implication the easy part and much closer to a real party game, in which you are allowed to use a thesaurus or a rhyming dictionary and anything else you can get your ears on. I believe that the phrase "A trip to the moon on gossamer wings" came from an ad for mattresses or bedsprings or some such, while the words "It's delightful, it's delicious, it's de-lovely" were originally intoned by Monty Woolley on a tropical night while they were off cruising someplace. As every comic knows, you can't beat the right cliché in the right place, in which spirit let's just say that, in lyric writing, anything goes. Well, did you ever?

But there was only one right tune, and Cole would sit at his desk with the dedication of a monk, abstaining from even the comforts of the piano until he had written out the gist of it. His words might have made it to Broadway at any time, but not by themselves, and it would take him the best part of a decade to get the tunes he wanted, that's to say tunes that could "touch your heart" or tickle your funny bone. Two songs may serve to measure his progress. In 1924, "I'm in Love Again" was his first genuine hit and probably the first one that you might find yourself humming without remembering anything else about it. And then "What Is This Thing Called Love" in 1929, which sounds exactly like what he was looking for.

But once he had turned this key, all of Broadway fell open to him at once: He wasn't just allowed onto the street, he owned it. And just like that, Cole Porter became synonymous with Broadway to an extent that not even Kern could claim. You were definitely not in Peoria tonight. Or were you?

On a closer look, even Cole's slyest lyrics could have been written with at least half of his other eye on Peoria. The fact is, Americans of all kinds seemed then, as they do now, to enjoy hearing lists of celebrities read, especially if you threw in references to cellophane and Mickey Mouse then (or to e-mail and Britney Spears now). And there is nothing especially arcane about the thought of "electric eels" and "lazy jellyfish" doing it. This is sophistication for the masses, well within the reach of a bright traveling salesman. As an old Peruvian himself, he knew that at least half the people in the outback would rather be someplace else anyway, and were planning to go there sometime. So why not take them there right now and give them an evening in Paree, or the Rainbow Room, or the South Pacific?

And clinching it was something else that Cole knew about Peru, and Peoria, and Podunk too. The West had *already* been melodically won by Irving Berlin and his little Jewish songs. When Jerome Kern said that Berlin *was* American music, he wasn't just referring to Broadway or the Brill Building. And now, by putting all his own various know-hows together, Cole Porter could start to "be" American music too.

In fact, for years he scored first on a list of America's tip-top favorite songs with five entries—which, since he wrote both words and music, made him the champ, one-two with Irving Berlin himself.

Grounds for envy, one might suppose—but not in this profession, or with these two men. Berlin and Porter really were too completely unalike to hate each other, and besides, each had something the other wanted. Before they even met, Irving was looking for fresh talent to stuff into his own little theater, the Music Box, and Porter was looking for a ticket to Broadway: and voilà! They were partners for a season with an interest in each other's immediate success.

And in a more general way, Berlin wanted to go more uptown with his music, while Porter wished to delve further into the little Jewish song, which Irving was still writing better than anyone. And then of course there was the inevitable Fred Astaire on hand to serve as an interested party and test site. The stagy number "Let's Face the Music and Dance" is widely considered Berlin's most direct response to Porter. But both men met in that amorphous concept known as the typical Fred Astaire song.

And another curious bond these three men shared was that they all had rich wives who were utterly out of place in Hollywood and culturally much too good for it, which made them a useful trio of muses for the work the men did together.

Berlin would tip his cap to the Cole connection by naming his second daughter after Linda Porter, while Cole would say thanks to Irving the best way he knew how, by comparing a Berlin ballad to a Waldorf salad and placing it at the top.

Linda had to be a muse in absentia for a while. Although she had been the perfect companion for an American in Europe, a Henry James character with an exquisite sense of style and nuance who had helped him to be a positively superb expatriate, Cole had done Europe now and was ready to go home to America—with all its slang and its swing, its intoxicating vulgarity and self-satisfied lack of nuance. More prosaically, as the twenties began to wind down, Cole must have seen that he couldn't very well conduct a Broadway career completely from Europe, and he returned to New York sans Linda. Possibly, she hoped he would just get his silly business over with—he didn't need the money—and he would then return to his senses and Europe quite soon. With still-fresh memories of a dreadful first marriage in America, Linda had no wish to return for a second. But artistic repatriation cannot be done overnight, and Cole had some catching up to do with the intangibles—the small changes of phrase and attitude that you can't hear from abroad, and such far-out developments as Ethel Merman or the nose of the great Durante.

From this vantage, his early shows, such as *Gay Divorce* and *Nymph Errant,* were like halfway houses, and could easily have been written in Paris or Venice. But his big one, *Anything Goes* (1934), was unmistakably American. "You're the Top," "I Get a Kick Out of You," "Anything Goes." I'm back! And ready to start a brand-new chapter, with new scripts and new stories. And the whole point of the Astaire figure is that he blends high style with a certain street authenticity. In a prototypical role, his real name is Pete Peters of Pittsburgh, P-A, but he is posing as the great Petrov, the ballet master, and he will finally turn out somehow to be both, an American gentleman whose innate classiness is worth any number of fancy titles. And here was a role waiting for Cole too, as that other plot device, the rich snob becoming a regular guy, with a touch of the great

Petrov too, the serious artist tapping his foot. But there didn't seem to be a part for Linda, at least so long as she remained an expatriate dilettante who wasn't about to budge.

Linda must have seen that the jig was up, and she agreed to come over, at least as far as New York, which must have seemed like a halfway house in itself, a kind of Europe West, which was not without its subtleties or its Europeans either, many of whom never got beyond it. And Linda could always decorate the Porters' suite at the Waldorf like Versailles and pretend. In short, the Porters as an entity still made some kind of remembered sense in New York. In Hollywood, Cole's next port of call, they would make none at all.

Before testing these next and perhaps final roles together, the Porters took off together on an epic around-the-world cruise in 1935 with Cole's old pal Woolley and his new working partner, Moss Hart, which would prove to be a Last Hurrah and Goodbye to All That to the beautiful life, and out of which would come not only the musical *Jubilee,* but also Cole's slap-happiest song, "It's De-Lovely," and his most rhythmically adventurous one, "Begin the Beguine." The chief musical gift the non-Caucasian world had to offer back then was a variety of exotic beats, and Cole would use these as a semisecret weapon to provide the kicker in his songs, in the form of vivid bass lines that worked like pistons under the melody.

But now back to America at its corniest, namely, Hollywood, which in that pre–Las Vegas dawn was still the undisputed world capital of vulgarity. Linda's love of appearances, both social and aesthetic, must have been affronted by every sight and sound of it. Cole, on the other hand, thought it was the funniest joke ever, a sublime parody of the land he loved, and to hell with sophistication. He ordered up a jacket made up of every sample in the store ("be a clown," the song says, not "be a fop") and got set to run amuck.

After all the tasteful years abroad, Cole gulped up this crazy new atmosphere as he had once gulped up Yale and Paris. And if promiscuity was what they did here, he would be the best at that too, vying with George Cukor to conduct the most star-studded gay salon in the West. Everyone in Hollywood was beautiful and everyone was tied up at the moment, so romances lasted no longer than shooting schedules. Now Cole even dispensed with the charade of introducing his lovers to Linda, leaving her to keep up grim appearances by herself, a game she continued to play so conscientiously that to this day people don't know if she had any sex life herself at all, and if so what kind.

It was startlingly cruel, and Cole probably knew it. The fickleness that so terrified and tormented him had always been first and last his own, and his dealings with Linda would be for a while a heartbreaking mixture of icy detachment and unflagging solicitousness, interspersed, since Cole never threw away anything, with flashes of the old feelings as well. Linda was still "nice to come home to" occasionally and "love" in one's fashion.

Finally, Linda could take no more. She offered to put Cole out of their mutual misery or else further into it, by telling him to choose between Hollywood and her. It was a dramatic peak. "How'm I riding?" he wrote around then. "I'm riding high." And he was. At his crest in 1936, he received two diplomas proving it, the more obvious being a lush three-year contract at MGM, the other a spontaneous compliment from a producer called Sam Katz. "That song is beautiful. Why, it's Jewish."

"Mission accomplished," although not in a flight jacket but a velvet smoking one. As we've seen, Oscar Levant says that Gershwin had gone West that very same year to snatch back his crown from Rodgers and Porter, and now, with his own death just a year away, he would get a chance to square off against one of these young pretenders. "I've got you under my skin," wrote Porter. "They can't take that away from me," wrote Gershwin, as if in answer. American popular songs never got better than that.

Maybe at that peak of fame and confidence Cole might have faced down his fears of abandonment once and for all by saying goodbye to a woman friend.

But before Cole could make his decision, a real horse, on which one day he was literally riding high, decided the question for him by first throwing him and then rolling over both his legs (like a hitman making sure).

Linda paused in the doorway. If she hoped that this would sober Cole up or even slow him down much, she was in for a nasty surprise. But at least she had a role again, if not her old one. Henceforth, she really could be his mother—she looked old enough at this point—and her first decision as such would be that Cole's leg *not* be amputated, for the sake of his pride—a choice that has since been debated almost as hotly as George Gershwin's brain tumor.

What we do know is that from now on, pain would be the invisible presence in every Cole Porter anecdote, and in every assessment of his character too. Some days it seemed that the postaccident Cole could be unbelievably bitchy (even Noël Coward found him hard to take), but on others, more frequent ones, he was preternaturally thoughtful and kind. And then sometimes a streak of snobbery flared up, although he despised it in others. The only constant was restlessness.

Whatever has been said about Cole in his later years—selfishness or altruism, lust or love—is undoubtedly true. But always there was pain too, coming or going or in full possession, and nearly always there was defiance. Cole's preferred attitude is best summed up in the report he broadcast himself as fast as he could get it out, that as he lay under the horse, he worked on the lyrics to "At Long Last Love." Maybe he did. But then again, maybe he had once served in the French Foreign Legion. All he owed the public was a good story.

And the big story now was that this thing had not gotten him down for a minute! At least to judge from the songs that never stopped coming, more ebulliently than ever. "If they ever put a bullet through your brain, I'll complain," "If you're ever . . . sawed in half, I won't laugh" he wrote in 1939, a time when extreme measures must have passed through his mind quite a lot. So he'd make fun of them and of everything else besides. "Astrology, mythology . . . stupidity, solidity, frigidity" he wrote for Danny Kaye, in one of his giddiest list songs.

In the years right after his accident, Cole wildly overindulged in his two favorite pain medicines: work, and play. If World War I had been a party for Cole, he saw to it that World War II would be a downright orgy, certainly proving that the greatest of all wars can be won with gays in the military. Or perhaps his handsome companions were just queens for a day, beguiled by a chance to sit with a celebrity around his pool in Hollywood or at the men's bar of the Waldorf-Astoria in New York, as he snatched at pleasure in mind-numbing quantities.

"Happy people don't need to have fun" as the late Jean Stafford would intone on bad mornings, by which gauge Cole must have been truly desperate. At around that time, Cole seems to have thought about Catholic instruction too, for a different kind of relief. His friend Lawrason Riggs, with whom he'd written *See America First,* had since fetched up as the Catholic chaplain at Yale, and he might have made an understanding guide for Cole through the barbed wire of moral theology. (My father, who knew and liked Mgsr. Riggs, found him a bit "perfumy" himself.) But Riggs's sudden death by heart failure in 1943 blocked off that particular exit for good. So, on with the orgy!

But all the pleasure in the world still left plenty of time for Cole to work, and he dashed off a couple of unsuccessful musicals. Just like that, the vultures were on him. Obviously, the old boy was beginning to lose it. Although he was still batting out gems like "I Love You (Hums the April Breeze)" and "Ev'ry Time We Say Goodbye," he was in his midfifties now, an age when the waiter looks over every few minutes to see if you've left yet. The war was almost over and the music was changing and a crowd of new customers was straining the rope to get in.

But this time the joke was on the vultures. Cole's alleged burnout proved to be a superb theatrical buildup to an astonishing comeback. *Kiss Me, Kate* was like a salesman's sample case, containing a choice bit of everything he did. Since the plot concerns some Americans putting on a Shakespeare play, Porter seizes the opportunity to divide the songs into two, giving the cast some jazzy, beat-driven ones ("Too Darn Hot," "Why Can't You Behave") to sing on its own time, and some traditional singer-driven ones ("Where Is the Life That Late I Led?") to insert into the play, plus subdivisions of both categories, before wrapping the whole adventure up in a swirl of timeless but curiously Shakespearean-sounding joy. Now I shall ever be, now I shall ever be, mi-ine, thi-ine: as if the composer himself was laughing in triumph at pulling off this caper. With this one score, Porter accomplished all he could reasonably have dreamed of, as a boy on a ferryboat, and a student of Shakespeare at Yale, and as a student of both jazz and classical composition in the bistros and classrooms of Paris. And Robert Browning, Irving Berlin, and both his mother and his father could all have felt equally proud.

After such an explosion, everything else had to seem a slight anticlimax, although two more of his shows, *Can-Can* and *Silk Stockings,* and one more movie, *High Society,* contained more good music than anything done by the postwar popinjays who had once challenged him. In each of these emanations, Porter would play the unlikely role of custodian to the great "Jewish" songs whose run on Broadway and elsewhere was now drawing to a close.

It's hard to keep the faith when the sounds in the air change, but Cole had worked too hard to write that way, and loved it too much to give it up now, and such later numbers as "It's All Right with Me" and "You're Sensational" sound as if the 1930s had never ended—which they hadn't yet if you didn't want them to. How long he could have kept this going against hard rock, acid rock, rap, we'll never know, because by then, "Miss Otis" had sent her last regrets. After a last round of pleasure trips that might best be described as "brisk and bracing"—the buses ran on time and you'd better be on them, and all the sights were seen and you'd better be prepared to discuss them—his legs finally gave out for keeps, both literally and metaphorically. The fun ended. The surgeons of the day, who seemingly never got anything quite right, but who never gave up on it either (e.g., Thurber's twenty-plus eye operations), decided after thirty or so in Cole's case that the right leg really had to go this time. Since by then Linda was no longer around to give them an argument, they went ahead and inevitably botched it, or so one assumes from the screaming, uncontrollable pain they left him in, and the mind-fogging painkillers that they thus condemned him to.

But perhaps the process had really begun a few years earlier with the deaths of both Linda and his mother in the early 1950s. If every goodbye really caused him to "die a little," these two long goodbyes must have caused an unearthly loneliness, as if all his bleakest lyrics had come true. "Don't you know, little fool, you never can win?"

So this, combined with martinis and painkillers, finally did what wild horses had failed to do. If it didn't crush his spirit, it did sap his will and his capacity to express it. Accounts from Cole's last years suggest a stoic down to his last hair shirt, keeping up appearances, sort of, and trying to take an interest, and still freakishly craving sex. But no more songs or jokes now. Most of the time the host just mutely stares at his dinner guests, of which he never invites more than two at a time. Any bright conversation has to come from them.

In that last sad silence, which one imagines broken by the scraping of chairs as his manservant tries to hoist him from the table while no one's looking, one gets a chance to consider what we've lost. Cole had lived every moment of his life till now as fully and entertainingly as a life can be lived. This, after the myths have been enjoyed and put away for the night, may be the reason his songs still work. They have a pulse, as if someone is still in there, a real pining lover in the serious ones, eating out a real heart; and in the funny ones, a kid showing off as merrily as ever, conquering Peru and Yale, Paris and Broadway, forever and ever, amen.

In a strange, throwaway ending, it seems that, although Cole had insisted on no religion or fuss at his graveside, he made two exceptions. He wanted the Lord's Prayer recited and he wanted the verse that states Christianity's central proposition to be read: "I am the resurrection, and the life; he that believeth in me, though he were dead, yet shall he live."

What was that again? Cole Porter with an inner life? It was the perfect curtain.

# Richard Rodgers:
# Dr. Jekyll and Mr. Rodgers

RICHARD RODGERS

*I*n drastic contrast to Irving Berlin and Cole Porter, Richard Rodgers gen-
erated practically no gossip and left behind no legend. Judging from his
amazing output, maybe he was simply too busy writing music to have an
outsize reputation, let alone invent one. Or maybe he was smart enough
to let his music do the talking for him. But the fact is that his identity is
quite hard to pin down in his music too. If personal style is what one falls
back on when one runs out of new things to say, Rodgers had either no
style or perhaps too many styles to count—a different one for every scene

of every show, in fact. So although his music is, by some accounts, the most often played of any composer in history, such was its sheer variety, melodic inventiveness, and lack of musical ego that his work keeps disappearing into the crowd of great American songs, like a huge anonymous donation, taking himself with it.

So to learn that he actually wrote a memoir called *Musical Stages* is rather like discovering that the Sphinx kept a diary: One turns to it eagerly, if not skeptically. How much can you trust a sphinx? Well, maybe if you read between the lines, and wait for someone else's book to compare it with . . .

His memoir immediately puts one on guard by lashing out at his family, telling us how impossible they were to live with—a charge that rings strangely down the years, because in an introduction to a later edition of this book, his daughter, Mary, levels exactly the same charge against him: not that he was a bad man exactly (he could be startlingly generous), just an impossible one. It seems the one gift this gifted family lacked through two generations was the smallest one: the kind of amiable in-house chitchat that happy families run on. The first sounds that young Dick's sensitive ears picked up in the family's city quarters were his grandmother's sarcastic tirades and his grandfather's defiant growls, broken only by his mother's occasional wistful piano playing between bouts—which may have given Dick his first, fatal taste for comfort music. His father, Dr. William Rodgers, preferred to spend his family time in lofty, apparently disapproving, silence. Although allegedly Dr. Rodgers showed quite a bit of charm with his patients, he wasn't wasting it on his family.

If words wounded, music healed. In no time at all, Dick Rodgers struck the piano himself, finding with almost the first chord that it could solve practically everything, bringing peace even to his grandmother. It also enormously enhanced his own status—if he could just get to the instrument before his envious brother, Mort, broke his fingers or set fire to the piano. In *Musical Stages*, Rodgers introduces the piano first. With time, it became his imaginary friend and alter ego, through which he could say everything he wanted and explore his own outer limits of tenderness and wit, while his impossible family looked on in admiring silence—or, at any rate, in silence.

The next lesson he learned from the instrument was that if humans *must* open their mouths, the best you could hope for was a song. His parents had a cheerful hobby of bringing sheet music home from new musicals and singing together at the piano while his mother played. And the apartment was transformed into a cloud-cuckoo-land. And Rodgers had found himself a lifelong model of perfect happiness. Harmony at home, love on the stage, music everywhere.

The piano never taught Richard Rodgers a better way to cope with domestic situations than just to play something, or shut up like his father, or turn truculent like his grandfather. Any finer points, such as manners or conversation, he would have to learn from the Broadway stage, which would become his spiritual home and family court from the moment he entered one at the age of twelve or so. From then on, his parents would magically cease to matter until they later showed up in the orchestra seats, warmly applauding their son—nice people, after all, in that context, who, rare among artists' parents, thoroughly approved of his chosen life: a life that he, perhaps in return, proceeded to keep as outwardly square as he possibly could, dressing and comporting himself like a banker, hiding any private sins in the best Ivy League manner, and eventually courting at full length a most suitable and ladylike young woman named Dorothy Feiner, to whom he tried vociferously to be faithful, for a while.

Meanwhile, back in his real life, he met the two most important elements in his coming career: the music of Jerome Kern, which combined for the first time the concepts "American," "classy," and "popular"— Eureka! And the indispensable Larry Hart, with whom Rodgers, at sixteen, would start almost immediately to unwrap his extraordinary gift for melody.

At first, *Musical Stages* seems to be completely candid about Larry Hart too, quite thrillingly so because this time the candor is 100 percent favorable. In brief, Rodgers was poleaxed by his new friend and galvanized to the point where you could almost see his own young life start to change as you read. And these few pages should be underlined and returned to, because the ebullient mood doesn't last long, but soon gives way to a viperish tone of condescending exasperation that can only give aid and comfort to the conventional portrayal of Hart as a funny-looking little guy who writes exquisite love songs and who cannot find love himself, so naturally drinks himself to death. In the silly movie *Words and Music* (1948), Mickey Rooney hammered this image home by playing Hart as a lovelorn dwarf, so perhaps it's worth noting that offscreen Rooney himself married the likes of Ava Gardner and Martha Vickers, proving if nothing else that dwarfs and near-dwarfs don't *have* to be lovelorn. And Larry Hart might have married just as well if he'd really wanted to. Witnesses attest that he could look positively handsome with a wave of his wit and charm. Like Cole Porter, Hart was a homosexual who genuinely loved women. However, unlike Cole, Hart desired them only to step out with and paint and repaint the town over and over—not to come home to and love.

The one thing that dwarfs really can't do is drink as much as the Jolly Green Giant, and Hart's attempts to do so would lead to most of the grief that followed. In the cramped world of psychohistory, nobody has ever gotten drunk just for fun, but only to escape from some problem he or she can't face. So the possibility that Hart might have had an inspired and highly productive capacity for enjoying himself is simply squeezed into a box marked "manic-depressive," from which nothing good or beautiful has ever emerged.

So it's worth repeating that *Musical Stages* gives absolutely no impression that the reader is about to meet a basket case when Rodgers first walks into the Hart apartment. On the contrary, Rodgers proceeds to find that Hart has easily the richest, most entertaining mind he has encountered in his sixteen years, a mind stuffed to the brim with both high culture and low—from the German operettas that Hart had recently translated (he was also distantly related to Heinrich Heine) to the latest word from the street (and below the street). Better still, here was a mind stuffed with ideas about both songs and musicals, which echoed and clarified Rodgers's own. In later years Rodgers would privately talk about "the statute of limitations on gratitude," but in this case it shouldn't be invoked for at least a thousand years, because in a crucial sense, he was born that day. The Rodgers-in-the-piano had finally met his match and his counterpart—not only a friend he could talk to, but one who could talk back, and who, while loving Rodgers unconditionally, would meet the first threat of Rodgers's disabling musical sentimentality with the cold eye and sour tongue of a perpetual hangover, and would interject a derisive lyric like a stop sign.

So Rodgers was forced to dig down beyond his natural facility into parts unknown. Alter egos have inner lives too. And the Rodgers-in-the-piano proved to be as subtle and witty and even likable as anyone in American music—so long as Hart was waiting next to the piano to guide and keep him company. In her introduction to *Musical Stages,* Mary Rodgers talks of loving her father's songs, and of that being enough. But if so, it was also enough to make one love Larry Hart. Because Larry, along with his gemütlich mother and his disreputable father, taught Rodgers that you could belong to a technically higher social class than his own without being the least bit respectable, thus (for a while) loosening the grip of Rodgers's nastiest attribute, his innate snobbery.

Unfortunately, the lesson and the likableness would last only as long as Hart did, and nature invariably sees to it that the greatest of partnerships—whether of George and Ira, or John and Paul, or Gilbert and Sullivan—never last quite long enough. But something else seems to have let them know that they'd better get moving right away, and by the time Richard Rodgers had reached a ripe seventeen, he and Hart had already written an establishing song to prove that indeed they could do it. "Any Old Place with You," with its immortal thought "I'd go to hell for ya, or Philadelphia."

Okay, you're songwriters, now grow up, on the double. Over the next few years, Dick would attend Columbia briefly and the Juilliard School (as it's now called) of music while intermittently writing varsity shows for both. After which, these two really poured it on for the next fifteen years, until they had piled up an oeuvre that a couple of centenarians could be proud of.

It's still a pleasure just to recite the titles and start the tunes spinning in one's head, beginning anywhere on the list and ending up anywhere else. "Where or When," "My Funny Valentine," "Little Girl Blue," "The Lady Is a Tramp," "With a Song in My Heart." A friend of mine recently gave a party just to celebrate the day when he and his brother and I had all discovered and first played and sung the Rodgers and Hart book. So that statute of limitations on gratitude still has a ways yet to go—at least for some of us.

"I can pee melody," Rodgers is alleged to have said, which also suggests a compulsion: When you've got to go, you've got to go, and at a certain point their assembly-line production turned out to be the pace that kills. Perhaps you can't keep revving up a manic-depressive like Hart without tearing something within. And soon Hart's alcoholism galloped toward the finish line in the manner of a Dylan Thomas and Brendan Behan.

But this was Dick's own schedule, and his whip was never far from Larry's back. By the midthirties, Hart responded by regularly disappearing for days on end (which I might have done too, if I had had to work with Rodgers) and scribbling his lyrics on envelopes and cocktail napkins and fraying any enchantment his increasingly prickly partner had ever felt for him, until probably the only thing keeping them together was the imperturbably high quality of these lyrics. "Bewitched" and "Falling in Love with Love"—the scores of *Pal Joey* and *The Boys from Syracuse*—were dashed off during these nightmare years, as if disappearing for days on end was just what Hart's craftsmanship called for, and as if to prove that the artist within him was ultimately just as serious and indomitable as the one inside Richard Rodgers.

Perhaps it was. But the facts on the ground said otherwise, and after writing a prophetic song called "I Didn't Know What Time It Was," it was all over. Hart died after literally lying in a gutter, in circumstances that truly deserve the name of classic tragedy. Dick felt as innocent of causing this death as Oedipus, but he may also have been just as cursed by it too. To sum it up quickly, Rodgers had wanted to write up a namby-pamby story called *Green Grow the Lilacs*, and Hart had not. So Dick wrote it with Hammerstein instead—nothing wrong with that so far, just a one-shot deal and then back to Hart for a revised version of their first great hit, *A Connecticut Yankee*, with sparkling new words from Larry that would include one of his coolest, driest lines yet: "I admire the moon as a moon, just a moon."

Away from the desk, though, or an envelope or an old menu to write on, Hart became a confused soul. The score Rodgers wrote with Hammerstein for the namby-pamby play, renamed *Oklahoma!*, seemed to explode with relief, as if Richard Rodgers had been simply dying to cut loose from Hart. The critics prattled on about breakthroughs and new beginnings—presumably involving Rodgers and Hammerstein. And against this—what?—a revival with Hart of a 1920s show? In 1943, Hart went to see both shows—his revival and Oscar's bombshell—and apparently liked them both, but he also talked loudly and drunkenly during them, to the point where Dick ordered their respective box offices not to let him in. So Larry went outside to lie down in his gutter, acquiring pneumonia from which he never recovered.

What else could Rodgers have done? Perhaps there's no good answer. But Dick never got that close to anyone else again. Instead the scene changes sharply from a 1930s tableau of kids putting on shows together to one of those slick 1950s offices from which Mr. Big, now Rodgers, emerges in time for the 5:25 to Greenwich every day and a cocktail on the lawn in his Bermuda shorts.

Of course, songwriters need to stay in tune with their times, but this was ridiculous. And even the family Rodgers returned to at night was a perfect period piece: happy on the outside, rotten on the inside. Its tasteful suburban façade proved to be an arena in which the latest ailments and prescription drugs slugged it out in human disguise, while the children, who assume that the whole thing is really about them, can start work on their own *Mommie Dearests*. In one corner, we find Dorothy Rodgers (anorexic, constipated), who turns into a raging, capricious monster—who wouldn't? And in the other, her husband (boozed, tranquilized), who seems permanently depressed and half-stoned. He comes to life one show at a time—just long enough to romance a new heroine, alienate the writer and the director forever, and kiss the whole chorus line goodbye before returning home to keep up appearances for the neighbors, as his father had once kept them up for his patients.

Needless to say, none of these ghoulish phenomena can be found in Dick's memoir, which doesn't tell any significant truths from Larry's death on. After a long and no doubt agonizing wait, his daughters finally commissioned that other book we've been waiting for—Meryle Secrest's *Somewhere for Me: A Biography of Richard Rodgers*—which contains the gist of their combined *Mommie Dearests*, which time has not mellowed perhaps as much as they had hoped for. The first question it answers is the one we began with, to wit, why did Rodgers seem so invisible?

Like each of the other four classic songwriters that everyone has still heard of—Jerome Kern, Irving Berlin, Cole Porter, and George Gershwin—Rodgers first made his mark in New York in the high noon and early sunset of the golden age of newspaper publicity, when there were allegedly a million stories in Manhattan, with reporters trying to cover all of them. And each of the others had learned how to be good copy and fun to read about, particularly if the reporter was lucky enough to catch Kern at the track or Porter in his gondola. But where would you catch Rodgers? And why would you bother? He appeared to possess no characteristics whatever, and worked with a lyricist who possessed enough color for two and a lifetime. The hyperactive Larry Hart could not only talk enough to fill whole newspapers at a sitting but could also carouse so conspicuously between times that keeping his name *out* of the papers became the issue. Rodgers came of age playing the sobering part of sometime guardian and straight man to one of New York's major characters.

So who, outside of Agatha Christie, would ever suspect *him* of anything? Since Hart was going to get the story anyway, who would notice if Rodgers had gotten a little squiffy as well, and appeared to be with a different chorus girl tonight? And one night led to another until by the time Hart had died and been replaced by the much milder Oscar Hammerstein, Rodgers was doing so much carousing that covering up for himself had become a necessity. Suddenly with Oscar, one had a sense of two straight men working together with no top banana in sight.

Did Hammerstein also have something to hide? Gossip should not be multiplied unnecessarily, although it has been. But let's leave it in here that Rodgers's name in particular never seemed to go out by itself anymore, but invariably became RodgersandHammerstein at work and DickandDorothy at play; in sum, he seemed to be the most dedicated partner and thoroughly married man in show business—a perfect ornament of the Eisenhower years.

Signing up with Hammerstein in the first place had been the artistic equivalent of moving to the suburbs, and Rodgers's literal move to the burbs would prove to be the perfect postwar blend of hypocrisy and wish fulfillment. On the one hand, his bilocation permitted his double life to go into overdrive between evening clothes and Bermuda shorts—but, as I learned from a friend of mine who knew him, Dick Rodgers also wasted several of his most celebrated years vainly trying to talk his way into a local country club that didn't take Jews or theater people or whatever. So even in his Connecticut castle, he could never just relax and be himself. You can't keep a good snob down forever, and without

Larry Hart to cauterize it, his snobbery apparently ballooned to Macy's Parade proportions.

Which leaves us with the unanswerable question: Why, with genuine royalty virtually at his feet, did Rodgers bother with the provincial nonentities at this snooty country club? Well, his father would have understood. By 1902, when Dick was born, Dr. William Rodgers had reached what might be called the awkward stage of assimilation. Professionally, he was almost too respectable. But he sent his two sons mixed signals by raising the family in the home of his much richer and cruder in-laws, who embodied all the harshness, noise, and sense of overcrowding of an earlier time.

Anyhow, maybe this contrast nudged Dick's imagination on the eventual road to quiet lawns and empty rooms, toward PTAs and country clubs. At any rate, that is where his Second Act found him, growing ever more remote and regal in his suburban casuals and even, like a regular mogul, writing a memoir to hide behind forever. Later, Joe Fox, his editor on that book, would confide his frustration at having to beg for a straight answer to the simplest personal question: "Was Larry Hart really a homosexual?" "I never noticed," said Rodgers.

Gentlemen may not notice things like that, but Rodgers most certainly had, and now that his family has also delivered on the second half of its one-two punch to Daddy's pretensions, we can also pick up his own tone in his breezy, sometimes bitchy, and always articulate published letters to his late wife. And one realizes, among other things, that his secret drinking had rubbed his own nerves raw years before and that his impatience with Larry had become almost as neurotic as the latter's response to it. "That little fag," he wrote several times, referring to the man whose orientation he hadn't noticed.

Like many tragedies, Richard Rodgers, Part Two, is basically a soap opera with the stakes raised—the stakes in this case being nothing less than the future of the American musical. And the tragedy, if that's the right word, is that in the end Rodgers's lifelong attempt to merge music, words, dance, and even scenery into something like great art would be deemed kitsch, and hardly art at all. His climactic masterpiece, *The Sound of Music,* has survived into this century as a festival of high camp.

As it was, he was stunned enough to find that later generations preferred his earlier work with Hart. Wasn't Hammerstein supposed to be the revolutionary around here?

But Hammerstein, as Rodgers might have known, if his literary taste had kept up with his music, wasn't even facing in the right direction. Back in the 1920s, while Rodgers and Hart were already talking about a new kind of American musical, Hammerstein was still cheerfully dabbling in old-fashioned operettas like *Rose-Marie* and *The Desert Song*. He obviously loved the form in all its artifice and sentimentality, and this antiquated taste would sabotage every later attempt to add realism. Are we meant to be in Iowa this time or Oklahoma, or possibly Connecticut? "Durned if I know." The effects are gorgeously inauthentic, and the judgment of the sixties would be cruel.

Yet one can seldom be absolutely sure that a genius doesn't know what he's doing. Since Rodgers wasn't going to find another Hart to jam with anyway, why not try something different? Instead of concocting tunes for the lyricist to chase, why not let him go first, as Hammerstein manifestly preferred, and see where that led? Any artist who wants to last as long as Rodgers did had better change his style at least once to keep the flow going; Hammerstein's proudly corny words tapped not only a new vein of ideas but also a new aspect of his talent. Even the fertile Jule Styne expressed amazement at the speed and sureness of Rodgers's response to other people's words. Just say something like "Bali Ha'i" or "Oh, what a beautiful morning," and out would pop the musical equivalent of these words, the perfect tune.

But not the perfect jazz tune. Hammerstein had turned his back on the Jazz Age from the first downbeat onward, and jazz returned the favor to him in the Big Band Era by cutting him off. Now in the postwar years of inventory, as America began to count its blessings and bask in old glories, he had once again become the man who wrote *Show Boat*, and even perhaps the man who would write the *next Show Boat* too. One could hardly become classier than that.

To be specific, Oscar's gentility seems to have leaned toward voices over instruments and leaned away from brass instruments altogether and the syncopation that went with them. Well, okay, compromising on tempo was no deal breaker for Dick, as it would have been for Cole Porter. His only trademark in this respect was a taste for unobtrusive, all-purpose waltzes, from the intense "Lover (When We're Dancing)" for Hart to the dreamy "Out of My Dreams" for Oscar, and the perky "Oh, What a Beautiful Mornin'."

Since he was now basically writing settings for Hammerstein's poetry, it made perfect sense to drop "that thing" and give Oscar the extra space for his lush emotions and warm humor that would take the place of Larry's irony and wit, to the delight of amateurs with big voices and to the massed yawns of interpreters like Sinatra and Sarah Vaughan, who instead kept finding more and more gems in the old Hart songbook, and erecting a monument of discs in their joint name that towers over Rodgers's oeuvre with Hammerstein. But perhaps genius still knew best in that Dick was at least still able to work with Oscar and the tunes did at least keep coming, as they would not with anyone else. And some of the tunes were beauties too, with or without "that thing." *Oklahoma!*, which was written under Hart's influence, and indeed when he himself was still above ground, is a perfect specimen of show-tune writing, with a song to cap every mood and occasion, all the while disguising its basic silliness. And even as Rodgers drifted farther from the jazz song, and from the scope of this book, he kept adding to the pool of melody for jazzmen to make into fresh jam, up to and including the elegant "My Favorite Things," which John Coltrane would redeem from its Austro-Hungarian trappings and transfer back to pure jazz.

After Oscar Hammerstein's death, Dick's first instinct was to write his own lyrics—maybe to prove he could, and maybe because he knew how impossible he was to work with. Anyone he had or ever would try it with would become part of an unhappy family of two; this had been the only model Rodgers knew. Hart had run away, while Hammerstein had worked in his own splendid isolation—I go first, you go second. There is no image of real teamwork even in this most famous of teams.

So Dick went solo on a show called (ironically?) *No Strings*. But although *No Strings* was a success, modest by his standards and colossal by anyone else's, perhaps he found something flat about it, or perhaps *he* didn't like working with himself either, for he never again tried a one-man turn. Instead, he proceeded to strike out with the likes of Alan Jay Lerner and Stephen Sondheim, merely the best in the business. And maybe even

worse from his point of view, he began to acquire the equivalent of a police dossier in gossip. If his drinking up till then had been a family secret,
it was all over Broadway now, and the street version was, if anything, even
worse than the family one.

Bad drunks leave bad memories, and we currently know much more
about the years when Rodgers was slipping than about his heights. Which
has left him with an irony that would have pained him beyond endurance.
Larry Hart, like Scott Fitzgerald, had gone down in flames early and has
been unequivocally admired ever since. Rodgers, like Hemingway, lived
longer and crashed slower and harder, and there seems no rush to dig up
either of them from the rubble. Each of them had made the further boozy
mistake of condescending to their more likable partners, using phrases
like "poor Scott" and "the little fag," for which they would end up paying
again and again. When vengeance and justice arrive at the same verdict,
it can be irresistible, but finally can any fellow human really be so easily
and decisively judged?

Well, maybe if the judge is on a tight deadline. But the longer this
essay sits on my desk, the more questions arise from it. For one thing, I
met Dick's well-balanced and good-humored daughter, Mary, and cannot
easily imagine anyone so manifestly functional emerging from not one but
two such monsters as her parents have been described. I've also met a
cousin who passes along an ancestral memory of Dick Rodgers and Larry
Hart actually playing together in the backyard around an old tree house
during what was supposed to be the peak of their alienation. And I quite
recently met a doctor from Sloan-Kettering cancer hospital who remembers Dick as a positively inspiring patient, which in hospital lingo means
cheerful, cheerful, and more cheerful—not an easy mood to sustain when
you suddenly need to have your jaw removed and replaced, as Dick did in
1955, seemingly at the height of his success. This leads to a final clue in
Rodgers's memoir itself, which might be called the dog that didn't bark, or
rather the cure that didn't work.

Faced at a certain point in his own story with the undeniable, he suddenly admits that, yes, he did indeed drink too much once upon a time
and succumbed to angst and existential aphasia and everything else that
has been said about him. But he sweeps the whole syndrome into a few

manageable months in 1957, some of which were spent in the Payne Whitney Psychiatric Clinic, where the shrinks would proceed to clear the whole thing up forever—a happy ending that has since been endorsed by absolutely nobody, perhaps because it is flatly impossible.

Once more, the last laugh is on him, because as everyone knows now but practically nobody knew back then, psychiatry can't do anything for addiction-depression unless the sufferer agrees to go on the wagon and stay on it—and not just the booze wagon but the pill wagon or whatever-else-you're-on wagon as well. Rodgers would unconsciously bear this out by feeling "cured" at Payne Whitney, just as he had felt so well at Sloan-Kettering. "Cured" not, as he now supposed, because of the world-famous head-shrinkage that was the main event at Payne, but because of the sideshow—temporary abstinence—that made him into a positive "doctor's helper," as he shyly and self-mockingly boasted of becoming while there.

This phenomenon is known to former drunks as the pink cloud, and is as insubstantial as it sounds. Just laying off the downers you've been taking makes you feel preternaturally buoyant at first, but if you sit on the cloud, you go right through it. So in no time Rodgers was back to stay on his booze and painkillers, a victim and perpetrator of not a crime but a sloppy cover-up of the pharmaceutical anarchy that raged in America after World War II.

So for the most part the man Mary Rodgers describes in her introduction sounds drearily familiar: a man without friends or hobbies or any life at all. Yet the malaise had not altogether consumed the Rodgers in the piano, who continued to fight his own private wars with the Death Wish and the Life Principle. On various occasions, Mary has talked of the piano as a hub of activity, and of it lugubriously falling silent for long periods, as the instrument waited for a great script to enter the room and activate it once more. In a devastating sentence that pares the situation to the bone, she says that her father actually had no interest in music as such, no matter how challenging, but only in telling stories, no matter how banal. It was his belief that all music was basically descriptive, whether it knew it or not. Three of his own best pieces were pure descriptions of, respectively, a *Slaughter on Tenth Avenue,* a *Victory at Sea,* and a Carousel Waltz, in the show of the same name. So now, in his solitude, why didn't he take one further step into abstraction by boiling down the basic formula—the boy, the girl, and the eye candy—and rendering *them* as pure music too?

The technical problem toward the end was getting him from his chair to the piano, and it never happened. But perhaps the last word should go to the demiurge in the music box, taken from the one occasion when it chose to speak to itself in *No Strings*. Two lines in particular seem to have survived the years since, one of them because it seems so acutely true, and the other because it doesn't. "The kindest words I'll ever know are waiting to be said." They are still waiting, as far as I know, but "the sweetest sounds I'll ever hear are still inside my head" seems far-fetched. The sweetest songs *I've* ever heard—perhaps not the best or most interesting, but definitely the sweetest—are safe and sound in the Rodgers and Hart songbook.

Yet Rodgers was speaking a songwriter's truth that I've heard echoed at least twice by other practitioners—by Gershwin, who said that he had more songs in his head than he could write down in a hundred years, and just the other night by my friend Cy Coleman, who confirmed that he, too, had more in there than he could count, so perhaps songwriting can best be defined as the wonderful ability to go in there and get them.

*Part Four*

Hollywood—The Sugar Daddy

# Hooray for Hollywood (Sometimes)

RICHARD WHITING

"*H*ow is your book on the great *show* songs coming?" Although I had never actually called them that, the translation was instantaneous and unanimous, because one of the sturdiest prejudices in this field insists that all the great songs began on Broadway. Nothing *that* good could have come out of Tin Pan Alley, let alone the crass movie business. From the moment that Hollywood opened its mouth to talk and sing, it seemed that you were either in thrall to the results or you despised them with all your soul. And while you were most likely to outgrow the first mistake, the second one, the unconditional contempt, could be a life sentence, as in the case of Alec

Wilder, who forever maintained that theater songs were better than movie songs . . . because they had to be. That's just the way it was.

Based on the stage writers' autonomy versus the movie guys' servitude, Wilder makes a plausible case too. For the most part, the best stage writers were free to score their own stuff, and decide on things like length and shape and musical arrangement. Trained musicians like Gershwin and Kern valued this freedom and made the most of it. But, significantly, a lot of others, such as Richard Rodgers, didn't—because, as Cy Coleman explained to me, while you were home arranging your songs, the producer and director were quite likely removing the scenes your songs were in and hence the songs too. And to completely counter Wilder's argument, one need only play one other card, which is that by his own reckoning each of the above-mentioned songwriters wrote some of his very greatest songs for movies, while as for length and shape, Harold Arlen's "Blues in the Night" and Rube Bloom's "Day In, Day Out" ramble on at interminable length and are as free-form as anything ever produced on Broadway.

In movies, the longer your song lasts, the more time the studio gets to show off its scenery and choreography, and how much better it can make a number like "Begin and Beguine" look than all the stage carpenters and small-as-life dancers of Broadway put together. Movie songs have another huge built-in advantage. Stage songs generally have to be part of a story or else they seem intrusive, but movie songs can play quietly in the background, establishing a mood, behind our backs as it were, and selling us on the tune before we're even aware of having heard it. It is a truism of the stage that even professionals can't always spot a hit the first time they hear it, while as for critics, there is a long honor roll of great songs that didn't make it into first-night reviews, for example, the mutt who found Kern's score for *Roberta* "sweetly forgettable." Yeah, right, so much for "Smoke Gets in Your Eyes."

In contrast, I recommend that you take a look at the great Bing Crosby and W. C. Fields movie *Mississippi*. Listen for the Richard Rodgers song "It's Easy to Remember." Notice how often it is played before Bing officially introduces it. By the time he does, it's like an old friend.

All the tunes used to be replayed so often that even the background music could be turned into songs, as in the case of David Raksin's "Laura," which wound up with a lyric by Johnny Mercer (and with the rare encomium of being the song Cole Porter would most have liked to have written himself). With bandleaders and singers and Hollywood itself beating the bushes for new material, no good tune went unheard. Eddie Cantor's archetypal film *Kid Millions* ends with a perfect metaphor for the situation: an ice cream factory stretching to infinity, with different shades of ice cream bursting from every pore while an infinity of kids pour through to become presumably, infinitely sick. By the time you left the movie house on a Saturday afternoon, the entertainment was coming out of your ears, but you knew all the songs too.

There's no need to catalogue all the usual horror stories about Hollywood, which were undoubtedly just as true, of talent ignored or manhandled. Two specimens cover most of this ground: Saul Chaplin had already passed the first and most important requirement for movie glory; he had "made it" in New York with a couple of hits, "Please Be Kind" and the immortal (i.e., Sinatra liked it) "Until the Real Thing Comes Along," plus another hit that he had by the tail, "Bei Mir Bist du Schoen," a song that he and his partner Sammy Cahn hadn't precisely written but had rearranged and signed.

Unfortunately, though, Saul never learned how to play politics in New York because Cahn played it for both of them from morning to night. This would be Chaplin's downfall because Hollywood was such a politician's delight that Sammy kept right on playing it until he had played himself into a whole new partnership with the red-hot Jule Styne. Saul didn't know what to do next, or what the first step was in this dance, so he finally retired upward into management, where he happily worked alongside such fellow drop-ups as Johnny "Body and Soul" Green at MGM and Victor "Stella by Starlight" Young at Paramount to help turn out the last great crops of musicals, in the forties and fifties, that Hollywood would ever produce. Finally, this is what makes it so hard to stay mad at Hollywood; even the losers got ice cream.

But even the winners had to play politics. And sometimes they lost and had to eat humble pie with their ice cream. As we have seen, even Berlin, Kern, and Gershwin got hazed at least once by the philistines before winding up in glory. The only one who was too proud to take it was Richard Rodgers. His brief film career proves a useful parable and recap of the songwriter's role out there. It reminds one, among other things, of how quickly the scene kept changing, of how much screen history might be crammed into a few years, so that "the good old days" could refer to any time up to last night, and the end of the world might have begun already.

When Rodgers and Hart arrived in late 1931, the first wave of musicals had just passed and Hollywood didn't know what to do next. For writers, it was like finding all the doors of the palace unlocked. The boys moved right in and, with the help of the adventurous director Rouben Mamoulian, produced a film, *Love Me Tonight,* that still seems avant-garde. For openers, the sequence of scenes that accompanies the hit song "Isn't It Romantic" is like a zoom lens that takes us from the big picture, of poilus fighting for France, to a smaller one of regular Parisians going about their business, to one street, and then to one shop and one man whistling, all done in the newsreel style that would later be used in *Duck Soup* ("Fredonia Goes to War") and makes a sublime overture to the operetta courtship that ensues between Maurice Chevalier and Jeanette MacDonald, which in turn is a study in felicitous high-comedy song placement. And the songs themselves, such as "Mimi," "Lover," "Isn't It Romantic," are so good that Rodgers and Hart went straight to the top of the class without quite knowing what was so unique about this movie that got them there. So after a routine musical with George M. Cohan flopped, the pair resumed the same general method of integrating songs and pictures with Al Jolson in *Hallelujah, I'm a Bum!,* which was a step backward, because Jolson was a step backward. Maurice Chevalier was a one-on-one entertainer, a confider of songs, perfect for the movies, while Jolson and Cohan preferred to work the whole crowd, which usually just looks silly in movies. Still, *Hallelujah* succeeded, just enough anyway to prompt MGM to sign up Rodgers and Hart with a flourish and a big banquet in their honor.

And then that same year *42nd Street* was released and with that, comic impressionism gave way to sexy sentimentalism and technological narcissism, and a moment later Rodgers and Hart found themselves out of style and almost out of work, taking stabs at projects that were soon abandoned, and wasting precious time rewriting, among other things, maybe the greatest song that never made it into a movie. Hart had written one set of words to it to suit one kind of movie, and then another set, and finally gave up and just wrote some words that could have been a parody and called it "Blue Moon."

At this point, it was too soon in musical comedy history to know just how long the latest trend would last. All Rodgers needed to do now was get out of town, and either do another stage show or go around the world. Then he could return to another banquet in his honor. Hollywood was always celebrating new arrivals, however often they'd been there before, and if you timed it right, like Gershwin and Porter in 1936, you might even become the latest trend yourself.

The year 1932 was not a good time to be anywhere. The Depression had finally sunk in all the way and musicals seemed to be dying on Broadway as well. For the hyperactive Rodgers, it was a taste of hell. Because he and Hart had apparently lost the war on both coasts to just the kind of tired businessman leg-waving that they'd been trying to drive off Broadway. What else was *42nd Street* and its gold-digger children than bits and pieces of the old Ziegfeld Follies photographed from the ceiling and wrapped in a flimsy backstage romance?

Fortunately, Broadway was resilient too and was just about to come back from the dead, as is its wont. Rodgers returned, a grumpier but wiser man, to make a huge New York splash with Billy Rose's *Jumbo,* and then a whole string of splashes which would eventually prove that if you sold enough Broadway musicals to Hollywood, you could make the same millions, revolutionize the stage musical to your heart's content, and never again have to go to the dreaded West Coast. And any second thoughts Rodgers might have had about leaving were erased in advance when he went around to say goodbye to the big MGM pooh-bah Irving Thalberg, who had originally begged to sign him, and now Thalberg didn't even recognize him.

That was how it went in Hollywood—feast or famine, a banquet or a stale ham sandwich. As Rodgers read it, in their hearts, movie people didn't really like Broadway people, beyond their publicity value, which was good for roughly one film and a half, after which the hacks with the connections resumed their sway. (For the hacks' point of view, see my chapter on Harry Warren.) So after one last, moderately humiliating trip back to make *Mississippi* for W. C. Fields, and at the last minute Bing Crosby, Rodgers swore never to return for anything. If the studio wanted his big Broadway successes, or even the original *State Fair,* they would have to come and get 'em.

A reasonable condition, one might have supposed, and one that most New York writers might well have imposed a few years earlier. The arrival of talkies in 1927 had coincided with the greatest year in Broadway musical history, with Youmans, Gershwin, Rodgers, and Kern all hitting their peaks at once. It must have seemed like the ultimate sellers' market for songwriters. Hollywood would need all the pretty sounds it could get, on the double, and it needed New York authentication for its artistic pretensions. From the start, the studios saw great profit in glorifying the Great White Way and keeping it alive through the Depression, so they could advertise their latest movies as coming hot from Broadway, all of which suggests that they wanted the composers to stay at their pianos and get on with it.

The balance of arrogance must have seemed to run even more in the writers' favor after everyone had seen Al Jolson's performance in *The Jazz Singer*. Al seemed so much smaller on the screen, as if his famous charisma had been left out in the theater lobby. If this was the "world's greatest entertainer," as he billed himself, spare us the minor ones. "Valentino Talks." Big deal. The Bearded Lady sings. The possibility that someday Fred Astaire might loom over both Jolson and Valentino as a film presence was not how people were thinking yet. (Could less *really* be more? The idea was in the air, but people always need more proof.)

Whatever you thought of the songs in *The Jazz Singer*, no one had to leave New York to provide them. The city was still coming into its own as a match for Paris and London as a great world capital. And as new buildings raced one another to the sky, in a joint leap of faith and vote of confidence down below, the legitimate theaters were multiplying like rabbits. And, as always, talent was flooding into town on every bus and train. Could you really tell them all to go back out West? Meanwhile, a sturdy little Broadway-based film colony had been growing up on Long Island to provide day jobs for all the new talent. And how much sunlight did you need for movies, anyway? They made them in Germany, didn't they? And wasn't it more important to be where the life was and where the culture was coming from? If you *have* a city like New York, for heaven's sake, use it.

That was the view from 1927, a most misleading year. Flash forward just a few years more: The market has crashed, and there is Gershwin all right, on his Hollywood estate taking home movies of himself with friends and starlets in the latest beachwear. George is definitely visiting royalty, but not city-style royalty. As with Kern and Rodgers before him, his West Coast lifestyle foreshadows the suburbanization of haute Broadway, with tennis and golf replacing booze and breakdowns.

That was one end of town, anyway. But if you could look simultaneously into the bar of Hollywood's Roosevelt Hotel, you would find that the lowlifes of Tin Pan Alley had actually re-created their own New York as if for a movie scene, drink for drink, gag for gag, and also bet for bet. For them, the one blessing of the West was the multiplicity of racetracks, where, if spotted, you could always claim to be trying to find Bing Crosby, or later Bob Hope, for your next movie.

But you couldn't have found these types on day one in 1927. No one was there yet. No one who was anybody, that is. There were, as always in Hollywood, at least a couple of nonentities-in-waiting ready to form an aristocracy, and while Nacio Herb Brown looked more like the gentleman's tailor that he was than Gene Kelly, and Arthur Freed, the one time I saw him, seemed like the last man in the world to "Make [Anybody] Laugh" like Donald O'Connor, these two did share the one indispensable gift that *Singin' in the Rain* is based on: *being* there when the bell rang and being ready for it as if they'd been preparing for it all their lives.

Young Nacio (or Ignacio) Brown had the unusual songwriters' distinction of being born in New Mexico, but his father had since moved on to become the sheriff of Los Angeles, so that his son had pretty much grown up with the film colony while it was still in its small-town phase. The VIPs hadn't yet hedged themselves off in their castles for tourists to dream about, but still walked the streets and talked to normal folk, so it was the easiest thing in the world for Brown to set himself up as a haberdasher to the stars, trading suits for connections, or later for song plugs. And it was equally easy for him to spread himself, like everyone else, into real estate so that in a pinch he could say, "If you don't need a suit today, how about a house?" Short of becoming a celebrity hairdresser or a bartender at the Brown Derby, it's hard to imagine what more the man could have done to position himself to catch the latest buzz and meet the biggest buzzards, which would include in the course of time Irving Thalberg, the boy wonder at MGM.

And after dark, Brown played the piano in a local bistro, on the

strength of which he hooked up with a hustler from all over called Arthur
Freed, who on the side wrote lyrics. Unlike Brown with his Southwestern
roots, Arthur Freed seemed to have touched base with all four corners of
America and several corners of show biz. Born in Charleston, he had
somehow managed to be raised in Seattle, and educated at Phillips Ex-
eter, although presumably not for the life he proceeded to live, which ran
from plugging songs and producing shows for the army to running a music
shop and even doing a stint onstage with the young Marx Brothers, who
were the last word in discombobulation. Perhaps Freed's most prophetic
achievement of all was the assemblage of the enduring standard "I Cried
for You," which may be the only song ever written by two bandleaders and
one jack-of-all-trades. Clearly this man knew how to put packages together and make his own opportunities. Combining him with Brown was
almost unfair. Not until Rodgers joined Hammerstein, or as J.F.K. might
put it, not since Irving Berlin dined alone, would songwriting see such
concentrated business acumen in one room.

So, what with Freed writing the lyrics, and Brown playing all his tunes
in every bistro for miles around, chances were that by the time *The Jazz
Singer* came out, Thalberg and the others had already heard all the songs
for MGM's answer to it, the first *Broadway Melody* of 1929, and for the
film after that as well.

The Broadway stick-in-the-muds finally got the message, some faster
than others, that Hollywood worked too quickly and spasmodically to wait
for you to mail in your songs. The highly successful and commercial team
of Brown, Henderson, and DeSylva was out there in a flash and wrote one
of the first anthems, "You Ought to Be in Pictures." DeSylva, the most busi-
nesslike of the three, proceeded into management, as would Freed himself.
If every writer in the world was coming out here, why tie yourself down to
one? Lyric writers as such are hustlers by calling and are also frequently
subject to the question, "But what do you *really* do for a living?" By 1960 or
so, Freed had developed a particularly satisfactory answer, namely, that he
had saved the American musical forever, or at least for a few precious
decades, by producing masterworks including *Meet Me in St. Louis, Easter
Parade,* and *An American in Paris,* which have so far proved immortal.

One last benefaction of Freed's second career was to the studio that
had housed him for so long and had bankrolled that whole gorgeous sunset

of the great musicals. If one had nothing to go on but the two *That's Entertainment* movies, one might suppose that MGM had been the undisputed king of the genre all along. But this is winner's history; by continuing to bet big bucks while the other players folded and left the table, MGM had picked up an Astaire here and a Crosby there, and then with a series of film bios, all the songs of Porter, Kern, and Rodgers and the team of Kalmar and Ruby, until finally, it had almost the whole deck in its hands. This was no great scandal or even a secret. Hollywood history works like that. You can buy all the rights to history itself, if you can afford it.

Yet from the writers' point of view, and ours, the multiplicity of studios may be the single most important fact in this chapter. If any one person ever really owned history, it would immediately stop moving at whatever phase the owner liked best. To put it dialectically, the czar of MGM, Louis B. Mayer, loved what he considered classiness, while the genius, Thalberg, believed that spectacle was the essence of movies, so the ideal for both of them was something like operetta with its massed choirs of braided uniforms and bobbing Adam's apples, playing a real palace. But at Paramount, Maurice Chevalier could do this same scene with a leer and a wink that changed everything, while at Warner Bros. the spectacle would be Americanized by Busby Berkeley into something flashier and less classy but more truly cinematic. And when all these cards had been played, a pair of Broadway hoofers at RKO named Astaire and Rogers would trump any number of MGM's epaulets and evening gowns and Warner Bros.'s leg shows too, with sheer gracefulness and art deco, and Bing Crosby would make things even simpler at Paramount in the role of a classy common man. All these changes and many more called for new songwriters, until every American who could carry a tune seemed to be under contract to some Hollywood muckety-muck or other. But once again, I'll choose just two representatives who played a modified form of leapfrog with each other at Paramount, which was incidentally the edgiest of the studios and perhaps the best candidate to put together a *That's Entertainment* of its own.

From day one, or at the latest day two, of the talkie era, Paramount began stockpiling writers, one of these being Richard Whiting, a jewel of the Chicago wing of Tin Pan Alley and a most unlikely man to find in Hollywood at all.

In fact, Whiting's presence at or near the creation of talkies was a great deal chancier than Nacio Brown's was, so much so that he even wrote a song about it, or the lyric of one anyway—he refused to take credit for the tune, although his fingerprints are all over it. "She's Funny That Way" is apparently a hymn to a wife's willingness to adapt to her husband's capriciousness, but the real life wrinkle is that it was actually Mrs. Whiting's caprice that got Richard out to Hollywood to try his luck in the Great Sound Rush, so that *he* was the one who had to be "funny that way."

Left to his own devices, it is questionable whether Whiting would ever have gone anywhere at all. A Midwesterner by birth and conviction, young Richard used up his whole supply of wanderlust early in life by attending a military school in California. After that, just getting him from Detroit to Chicago was almost more trouble than it was worth, while he didn't get as far as New York until the 1920s were almost over. Yet during that decade, he wrote some of the nation's hippest songs from right where he was. Although the Chicago wing housed only three names that anyone still remembers, all three were, as Spencer Tracy put it, "cherse": Gus Kahn, who came closest to being the official Alley lyricist to the decade without abandoning his base; Isham Jones, a taciturn coal miner turned bandleader, who wrote, among other hits, the trailblazing tune for "It Had to Be You," which Johnny Mercer considered the perfect song; and Whiting himself, who kicked off the twenties with such with-it numbers as "Japanese Sandman" (words: Raymond B. Egan) and "Ain't We Got Fun" (Gus Kahn and Ray Egan) and went on to such period excellences as "Sleepy Time Gal" and "Breezing Along with the Breeze." So who needed New York?

But Hollywood in the 1930s was something else. Even homebodies like Kahn and Whiting had to get out there and play their songs in person, during what must have seemed like a perpetual casting call from contract to contract and job to job. Perhaps the studios felt that if the writers ever got comfortable, they'd all fall asleep. So even after they wangled that first precious two-year contract, the boss knew how to keep everyone sweating, most notoriously by assigning the same picture to all of them at once or else by gutting the latest Broadway scores of everything but the hits and handing the carcasses over to the studio's geniuses for embalming.

Yet the force of inertia is awfully strong out there. Its racetracks and golf courses tended to be full of musical talent all the time. By establishing himself so early out there, Richard Whiting was the closest thing to Old Hollywood, and it was only half a joke that Johnny Mercer talked about him almost as if he were the resident golf pro. Since golf was also the pastime of the elite writers, the Jerome Kerns and the Harold Arlens as opposed to the barflies of Tin Pan Alley, Whiting's social set was partly determined for him by his sheer skill at the game. And what could be more appropriate than that he end up playing it and writing songs as well with Johnny Mercer of the Savannah Mercers?

But before getting to Johnny, Whiting had already written his identifying songs with the *other* nicest guy in the business, Leo Robin, who was very much a Broadway lyricist in his heart, and who would later achieve his dream of actually being one with Nice Guy Number Three, Jule Styne, for the score of *Gentlemen Prefer Blondes*. Since Robin would prove to be Whiting's best other half, platonically speaking, he deserves a few words on his own.

Leo is probably best remembered now for a few unforgettable lines, "It's then that those louses go back to their spouses." From *Gentlemen*, "Strictly between us/you're cuter than Venus/and what's more you've got arms" from the movie song "Love Is Just Around the Corner," and "Thanks for the Memory" from one thousand years of Bob Hope.

Robin's other specialty, which he shared with Whiting, was writing great theme songs that fit the singers they were aimed at so well that he or she would need no other. With Whiting, for instance, Robin wrote "Louise" for Maurice Chevalier, which forced its way straight to the top of Chevalier's mostly French repertoire, and also for Maurice, "One Hour with You," which *he* didn't adopt, but which Eddie Cantor did for his long-running radio show; and for Jeanette MacDonald a quintessential number that could almost serve as a career résumé. When "Beyond the Blue Horizon" is played as it was in the movie with an express-train accompaniment, it conveys all the melodramatic, high-octane optimism that would eat poor Nelson Eddy alive in film after film and would, with a little help from Eddy's wimpishness, turn a pleasant light comedy actress into a dragon to reckon with.

The key to such songs is obviously empathy and interest in other people, and in this respect, Whiting's and Robin's legendary niceness may actually have helped them professionally. "I haven't seen it yet," Jonathan Schwartz reports Robin saying about some show or other, "but I'll bet it's good." Robin and Whiting both *wanted* people and things to be good, and anything they could do to help was gladly done. Thus, without each other, Whiting also wrote "On the Good Ship Lollipop" for Shirley Temple, and Robin, with Ralph Rainger, batted out "Please" and "Love in Bloom" for Bing Crosby—although the latter was grabbed by Jack Benny for his radio show—and of course for Hope, "Thanks for the Memory."

One other song Whiting wrote for Chevalier insists on being mentioned, if only because it was his own special favorite, "My Ideal." This song would also make my own top ten, for what that's worth, if simply for the second A section, which like that of Rodgers's "A Ship Without a Sail," takes you at least one step further into the unknown than you thought possible, and unleashes a terrible beauty.

With that one, Whiting touched greatness, yet Paramount kept signing up more songwriters anyway, including the aforesaid Rodgers, who worked with Chevalier, whom Dick might have considered his own personal property. As the oldest settler, Whiting was also one of the first to illustrate another great law of Hollywood life, namely, that the longer you stayed in one place, the less respect you got. In fact, Whiting might have lost any of the remaining clout he still possessed had Chevalier carried out his threat to go home to France before his novelty wore off, and be completely replaced by the new house star, Bing Crosby. Crosby, in his acting style at least, was no respecter of persons of any kind. It was his first order of business to lower the tone of any joint he was in, and the tone of the songs as well, which would now need to contain more jazz and more schmaltz to service the famous throb of his own voice, a sound more Tin Pan Alley than Broadway.

Although I don't know the particulars of Whiting's decision, I do know that he jumped ship to Fox for a short while for one contract, while Bing and his boyos settled into Paramount. The Crosby gang was made up of various combinations of Arthur "Pennies from Heaven" Johnston and Jimmy "You Made Me Love You" Monaco on the tunes, and increasingly Crosby's New York pal Johnny Burke on the words, which combination was starting to give Paramount a blue collar bull pen all the way until the arrival of a new compromise candidate named Ralph Rainger, who while not Broadway in the highest sense was not quite Tin Pan Alley either. Like Carmichael and Schwartz, Rainger had gone the same law school route for the same reasons—to play the piano a bit longer—and he was now manifestly acceptable to the uptown crowd. He would even supply the music for a Dorothy Parker lyric, the haunting "I Wished on the Moon," which is typical of both her and him.

Above all, Rainger was preeminently what you had to be in Hollywood: intuitive and adaptable. Without realizing it, he had discovered that he was a songwriter by composing the perfect piece of material for the singer Libby Holman, for whose latest show he had been working as a rehearsal pianist. "Moaning Low" was one of those "found" songs like "Smoke Gets in Your Eyes." It suited Holman so well that it probably saved her young career from crashing before takeoff, and it seems likely he got the idea for it from just being around her.

So what might being around Bing Crosby produce for him? Rainger didn't have to wait long to find out, because his first song for Bing was an enduring hit, and worked as a magical calling card for himself at Paramount. "Please," as Leo Robin's plaintive lyrics add, "lend your little ear to my pleas." The tune whines in the plaintive style of the young Crosby, but it whines classily, if that's possible. And for Rainger's next go-round with Bing in *The Big Broadcast of 1936,* the hit "June in January" seemed to keep step with Crosby's own evolution from a groaner to the streamlined crooning machine that people remember today. Rainger was right there with him.

Perhaps Rainger was almost too much in tune with his own times and what was happening for him to last into ours. It is hard to believe what huge stature he once had in the Hollywood music game—even people outside of Hollywood had heard of him—and how small a figure he cuts in history. Never underestimate the journalistic value of a catchy name, of course; but unfortunately Ralph was also a master of the A-minus and B-plus song that doesn't quite make it into the future. See the funny movie *Moon over Miami* sometime (it's still around, thanks to Betty Grable) and you'll hear a charming score without a single standard in it except for the title song, which wasn't written by Rainger. And before Ralph could pick up the accelerated beat and inspirational charge of wartime (Write a song for your Uncle Sam!), he died in one of the epidemic plane crashes of the day.

In his interview with Max Wilk, Harry Warren, the King Crab in Hollywood, complained that you had to have a Broadway reputation to get treated right in Hollywood, but he admits in another connection that the work never stopped coming for him. And as we have seen, the work did stop coming for Warren's fellow sourpuss, Richard Rodgers of Broadway.

Anyhow, as we have also seen, musicals were hurting all over by the end of 1931, and with even Chevalier threatening to return to France, Whiting jumped ship and signed on with Fox. And within a few months Warren and Dubin's *42nd Street* had saved musicals all over, and Bing Crosby had saved Paramount, so what, Whiting may have wondered, had been the point of moving?

Whether one's Hollywood moves worked or not, one kept on making them—anything else was a sin against optimism, but Whiting's last one was a beauty, a rendezvous with Mercer at yet another studio, Warner Bros. At age forty-five, Whiting was by then a grand old man, in pop music time, and Johnny Mercer had had lots of time to venerate him. And Johnny was unbelievably hot just then, and happy to share his heat with Whiting in a spray of new songs, two of which are probably now played more often than the rest of his work put together. "Too Marvelous for Words" was produced in a style worthy of a going-away present to himself. Looking at it today, one would swear it was choreographed by Busby Berkeley, since it was tapped out by a group of chorus girls on the keys of a kind of giant piano that at one time only Busby could have thought of, but that anyone could imitate now, and which eventually no one would be able to afford anyway. In this case, as in so many, Whiting's tune is immortal because Mercer's words are too. Even lyrical-amnesiacs can always come up with "that old standby amorous" and "Webster's dick-shun-ary," and once you have those, you have the whole song. In the matter of teamwork, both men had met their match and would meet it once more before parting.

"Hooray for Hollywood" has remained an anthem because both men were equally plugged in not only to each other but to their peculiar time and place, Hollywood in 1937, where "every barmaid can be a star made," or alternatively you could always "go out and try your luck, you could be Donald Duck." And with that you can see it all: the orange juice stands and the jalopies covered in funny sayings ("Aw faw down go boom"), and filled with good-looking or funny-looking kids who had gone out there to make it. It has often been said that Hollywood never made a real movie about the Depression, and yet if you saw it in person, apparently the whole place seemed to be about the Depression and its dreams.

In the early black days of the slump, one dreamed about impossibilities like ocean liners and dancing with Fred Astaire. "If I Had a Million"? Yeah, sure. But by Roosevelt's second term, things really did seem to be looking up, as the Gershwin song assured us, and some serious daydreaming seemed to be in order, not about Ruritania anymore, which Hitler seemed to be sealing off right then, but about yourself making it right here in the U.S.A., and specifically in Hollywood, where Lana Turner had just been discovered on a drugstore stool, thus changing a whole nation's consciousness. So perhaps Fred Astaire was still out of reach, but Mickey Rooney? Come on! Or possibly Shirley Temple? You bet that your daughter could look just as cute if they could do something about her teeth. From 1938 on, the musicals increasingly started to use real surfaces for their fantasies. Even at the old house of fantasy, MGM, the first thing they showed visitors now was Andy Hardy's hometown, and the master daydream in this real land of Oz was of having your car waved through the gates. "Good morning, Mr. Gable. Mr. Mayer is expecting you."

Mercer and Whiting were right next door at Warners in the cusp year 1937, capturing the whole sense of possibility in both music and words. Never mind whether "the dreams that you dared to dream" ever actually came true, because by then you'd be dreaming something else. In Tinseltown, the dream itself was the message, as Marshall McLuhan would say. The real story might end in the bitter confusion of Nathanael West's worst day of the locust, but it began with hooray for Hollywood. When I found myself there in 1950, they still seemed to be dreaming it. Every waitress and bellhop was good-looking and every one of them had a style and a shtick, if you'd just give them a moment.

It was a great note for Richard Whiting to end on. He was not out of it, after all, but had again become the latest thing. So he had his own dream to ride out on when his death came suddenly in February 1938.

"Richard Whiting was an original," said Mercer, and one reflects again on how many of these people were original, although they were consigned for the most part to the same thirty-two-bar choruses and identical tempo and other conventions. There is no mistaking a Whiting song for a Walter Donaldson or an Arthur Schwartz for a Burton Lane. Richard Whiting might be thought to have brought something new from the Midwest, as Hoagy had, but with everyone now primed on the same movies, records, and radio shows, regionalism quietly dropped out of this kind of music to burrow further into "country" and the less familiar "Western." Otherwise, whether you came from Texas or New Jersey was hardly worth mentioning. Once the jazz song cut its guide ropes to New York City, it became just plain American—perfect for World War II, but less so afterward. Meanwhile, back at Paramount, Ralph Rainger's timing and luck might have seemed better than Whiting's, but they weren't really, because he never could become the sole proprietor to Bing Crosby, which was the name of the game in the thirties. So when his contract came up for renewal in 1938, it apparently struck him as a good time to leave. He had struck gold once with the new boy on the lot, Bob Hope, but the sequel to "Thanks for the Memory" was assigned to the team of Hoagy Carmichael and Frank Loesser. Besides, Hope was becoming more exclusively a comedian and was just using whoever his partner Crosby liked at that moment, which usually meant whoever Bing's friend Johnny Burke liked, and that wasn't Rainger's professional set.

So Rainger jumped to Twentieth Century, which Darryl Zanuck was already turning into a haven for musicals. There he ran into a buzz saw called Harry Warren, who could, and very nearly did, write all the studio's musicals himself. And then Rainger's story suddenly ended with that plane crash. Even in retrospect one would hesitate to give advice to any of these men, because everyone else was moving around out there too. New people were entering, and no doubt, had Whiting and Rainger lived, they would have bumped into each other again, at least once.

Those two were a pair of stay-at-homes next to the ultimate politician, Jimmy McHugh, who, if not for music, might have wound up running a political machine in his native Boston and earning his own last hurrah that way. As it was, McHugh graduated from a job at the Boston Opera House to a composing one at the Cotton Club, and thence to the movies, revealing along the way a pure musical gift to match his calculating heart. For all his undoubted excellence, which included some of the most pleasantly surprising bridges I know of, and some of the cleverest tunes, such as "Don't Blame Me" and "Say It (Over and Over Again)," McHugh is best remembered for a couple of rumors about him, and the damning fact that these rumors are still believed by many.

Everyone in town knew that young Fats Waller would sometimes try to peddle his latest tunes around the Brill Building in exchange for all their worth in gin. But since there was nothing to keep him from selling the same song to someone else on the next floor, he didn't find many takers, and the only actual songs to emerge from the rumor mill were "On the Sunny Side of the Street" and "I Can't Give You Anything but Love," both ostensibly by McHugh and his partner, Dorothy Fields. The only reason I don't believe these rumors myself is Fields, who was a lady, and would also give Wilk a most circumstantial account of hearing the words "I can't give you anything but love," whispered by a swain to his sweetie just outside of Tiffany's.

Besides which, Dorothy Fields had no reason to front for Jimmy McHugh, who had once bummed a few bucks off her himself by demanding a piece of her lyric royalties to Kern's *Roberta*. This was big league caddishness, and when Wilk asked her to assess working with McHugh, she answered with the faintest praise applicable. "Professional," she said. And that he was, down to the smallest detail, such as (again, according to legend) hanging out with the portly Louella Parsons, whose gossip columns were law in Hollywood.

As a married Catholic, McHugh was assumed to be making the most of the Spencer Tracy privilege, which entitled one to unlimited whoopee so long as one is truly sorry for it at least once a year, and thus it was inevitable that the rumors bubbled up about him and Dorothy Fields, which there was no particular reason to believe. What is not fair to assume in a case like McHugh's is that all his (many) good deeds were pure hypocrisy. Like Richard Rodgers and so many others, McHugh lived his whole life theatrically, bordering on operatically, with his outsize virtues and vices slugging it out on a scale of overgrown contraltos and bassi, with his own soul going alternately to heaven and hell, sometimes in the course of a single evening. Thank God I am not called upon to judge any of them.

Where McHugh's professionalism did spring a leak was in his tendency to be in the wrong place when the good movies were handed out, as you'll see his name on a raft of clunkers. Still, as Mercer tells us, anyone could get lucky out there, and McHugh would also find himself in line, with the excellent lyric writer Harold Adamson, to write the songs for Frank Sinatra's first movie, *Higher and Higher*. Luck followed him to the keyboard on that one, where he wrote the superefficient "I Couldn't Sleep a Wink Last Night," which sticks in your head like flypaper on contact, and the gorgeous "A Lovely Way to Spend an Evening," which has a bridge that reminds me of one of those small real ones occasionally found in gardens, a splendid little artifact.

Whiting and Rainger and McHugh were just three of the writers throwing the dice year after year and film after film. To throw a final bone to Hollywood, everyone wanted these writers to get lucky, and even conspired toward it. Unlike the witless owners of baseball teams, the studio heads had the sense to realize that they were partners as well as rivals and that their joint goal was just to get people to the movies, *all* the movies, and get them to buy all the songs on the way out as well. Anyone who learns one lyric will learn two, or twelve. Studios were in the habit-forming business, and every little bit helped.

With this in mind, these greedy, unscrupulous cartoons would actually lend each other their contract writers as they lent their actors for particular projects, making the best exchange they could get for them on the spur of the moment, and even allowing the writers a say in the transaction, to wit and as follows: Jule Styne, who had begun life as a classical prodigy and gone West as a voice coach, had apparently come to a dead end at Republic Pictures writing songs for cowboy movies, presumably to be sung to the horses. But when they asked him who he'd like for a partner and he said Frank Loesser, they actually borrowed Loesser for him from Paramount in its unofficial rent-a-writer program. Just like that, Jule became a real songwriter, simply by handing over his best tune and having a third-rate poem but absolutely first-rate lyric stamped on it. The result, "I Don't Want to Walk Without You," also helped Loesser, who, after fobbing off Republic with some real horse music, smuggled this gem back to Paramount, where it enhanced his standing enormously. Nobody complained—that was how the game was played.

With which, I rest my case. With so many talented people scheming between golf shots to place their material, and receiving so many chances to do so, something good had to happen—as well, of course, as something bad. To throw a last bone to the naysayers, a film called *That's* Not *Entertainment* could probably fill a few hours too.

But perhaps not so very many. Hollywood was so rich back then that, like the government, it could afford to pay writers *not* to produce, or at least not to publish. Warren talks of writing eighteen tunes for one movie, and of publishing maybe four of them—nice odds, although not foolproof. If even one of these songs became a standard, thank Hollywood for spending like a drunken sailor on these lunatic investments. The Great American Songbook would not be the same without them.

# Harry Warren: The King of the Unknowns and His Quiet Reign in Hollywood

HARRY WARREN

*I*nsofar as Harry Warren is famous for anything at all, it's for not being famous—so much so that I've never heard him discussed without that subject dominating the conversation.

A lot of things had to go wrong to produce such majestic anonymity as Harry's. Had his father, Antonio Guaragna, just stayed put in his native Calabria, our subject, born Salvatore Guaragno, might have succeeded his idol, Puccini, as the last of the classic Italian opera writers; or if Antonio had stopped at his next port of call, Argentina, the title "King of the Tango" might have been Salvatore's for the taking.

But Antonio kept moving until he settled down in Brooklyn Heights,

New York, which pop-musically speaking placed his boy practically in the middle of the cattle call. Yet even that might have worked out if he hadn't also decided to Americanize the family name into the most forgettable one in the whole show biz register. A young man named Salvatore Guaragna might have stood out even in the crowd on Tin Pan Alley. Or he might have stood out under any name at all if he'd had the time and opportunity to write a few really big Broadway shows. But the Depression came along shortly before he could do that and, as Harry Warren, he decamped for Hollywood—where his luck got both better and worse. Warren became such a prodigious success out there that he could never quite afford to leave "just yet." And by the time he could finally afford to, he'd been hopelessly typecast in the trade as a movie writer and was by definition not classy enough for Broadway.

So Antonio Guaragna's son disappeared into Warner Bros.'s studio, and was never heard of again—until, that is, he eventually became an archivist's delight as the king of the unknowns and the prototype to the point of caricature of all the New Yorkers who went West in the 1930s, kicking and screaming, and stayed there moaning and groaning, and vanishing one by one from public view, like a pack of Cheshire cats, leaving behind not smiles but forgettable movies and unforgettable music.

In his role as King Anonymous, Warren illustrates to profuse perfection how Hollywood could immortalize a song like nobody's business, while deep-sixing its creators beyond recall. To be fair, Tinseltown handsomely delivered on both ends of the deal, and still does in some cases. For instance, quite recently, Warren's flagship "I Only Have Eyes for You" could be heard in the background of three new movies in the same year, making it one of those rare songs like Rodgers's "Blue Moon" and Carmichael's "Georgia" that seems to roll over into the next generation and the next and just keep on rolling. And by selling its old films to TV, Hollywood has conspired to keep several other Warren standards around in the half-light of the nation's subconscious. Is there, for instance, anyone in America who hasn't heard "Chattanooga Choo Choo" or "(I've Got a Gal in) Kalamazoo" at least once? Or some scrap of music from the *42nd Street* cycle ("Shuffle Off to Buffalo," anyone? Or "You're Getting to Be a Habit with Me"?) Or, failing that, one or both of his swan songs, sacred and profane—the haunting theme music of the Grant-Kerr edition of *An Affair to Remember* or our subject's last tip of the cap to his own origins, the droll "That's Amore," which parodies Italian pop so well that it's become part of it?

Then there are the TV commercials that keep so many old songs in subliminal circulation, but most recently Warren's "At Last," "The Gold Diggers' Song (We're in the Money)," and "About a Quarter to Nine," all of which I've heard peddling products, and I'm not even a serious couch potato. TV has also dished out numerous Warren classics in its retrospectives of other people that he helped to make famous, most particularly Busby Berkeley, who seems to be being celebrated every time I turn on the set, but also of Betty Grable, Ruby Keeler, and the Glenn Miller Orchestra, among others. Although Warren was never sure that Busby even liked music as such, Buzz was obviously the right scene-designer-cum-drill-sergeant at the right time in movie history, so his name is now the only one on the old musicals (as in Busby Berkeley's *Gold Diggers of 1933*) while Warren, whose songs old Buzz depended and insisted on, left his name on nothing.

In fact, as a kind of postmortem pie in the face, two main studios, Warner Bros. and Twentieth Century–Fox, even managed to leave Harry's name out of their own self-congratulatory retrospectives toward the end of the last century. They were both (quite justly) as pleased as punch over their great musicals, and about such performers as Keeler and Alice Faye and the Nicholas Brothers, but modest to a fault about the songwriter they'd hired to supply the music. And Twentieth Century really rubbed the whipped cream into Harry's headstone when it showed a clip of Irving Berlin instead, sitting by his obligatory pool. Although Irving had indeed batted out a couple of those famous musicals for Fox, he was better remembered for his work at RKO and Paramount, and was not in the least central to the Fox story.

So okay—they weren't really all out to get Harry. Popular history goes with the names everyone knows, and you don't clutter people's minds with new names at this late date. But it wouldn't have fooled our subject for a moment because the studio had retroactively played right into the great Harry Warren–Irving Berlin joke—a mock-epic feud between the two men, which, as Burton Lane assured me, really was a joke—up to a point.

The best way to picture Harry Warren is, I gather, to imagine a sensitive little guy with a Roman nose and the conversational style of an old-fashioned New York cabbie, which meant that he always sounded annoyed about something or other, but how annoyed was he really this time? Since the complaints never stopped coming, they served as a perfect cover for the speaker's real feelings. One never knew for sure whether the cabdriver really hated the mayor, or whether Warren hated Berlin. Over the years, Harry played every kind of riff on his major gripe, namely, his world-famous anonymity, about which he could be genuinely humorous, à la mode de Rodney Dangerfield, or unmistakably bitter, when his lifelong rash got the occasional better of him.

But as with the old cabbie, the overall impression Warren made was of a man with a basically good nature, and he wound up one of the most popular guys in what remained of Hollywood. And, after all, he did have something to grumble about. During the years they were competing, Warren actually had more songs on the Hit Parade than Irving Berlin, but you'd never have guessed it from the papers or the fan magazines or even from the conversations of quite knowledgeable people, many of whom have still never heard of him. If Irving Berlin was a King Midas who didn't even have to touch things to turn them to gold, Warren was the Invisible Man. He could make a fortune too, but he couldn't show up to claim it— almost literally on one occasion. When he turned up at the Academy to pick up his Oscar, at first he wasn't allowed in. He didn't look the part.

Harry got the joke and knew it was funny, but it was also maddening, and it had gone on too long. Still, friends like Burton Lane and Harold Arlen took advantage of this competition with Berlin, fanning the feud every chance they got, one time going so far as to print up a playbill proclaiming "Irving Berlin's new production of *42nd Street*" in the hopes of hearing a gratifying growl out of Warren, and perhaps a funny line, such as his most, and only, famous one in World War II, "They bombed the wrong Berlin."

But even this apparent score over Irving wound up being just another joke on Warren himself, because (1) the line became famous immediately but Harry didn't and the crack about him soon became "His name could vanish from the page while you were looking at it," and (2) life would eventually imitate jest by producing some *actual* playbills that read "David

Merrick's *42nd Street*," omitting Harry's name yet again for the whole ten years that show first ran on Broadway and replacing his name with that of a *real* megalomaniac.

And although he has picked up some random champions over the years, including Michael Feinstein and a guy I heard from in the Kalamazoo area who persuaded Mayor Giuliani to name a Brooklyn block after Harry, his luck never seems to turn enough to stay turned. As I write this, *42nd Street* is back where it belongs and occasionally honors his name. But the name refuses to stick or really register. In a recent uncomprehending biography of Irving Berlin, the author doesn't seem to know much about Warren except for his obvious credits, and "the joke," but he adds gratuitously that he doesn't know if Warren was anti-Semitic.

Seldom would evidence have been easier to find if he'd felt Warren was worth looking into. Just about everyone who counted in Warren's life was Jewish, most particularly his closest friend, Harold Arlen, with whom he toured Europe in the 1950s, and his beloved partners, Al Dubin and Mack Gordon, as well as his living hero, Jerome Kern—who was not only Jewish but almost as famous as Irving Berlin (fame in general was not a problem for Warren, just Berlin's fame). This was the gang Harry chose to run with in Hollywood, as opposed to, let's say, the Walter Donaldsons or the Jimmy McHughs. And before that he had kept the same sort of company in New York, working with and enjoying among others his soon-to-be lifelong friend Ira Gershwin and the nerve-racking Billy Rose, who took big bows and major money for just supplying the title to Warren's early hit "I Found a Million Dollar Baby (in a Five and Ten Cent Store)." Rose was widely resented by other writers for just such tricks, but not by Warren, who admired Billy for having precisely what he lacked himself, the gift for promotion. He felt Rose's salesmanship, which would later run to aquacades and live elephants, was worth his cut anytime.

But perhaps the real reason he liked Billy so much was that the little man's vitality, inventiveness, and mind-boggling audacity reminded Warren of New York, and Harry loved to be reminded of New York. Which brings us to Warren's defining crotchet number two—giving Irving Berlin a rest. ("Let the bum get his own chapter.") By the midthirties, Al Dubin must presumably have had at least two earfuls of his partner's homesickness and decided to give the old boy a present in the form of a lyric that expressed the problem perfectly. Although the words of "Lullaby of Broadway" probably described Al Dubin's nightlife a lot better than Harry's, the sounds are all Warren's and all New York, with its rumbling subways and rattling taxis and its inimitable phrases. "The daffydils who entertain at Angelo's and Maxie's"—where else would you hear them called "daffydils," or did Dubin make that up himself? New Yorkers were always doing this to you—coining new words, or borrowing them from other countries or parts of this one. Times Square alone was and is a great clearinghouse for words, and Harry with his great ear must have missed them a lot more than he missed Angelo's or Maxie's. So if you're lucky enough to hear Warren sing "Lullaby" himself (a rare tape exists of this), you're probably as close to his essence, his soul, as one could get. This is Harry's signature song and his signature voice too—light, breezy, and smart—and you realize that perhaps his accent and his attitude were themselves mementos of New York, lovingly preserved in brine and marinated in the toxic air of Los Angeles. When his young friend and disciple Michael Feinstein asked him one day about his somewhat stylized grouchiness, Harry was at something of a loss to explain it. But perhaps it's obvious: He grumbled because New Yorkers grumbled; it was the first sound you heard in those days. Even the daffodils grumbled between numbers. And everyone in L.A. was so damn upbeat and positive, *some*one had to complain around here.

And while I'm reading his mind, I'd guess that much of the fuss with Berlin dates back to "Lullaby" too, which beat out Irving's entry, "Cheek to Cheek," for the 1935 Oscar, to the reported annoyance of Berlin. But "Lullaby" had as many associations for Warren as "Always" had for Berlin and was definitely the wrong song to pick on. And no doubt Harry thought, doesn't Irving have enough awards already? Aren't I allowed to win at least once around here?

Berlin was only a symbol of Warren's anonymity, and incidentally Harry wasn't the only songwriter to jeer at Irving for hogging all the fame. In his usual self-mocking mode, Harry might have pointed out that he had never had a chance anyway, Berlin or no Berlin, because he'd been born on Christmas Day, which meant that he'd been upstaged from day one. By which reading, God undoubtedly summoned up the Great Depression just to annoy Harry Warren, and invented Hollywood too, in the same malicious let's-get-Harry spirit.

But on more serious inspection, Harry's bad luck looks much like everyone else's bad luck, except that he had more of it. When people hear a tune, apparently it's not in their nature to ask, who wrote that? But in New York, they tell you anyway, loud and clear. In movies, they told you once quietly, and it didn't stick. You were lucky, in fact, to keep the reputation you came in with.

It's a toss-up. Different names stick in different heads. Sammy Fain is an easy one, because it sounds like Tin Pan Alley. Likewise, the team of DeSylva, Brown, and Henderson stayed familiar for a while after its heyday in the 1920s, but only in that form. You had to be a real fanatic to know which one wrote the tune, or even what all their first names were. And when DeSylva quit, Brown and Henderson sounded completely unfamiliar. Better to be called Tin Pan Alley–sounding Sammy Fain, or Ray Noble, which arrestingly changes the subject, or just about anything but Harry Warren, who had a further handicap: He wrote so many hits that they began to sound like typical movie songs, straight off the assembly line.

The idea of a one-man assembly line turning out quality products might spell genius on Broadway, but was just more mass production in Hollywood, where the more hits he wrote the more of a hack he was assumed to be. If only he'd made his mark earlier, like Rodgers or Porter, or even been born later like Jerry Herman and Stephen Sondheim—when Broadway was un-Depressed and there was no Hollywood left to get lost in. So Harry's worst luck was simply having had all his best years during the great movie blackout, and what made it hurt so much is that they were such very good years. If you enjoy the sight of jaws dropping, read a list of Warren's movie titles and stand back. Of course, by now these don't sound particularly commercial, any more than Gershwin's movie songs do.

Yet in another sense, he wasn't unlucky. If one takes fame off the scale for a moment and measures his actual life next to those of the other superstars, his life looks pretty darn good, starting with his birth into a congenial family in a gorgeous part of New York and ending with his peaceful death in Hollywood some eighty-eight years later surrounded to the end by all the creature comforts a rich man could want, and always by enough friends and admirers never to feel abandoned or insignificant. "Isn't it ridiculous that Harry isn't famous?" Everyone felt exactly as he did about it.

Like his fellow Brooklynite, George Gershwin, Harry Warren's talent appears to have come to him from out of the blue, genetically speaking. His family was of the cheerful Italian persuasion that, if you wanted to listen to some music today, you sang it yourself. And presumably, if you wanted to turn it off, you yelled, "Shut up!"

So, if that was how you did it, Harry would just do more of it. He would later describe his gift in terms of pure appetite, not necessarily for composition but simply for music itself. And in this spirit, he joined the local church choir—and here his luck ran very good indeed, because Brooklyn Heights boasted one of the rare Catholic churches in America to concentrate on the classical masses of Bach and Palestrina, which plunged Harry into both polyphony and plainchant faster and better than any music teacher could have. And Harry would always be preeminently a composer for the voice first, and for the ensemble of voices and instruments second.

So far, Harry's luck had begun okay and would continue so for a while when he got a job in a store that sounds too good to be true—a barbershop that sold musical instruments on the side. Naturally, in his greed, he learned all of them at once. And it is pleasant to picture, in a movie-biography sort of way, an unusually small kid in knickers feeling his way with a trombone slide as the full Glenn Miller Orchestra begins tentatively to play "Serenade in Blue" or another of Harry's grown-up songs on the soundtrack. Henceforth, all the odd jobs in Harry's life centered on music, one way or another, whether it was serving stints as the world's shyest song-plugger, or strumming piano chords to go with silent movies, and learning incidentally how to fit them around the contours of the storytelling. Long before talkies, accompanists were learning how to heighten movie themes with just the right music, or the right silence.

Songs have so many facets that every different job seemed to teach him something else about them, and Harry's occasional gigs playing home-style piano at parties perhaps also instructed him as to what people liked to dance to all night and what contrariwise would bring them around the piano attempting to sing.

The actual call to write his own songs came to him on his one ostensibly nonmusical beat as a humble employee of the U.S. Navy stationed peacefully and dreamily at Montauk, Long Island, during World War I. Once again, Harry got lucky in a small way. Stateside service can be a great incubator of talent, and as the closest thing to an entertainer at that particular camp, he got lots of chances to play for a captive and most contemporary audience.

One of the most surprising things to learn about this great writer of, among other things, love songs, is that he himself got married in 1917 in his twenty-second year, before he'd even been published, and he stayed a homebody all his life, later claiming that he had never been to a single Hollywood party, at least in the grand sense of the phrase, and that he couldn't make even a short public appearance without getting slightly lit beforehand. (I've heard a tape of him slurring an acceptance speech and can attest that he sounds like a most amiable drunk, when he had to be.) Harry loved people, but not in bulk, and he liked to talk, but he wasn't a word-man, and one senses that his grumbling was partly a resort to verbal formulas that seemed to amuse people.

The obvious question is, Why on earth should such a quiet soul love New York so ardently, and hate Los Angeles so? Give or take a swimming pool, what difference did it make? The answer, as always, is music, and the pleasure of learning step by step that he could create it himself, and that he loved the other people making it, and best of all, that he could hear it all over town, leaking out of theaters and drumming through publishing offices and at the parties he did go to in those days, in the only way he felt comfortable, as a musician. To those of us who don't have the call, the total confidence this shy man felt at the piano is the astonishing part, because truth to tell, he wasn't all that good at it. ("I play better than Berlin, though," he told Max Wilk defensively. "And Jerry Kern too.") But the thing was, Harry was at home in music, and felt easy and unembarrassed as he slopped around his musical home.

Warren's songwriting career got off to a stuttering start, as if he didn't really believe it yet. His first minor hit, "Rose of the Rio Grande" (1922), was followed by nothing much—a light patter of forgotten titles—until he suddenly broke out in 1925 with a really big one, the utterly 1920s-sounding "I Love My Baby (My Baby Loves Me)," which encouraged him to step up production to something like full-time. But the dam hadn't yet broken by any means. Around the same time, he wrote a funny little immigrant song called "Where Do You Work-a, John?" that the school kids were still singing when I came to the States a generation later. Then in another two years one more, "Nagasaki," and that was it until after the market crash—a pleasant trickle of minor titles that left Harry serenely jogging in the middle of the Broadway pack as the good times ended. On a happiness graph, he'd had a wonderful decade, and it would seem a bit more wonderful every year he moved further from it. But there was precious little about his track record or his personality to suggest anything like greatness or even a wish for it. He wasn't built on that scale and apparently didn't want to be. "One of the boys" is a nice thing to be too, and his lack of recognition should have made it easy to remain one for the rest of his days.

A teaspoon of ambition sooner might have saved him a lot of groaning later. Because things really began to happen in 1930. There were some hungry lyricists and entrepreneurs wheeling around Broadway that year, as if they knew the end was coming, and Harry began to get enough assignments to qualify for the law I've named after him, that if you get to bat often enough, both your game and your chances improve exponentially, and the hits come. At any rate, that year he wrote his best song so far, with Billy Rose and an ex-vaudevillian, Mort Dixon, called "Would You Like to Take a Walk?" and a charming number with the already famous Ira Gershwin, "Cheerful Little Earful," a step up in itself, and then as a harbinger of things to come, his first song for the movies.

Hollywood had just bought the Rodgers and Hart show *Spring Is Here,* and as usual, gutted it, and was looking around for parts. Harry took his first trip West—and hated it on sight. After contributing an ephemeral hit called "Absence Makes the Heart Grow Fonder (For Somebody Else)" he hightailed it back East, no doubt complaining all the way. He had seen the future, and it was awful. "It looked like a small town in South Dakota" was how he described his first impression of Hollywood to Terry-Thomas, or "like being on an Indian reservation." I can verify that as late as 1950, when Warren's best years were behind him, Los Angeles still seemed like a cow town to eastern eyes, with a defiantly antiquated-looking trolley clanking its way from a vestigial downtown to a string of minimalist beaches without a dune or an honest-to-God wave to be seen. The water moved just enough to prove it wasn't a lake, and it didn't so much invite you in as put up with you when you got there—if, that is, you were one of those eastern nerve-cases keen on swimming. For everyone else, the beach was just another place to have one's picture taken and to be discovered by a famous producer.

It was almost enough to make a man miss Coney Island on a steamy Fourth of July weekend, and Harry raced back to New York as fast as a three-day train ride could carry him. This so-called Depression couldn't last forever, could it? In the years 1929 through 1931, the whole nation was holding its breath about this, and Broadway buzzed with nervous energy and spasms of wild optimism. Harry wrote two more megahits, "I Found a Million Dollar Baby" and "You're My Everything," which might have attracted more attention if Cole Porter and his first songs hadn't hit town around the same time. Still, they got just enough notice to place Warren on the brink of fame, if Broadway would just hang on a little bit longer.

It seems in retrospect as if Broadway might well have weathered the Depression just fine if that had been its only problem, as the London West End would survive World War II. Theater thrives on hard times. As Londoners later testified, the London Blitz actually made theater-going more exciting. There's nothing like the sound of bombs falling outside and the sight of ushers sealing up doors and windows to keep all the light inside to bring Shakespeare to total life.

But what Broadway could not so easily compete with was the news of good times happening somewhere else in the country. And as the Depression dug itself in, the combination of high movie salaries for the actors, cheap movie tickets for the public, and the sheer novelty of a new art form that made the stage seem obsolete, began to strip Broadway of both talent and customers—not all of either, fortunately: Broadway survived the thirties and had some glorious moments too, but they were partly subsidized by Hollywood and there were never enough to go around or to provide a reliable living for more than a few people. So Arthur Schwartz made it on Broadway, but was unlucky in Hollywood. It was still the wrong way to bet, and by 1931, just about everyone you'd ever heard of, including all the famous songwriters, had been to Hollywood at least once; and while most hated it every bit as much as Harry did, they would all be back.

Well, at least Harry liked train rides. He also got some great songs out of them and the places they went, like Buffalo and Chattanooga, and even out of the train lines themselves, like the famous Atchison, Topeka, and Santa Fe Railway. By 1931, it must have been clear that while his star might be rising in the East, the light itself was failing in that area. Like it or not, he had better go West again at least for a while. (Nobody ever went yet for more than a while.)

By chance, Warner Bros. had reached the same conclusion. While his relatively hot streak lasted, they wanted Warren out there immediately to write the music for a new musical called *42nd Street.* It was a fateful moment, because after the first flourish of movie musicals, the form had started dying almost immediately. The studios would never fathom the fact that musicals are always dying, or else being reborn, or both at once; they need constant resuscitation by new talents and styles, from, for instance, Maurice Chevalier to Bing Crosby to Dean Martin and Jerry Lewis to the end of that particular line.

Anyhow, the Warner execs dramatically decided to terrify the bankers with one all-or-nothing roll of the dice. Since movie musicals always died of the same thing, namely, costing too much, the studio chose to fight fire with fire by spending twice as much as ever for this next one, and as proof of intent, they signed up Busby Berkeley, the boy wonder and budget-buster extraordinaire. A modest success would get them nowhere. The musical *42nd Street* had to be a smash, or it would serve as the last great meal the movie musical would have before its execution.

Harry Warren was ready for the pressure, and ready also to go from two hit songs a year tops to sometimes two or more hits a movie, starting with this most crucial one. The title song itself has an epic quality to it, as if to say "I now declare this era open." The movie *42nd Street* gives you not just New York, even better to my mind than "Lullaby of Broadway" does, but almost the exact year in New York, something Harry had never come close to while he was still living there. Like Thomas Wolfe in London and James Joyce in Zurich and Trieste, it seemed he needed to step this far back from his subject to see it properly. But like Wolfe's Asheville and

Joyce's Dublin, the Warren version of New York would remain stubbornly in the past. Later in life, when he might easily have gone back there to stay, it wasn't there anymore. So he stayed in the land he hated, for keeps.

But it was too soon to worry about that now. In 1931 (and in 1932 and 1933 and 1934) Harry still planned to take the money and run back to God's country (and Gershwin's), where he belonged, not realizing yet that, as S. J. Perelman put it, they paid you in magic money out there that vanished as you flew over the Rockies. Right now Harry was hot, and his title song for *42nd Street* was joined by two other gems: "Shuffle Off to Buffalo" and one of Sinatra's hardy perennials, "You're Getting to Be a Habit with Me," which makes as good a place as any to introduce Harry's new partner, the one made in heaven for him, who had just helped Warren as he had never been helped before. Harry had already worked briefly with Al Dubin in New York, but that didn't count because that was when he was working with everybody. The Hollywood contract system allowed for no such promiscuity. The studios couldn't afford to sign up an alley full of guys and wait for them to find each other. If you didn't have a partner, they matched you up with someone from the office pool and hoped for the best.

Sometimes arranged marriages work out better than love matches, and besides, these two guys had something important in common. Each had been groping his way through the transition from the mostly funny song to the great ballad takeover. Dubin had already scored a major hit in between modes with "Tiptoe Through the Tulips" (music: Joe Burke), which was such a prime example of a funny-tender compromise with whimsy and sentiment that he too had received an RSVP from Warner Bros. that coincided with Harry's. So *42nd Street* was crucial for Al too, and blessedly the script was right up his street, because it was about the world they had both just come from, and it seemed to be set in the year before last, their best year, so there was nothing stopping them from homing in on the territory of Arthur Freed and Nacio Brown and getting it right this time. Where *The Broadway Melody* had presented an elegant fantasy of Broadway made in Hollywood, *42nd Street* was the real thing and one knew it right away.

Away they went, in a cloud of song titles, which in no time had become pretty much transferable from one silly story to another. The speed of this is worth stressing because Warren's best shot at recognition had probably already come and gone with *42nd Street*. At that point, he had just helped to bring movie musicals back to life and thus incidentally kept the business open for countless entertainers and colleagues who now had no place else to go—no vaudeville and not much Broadway. But if he expected a round of applause for this, he didn't know Hollywood. Certainly none of the other concerned parties were talking about him. The actors had their own places in the sun to worry about, and were fully occupied just trying to keep Busby Berkeley from absorbing all the rays himself—a contest that the studios viewed benignly. May they both win! But the writers—what writers? Movie songs were just there, don't worry about it. Go back to your nice dream.

The time was never riper, but if Warren wanted fame, he had to get it himself, preferably by doing something completely irrelevant, like suing the studio, or joining the Abraham Lincoln Brigade or setting fire to his contract—anything but writing. The one way he could never get it was simply by writing more great songs.

Unfortunately, that was the only way he wanted to get it. The second best-known story about Warren tells of how he once hired a press agent, and fired the man almost immediately for getting his name in the paper—probably for being sighted at a screening, or some other incendiary event. Like many people who have had to work all their lives, Warren knew the value of a dollar. Reading about where he'd been last night was not it.

So his lifelong attitude began to form: of resignation, anger, irony, and perhaps maddening, indestructible hope—dashed again and again—that this time would be different, and that one more hit might win him his elusive fame.

But if such a song or show existed, he had already written it with *42nd Street,* or if not that one, with his next, *Gold Diggers of 1933*, which also stands out from the pack because at that primal stage, its formula of showgirls "making it" still seemed fresh, even to moviemakers, and the Depression itself seemed relatively fresh, a scary but perhaps manageable blip on the business cycle that would be ironed out any day now by sheer high spirits and optimism. Anyhow, Hollywood did its bit, and here was its latest pitch: that for every old-timer moping around cadging dimes, there was a kid out there who was "in the money," having found shiny new opportunities in the debris and most particularly in show biz, a miracle industry that seemed to be laying on new workers almost as fast as the other businesses were laying them off. So might it not be possible for show business to turn this whole thing around single-handed? "Old Man Depression, you are through, you've done us wrong."

Those first Warren-Berkeley movies have an additional poignancy because they ignore the extent to which Hollywood had already killed off so many other forms of show business. In those early days of talking pictures, it still seemed possible to think of Broadway as the Great White Way to fame and fortune, because in a way it still was—but not in the old way.

Although *Singin' in the Rain* exaggerated the problem of turning silent actors into talking ones, it was a real problem, and the studios still hadn't figured a better way to find and groom the latter than to grab them ready-made off the New York stage. So it was very much in Hollywood's interest to glorify Broadway and exaggerate its importance. "You're going to come back a star," says the producer. But in real life his next words would have been, "So I'll see you in Hollywood," as he waved his own ticket. Ginger Rogers, who first sang "The Gold Diggers' Song (We're in the Money)," nicely illustrated the way things really worked. After just one leading role on the stage, Ginger proceeded to a long career in movies, with an immortality bonus that the theater no longer guaranteed. Stars might be born on Broadway, but they grew and bloomed forever in Hollywood.

Not so with songwriters. They had to be big indeed on arrival to retain any size at all out there. Otherwise they shrank to the size of screen credits, and were almost as invisible as screenwriters and photographers.

What happened in between vestigial recognition and none at all could be summed up in a single phrase: "double features." In what looks from here like in no time flat, the talkies mutated from special events that you dressed up for to the stuff of habit and blue jeans. Distributors took to treating them that way by piling people's plates high twice a week with the audiovisual equivalent of junk food, mostly based on tiny variations on the exact same theme: different cartoon but same characters and setup—cat chases mouse, gets clobbered. Fade to newsreel—different beauty contest, same old Joe Louis; to travelogue—different island, same contrast of rich and poor, old and new, same regret upon leaving; to coming attractions, adventure serial, funny subject, and what have we here? The new Charlie Chan? Or the last Mr. Moto held over?

It was the second feature that clinched the incoherence, because even the voice over the telephone, supposing you could reach one, could no longer tell you within the nearest hour precisely when the main movie came on. And after a while, it seemed pretentious to ask. So you just "went to the movies" like everyone else, and enjoyed the total experience, buying popcorn during the credits, shushing new arrivals at big moments, and trying to remember when you came in yourself. ("Didn't we see this already?" "No, I think that was last week.") Also, you had to decide if you really wanted another set of dishes.

It was all highly exhilarating and American and vague, and a pop quiz afterward would have yielded a lot less information than the most amateur film buff knows today. "So what was the name of the second movie, anyway?" "I'm not sure, but I know the music was by Al Dubin and Harry Warren."

Fat chance. What you did remember in descending order of vividness was (1) the clumsy hippo who stepped on your foot, (2) the lady with the Carmen Miranda hat that she wouldn't, or perhaps couldn't, take off, and (3) the names of the stars, which in a couple of years the studios had learned how to mass-produce in daunting numbers. MGM boasted that it actually housed more stars than the sky itself, and would sporadically prove it with regimental photos covering every inch of the *Life* magazine centerfolds. And kids who couldn't even find World War II on a map had no trouble identifying every one of them. In a word, they were gods; and gods don't need writers.

That's where Harry's fame went, somewhere between "Coming soon to this theater" and "That's all, folks." It was almost enough to make a man move to Europe, where Harry had become famous almost immediately because the natives watched one movie at a time and the credits were part of the show, so you might as well enjoy them. Okay, it was only Europe, and he only learned about it twenty years later when he finally went there. But at least Hollywood had paid Harry handsomely for his anonymity, in terms not only of cash but with assignments, and all the times at bat he could handle. Two sets of double features a week adds up to an awful lot of films to fill with music, quite enough to exhaust a thin talent or, in Warren's case, to reveal a major one. To the puzzlement and admiration of old friends like the Gershwins, Warren got better as he went along, until even he must have wondered whether Hollywood might in some strange way be good for him. After all, no one in his New York days had ever compared him to Irving Berlin, but that was because back then he really, by sheer weight of numbers, wasn't in the same league. Now he was, and the people who counted knew it. And if he didn't have fame, he won the two next best things—grounds for endless complaint and a suspiciously good life.

There were a lot worse ways to pass the Depression than playing golf every afternoon with one's fellow writers—one's favorite game in one's favorite company—or, if you were Warren's partner Dubin, drinking and eating your heart out at the Brown Derby, and if you were either of them, cooling off as needed in the world's snazziest swimming pools.

And then there were the studios, which dotted the landscape like shopping malls or fortified medieval towns, and which collectively were Hollywood, the closest thing to a city you could find out there. And what the commissaries lacked as restaurants, they made up for in the quality of their customers, who constituted everybody who was anybody, and in their gossip, which was of the very latest and dirtiest.

All these people knew who Harry Warren was and how good he was, except, apparently, one lady who turned up in a typical Burton Lane anecdote that I wish I remembered better. It seems that Harry was also the spitting image of the MGM studio doctor, so this lady ran up to him in distress one day to tell him that his latest prescription had brought on all kinds of horrible side effects, such as palpitations, itches, and God knew what all, and he answered, "If I were you, I'd stop taking it immediately," before disappearing through the nearest door. Lane was in high spirits himself as he told the story, but Warren didn't sound like an unhappy man. And certainly when he and Dubin wrote their defining hymn to hard times, "Remember My Forgotten Man," nobody supposed they were talking about themselves, affluent songwriters who couldn't get their names in the paper. Well, boo-hoo.

So Warren joined the crowd and complained about the boss instead (at Warner Bros.), and when the boss turned out to be okay (at Fox), he complained about the boss's lawyers, and finally, when there was no boss left, what was happening to the nation's music. The arc of Harry's gripes tells the tale. In the first gold-digging days of talkies, amateurs such as producers and even the moguls themselves thought that they knew all about music, and you were lucky if they didn't think their nephews did too. So Harry resorted to playing one of these geniuses off another. "You don't like this one? That's funny, Jack Warner does."

Gradually, the real experts took over, but it still helped to play politics. Comparing Harry's groans with those of the East Coast champion, Richard Rodgers, one finds that the latter got a ceremonial welcome out of Louis B. Mayer, but no work to speak of. Meanwhile, Harry "got no respect," but more job offers than even he could cope with. So naturally he railed against the Broadway hotshot like Rodgers who got all the glory, while Rodgers himself whined about the studio hacks who got all the plum assignments.

Time in Hollywood starts and stops and starts again, but the one thing it has never done is just keep rolling peacefully along for a few years. While it may have looked for a moment as if there'd be no end to the Busby Berkeley cycle, suddenly it was over. And Warner Bros. hired the new rage, Johnny Mercer, with a view perhaps to replacing Dubin, who could take a hint and moved to New York, where he more or less imploded, from too much of everything you can have too much of, although the food alone would probably have done it. Three hundred pounds must have seemed even bigger in those days, and as he wrote in one of his last songs with Harry, "Just a little filthy lucre buys a lot of things." So he hit New York again to see how far his Hollywood lucre would go. After all, Harry had only written the tunes; the daffodils and Broadway babies were Dubin's ideas. And he would die of an excess of everything before the lucre ran out.

Thus ended the first phase of Harry's career, with all guns firing. "Lulu's Back in Town," "She's a Latin from Manhattan," "September in the Rain," and a lot of filthy lucre in *his* pockets too. Also already present, a legendary hatred of Hollywood that he could dine out on forever.

So why didn't Harry go back to New York too? Perhaps he liked Hollywood better than he pretended—or perhaps his wife did, or his children. They counted too. Harry's life was far from a typical show biz one, full of flashy career moves and caprice. And something else happened the year

Dubin left. Harry would always call himself a good family man, but he didn't say anything about being a happy one, and from 1938 on, he almost certainly wasn't one, because that spring the Warrens' nineteen-year-old and only son, Harry Jr., died of pneumonia, and it seems that it was possible to blame Harry for not getting him to the hospital in time. In the best accounts of what happened next, his wife never quite forgave him; and in the worst, she had no more to do with him at all.

There are always huge blanks in any marriage, and there may have been some good days even at the Warrens'. But it seems like thin pickings for a family man, even if you throw in a lovely daughter and a couple of grandchildren; and a contemporary reader has to wonder why Harry didn't just listen to his own songs and swing a little, like his fellow Catholics Jimmy McHugh and Bing Crosby, who, at least intermittently, made out like bandits under cover of Catholicism. This was Hollywood, after all, which was an occasion of sin in itself. So make a good confession, my son, give lots of money, and try to be a good example when you have a moment and somebody's watching.

Yet, allowing again for blanks, the answer seems to have been probably nix on the swinging. Since Harry had sung in all those good choirs as a kid, chances were he'd learned something about the Church as well, and knew that the Spencer Tracy Exception, as we'll call it, was just a little too good to be true. Spencer would fry for it someday, or at least do some serious time in purgatory. Instead, Harry most likely joined that small legion of "Graham Greene" Catholics who believed that being true to a bad marriage was the heart of the matter.

Of such types, and there were a lot of them, I can say from fuzzy, youthful memory that they did not necessarily act particularly gloomy, but seemed to draw genuine strength from their faith, along with a serene conviction, rare in anyone, that they were somehow on the right track and that their lives meant something.

The other thing about them, which fits Harry too, is that they tended to fill the empty spaces in life with sheer hard work. The Warrens' marriage may have died in 1938, but his talent rose from the ashes soon afterward, and kept on rising. "You'll find your life will begin/the very moment you're in Argentina" is not a song line you'd normally associate with a broken heart, nor is "Chattanooga Choo Choo" two years later. By then,

World War II was breaking up non-Catholic marriages as well, quite bru-
tally, and smiling through the tears and soldiering on were much in vogue,
so that perhaps it's no coincidence that novelist Graham Greene and his
fellow Catholics harped on it so much in wartime and right afterward. But
I should stress here that I'm just guessing about Harry, as I am periodi-
cally about all these guys. Harry definitely belongs to the school of
Catholics that does not carry on about it, and I'll gladly follow his lead on
this.

So Warren, equipped now with a sad home life, acquired an unpromising partner at work, lyricist Mack Gordon. Frank Loesser describes Mack
as ranting on about something or other at an ASCAP meeting while the
audience slept, and while Johnny Mercer actually read a newspaper, and
a friend once told me a firsthand, slightly slanderous anecdote concerning
Gordon's unrequited love of a chorus girl, all of which adds up to a bore
by day and a strikeout at night.

Luckily, Gordon's lyrics were, in Mark Twain's phrase, quite a bit better than they sounded. To begin with, Gordon offers an advanced lesson
in why good song lyrics don't have to be great poetry. For a reputed wind-
bag, he had a wonderful ear for the regular phrases people were using that
year. "I'm going to send a wire, 'hopping on a flyer,' leaving today." Only in
1941! And an even better ear for fitting them on the right notes, for example, the innocuous phrase "how long can a guy go on dreaming," which attached to Harry's tune "I Had the Craziest Dream," still brings back World
War II as vividly as any line I can think of, with the possible exception of
Frank Loesser's "Why'd you have to turn off all that sunshine?" The scene
I picture in both cases is someplace like Penn Station, piled high with
duffel bags and lined from wall to wall with gobs and GIs waiting, waiting,
waiting . . .

It wasn't literary, and singers with a taste for good writing tend to shy
away from Gordon's lyrics. "The More I See You," for instance, has a wonderful singer's melody—but who wants to get his chops around "I know
the only one for me could only be you"? If, as Samuel Taylor Coleridge
says, a poem is like a palace that must also be a good house, this lyric is
like a Quonset hut that hasn't been lived in yet. And the lyrics of "At Last"
or even of Harry's biggest hit, "You'll Never Know," are not much better.
The words of the ballads are consistently undistinguished second-class

verse saved by the music. No wonder Gordon's own love life was not an unbroken success. Admittedly, he picked up nicely for half-funny novelty songs such as "Chattanooga Choo Choo" and wonderfully for the handful of Brazilian imitations he and Harry concocted for the Portuguese bombshell Carmen Miranda ("Boom-chicka-boom"). But when it came to the million ways of saying "I love you," he returned to the back of the line. But oh, those tunes. At least Gordon obeyed the first rule of the lyricist's code, "at least do no harm"—and is it possible that just in terms of sound he might have done something to help?

For an answer, one turns to Warren's most beautiful song of all, "There Will Never Be Another You." There one finds, amid the clumsiness and the clichés, four ordinary little words that turn a good number into a great one, "There will be other songs to sing (pause) Another fall, another spring." Not beautiful perhaps, but beautifully efficient, and Warren himself put his finger on how this worked when he said, "He had an innate sense of song."

Apparently Gordon needed to hear each new tune over and over again like a musical illiterate, but when he got it, he got the whole thing from the punchy first line to the well-articulated caboose. "When I hear that serenade in blue," sounds in performance much more powerful than the words deserve. The trick for the listener is to turn off the switch that tells you what words mean. Forget you know English altogether if you can and just listen, for instance, to the pounding of that bridge, "It seems like only yesterday a small café, a crowded floor . . ." That goes double for "I Know Why." You'll find yourself listening closely to the first line and you'll remember it forever, "Why do robins sing in December?" But your attention veers off from there. Who really cares why the little so-and-so's sing then, if they even do? This is the standard song about a guy falling in love and hallucinating, right? Enough said.

Like most teams, Warren and Gordon arrived at these blends of great music and mesmeric words along the following conventional lines: The lyricist comes up with a theme and a title, which the composer tries to translate into music before handing it back to the other guy for further decoration, or "songing." And the main question is, do we have to fit this into a story of some kind or can we just concentrate on selling the mother? Clearly, the proof of this latter kind of writing was on the Hit Parade, and

Gordon did so well on it that you could almost suppose that he had crammed for it like for an examination, as if his life depended upon it.

By this time, Warren had become a very big man indeed on campus, if nowhere else, and helping him onto the Hit Parade seemed like the minimum requirement for working with him at all. Otherwise there were several hundred perennial lyricists out there forever ready to pounce, who made their living from pouncing, in fact—and maybe the best of them, Leo Robin, would write a warning wartime hit with Warren right under Gordon's nose. "No Love, No Nothin' " was not just pretty but was clever enough to be on Broadway, maybe even taking Harry with it someday.

But in the suspended animation of wartime, the Hit Parade was still the accepted stock exchange. Nobody was about to argue with it until at least V-E Day. So Gordon concentrated on making Warren's sounds as catchy as they could be, and the hits kept coming and have astonishingly been enjoyed to this day by all the world, as if they really were great, words and all.

After which, Harry changed studios, and Mack was out on the street—not because he had done anything worse than usual, or even because Warren was trying to get rid of him. Warren was as loyal to individuals as he was vindictive about institutions. He seemed to have been genuinely sorry to lose any partner to the system. But his vendetta against Fox's lawyers remained the first order of peacetime business. It seems these shysters had once taken him off salary while he sweated out an inconvenient attack of pneumonia, and although he was no Tony Soprano, some scores must be settled. And it might be worth recalling that his own son had died of pneumonia just a couple of years earlier. Getting it himself may have been an unusually intense experience for Harry.

On the other side of the fence, Arthur Freed had his own list of favorite lyricists, very much including himself. Even before Warren technically left Fox, he found himself collaborating with his future employer on the beautiful "This Heart of Mine," for use when he got to MGM. Thus began what Harry Warren always swore were the happiest days of his life.

Warren's insistence on the absolute wonderfulness of his MGM years gives rise to several thoughts and guesses, because professionally speaking, only one of these years was really good, while the rest were so-so verging on ominous. If Harry had simply wanted what we all want—less work for more money—after the grind of Warner Bros. and Fox, okay. But that is one of those dreams you have to be careful about, because by the time he had left his utopia a half decade or so later, he was down to almost no work at all.

Still, he held tight to his memory of unalloyed happiness throughout, and there's no reason not to let him have it, if only in comparison with most other writers who were getting no work at all. Nevertheless, only his first year was really good by his own standards.

Every serious grumbler needs to have something ideal to point to just to prove that he knows the difference. Being hard to please is fine, but being impossible to please is just annoying. So attention should be paid to Harry's good year, and bits of the others. To begin with, the chances of any kind of happiness at MGM hung entirely on the whim of Louis B. Mayer, a guy famous for making life a living hell for people he didn't like—for example, the Marx Brothers. However, Louis B. could also make life pleasant indeed for those he fancied. And whatever his personal feelings toward Warren (if he had any—he could be vague about the identities of underlings), he decided just then that he loved musicals, classy ones, that is, and would make the whole operation positively heavenly—for a while. Through Freed, he would grant Warren his own bungalow, or home away from home, and the run of the Versailles of movie studios in its last gorgeous flush. And on the professional side, Harry also had the run, via Freed, of Louis B. Mayer's wallet. So what lyricist would Harry like today, besides myself, of course? And what actors and directors?

The result was one of the last great original musicals to come out of anywhere. *The Harvey Girls* had words by Johnny Mercer, and starred Judy Garland and Ray Bolger, all at their very best. Warren's score too shows him not just shining but incandescent, courtesy of all the overwork he'd recently been getting at his previous sweatshops. Warner Bros. and Fox might have worked him like a dog, but they bred a champion, and to borrow a phrase ballplayers use during the World Series, he would have all winter to rest.

Starting almost immediately. It was still only 1946 when *The Harvey Girls* came out—still wartime, culturally speaking, but without the rationing. But already TV was rumbling in the distance, and Hollywood would soon be hauling out its biggest guns to counter it, such as the best of the Gershwins for *An American in Paris,* Arthur Schwartz for *The Band Wagon,* and Rodgers, Kern, and Porter for what were laughingly called biographies but were more like music racks. And Freed found a few minor names that could be turned into big guns too, for at least one movie. What separated the great writers from the good ones was sometimes merely their sheer volume, and if you could make, let's say, five or more great films out of Gershwin, maybe you could eke out at least one (*Three Little Words*) from the great vaudeville team of Bert Kalmar and Harry Ruby, and another from Arthur Freed himself and his buddy Nacio Brown. Arthur was not the least shy about invoking his own droit du seigneur, or boss's privilege, and he asked the great writing team of Comden and Green to "make me a star," or at least immortalize my songs, and oh my, did they ever! *Singin' in the Rain* would turn out to be the biggest gun ever—the joke being that I possibly saw it just once in a movie house, and at least a dozen times since on dreaded TV, that medium the movies never managed to kill.

In the face of this gaudy barrage of masterpieces, even the best original musicals inevitably began to seem quite pale. Using a simple memory test, I find such average scores as Warren's *The Barkleys of Broadway* and his *Summer Stock* have faded almost completely while several others are now completely unfamiliar, maybe because they didn't last long enough or get distributed widely enough to be generally seen. Suddenly the odds against them were too high. Even the original *42nd Street* or the miraculous early Astaires had never coughed up more than four or five great songs, but Freed's all-star teams routinely carried nine or ten. Even Harry couldn't compete with MGM's whole inventory, which now contained everything Freed wanted. So if my cast-iron prejudice is the least correct, that musicals are basically only as good as their songs, the jig was almost up with new musicals even before TV had completed its conquest.

Hollywood had cut its own throat in anticipation but, incidentally, left a few necks like Warren's hanging by threads in the process. After all the modified, "writer-cized" hoopla surrounding Harry's arrival at MGM, the enthusiasm for him proved to be as ephemeral as most Hollywood enthusiasms. By the time his contract with MGM was over, circa 1952, he was happy to accept a one-shot call from Bing Crosby at Paramount (hit song, "Zing a Little Zong," words by Leo Robin) and others from Jerry Lewis, who needed songs for his still relatively shy partner, Dean Martin, and who would get almost more than he could have bargained for. It was as if Harry, fully aware of his mortality by now, killed two birds with one song. Not only would Warren give Martin the best, most characteristic piece of work in Dino's career, but Warren also proved that he himself was as good and unbelievably versatile as ever. Although upon first thought "That's Amore" (words: Jack Brooks) might seem like the exact opposite of a great song, at that time and in that situation it took a great craftsman to write it.

It's hard to believe, but we've still only reached 1953, because by then the writing was all over the wall for Warren. Arthur Freed even contemplated a drastic reduction of his *own* schedule. So much history had come and gone that World War II seemed like ancient times; Stalin's death, the rise and fall of Joe McCarthy, and the beginning and end of a whole new war in Korea, with its own little postwar. It was time for the music to move along as well, and for the revival houses to give up or turn into TV studios, and for the writers to go into their final grumbles.

The endless natural war between musicals and inflation was well and truly over if the musical itself wasn't that popular anymore. Within not much more than a year, the remaining writers in Hollywood found themselves down to their last gimmick—title songs. Or at least so the Oscars say. In 1953, Sammy Fain won the top prize with a traditional and quite characteristic jazz song, "Secret Love," which might have won in any year, but he then came back in 1955 to win it again with a piece of featureless mush called "Love Is a Many-Splendored Thing" that might have been written by anybody. In between, Jule Styne played hooky from Broadway, where he was still safe, long enough to win the 1954 Oscar with "Three Coins in the Fountain"—mush to end all mush! Without being told, you *know* it's a film title. And here the bull session aspect of this book must take over for a moment, as one recalls the novelty of seeing bits of the movie run before the credits, and then run right in back of them—wow, typescript and music and action all at once—and the novelty of hearing title songs that were literally about the movie. *High Noon* kicked off a bunch of those—"He made a vow while in state's prison."

Any way you sliced it, it came down to just one song per movie, and even that made a weak reed for a whole profession to lean on because it was only as sturdy as the gimmick itself. Perhaps that was only there to keep ASCAP happy until the studios were safely out of the music-publishing business altogether, and could let it sink quietly back in the East.

Since theme music was virtually the last game left, it seemed only fair that Warren should take twice as much time as usual to provide maybe the best ever piece of it before going down with the whole ship himself. The Charles Boyer classic *Love Affair* was about to be handed over to the new king, Cary Grant, and by the time everyone had calmed down and finished the coronation, Harry had worked longer on the title song, "An Affair to Remember," than he had usually been allowed for whole movies. He had turned it into haunting background music as well, and a successful pop song in its own right.

He had not planned for it to be his swan song, and in a strict sense it was not. But for all that history cared, it could have been—unless, that is, history discovers something new. For instance, my own scorecard gives Warren five more years, courtesy of a beautiful Latin mass that Michael Feinstein sent me part of recently, which Harry had finished in 1962, the year Catholics went off the Latin standard. But the Church has been known to change its mind over the centuries, and maybe Harry will be revived in vestments someday as a good Catholic boy. He earned it.

And who knows what else Michael might come up with? Right after serving hard time at the Gershwins, Feinstein went to work on Harry's files and found him a much more congenial host. And perhaps the arrival on the scene of such a brilliant archivist-musician might in itself be considered a mark of fortune's favor, as if history had finally decided to give Harry a break—long after he'd left the room, that is. In fact, his life had already ended on a typically mixed note.

On the plus side, the rapacious David Merrick undertook the first stage version of *42nd Street*, which would balloon into the best anthology a writer ever had, giving Harry Warren the longest hearing he could ask for—almost ten years that first time, and four years the next, and who knows what the future may bring?

On the minus side, the thought of all that ink going to someone like Warren might have been too much for Merrick. In the cloud of acrimony that followed this man wherever he went, Merrick yanked Harry's name off his creation and confirmed the legend of triumphant songs and an unknown, unknowable writer. Period. He had finally gotten Warren onto his beloved Broadway, but left off the name.

When Harry died, it only seemed to confirm his anonymity for eternity.

Or so it seemed at first, as I and other diehards gloomily continued to ask our reasonably knowledgeable friends if they'd yet heard of him. But with its return in 2001, with his name attached, the show began to reveal an unearthly streak of stubbornness. The musical *42nd Street* may just not leave Broadway until *somebody* learns where it came from.

There the matter rests. The pantheon of great writers has been fixed in the stars for a long time now, and Harry's name is a tough sell in any circumstance. Every now and then, I sense a crack in the amnesia. And who knows what another millennium may bring? If Harry Warren miraculously lost his anonymity, he'd also lose his chief claim to fame. Meanwhile, I can't help wishing they could find a way simply to change the guy's name back to the more ear-catching Salvatore Guaragna and do the "Who?" era over.

# Jimmy Van Heusen:
# On the Radio with Bing and Frank

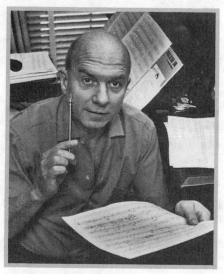

JIMMY VAN HEUSEN

Compared with writers like Harry Warren—but perhaps only compared with them—Jimmy Van Heusen was practically a household word for a while, partly because of an eye-catching last name. Could Jimmy possibly be related to the shirts of that name? And partly because he wrote a lot for Frank Sinatra, who was punctilious about naming names and attaching compliments to them, as in "a wonderful song by Jimmy Van Heusen brought to you by the wonderful band of Count Basie."

But Van Heusen was more famous for his less formal relationship with Sinatra, which consisted of hanging out with him after the music stopped, when the band and the serious people had gone home, leaving the scene to the parasites of night, the gossip-writers and paparazzi, to whom Van Heusen was basically the other guy in the picture and the unidentified witness to the latest Sinatra scene. In her interminable hatchet job on Frank, Kitty Kelley mentions Van Heusen several times while barely mentioning his profession. This probably suited Jimmy almost as much as it would have disgusted Harry Warren. As the younger of the two, Van Heusen had grown up to see the gap widening between celebrity and actual accomplishment, and it may even have tickled him to be good at one thing and famous for another.

"Broads, booze, songs, and Sinatra" was how he preferred to list his interests, thus slurring over one of the last truly classy catalogues, as well as one of the great musical friendships, in the whole archive of pop. In his own way, Van Heusen worked just as hard as Cole Porter at the gentlemanly convention of hiding both his work and his feelings, so that the only proof we have of either of them has to be found in the songs themselves. "Here's That Rainy Day," for instance, has a melody so sad it squeezed tears out of the stoical Johnny Carson on his last broadcast, but nobody ever caught Jimmy having a rainy day himself, unless you count hangovers. "But Beautiful" is such a moving tribute to love that it verges on a hymn, yet Van Heusen's own love life was anything but holy. His little black book was said to be the envy of Hollywood, which is like being praised for your cooking in Paris.

"Van Heusen never got past the age of nineteen," says Jonathan Schwartz, who knew him well. And the first thought that occurs is that nineteen was also exactly the age of his target audience and thus a good place to stop. Almost all great love songs are written either for nineteen-year-olds or for, as in "Rainy Day," people who remember nineteen all too well and only wish they could do it over again.

"Maybe I should have saved those leftover dreams," says the song—but why save them in the first place?—was Jimmy's philosophy. Why not spend them right now and dream some new ones, then spend those too? If one accepts the Cole Porter principle that falling in love is the Research

Department of songwriting, then Jimmy becomes one of the most consci-
entious craftsmen in the business.

And so too with Sinatra, whose singing seemed to get wiser as his life
got sillier and more childish. To hear Frank pour his soul into Cahn and
Van Heusen's stark little tribute to monogamy, "All the Way" ("Through
the good or lean years . . . come what may"), you could swear this was a
grown-up singing a grown up song. Yet perhaps later that night, two of the
song's perpetrators might have been observed winging their way across the
continent to wake up Sinatra's pal Jilly in New York for some drinks and
laughs that couldn't be found right that minute in Vegas or Palm Springs,
and then maybe picking up some chicks they'd overlooked last time. The
true signature song of their friendship was not one of their grown-up ones
but a celebration of the great game of hooky, "Come Fly with Me," which
was written and sung in their preferred mode of one nineteen-year-old to
another. Another obvious reason Van Heusen was indispensable to Frank
in his rodent phase was his pilot's license, and his willingness to use it at
any hour of the day or night, drunk or sober. Van Heusen could usually
drink Old Blue Eyes under the carpet and still fly a plane perfectly, at a
point when Frank could barely have mounted a bicycle, which gave
Jimmy another good reason for staying nineteen: He was so good at it, particularly in comparison to Frank and his little band of middle-aged amateurs. (Peter Lawford? Are you kidding?) The saying in Hollywood was
that "Sinatra would have been Van Heusen, but he flunked the physical."
Yet if Jimmy ever took any exercise at all, it was another of his secrets.

In his ego-soaked memoir *I Should Care,* lyricist Sammy Cahn, who
also flunked the physical, reveals a glint of some hard metal in Jimmy's
character, when he reports that Van Heusen couldn't stand being around
sloppy drunks. Surely, this had to include Sinatra once or twice. Jimmy
further qualified his taste for Chairman Frank in his own words: "He was
a bastard when I met him forty years ago, and he's still a bastard."

He was kidding, of course, as show biz guys usually are when they talk
about or to each other, but the tone of this crack establishes that here was
no camp follower talking. By staying up so late, Jimmy had seen many
sides to his friend, from the sublime to the stomach-turning, and he
didn't have to like all of them all of the time. Just one. The secret that

even Kitty Kelley couldn't tell, because it wasn't in her language, was that every session between these two was a potential working session, even one well disguised as an orgy. Booze and broads provided not just their own reward but also an excellent cover for an endless if choppy professional dialogue between the two reprobates. Music hovered just above Frank's head like a comic-strip bubble. An evening with him could lead practically anywhere, from the local police station to a celestial new song.

So in a sense, Sinatra was Van Heusen's work, the way Dr. Johnson was James Boswell's. Tonight you might get a great epigram, tomorrow a not particularly funny insult. But this was the guy he was writing both for and about, his model and canvas, so the time wasn't wasted for either of them. Sinatra could always find lots of other people to play with, but how many of them could he trust to pause in middrink and give him priceless advice about what to use on his next album? The sober truth is that Van Heusen and Sinatra were artistic soul mates who needed each other equally. And in this aspect, they had no choice but to "go all the way" together, "through the good or lean years," and the bright, fat ones as well, because no one else could go with them.

"If you had the only voice in the world and I wrote the only songs." These two characters were about all that was left in the garrison after Elvis and his hordes swept through. And they had unwittingly spent their lives preparing for it. Both exploded onto their respective scenes about the same time, the golden cusp of the 1930s and '40s, and this coincidence became more crucial as the music around them changed, and the ranks of survivors thinned. Like a blind man and a deaf one in the wilderness, Sinatra and Van Heusen kept each other on track with the Tradition, so long as they stayed together. And although they both would probably have done ever better work if the national style hadn't changed so much, the fact that they did any work at all in the alien air of the late fifties and early sixties was a triumph of—and I'm glad they're not reading this— character.

Sinatra and Van Heusen actually began working and talking music together way back in 1940, when Frank's record of Jimmy's "Imagination" was a major hit for both of them. But before they could become full-fledged partners, both had appointments to keep, Sinatra's with his young bobby socks fans, who screamed so loud you could barely hear the songs—"I'll never smile again—" "Frank-y-y!" All he needed was a great first line and the rest could be taken on faith. And Van Heusen had Bing Crosby.

Like Richard Rodgers, Van Heusen comes in two distinct parts. The parts weren't just divided by different lyricists but by singers as well. The songs Jimmy and his first word-man, Johnny Burke, tailored for Bing Crosby were as different from the ones he and lyricist two, Sammy Cahn, wrote for Sinatra as the two singers were from each other.

Which is to say, *very* different by the standards of their day, but not so different from this end of the telescope—not as different as, say, Pavarotti and Guns N' Roses. Bing and Frank had one crucial thing in common besides their allegedly happy-go-lucky personas, which made them just right for Van Heusen. They were both primarily microphone singers who, if anything, sounded better on radio than in person. Van Heusen belonged to the first wave of songwriters to grow up almost exclusively on radio music, with its mixture of coolness and intimacy. You didn't have to raise or project your voice on radio, or seduce more than one person. And you didn't have to come from a big city.

With the fascinating exception of Cole Porter, who later made up for it by becoming the most urbane of them all, all the first-wave geniuses of the Jazz Age were city guys writing primarily for city people. But as radio got big in the late 1920s, the Lower East Side suddenly reached to infinity and the progenitors could come from any place and beam their stuff at anybody. Where a Gershwin song had once said "Made in New York— Place in a crowded theater immediately," a Van Heusen song said "Made in the U.S.A.—Sounds best in a lonely bar or an empty apartment where the owner is experiencing sleeping problems due to heartbreak."

And another note might be added in large type, "Safe to use in a moving vehicle." With the coming of car radios came a need for songs to drive by at all hours, songs not too soporific for the late shift, or too stimulating to hold still for, sung by voices that were first and last good company, perfect passengers who could turn into whoever you wanted, the guy overseas or the girl next door.

And if there must be other talk as well, please try to keep it short and smooth so as not to break the spell, by either waking the driver or putting him all the way to sleep. Thus was born the disc jockey and thus died the average songwriter's last chance of name recognition, because even when the obligatory names like Gershwin and Porter were spoken, they had to be spoken often indeed to sink in and suspend the human Will to Dream. "It never occurred to me that the songs were written by different people," as Cy Coleman put it. "They were all just The Radio." And he actually cited the box itself as his first major influence.

So Van Heusen and Sinatra shared a generational secret that remains the key to performing this type of music. Pre-radio singers like Al Jolson and writers like Irving Berlin and George M. Cohan needed you to register their names—their livelihoods depended on it. Much, much later, of course, when video took over, the singing songwriters of rock would need to show off even more to sell the whole package.

But in the quiet years between, when the only sound was the song itself, music alone was center stage, and the experience of the music, as brought to you by whichever name you had heard before the hypnosis began, be it Bing Crosby or Connie Boswell, Glenn Miller or Harry James. These performers proceeded quietly but insistently to stamp their styles on each song, and make it theirs, a typical Peggy Lee or a vintage Tommy Dorsey. The composer became a ghostwriter indeed, without even the equivalent of a screen credit. I suspect in many cases that even the disc jockeys hadn't heard of them.

If it was Harry Warren's comic fate to serve his apprenticeship in the Boom and cash his chips in the Depression, Van Heusen had no such problem. By the time he hit New York in the thirties the issue was not between fame and obscurity, but between working and not working. You could eat anonymously with Mr. Big and the Company, or you could starve anonymously with the Okies and grape pickers.

And anyway, Jimmy had been majoring in anonymity since the age of fifteen, when he applied for a job at what must have been one of the first radio stations in the Syracuse area, thus moving right into the epicenter of anonymity. "Abandon self-promotion all ye who enter here" might have been the station's motto. The first glimpse we have of small-fry Van Heusen finds him actually listening to other people's latest songs on the radio, with a view to stealing them by copying them down in shorthand and singing them himself on his channel as if he had just thought of them. "The Best

Things in Life Are Free" might have been the radio station's other motto. When memory failed him, he probably wrote a few bars himself.

Van Heusen even got his name from the radio, in a roundabout sense. Unlike most stage names chosen for their all-American, that is, Englishy, sound, Jimmy leaned for his an inch or two in the other direction. There is such a thing as sounding *too* English, and the station manager made it clear right away that the new kid couldn't go on the air or stay there with a name like Edward Chester Babcock, which was the name real life had thrown Jimmy's way. He changed it on the spot to another one that he just happened to see on a truck sitting outside the window. Or so the story goes. Presumably, if some store in Syracuse hadn't ordered a consignment of Van Heusen shirts that day, we might know him now as—well, what? Johnny Kleenex? Herbert Hoover? Elmer Street?

Anyway, an alias suited Jimmy fine because he didn't particularly want the powers that be at his current school, or in his own house, to know that he was moonlighting as a premature disc jockey. And perhaps he was already used to the idea that writers don't have names on radio.

Middle-class families tell no tales, and the rest of Jimmy's childhood and adolescence tends to get summarized under the rubric "kicked out of school again," a phrase that occurs suspiciously often in celebrity bios. It adds a raffish touch and no one ever checks on it. What one does know is that boys with names like Chester Babcock usually wind up graduating— it's a yearbook kind of name. And this particular one would eventually wind up in the Syracuse University Hall of Fame.

More to the point, we also know that his father, Arthur, was an amateur cornet player and that his mother, Ida Mae, claimed descent from the ultimate layabout, Stephen Foster. So they must at least have appreciated his piano playing, which would later be called the best for party purposes in Hollywood. His family must also have realized that in this family, being a black sheep obsessed with pop music wasn't the worst thing that could happen. And, more seriously, I just discovered one last trace of his family, which would otherwise disappear obligingly from the scene. (They were nice people, but not part of the story, the legend, and tempermentally speaking, they needed attention even less than he did.) It seems that Jimmy had a schizophrenic brother, on the strength of whom he decided never to marry and have children himself. So perhaps the eternal nineteen-year-old did know something after all about shadows and rainy days.

The next step for any songwriter then was to head for New York and simply start mixing, and in no time Jimmy would find a fellow out-of-towner to write some words with him, namely, Harold Arlen's brother, Jerry, who lived in the anteroom of Tin Pan Alley all his life, singing with young Johnny Mercer in the second generation of Paul Whiteman's Rhythm Boys, and writing words for anyone who would have him. It must have been a delightful life for all concerned, and Van Heusen lingered in it for a bit, not breaking through like a boy wonder, but singing here, writing there, and haunting publishers' offices, so that when he did start publishing he was already at his best. His first big hit carried a disclaimer testifying to his eclectic modus vivendi in the person of a Johnny Mercer lyric. "I Thought About You" finds him bursting from the gate at the height of his powers and already blending perfectly with Mercer. Although I've never actually heard Mercer sing it, I can't imagine anyone doing it better, and it is tantalizing to think of all the other songs Van Heusen and Mercer might have given us. But Johnny was already famous and had begun trading his services farther up the food chain, most especially with Harold Arlen, the one you got for first prize. Jimmy and Johnny had to settle for this one collaborative masterpiece.

That song plus a couple or three others he wrote first off the bat would actually outlive most of the stuff he wrote later, which suggests that in work as in life, it suited him to jump from one partner to another, thus avoiding a rut. For instance, another of those first standards, "Darn That Dream," was written with the expert handyman Eddie "Moonglow" DeLange for Louis Armstrong to swing the life out of in a crazy, swinging, all-black version of Shakespeare called *Swingin' the Dream*. You can't get much more promiscuous than that. It is probably the jazziest thing Jimmy ever wrote. Jazz groups still seem to think so anyway, and again it suggests how far Van Heusen might have gone in that direction if his career and his personality had taken the same kind of turn as, say, Duke Ellington's and he had found himself composing jazz through the medium of other musicians.

But Jimmy preferred working *around* jazz, dropping in and out of the neighborhood rather as the swing bands did, thus catching the sound of that era better than anyone. He definitely did not have the job profile of a bandleader, or of any other kind of responsible citizen. Eventually World War II would blow his cover and reveal him retroactively to have been capable of enormous self-discipline all along. Of all his concealments, this was his most thorough. Without breaking stride, he continued his whole life to project the air of a borderline delinquent rescued—but only just—from becoming a total deadbeat by music, the way inner-city kids are saved by boxing. If worse came to worst, perhaps he could make it as a soldier of fortune. But he was definitely not a leader of men.

Yet he seems to have worked wonderfully well with all his lyricists, as you might actually guess by looking at a photograph of him, and it's a pet theory of mine that he may even have let the bridge of "Darn That Dream" go slightly astray to accommodate DeLange's lyrics. But when I mentioned this to Sammy Cahn, he said that Van Heusen had never done that much for him.

In the few photos I have seen, Van Heusen looks something like Senator John McCain, which is to say a comfortable, good-natured fellow, somewhat prematurely bald in a friendly sort of way, as if hair were pretentious. And he always seemed happy to sit in the corners of other people's pictures. Working with him seems to have been anything but a clash of egos. A Babcock doesn't need to prove anything, except that he is not a creep.

In the cutthroat era that gave us Kern and Berlin, egomania was a necessary tool of the trade, and Kern in particular would not have changed a note for Shakespeare himself. "Write another soliloquy, we've got time." A generation later, Gershwin would at least have shelved the tune for him or written another one, but Van Heusen, I suspect, would have let Bing Crosby change it on the spot. Cahn describes him as a what-the-hell kind of guy, from the moment he rolled out of bed around midday, yawning and scratching, and doing his chores at the piano, until the moment he sensed he had caught his fish for the day and could really start living. Writing hits was nothing to lose sleep over, an attitude that sounds more like Bing Crosby than Bing himself did in real life, just as Van Heusen's daily hangovers, real or feigned, would also make him the perfect partner for Frank Sinatra.

Van Heusen's empathy for such happy-go-lucky types might, I suppose, have been feigned sometimes too, but if so it was certainly not something he had to work on very hard. His lethargy, real or posed, would almost immediately make him the perfect tailor or court-composer for Crosby, but fortunately he was not confined to that exclusively. During the tantalizingly short while it lasted, the entertainment fever of World War II kept Jimmy bombarded with a fury of assignments from all over, and four of my own all-time favorites would be written for such a tatter-demalion cast as Harry Babbitt, "Humpty Dumpty Heart"; Ginger Rogers, "Suddenly It's Spring"; Fred MacMurray, of all people, "It Could Happen to You"; and Dinah Shore, "Like Someone in Love"—in other words, whoever the studio rotation made available that month.

The one constraint on his freedom was that he was handcuffed to lyricist Johnny Burke, which was no constraint at all. They had been a dream team from the start, and two of the three first hits they wrote have almost outlived anything either did later. Only the first, "Oh, You Crazy Moon," may have slipped even slightly, and significantly this is the only one that sounds like a "typical" Van Heusen tune in that it never really takes off but plays beguiling and ingenious games on the runway, a formula he fell back on quite a lot in his later songs with Cahn and Sinatra. But the other two songs took off like rockets. Since "Imagination" was number one on the Hit Parade the week I arrived in this country, it still sounds to me like the whole American continent. In contrast, their next, "Polka Dots and Moon-beams," seems more specific and is set not far away from wherever you are in the cardboard village of Tin Pan Alley on the Wabash, where it begins with a garden party and ends in a cottage for two, a million miles away from Caesars Palace and the ring-a-ding world of Frank Sinatra that Van Heusen and Sammy Cahn dealt with later.

With these two songs, Johnny Burke and Van Heusen made a Siamese connection, sounding like one writer, not two. Even better, they were on a roll and had a contract. Johnny Burke had been a Paramount writer for some time and had become the perfect mouthpiece for Bing's supposedly lighter side, with lyrics like in "Pennies from Heaven" and in such corn-pone soufflés as "Sweet Potato Piper" and "That Sly Old Gentleman from Featherbed Lane"—which might not have gone too well with Jimmy's hangovers. (Burke's hangovers were bad enough.) But fortunately, by 1940 the chief order of business for the new team would be the *Road* pictures with Bob Hope, in which the cold, dark side of Crosby was finally given a hilarious airing for the world to see and laugh at. Perhaps not since the plays of Ben Jonson has comedy gotten any blacker than it does in this running saga of betrayal and double-crossing between friends.

The good news for Burke and Van Heusen was that they did not have to sound pixieish for the new Bing. Although Crosby was still supposed, incredibly, to be Mr. Relaxation without a care in the world, this didn't have to be a virtue anymore. The breezy songs the boys wrote for him, like "Ain't Got a Dime to My Name" and "My Heart Is a Hobo," could also be consonant with total irresponsibility and cynicism; this was not necessarily a nice guy, just a supremely lazy and selfish one who would later be consigned by Father "Bing" O'Malley himself to his famous menagerie of delinquents. ("Would you rather be a fish . . . or a pig?") Van Heusen had no better training for the *Road* pictures than getting kicked out of school regularly.

And the boys quit kidding occasionally and got to write some great love songs that sounded particularly good on Crosby, like "Moonlight Becomes You," "It's Always You," and "But Beautiful" as well as some fine edgy duets for Hope and Crosby, like "Put Her There, Pal," and the title song of the *Road to Morocco* that nicely captures the Friar's Club Roast aspect of their friendship while setting the table for the feast of amorality to follow. The *Road to Morocco* theme song actually reminds me of a Greek chorus on its day off saying what it really thinks. In their courtly way, they even concocted a perfect showcase for the generally underscripted Miss Lamour, a song titled "Personality," "What did Romeo see in Juliet/or Pierrot in Pierrette/or Jupiter in Juno?/(pause) you know."

This one was from *Road to Utopia* (1946), a funny movie with a great score that included, by way of contrast, the lush "Welcome to My Dreams" and the beautifully understated "It's Anybody's Spring," and as the trailers never got tired of saying, much, much more; but it was also, in retrospect, a film with the hint of a death rattle. Bing and Bob were now manifestly middle-aged men, still acting like college boys but *old* college boys, paunchy and sly and on the verge of being out of wind. The next *Road*, one senses, would be Sunset Boulevard itself for all of them.

In this, the *Road* pictures symbolized the life span of a whole profession. The Hollywood songwriters had entered the war a short while before as fresh and bouncy as the annual New Year baby, and they were already leaving it as old men and has-beens, their best work behind them.

Like the army itself, the great original musicals and their providers took their time demobilizing, and the songwriters didn't all get kicked out on the same day. Burke and Van Heusen stayed on at Paramount several more years, but there was increasingly less to do except hang around the club and check the mail. Their glory days were over and, ready or not, so were their primes—which in Hollywood are allotted to you by a Higher Power, aka the marketplace. In the great postwar drought that hasn't ended yet, Hoagy Carmichael was surely not the only writer to regret not having tried harder when the going was good, most specifically during the war itself. It is a law of life in this business that whether you're an old-timer like Jimmy Monaco, whose big hit "You Made Me Love You" had actually been written in 1912, or a new kid on the block like Gene "I'll Remember April" DePaul, who began during the war itself, you'd better be at your best when the gold rush is announced. Forget your biological clock or the arc of your creative development; the market will tell you when your prime occurs—or else tell you, "Whoops, you missed it. Better luck in the next life."

Compared with those extremes, Burke and Van Heusen were among the lucky ones, but they could have been luckier. Their careers stood at high noon as the war arrived, and by the time it was over they had enjoyed a very good war. But it could have been better, if it hadn't been for Van Heusen's other war work, which virtually no one knew about at the time and which perhaps tells more about his character than all his salacious press clips put together. As he told it later, and without heroics, to David Ewen, Jimmy's 1942 through '44 schedule went roughly like this: Four days in a row, up at four A.M. to test-fly new Lockheed warplanes until noon, under the name of Chester Babcock; then off to Paramount to write songs for the rest of the day as his other self, Jimmy Van Heusen; then, a two-and-a-half-day break, during which he only had to get up whenever the studio did, to write songs all day this time. Then back to Go, and you can sleep as long as you like when the war is over, buddy.

Okay, things were tough all over. Testing airplanes was always danger-ous, especially when they'd been built at breakneck speed by overworked, undertrained amateurs, and which may well have embodied technical breakthroughs each time, but at least he didn't have to do it under enemy fire, so Jimmy wouldn't have assigned himself to the World War II Hall of Fame.

What twenty-first-century sensibilities might find harder to grasp is not the deed but the cover-up. Imagine the glory at the Lockheed base if he ever so much as let one colleague know that he had recently written that song they were all humming, "Sunday, Monday, or Always"; and imagine the megaglory of tipping off Louella Parsons, the gossip queen, that you were not just another Hollywood draft dodger, the kind people hooted and whistled at in the street, but a hero on two fronts, the entertainment one as well as the real one, in which he was entrusting his life again and again to the skills of Rosie the Riveter between songs. Ronald Reagan would have told Ms. Parsons even if he *hadn't* done it, as an inspirational story. But the hell with it. Jimmy was not the inspirational type, and besides, he was only a great songwriter, not a minor movie star, so he mightn't even have inspired anyone that much. And finally, of course, there was his job at Paramount to worry about. No doubt his bosses would have crooned his praises in public—but who wants to make movies with a guy who might go down in flames any minute, and hold up your next picture? Who did this guy think he was anyway? Joan of Arc?

In retrospect, the myriad changes of sensibility that occur in this country seem like earthquakes that no one notices at the moment they occur. In the 1920s, a writer could genuinely think of himself, and be thought of, as a star. In the thirties and forties, he was just a working stiff to all concerned. From the 1990s until today, a guy with Van Heusen's war record would undoubtedly have sold the book and movie rights and established his own website as the Singing Test Pilot or the FlyingTroubador.com. In the 1940s the worst thing that you could be was a hotshot or a big deal. "What are you?" as the kids used to say. "A wise guy or Boy Scout?" To this, there was no correct answer except to put up your dukes and pray.

Further proof of Jimmy's character would be considerably less spectacular. To put it briefly, he survived in a dying business. Most didn't. Anyone can be a hero, but getting out of bed every day takes real character, and resisting the noonday devil, aka the third dry martini, and taking jobs he wouldn't even have looked at a few years before. Peacetime can really take it out of you after a while, because it is at once pointless and unpredictable. During the war, everything that could be stabilized had been, even fame, so that if you didn't go down in flames, you stayed up there forever. No celebrity ever faded away in those days, although several, like Al Jolson, came back to life.

So the hardest work a writer had to do back then was hitch his wagon to a fixed star and watch the money roll in. And, as Jonathan Schwartz pointed out to me, Jimmy's smartest career move had simply been to buy a house in Palm Springs, which would place him with one stroke of the pen in the same playground as first Crosby, and then Sinatra, a one-two punch that should have been good for a lifetime—and was, in a way, although probably not as good as it looked at the time.

Van Heusen indeed needed them both, because in the acceleration of peacetime, they were suddenly the only games in town—when, that is, they were available, and so long as they were able to keep surviving themselves. In the new Hollywood, no star was that fixed anymore, and Jimmy was in for a bumpy ride indeed, as both Bing and Frank fought to redefine and resell themselves in the brave new world. The second half of Van Heusen's career would be defined by these bumps—a tale of two singers taking their own lumps every time fashion hit a curve, then passing them on to Jimmy. None of this was clear at first. As peace arrived, Bing at least looked like money in the bank. As Bob Hope would later learn and go to exhaustive lengths to prove, an audience of soldiers can serve as the closest thing we have to a fountain of youth for both a man and his work for several lifetimes, and as an embalming fluid after that. Crosby splashed deep and well and emerged from the war as perhaps the nation's ultimate entertainer, or, as Alec Wilder would put it, the first guy you would send for if your theater was on fire and you wanted everyone to keep calm.

At this point, Sinatra's position was considerably trickier and uniquely modern. Like Superman, Francis Albert came in two distinct aspects. At one moment, he was the skinny little kid that half the country made fun of, and at the next, he was the greatest sound ever to come out of a radio. This side of him was simply called the Voice, a spectral figure who had somehow leaped over the technology in a single bound to broadcast from inside your own head, not just singing to you but at certain points becoming you and singing to the girl, or the whole sex, that you loved. It sounds impossible and was presumably never that clear-cut, but it still certainly is possible to love listening to him without having any particular personal feelings about him, one way or the other.

If the army had ordered him to specifications, they couldn't have come up with anything better. As a voice in the dark and as everybody's closest friend, Sinatra offered the last word in specialization: a buddy with all the bugs removed, and 100 percent guaranteed not to get on your nerves or die at your side. In other words, he was perfect company for men over-seas—so long as they stayed there.

As for so many, the problem would be peacetime, which means day-light. Daylight wakes you from the good dreams as well as from bad ones. So even if the real live Sinatra turned out to be perfect, he would have been disappointing, if only because, let's face it, he was another male, a biological rival, and as such a stranger. The part he'd been playing doesn't exist in real life and would soon be blown away completely as the faucets and fire hoses of gossip turned on again. But before this could happen, Sinatra signed up with one of the great protection syndicates, which would prolong his cover for a bit longer. If you worked for MGM, you au-tomatically became whatever they wanted. And what Louis B. Mayer wanted was for Frank to go on with the fan-magazine version at its most simpleminded. Although Old Blue Eyes is now widely remembered as a cross between Don Corleone and Francis of Assisi, a thug whose good deeds held world records, he came across in the 1940s more as an Ital-ianate Andy Hardy, everybody's kid brother who had, as the GIs might un-fortunately recall now, stayed home with the girls while the grown-ups were off fighting and dying. But that was all right, I guess, because he was obviously still a kid, still called "Frankie," not "Frank," let alone the "Chair-man of the Board."

As if to ram this home, Sinatra also contrived to have one of those chil-dren's book marriages in which the tender smile and the melting glance are the hottest units of exchange and which didn't count at all against your juvenile status. Any babies born to such babies were invariably bun-dles of joy brought by a friendly stork directly from the angel factory. A grim little slice of sociology packaged in a song called "I'll Buy That Dream" spells out the peacetime promise of such marriages with ghoulish touches like "Imagine . . . you thanking Dad for my dowry" and "Someone like you in the nursery." "I'll Buy That Dream" quotes a slaphappy GI before he has even had a good chance to look at the contract, not realizing that this may be the last love song he will ever be allowed to sing, unless he has a cheating heart and a first-rate lawyer.

Somebody would have to pay for this someday, and that somebody might be Frank if he ever broke the rules. But meanwhile, in the limbo of the late 1940s, Sinatra stumbled upon another way to be two people at once. On-screen he remained the perfect middle-class boy-man, fetched out in a cute little sailor suit to prove it, while on radio and records he was still the Voice who had so recently brought love to life for thousands of grateful adults, in direct and day-to-day contrast with death. But then for a moment, the Voice itself seemed to split, as Sinatra busted a gut trying to figure out how to keep up with the current taste.

The cusp of the 1950s marked the only period when Frank's voice was ever untrue to itself, as he struggled to get his chops around the latest baby boomer novelty numbers. The day on which he recorded "Mama Will Bark" for the Mephistopheles of pop, Mitch Miller, seems in retrospect like a total eclipse of the sun. After that, even so gifted a singer as Frank would have to give up and find a new style, a singing self that suited the times, but did not belong to them. "Songs," as he might say, "for swinging grown-ups."

The kid brother persona wasn't working that well either, on the screen or at the box office. The real big brothers were back, so who needed kid ones? The only catch was that Franky couldn't seem to stop playing one anyhow, whether to Gene Kelly or Marlon Brando, to Bing Crosby or even Keenan Wynn. Never mind how tough he wanted to be now, it wouldn't project that way. As a frail kid in a tough world, and as a lifelong mama's boy to a powerful and socially ambitious mother, he had developed a style he could never quite shake. With time, his cuteness would wear off (there are few cute middle-aged men) but the boyishness remained like a tattoo to narrow his movie possibilities in an unusual way, that is, it was always easy enough to find parts and movies for him, but hard to make him the star, the hero.

So Franky did the next best thing; he dropped the *y* from his name and learned how to act. For one thing, kid brothers can suffer, can't they? They could become drug addicts (for *The Man with the Golden Arm*), and they could sing about going "All the Way" (for *The Joker Is Wild*). And best of all, they could become obnoxious bums. And here real life would help him out with one of the best-disguised blessings in history by turning him into Public Enemy No. 1.

It is hard to convey now, and even harder to believe, the atmosphere in America just a couple of years after World War II. But imagine it this way: The public celebration is over and people have finally run out of excuses, but some of the crowd hasn't gone home yet, and is now spoiling for a fight with someone, anyone, before they have to disperse back into privacy. "Too much laughing turns to crying," as my grandmother used to warn, and somebody usually has to pay for getting you so drunk last night. So who can we still get mad at in the name of the U.S.A.? Although we didn't have enough outright traitors to keep the bonfires going, we did have communists, real and suspected, and comsymps and fellow travelers, and the ruckus we were able to make over these should have been enough vengeance for anyone. But puritans can be hard to satisfy, and there were a few other folk out there who had let us down badly, weren't there? And while we still had this length of rope anyway . . . And thus one arrived at perhaps the two most unlikely war criminals of all time: Ingrid Bergman for sinning against her role in *Casablanca* and running off with a foreign (ugh) film director, and Frank Sinatra for betraying his own publicity and doing what practically every man in America at least wanted to do—cheating on his wife and chasing after Ava Gardner.

Now wait a damn minute—isn't this the guy who sold us that dream? One of those guys, anyway. About thanking Dad for her dowry? Not that every postwar marriage in America had gone bad quite yet, but all of them had proved hard work, and precious few were like songs. And here was a guy who could actually afford babysitters and all the vacations he wanted, giving up on an allegedly perfect marriage. And Frank only got himself in deeper by singing a gorgeous Van Heusen love song to one "Nancy," which had in fact been written for somebody else's newborn baby, but which also happened to be his own picture-perfect wife's name, and that settled it. "Don't bother to explain. Never do we want to hear another note from this bum," who didn't sound that good anymore, anyhow.

Thus, one small footnote to history and one huge kick in the head for Burke and Van Heusen, who would thereby lose the use of half of their nest egg for another few prime years, and the full use of it forever, because when Sinatra did fight his way back into acceptance it was as a straight, nonmusical actor on-screen and largely as a singer of already-written standards on wax. And before things got even a little bit better, Burke was gone.

Which left the team with Bing Crosby and nothing but Bing Crosby—when he wasn't too busy. The trouble with Bing was that there wasn't enough of him to go around. Ominously, none of the occasional new singers that Hollywood was now trying to make into stars, from Howard Keel to Mario Lanza, was of a kind to share Crosby's workload. Which meant that although Bing might be overworked at the moment, he probably wouldn't be for long because his work was out of date; and when he closed up shop, that shop would not open again. The casual, unspectacular, original musical would be no more.

Thus, in bits and pieces, and in a deceptive fever of activity, Death began to make its presence clear to the old Hollywood. The Marx Brothers, for instance, made a new movie. For a second, it seemed like a comeback, but it was just a chance for them to take a last bow. And "Gable's back and Garson's got him" screamed the ads, but not for long. An old man returning to an old lady was really nothing to get excited about, or at least so it seemed to those all-important kids, of which, incidentally, I was one myself. And when Fred and Ginger put on their taps once again, they seemed older than time itself, even to young me, their keenest fan of my age in America. There's a limit to how much you can doubt your own eyes. Even half-blind with idolatry, I found myself wishing that Ginger at least would retire for good and Fred could just stick to dancing from now on and leave the romance, which was a bore anyway, to the kids—a heresy that I would take back after his next movie and never commit again.

By keeping his continuity in our eyes right through the war, Crosby did not yet seem so moribund, but the clock was ticking on him too. The remaining songwriters all wanted to grab at least one more ride on the old Bingo Shuttle, until there was hardly room for Van Heusen himself on his own life raft.

Meanwhile, Emerson's famous "Imp of the Perverse" entered the picture. In 1943, Bing with justified misgivings made the mistake of playing a priest on-screen in *Going My Way,* and now the Catholic hierarchy was holding him to it, not just in terms of future roles, but in terms of his off-camera behavior and image. Once a good example, always a good example, and suddenly Bing's natural tendency to keep his sins under his hat anyhow found itself reinforced by clerical mandates. As Gary Giddins showed in his excellent biography, Bing's sins became worse as his image got better, and apparently his sins worsened with every screen appearance. Burke and Van Heusen were stuck with the image, and a truly exasperating problem—Sinatra too sinful to get any part at all and Bing so virtuous his writers had to work the sunshine shift and write just the kind of "smile, damn you" songs they'd managed to avoid before.

Considering the extent to which it ran against their collective grain, the score Burke and Van Heusen concocted for *Going My Way* was astoundingly good, in the same way that *Oklahoma!* was in that same year—which might suggest that a sophisticated man can get away with one corny show, but he'd better not make it a habit. Because naturally they were asked immediately to do *Going My Way* again in the form of another priest movie called *The Bells of St. Mary's*. And this score would seem eerily professional—just right for a thoroughly second-rate occasion, but totally unlike themselves.

Okay—no sweat, just some time wasted and perhaps some sweat to come. Perhaps an expert on postwar booms could have seen what was coming. But *The Bells* exemplified the next problem around the corner: how to keep busy while protecting your talent, by absorbing the musical changes around you into your style so that you seem to have thought of them first. So that if you're suddenly asked to write, say, a mambo, it will be a Van Heusen mambo and not just an exercise in mambo writing. But suppose the public wants a mambo at one moment and a Charleston the next? The first years of peace could be called the years of cultural indigestion, as Americans wanted to try everything they had been missing, all at the same time, through a background ringing with salesmen and driveways honking with new cars as the austerity of wartime began to fill up like a Christmas pudding.

So what kind of music would you like to go with all this? Well, everything ever written would be nice. Thus in some suburban ranch houses and split-levels you might hear the latest LPs playing in one room while kids harmonized to "Moonlight Bay" in the next, or attempted to learn the rumba. And meanwhile, in the kitchen there was this guy demonstrating pressure cookers or ice cream makers, while in at least one of the five rooms, new radios blared selections from the world's million greatest hits.

That's what it seemed like, anyway, to a kid returning from England in 1947—or half of what it seemed like. The other half, the bestseller list and the Hit Parade, seemed to show no variety at all. One day, for instance, it seemed as if the whole city of New York had conspired to play the exact same record out of every door and window I passed, a dental drill of a song called "Near You" that apparently had the power to keep itself playing indefinitely. "There's just one place for me—near you." Couldn't there be at least two places for me? And was America really down to just one record?

One at a time, it seemed, until you got it home and looked at the mail-order catalogues. Later that same day, I visited an old friend's apartment and found a trove of great records that had just become available for the first time in years and featured enough old songs that I had never heard before to seem like a whole new movement. Thus a sturdy little betwixt-and-between generation was born that fell in love with the standards just as they slowed to a trickle, and then stopped altogether.

It was, as it always is, the best of times and the worst of times, but the good parts tended to be more and more private and the bad parts inescapable. It seemed that by 1945, the kids had seized control of all the jukeboxes and radios and wouldn't let go for a moment. And just like that, the magical coincidence of quality and popularity was over, the music in the public square was nowhere near the best music anymore. Listening to a program recently of the top pop hits from 1940 to 1955, I was startled all over again at how sharp the break was at the end of World War II, as if the bad stuff had been waiting for its cue. And perhaps it had, because several of the new hits seemed to depend on the latest gimmickry and special effects, to celebrate technology more than music. The kid at the piano syncopating everything had died in the war and been replaced by his country cousin.

As far as the number-one hits were concerned, the great Broadway shows had never happened, couldn't have happened. To cut a short story shorter, we lived in two musical worlds then, and the jazz world was losing. And Arthur Freed's great compilations of songs by Gershwin and

Kern, and so forth, were indeed "classical" now in the sense that the kids didn't listen to them much. Without new babies, the greatest nation perishes. And the mass audience was not willing to pay good money for any more new jazz babies.

So here was Van Heusen, still trying to churn them out on the piano as though nothing had happened. And his best bet was still to churn the songs through Bing Crosby, who seemed to enjoy some kind of immunity and could probably have made a gold record out of "Alice Blue Gown" or "After the Ball" in that peculiar time.

But the sunlight had begun to get in its licks on Bing the movie star too, if not Bing the singer. I remember wondering as early as his *Mr. Music* in 1950 whether "The Groaner" might be just a little too old to be courting this particular girl. It was a rigidly conventional time in our national history, as I recall, meaning that an actor only proceeds on such an unwholesome course if the lady insists on it.

As the English say, "Time, gentlemen, please." Or almost time. From roughly now on, Crosby would be down to playing married men or, God forbid, more priests, neither of which groups tended to march to the same drum as Jimmy Van Heusen, so perhaps it's not too surprising that Bing's only two Oscar nominations in the early fifties were both written by older, married men, which, on second thought, describes all the other songwriters left in Hollywood: "In the Cool, Cool, Cool of the Evening," by Mercer and Carmichael, and "Zing a Little Zong," by Robin and Warren.

Well, married men probably don't sing that much anyway, except to themselves (though Kathryn Crosby says that Bing never stopped singing around the house). By the time Sinatra came back in favor as a straight actor, Bing was heading the same way from the other direction, playing parts that had either no songs at all or that had just an occasional one or two to prove that he, like Frank, could still do it, as with the gorgeous Van Heusen and Cahn "Second Time Around" for Bing and their "High Hopes" for Frank. It was a starvation diet after the banquets of wartime. Jimmy eked it out as best he could with such crumbs from the commissary table as movie title songs to accompany the latest fad—protracted screen credits for films like *Indiscreet* and *The Tender Trap,* and occasional odd-job songs to cram into musicals like *Anything Goes* and *Star,* which needed a whiff of new stuff to go with the old stuff that was already in there, or genre songs like his virtually last "Thoroughly Modern Millie" to remind viewers of a particular time and place.

A diet consisting almost entirely of snacks is inevitably a thin one, but it was still better than anyone else's for reasons of his sheer consistency, and perhaps of studio politics, as played by his second and last new partner, Sammy Cahn. Van Heusen kept on getting assignments long after everyone else but Henry Mancini had packed in their music sheets.

Once again Van Heusen's technique for advancing himself had begun with simply making the right connection and letting nature take its course. The exact story of how Jimmy came finally to split up with Burke and proceed with the braggadocious Sammy Cahn has been somewhat muddied by Cahn's own inevitable boasting and everyone else's reticence. In Sammy's version, Frank Sinatra was always so eager to have Sammy write his songs that he personally engineered the partnership, in the manner of a Godfather, or the capo de capo to the stars that Frank liked to come on as.

But an equally plausible counterversion has the boozy but ferociously disciplined Bing Crosby ordering Burke to quit drinking, or else. Johnny, who might well have been bored and frustrated by postwar Hollywood by then anyway, shrugged and pushed off to the more congenial climate of New York—not exactly Siberia—where he and Van Heusen would actually write their last masterpiece together, "Here's That Rainy Day." Drunk or sober, Burke would also write maybe his own best-known words of all after that to go with Erroll Garner's classic "Misty." As with his fellow lyrical lushes Dorothy Fields and Larry Hart, Johnny Burke's real or imagined drinking never showed in his work.

Van Heusen himself never said why Burke quit. But Sammy Cahn made obvious sense as a replacement. To survive in a shrinking business, it was no longer enough to have talent or even character. What you needed most was hustle. And Jimmy, like many gifted people, was always happy to have other people do his hustling, as well as help give him a new sound and a new subject matter in lyrics. In short, being born again was suddenly the only way to go for him *or* Johnny.

In contrast, nothing had ever come easy to Sammy Cahn, and he wasn't geared to quit, now or ever. In the midthirties, when Sammy had come along, the country was falling down with would-be songwriters, and he was just another funny-looking kid from the Bronx trying to get noticed by someone. And he tried so hard that he would become kind of a joke in the business, as in "You're pulling a Cahn on me" or "Quit Cahning around." Like other hustlers, he never grasped the fact that at a certain point it's safe to stop boasting and let someone else do it for you. In his heart he seemed to feel that the only thing standing between himself and complete extinction was his own tongue. Of course, if Cahn hadn't had that particular temperament, we might well have never heard of him. And it's possible that we might not have heard quite so much of Jule Styne or Jimmy Van Heusen either.

What is particularly funny and touching about Sammy is that once he began writing for Sinatra again, he also wanted to be recognized as a member of the Rat Pack in full swing. Thus, he may actually have underplayed his real service to Sinatra, which was *not* to swing with him but simply to get himself to bed every night and to get Van Heusen out of bed the next morning to write the songs that made Frank seem what he no longer was, up to date.

But Sammy insisted on being a swinger, and in his memoir, *I Should Care,* he wastes no chance to assure us that he too had plenty of broads, thus paradoxically reminding us of the most repulsive side of Sinatra too—the celebrity arrogance that mistakes broads for real women and one-night stands for romantic conquests.

One now sees a cultural disconnect between what the Pack thought it was doing and the public's actual perception of it. In the original *Ocean's Eleven* film, for instance, Frank and the boys posed as their dream selves—combat veterans, which none of them was, who wanted to recapture the happy-go-lucky spirit of World War II with one last operation, a coordinated scam in Las Vegas that required more planning than Normandy itself. No doubt some cashiers and other small fry would lose their jobs, of course, but ho, ho, ho!

But no "over thirty" person can really fool a young one in any decade, let alone the sixties. We knew who they really were—a bunch of middle-aged 4-F millionaires on an endless spree, who are happy-go-lucky mainly because they have chauffeurs to drive them home later and lawyers to clean up the mess. They could never become what they thought they were, the advance guard of an edgy counter-counterculture that brought the generations up to par. They reminded hippies too much of their own daddies, and they probably even had trouble keeping up with Hugh Hefner and his Playboy mansion, where the real swingers lived on carrot juice and marijuana, and where Sinatra's Jack Daniel's bottle would have seemed like an antique.

There was one respect in which Frank Sinatra did remain up to speed—his music, which had a leanness and a sharpness that fit the changing times better than his smug, out-of-shape persona did. Singing, Sinatra could pass the Van Heusen physical, and the Mick Jagger test too. And it gave him some credibility with the young fans who ultimately determine who lives and who dies these days. Lots of fossilized entertainers were living out their days in the dry air of the desert, not changing a thing and knocking them dead at the Sands or Caesars Palace until both they and the audience were carried out for good. But Sinatra continued to be a presence to the whole nation's youth, and he owed an awful lot of it to the team of Cahn and Van Heusen.

Both of them. To hear Sammy tell it in his last years (as I did a couple of times, at exhausting lengths), he wrote the songs virtually by himself. But Sammy's self-promotion set up a critical counterforce. And some fans, myself included, have been tempted to go the other way and give him no credit at all. Since the songs Van Heusen wrote with Burke were on the whole unarguably better than the later ones with Cahn, Sammy must be to blame, no?

Yet with both men, Van Heusen's tune came first, and after much listening, I can't imagine how Sammy could have caught those particular notes better. His lyrics were every bit as right for Frank and his times as carrying moonbeams home in a jar had been right for Bing and his. It's just that polka dots and moonbeams were out and blowing your own horn and going all the way were in. By the same token, Jimmy's old tunes might have sounded almost too pretty to be true in an age of hard rock and heavy metal. Charm was out now, and machismo was in. Even a truly tender song like "All the Way" sounded, if you didn't listen too closely, like an ad for Viagra or whatever snake oil they were using back then. So Cahn did precisely what he had signed on to do: He found them both a way to change their styles without losing them.

But it isn't just sweetness that Van Heusen's later tunes lost, but also some freshness and unexpectedness. This was not the fault of either man. Sammy's songs with young Jule Styne sounded fresher too. As the last practitioners of a dying form, it was all they could do to avoid catching the plague that was killing all the other music. The one-shot deals that Van Heusen and Cahn were getting now, all those title songs and that "special material," were a far cry from the bonanzas of yesteryear, for which a studio writer like Warren might empty his desk drawer over the studio's head and be sure of one or two hits tumbling out. The creative law of averages that roughly regulates the ratio of hits to misses and of rosebuds to lemons had just been nullified. There was simply no time for all the misfires and wrong turns from which greatness unpredictably emerges. Where Jerome Kern had once said, "I don't do auditions," now each individual song had to audition and sound at least moderately good to some not-particularly-musical executives at first hearing, if the songwriter wanted to keep the shrinking field of other writers from beating him to the next assignment. To the highest batting average went the spoils, so Van Heusen began, perhaps unconsciously, perhaps not, to concentrate on that, and to depend more and more on formulas of which he was a master, just to get on base, never mind the home runs anymore. Henry Mancini later expressed his enormous admiration for Van Heusen's "logic," which was indeed extraordinary. Jimmy once showed Jonathan Schwartz precisely how to write a hit song from A to B and back—"Here, you take it. You write the rest of it, kid!" But, of course, neither Jonathan nor anyone else could write the rest of it without Chester Babcock guiding his fingers.

Van Heusen's formulas were instantly recognizable after you'd heard them, but nobody else could make them work because there was always at least one original twist among the theorems and equations that made the formulas jump to life. Jimmy probably held the lead in the "Why didn't I think of that idea?" stakes, and began piling up the Oscar nominations, but the best young talent was now in rock and roll, which is neither flexible nor modulated enough for the average movie's agenda. You can't play rock and roll in the background. And the other old-timers and would-be old-timers seemed to be cut off not only from the music in the air, but from their own life supports. You can't receive all your inspiration from listening to old records; it's like receiving your fresh air in cans. With all the skill in the world, a writer in the 1970s can only write an imitation of a 1930s song, not a real one.

Yet the new music had cut the old-timers off too. For a large part of the twentieth century, writers like Warren and Walter Donaldson had brilliantly adapted to changes of fashion in the jazz song. Several like Sammy Fain and Rube Bloom had made a fairly good fist of it with the bland, unaccented music of the fifties, with such margarine items as "Dear Hearts and Gentle People." Van Heusen and Cahn's first hit together, "Love and Marriage," demonstrated an equal willingness to play ball, within reason.

But rock was thundering and disorienting—not just a change of fashion, but total nudity, or something equally drastic. And the older songwriters couldn't really stand it, which didn't help. You had to think differently to write a rock song. Yet once your ears filled up on the stuff, it was hard to write anything else. "Selective deafness" was Cy Coleman's answer to this, shutting off the music in the air and on the jukebox and improvising on his memories. It may have worked for him, but for most people, listening only to the voices of the past is like living full-time in a museum. The best you can hope to produce is museum pieces—not collectors' items either, because great artworks have at least been out in the fresh air once.

And it is against this background that the later work of Van Heusen must be judged. Never mind how it compares with his best earlier stuff or how, incidentally, Cahn's lyrics compare with Johnny Burke's, but how does it stack up against Green Day's "American Idiot" or Christina Aguilera's "Beautiful"? Immortality can wait.

Van Heusen still had Sinatra, who needed him almost as badly. The class of 1940 was down to its last trick, and Sinatra had to decide year by year whether to stop running and become a monument, living on as a great but slightly out of it celebrator of last year's roses, or to wade into the latest catalogues, searching vainly for a few bars of music worthy of his golden but aging chops. The Greeks or someone must have had a myth about all this, of an old king and a receding tide, but by the end, Sinatra's incomparable technique was too subtly nuanced for the new songs, and one sometimes got the feeling that he was only singing them under protest and as badly as he could. Then a surprise like Kander and Ebbs's anthem "New York, New York" burst out, reminding one that Frank would never be completely out of it so long as there were still writers around who had been influenced by him. And one senses an answering spurt of youthfulness and gratitude on his part as he rises to meet, say, George Harrison's "Something" (in the way she moves).

There was still the team of Sammy, Jimmy, and Blue Eyes, until one day there wasn't. Although Jimmy lasted several years longer than almost anyone, he also walked away more briskly than most—and probably much more so than his feisty partner Cahn, who in a sense never quite walked away at all. Cahn went on like Yip Harburg and others, writing light verse for his own amusement and for anyone else he could find to listen, and to supply Sinatra with fourth and fifth choruses as long as Frank stayed open. As noted earlier, lyricists can go on adapting for at least as long as the average lifetime. But there does come a time when even a Sammy Cahn's phone falls silent.

Offstage, both Van Heusen and Frank finally wound down a bit too. Sinatra made a respectable marriage for himself outside of show business, and as far from another Ava Gardner fiasco as he could get. Van Heusen stunned his crowd by getting married too, not to some tomato, chick, or broad, but to an old girlfriend of Crosby's. Jimmy's friendship with Bing had been quieter than his lifelong spree with Frank (Bing was less ring-a-ding-ding than buh-buh-buh-buh), but it was every bit as steady, and amiably boozy too. So—the party was over, and as if to underline it, Bing's second wife, Kathryn, told me that Frank wrote a note to her husband not long before he died, expressing concern over Jimmy's drinking. "I know," she said with a smile, "I know." Any one of them could have written the note about any of the others.

Sinatra's records sound better than ever, Crosby has just been revived, and no doubt will be again, and to my ear Van Heusen's songs lasted the best of all—in the friendly hands not only of his buddies but of generations of jazz musicians who recognize that he had simply taken this kind of music a step further than anyone else had, except possibly Harold Arlen. Good music can now be brought back to life within seconds (as can bad music, of course). But some music comes back to life sounding old, and some young. Van Heusen's songs sound as though they were written this morning.

# Johnny Mercer:
# The All-American Voice

JOHNNY MERCER

"You have to start with John," Alec Wilder said to me one night. We sat on the porch, talking about that book we never got around to writing. Alec didn't need to say who John was. As mentioned earlier, in his pantheon there were just two first names, two saints, if you will: John (Mercer) and Frank (Sinatra). Everyone else had to grub along with two names.

"All roads lead through John," he added, and for a while that must have seemed true—not just the road to the writers but the road that ran between the past and the future. In the 1930s, Mercer's lyrics had done more than anyone's to split the difference between Tin Pan Alley and the Great

American Outback, between Broadway and Hollywood, thus widening the vocabulary and subject matter of the New York–based standards to embrace a new generation of audiences from all over. As the thirties moved along, Hollywood ceased to be New York West. Old vaudevillians like Bob Hope had been absorbed and reconstituted as Californians, other constituencies began to be heard from in the form of dancers like Buddy Ebsen and comics like Judy Canova, who would have looked just plain peculiar in evening clothes. And seriously—considering the number of kids who went to the movies now—wouldn't Gene Autry, the singing cowboy, really make a more suitable role model than Scarface?

The wave of primness that swept in as Prohibition swept out heavily favored country values over city ones. Jazz songs were speakeasy music— music to get drunk to, and worse. In fact, they were just right for 1940s film noir, which was all about cities and sin. There might be nothing positively sinful about this Gershwin fellow, but he undoubtedly wrote city music and indeed speakeasy music. Now that Daddy was out of the saloon at last, couldn't we try some family music for a change?

Although it seems far-fetched, the cycle actually would play itself out after World War II. Music lost its edge under Perry Como, and sin came thundering back in the new guise of Elvis Presley. But in the late thirties, there were still a couple of breakwaters against wholesomeness—the swing band movement, and the continued presence of the great songwriters. With Cole Porter in full spate and Mr. Kern just learning to swing, the jazz song was still mainstream enough. And if the words of the new songs said "From Natchez to Mobile, from Memphis to St. Joe," and celebrated the Atchison, Topeka, and Santa Fe Railway and "the visiting firemen from Kansas City," who cared where the tunes came from?

For once, the tyranny of lyrics came in handy—these were Mercer's songs and no one else's. And mind you, this wasn't just some city slicker with a road map of Dixie talking, but a regular good old boy. If Johnny Mercer wrote it or sang it, it automatically became country and western, and north and south too. So a couple of years later, in the forties, when America was called upon to perform its occasional miracle of seeming like one country, instead of fifty or a hundred, it needed a sound that could immediately remind kids from Brooklyn, Texas, Alabama, and the Pacific Northwest equally of home. Who better to turn to than Johnny Mercer? His voice was probably not quite the sound of your own neighborhood, but it definitely came from *a* neighborhood, a real one, a very American one, and one very much worth fighting for. So what if it also reminded you that America was very big? "My Mama Done Tol' Me" and "Accentuate the Positive" belonged to all of us, as did their author. As an average ten-something of the period, I can still remember Johnny as one of the Big Faces, next to people like Harry James, Der Bingle (Crosby), and the Andrews girls, with only two other songwriters in sight—Irving Berlin, who was left over from the last war, and Johnny's old partner, Hoagy Carmichael, who significantly also performed his own songs.

In reality, most of the lyrics our boys marched off singing were not by Mercer at all, but were merely of the "school of Mercer." Like Cole Porter, Johnny so dominated his corner of the musical universe that by December 1941 all songs of a certain kind were reflectively attributed to him, from Frank Loesser's "Small Fry" to Mack Gordon's "Chattanooga Choo Choo" to Tom Adair's "Let's Get Away from It All." Gossip, which is the research department of the obituary page, also prefers one superstar to several nebulae, and once established, Johnny's fame was self-perpetuating because his name was mentioned on radio, and other songwriters' weren't.

It was a vicious cycle to those who weren't in it, because Mercer's singing not only made his own songs famous, and vice versa, but it also put a lien on everything it touched. Johnny Burke's "Personality," for instance, is always assumed to be Mercer's because Mercer made the hit record of it. And Mack Gordon's "I've Got a Gal in Kalamazoo" goes to Mercer too, because Tex Beneke made the record and Beneke had a twang kind of like Mercer's, and besides has a name that takes at least twenty seconds to memorize, and who has the time?

To clinch his monopoly, Johnny looked and sounded exactly like people wanted him to: with a Huck Finn face, a gap-toothed grin, and an old shoe of a voice that reminded bandleader Paul Whiteman of a man singing in his sleep. Most of the great songwriters, as we've seen, looked like something else, but Mercer could have won an open casting call for the part of himself. When an artist resembles his work (as did Picasso, Gershwin, Hemingway), he seems twice as much of a genius, and frequently picks up all the marbles for his generation.

Yet although Mercer's reputation is by now almost as padded as

Dorothy Parker's with other people's creations, one finds little or no trace of serious resentment among his contemporaries. The consensus seems to be that (1) Mercer was simply too nice a guy for even a writer to resent, and (2) like Parker, he deserved his reputation, because he simply wrote better "Mercer" songs than anyone else. In terms not only of versification but also of sheer effectiveness (i.e., hits), Mercer's words were never just clever but extremely functional: "Bye bye baby/Time to hit the road to dreamland/You're my baby/ Dig you in the land of nod" caps its notes perfectly, punctuating them on the nose and making them sound as good as they possibly could.

Mercer may or may not have been the best poet among the lyricists, but he was one of the most musical, and he wrote enough "just right" tunes of his own to prove it. "I Wanna Be Around (to Pick Up the Pieces)" and "Something's Gotta Give" could not be improved melodically by Richard Rodgers himself, because Mercer—like Berlin, Porter, Loesser, and other complete songwriters—knew exactly what went where in a song and could always make up in aptness for what he lacked in musical brilliance. Mercer's special gift was to feel as at home with other people's tunes as with his own. If a hit could be found in a piece of material, Johnny would find it, or else he might put it there by changing a note or two. So the high road to Mercer Junction jostled with tinkers bringing their pots and pans, sharps and flats, to the old alchemist in hopes of a gold record.

But the roads Alec Wilder was talking about were also packed with old friends coming back for more. Anyone lucky enough to have caught Mercer's classic evening at the Ninety-second Street Y in New York in March 1971, or even to have heard a recording of it, can attest to the astonishing pleasure of his company. Mercer wasn't only entertaining but curiously authentic: Courtesy wasn't second nature to him; it was his essence. He didn't need to turn on the charm; he just had to be himself.

Above all, he didn't have one face for the public and another for friends. Everyone got the same Mercer, and as if to prove it, he warbled special greetings that night to some real pals in attendance—his old partner Harold Arlen; his teacher Yip Harburg; and Burton Lane, who just wrote songs—which warmed the whole audience the way great entertainers do. The entertainer whispers a private message, and a million people swear it's for them.

Like Frank Sinatra, Mercer never seemed to be addressing more than one person at a time—a person of immense importance to him. So if he was by chance addressing you, with the jokes and the compliments specially tailored for you, you would presumably walk through fire to keep in touch. And that's pretty much what you had to do, except that the fire usually came on your way out because Mercer also happened to be the meanest, cruelest of drunks this side of James Thurber.

As Wilder described it to me, when the bottle reached a certain level—he pointed to a spot two inches or so from the bottom—Johnny switched from friend to enemy in the course of a single sentence, flaying you alive with the nastiest crack he could think of. (He allegedly told Irving Berlin he had no talent for writing lyrics.)

Fortunately, Wilder, who had once suffered from the same malignancy himself, also knew the antidote: You sang a certain tune (he told me the name once, but I forgot it, and when I asked again, he'd forgotten it too), and Johnny would immediately burst into tears and forget what he was mad at. As every bartender knows, sadism and sentimentality are so closely wired in the human psyche that they constantly trip over each other in a drunk's head. But apparently only this one song would do it for Mercer, and if you didn't know it, you simply had to sing everything you knew while enduring the Jekyll-and-Hyde transformation and wait patiently for Johnny's flowers of remorse and the funny note that came with them the next day. Since Johnny could seldom remember whom he'd insulted, there must have been a lot of unexplained gifts. All his friends knew exactly what singer Jo Stafford meant when she said, "Please don't send me flowers tomorrow, Johnny."

Why a man drinks until his heart turns so black that he even hates the cat is a mystery understood only by the one doing it, and only while he's doing it. But one reason Johnny didn't quit is that it seems to have cost him no friends that he couldn't win back the next day. Nobody took it personally, for long at any rate. Whoever this foul-mouthed demon might be, he clearly wasn't the real Johnny Mercer.

So where *was* this unreal voice coming from? Drunken blather is a maddeningly opaque source, but one might find an echo someplace in the shadows and echoes of Savannah, Georgia, Johnny's hometown. He certainly came from pugnacious stock. An ancestor no more than four or five

generations earlier had gone down fighting in the Battle of Princeton during the Revolutionary War, while his great-grandfather Brigadier General
Hugh Weedon Mercer seems to have left the Confederate Army under a
cloud after the Civil War, brought on by his trial for the murder of two de-
serters. Perhaps old Hugh was doomed to roam the earth and pour his un-
used rage through the mellifluous pipes of his amiable descendant.

Such unearthly goings-on seem entirely possible as you wander the
moonlit squares of old Savannah, where the haunting of houses and of
people is like a plain fact of life. A young poet growing up here might find
it almost too rich, too overwhelming. What on earth could one write to
equal it? But at least Johnny was spared the handicap of living in a great
house or coming from a top family. The Mercer residence was and is a no-
big-deal affair on the outskirts of town. And, socially speaking, the Mercers were virtually arrivistes.

So Johnny grew up with an artist's double vision of Savannah, part
F. Scott Fitzgerald peering through the rich folks' windows, and part in-
sider, much too proud to be bowled over by what he saw. From a certain
point of view, he was in a rare position to look down on the town if he felt
like it. The Mercers were originally a great Virginia family, and when his
violent great-grandfather, General Weedon Mercer, married into Savannah in the 1840s, he had graduated from West Point and probably thought
he was doing Savannah a favor. Weedon Mercer would leave behind a decidedly mixed inheritance. On the upside, he built one of the greatest of
all great houses, thereby implanting the family name like a memorial in
the heart of the town, but then he saw to it by his army disgrace that no
Mercer would ever live in the Mercer house. His own last days were spent
out of gossip range in Baden-Baden, Germany. Meanwhile, he'd sown the
seed that would end up inside a man who could someday write "Any place
I hang my hat is home," which is either a very democratic thing to say or
a very arrogant one, depending on how you say it.

An artist never completely lets go of anything, but on a conscious and
working level, Mercer's drunken nonsense really did come from a phan-
tom of sorts, namely, the self he might have been if he hadn't been sub-
verted by American popular music from the age of six months, when he
hummed his first tune. Although his parents sent him to a posh Virginia
prep school called the Woodberry Forest School, he had already received

his basic education from the Victrola in the parlor, to which he listened with a child's ravenous capacity to learn, memorizing everything he heard and singing along with it.

Listening to those old Victrolas was an intense experience. The machines constantly needed cranking and the cylinders or records had to be changed every few minutes, and you'd better be paying attention. For the three minutes or so it lasted, the song was your whole universe, subsuming everything around it. To this day, I can remember the furniture around me as I sat listening to Mercer's early hit "I'm an Old Cowhand" as a tot in England.

If he'd heard anything but songs on the Victrola, he didn't bother to mention it. Basically, music for him would always be something that came with words. You might call the notes do-re-me or B-sharp and E-flat, or you might call them "I'm an old cowhand"—they answered to a thousand names, depending on the context, and matching them up became an early hobby. (He wrote his first complete song at age fifteen.) The only instrument he ever mastered was the human voice, which had to serve him as pianos serve other writers, as his lab, workshop, and rumpus room.

While still in his garbage-can years, absorbing everything, he picked up maybe his only non-American influence: W. S. Gilbert, who would become a crucial part of the mix. In most respects, Mercer might have come from a different planet than did Ira Gershwin and Yip Harburg, yet all three learned their ABC's from this same teacher, a Victorian English wit working in a language as remote from Southern vernacular as it was from that of the Lower East Side. No one trained in this school could ever be tempted by a rhyming-dictionary rhyme or a stale thought or a shabby word. Although Mercer would continue to use the dialect of his region, and everyone else's, he did it with the snap and the literacy of a Gilbert and Sullivan patter song. "But who was in the pantry a-laughin' and scratchin'/The waiter and the porter and the upstairs maid" (words and music: J. Mercer) isn't Broadway, but it isn't Tin Pan Alley either. It's what might be called "the Mercer compromise," a mishmash of high and low idioms that's both slangy and classy, an American *Upstairs, Downstairs* set to a jazz beat, and a quaint fragment of Mercer's autobiography, if you translate it a little.

Nothing sharpens the ear or the tongue like going from one social class to another, and that's pretty much what Johnny had to do, slipping out of the stuffy front rooms of Savannah society and into the pantry to find his voice and his material. At some unknown early date, he took to crossing over regularly to the black side of town, where he immersed himself so deeply in jazz and blues that he would one day receive a citation from a black social group calling him "our favorite colored singer." As Hoagy Carmichael, his partner in jazz, would say, "Johnny knew." For all his adaptability, there was a black-jazz base in everything Mercer wrote.

But the parlors of Savannah had their own siren song, and he never fully gave up his citizenship there either. In the sixties, when the writer Budd Schulberg asked Johnny if he could bring the great black pianist Hazel Scott to a party Johnny was giving, Johnny said, in effect, "I don't think it's that kind of party." The waiters and porters and upstairs maids might be his superiors in some ways, but he wouldn't know what to say to them if he found them in the parlor. In an old clip of Mercer appearing on the Nat King Cole TV show, Johnny looks friendly enough (he's there, isn't he?), but for once utterly tongue-tied, sheepish, and unsure of himself. He undoubtedly venerated black musicians: He led the singing of "Happy Birthday" on Louis Armstrong's fiftieth birthday at the Newport Jazz Festival in Rhode Island, and there's a picture of him in Bob Bach and Ginger Mercer's book *Our Huckleberry Friend* posed manfully cheek to cheek with Lena Horne. No one ever accused him of faking these overtures. It's just that in all his trips to the black side of Savannah, there is no record of his ever talking to anyone or making any friends. His manner with Nat King Cole is not that of an arrogant racist, but of a small boy who has never gotten over his shyness and slight fear. It may be that he crossed the tracks too early, before he could cope socially, but he had to be that young to get the gold, the beat.

Luckily for his peace of mind, Johnny's break with the upstairs life of Savannah was rendered infinitely easier by the Depression, which emptied a lot of parlors like his and removed yards of stuffing from American society. The real estate business of his father, George Mercer, went bellyup, and any thoughts the son might have had of writing for the Whiffenpoofs of Yale or the Triangle Club of Princeton went out the window.

Johnny had already been to New York, his dream city—the first time with a local stage company and the second time as a ship's stowaway—and he'd played a few bit parts in legitimate theater.

But then suddenly the sky was the limit. Survivors like John Cheever and Walter Kerr have testified to the giddy freedom young people felt during the Great Depression. "Goodbye, family business" was the song they were singing. "Farewell, old school tie." You were free at least to wait tables and wash dishes to your heart's content, and write songs and "dream, dream, dream," as Mercer's own song says.

The closest Johnny would come to washing dishes was serving as a Wall Street runner. But for once in history, songwriting proved a more solid profession than brokering. (People were doing a lot more singing than banking.) And in no time, Johnny was placing lyrics in shows and edging his way into the fraternity. His first sale, a bouncy number called "Out of Breath (and Scared to Death)" appeared in the Garrick Gaieties revue alongside an early effort by his next great friend, Yip Harburg, while a singing job with Paul Whiteman got John into a trio with Harold Arlen's ubiquitous brother, Jerry, who, as we've seen, would soon be writing lyrics with another future partner, Jimmy Van Heusen. So it went, like some hilarious frat party, as a brilliant new generation pulled into town, all set to take over from fuddy-duddys like Jerome Kern, Sigmund Romberg, and Vincent Youmans.

New York lived up to Johnny's dream so well that he remained somewhat starry-eyed about it until the day he died. By all accounts, the city has never been more charming than when it was dead broke and down at the heels, and there was no better place to watch it from than Paul Whiteman's bandstand, which seemed to be situated in the eye of the party. Everyone in music seemed to pass either through it or by it, and the gleeful Johnny met not only his heroes, the great songwriters who had raised him, but half the guys he would be working with in the coming years, including Whiteman's trombonist-singer, Jack Teagarden, his ex–Rhythm Boy Bing Crosby, and his violinist-arranger, Matty Malneck, with whom Johnny wrote "Goody Goody" and other goodies. Even Hoagy Carmichael, who would coauthor Johnny's first big hit, "Lazy Bones," had cut his first record of his first song with Paul Whiteman, the talent scout of the era.

In these circumstances, there was nothing to do but go ahead and become a songwriter. The choice may seem like a foregone conclusion in retrospect, but Mercer apparently couldn't believe his luck at first and was convinced only by his extraordinary success and the huge amount of work the boss gave him to do. Whiteman hosted a weekly radio show, and feeding special material to this monster is probably what made Mercer finally feel like the professional he'd been all along. Early hits like "P.S. I Love You" (music: Gordon Jenkins) suggest he was born professional, but it took a while for the country boy to stop scuffing his feet and calling people "sir" and "ma'am" and come into his estate.

He made the break with Savannah's rules official by marrying a New York showgirl named Ginger Meehan. Notarizing the split in his personality, so to speak, he marched off with the rest of the gang to Hollywood, which, as the Depression deepened, seemed like the last room in the house with the lights on. In 1935, Mercer signed on briefly as a writer and singing actor at RKO, but after two crummy movies, no one ever called him an actor again. As Mercer's name continued to penetrate the great American vagueness with songs he could sing himself, like "The Old Music Master" with Carmichael and "Bob White" (music: Bernie Hanighen), it didn't matter how hard the studios tried to bury his name between the art director's and the costume designer's; he was a star. "If you were a composer," says Margaret Whiting, "you tried to get Johnny Mercer or Frank Loesser, or else it didn't matter." And even Loesser felt Mercer was getting all the best assignments. Johnny reigned alone, in the public mind and in fact.

Thus, by his late twenties, the only question left to answer in that slaphappy community was: Who was lazier, he or Ira Gershwin? With Johnny and, I suspect, with Ira too, it was largely a matter of style. Although Mercer got through a prodigious amount of work, he appeared to do it all, like his singing, in his sleep. His preferred modus operandi was to lie on his back with his eyes closed like a psychiatric patient, as if he could dream songs into existence. But when Harry Warren tested this by saying, "How's Ginger?" on his way out to lunch one day, Mercer said, "She's fine," when Harry got back.

These naps must have been hives of activity as Mercer first mastered the tune, amazingly fast, and then laid various versions on it. Sometimes he opened his eyes with a complete lyric, and sometimes he came up empty. This kind of creation went in fits and starts. One particular assignment took him so long that Carmichael couldn't remember having written the tune when he finally received the finished song, "Skylark." But fast or slow, Mercer's style suited the image of casualness and added a finishing touch to his public persona. Movie people of the 1930s didn't have lives at all in the New York sense; they had anecdotes. And Mercer's laziness took care of all his duties in that department.

The shallowness of the legend can be gauged by a story Margaret Whiting tells. It seems that when Warner Bros. offered him the use of either Harry Warren or Margaret's father, Richard Whiting, as a partner, he said, "I guess I'll have to go with Dick—I think he can help me with my golf game." What Johnny remembered saying in his own, more sober, version was, "I'd rather work with Dick Whiting than with anybody," because he hero-worshipped Whiting for his work in the twenties even more than he hero-worshipped Warren. In the end, he managed to write with both of them: "Jeepers Creepers" with Warren and "Too Marvelous for Words" with Whiting. His golf game was never heard from again.

Likewise, the real Johnny probably closed his eyes not to relax but to "get in tune with the infinite," as he told his father. But he wasn't brought up to talk like that in public, or to talk about himself at all for more than a few minutes. So we'll never know. "I could tell you a lot/But it's not/in a gentleman's code" is how the lines originally read—and that went double for Johnny.

"Hooray for Hollywood," he wrote ironically (along with Richard Whiting), but artistically speaking, crazy old Hollywood gave him a lot to cheer about. The luck of the studio draw may have kept him from writing with Carmichael as much as nature had intended, but it gave him Harold Arlen instead, an even better partner in some ways. Mercer and Carmichael were so much alike, it might have been one man writing; with Arlen it was definitely two, each with an infinite capacity to surprise the other. "Blues in the Night," "One for My Baby," "That Old Black Magic," "My Shining Hour." What will he think of next? one imagines each of them thinking as he plunged in for more. And the system also gave him one dance with Jerome Kern, of which Johnny made the most. The persnickety Kern was so tickled by the lyrics to "I'm Old-Fashioned" that he summoned his wife to come listen—not an everyday occurrence in the Kern household. Mercer wrote just as well with Rube Bloom ("Fools Rush In") and Victor

Schertzinger ("Tangerine") as with the masters. Johnny Mercer was in the middle of a lifelong roll, and he wrote (and sang) like a happy man. Founding and helping run Capitol Records would be fun too for a while, giving him a chance to launch his spiritual daughter, Dick Whiting's orphan Margaret, on her great career and to give us the best of Jo Stafford. His records with Bing Crosby sound like a gas, as those two tightly coiled men vied with each other in feats of relaxation. "Allegretto, Mr. Crosby?" "Alligator, Mr. M." Singing with Crosby felt like family, as singing with Bobby Darin later would. It was the only style he knew.

Today his real family remains as private as ever, by unanimous consent. His marriage was perfect on the surface, as marriages were in those days, although people tend to roll their eyes when you mention Ginger, indicating perhaps that she was, or had become, a handful. His children, Amanda and John Jeff, were perfect too, as of course were Bing Crosby's and Joan Crawford's, but the real difference was that no one has ever wanted to write anything bad about Mercer, nor has anyone ever wanted to read it. Even the prodigious gossip mill has managed to cough up only one rumored affair, with Judy Garland. In movies, Garland never made a convincing romantic lead, but Johnny might have responded to the great singer and interpreter within.

Foraging for clues in the texts, one notes that he wrote not one but two mouthwatering songs of vengeance, "Goody Goody" and "I Wanna Be Around" ("And that's when I'll discover that revenge is sweet/As I sit there applauding from a front-row seat"), as well as some of the most roundabout love songs to come out of a most roundabout period. Like most American males, Johnny had a devil of a time with "I Love You," which the cheek-to-cheek dancing of the thirties and forties demanded a lot of, and he frequently resorted to far-out metaphors. The narrator of "Day In, Day Out" (music: Rube Bloom), for instance, feels a pounding in his heart whenever he even thinks of his loved one, which escalates abruptly into an ocean's roar and a thousand drums beating, the moment he makes contact. Clearly, this chap is inches away from cardiac arrest and must never kiss anyone again—or try to sing either.

But you don't take in the prose of the matter as you dance and hum across the floor, just sense a surge of primal feeling that seems to come from the music. And that's all that a love song strictly requires. Mercer piles the gorgeous sounds up to the roof, and if you wind up thinking, as I did for years, that this song is set in the tropics, so much the better. Johnny plants these travel-guide images subliminally enough for lovers to miss, with a dab here and a dab there, going (in "And the Angels Sing") from "water and moonlight beaming" to "long winter nights with the candles gleaming" and home again, like Dorothy returning from Oz, and you leave the floor thinking you've just had a wonderful dream.

Johnny's ballads are not great or even fairly good poetry, but they're superb musical poetry because everything fits. In his interview with Max Wilk, Mercer doesn't even mention poetry but talks about tunes, and the value of having a feel for them, of recognizing them, as Michelangelo allegedly recognized King David in a block of stone. Then, in the words of his colleague Oscar Hammerstein, "never let her go," and almost any old lyric will do. Mercer's own favorite song of all time, "It Had to Be You" (music: Isham Jones; words: Gus Kahn), bears a lyric of no distinction whatever, except that you remember it forever, after one hearing, because everything fits.

In short, Mercer was 100 percent professional, revealing next to nothing about himself in his work while seeming to reveal everything. A later partner, Bobby Dolan, used words like "listened," "learned," "absorbed," "transformed" to describe Mercer's trade secrets. His rumored laziness was long forgotten in his later period. Johnny was all business.

But there's always a little something besides professionalism in a Mercer song. Hacks walk away untouched when the job is done, but real artists go deeper, leaving behind bits of themselves. You'd swear there was a drop of Mercer's own blood in the gallon the man is bleeding as he sits at the bar, wailing about his code and his baby, although they may not be bleeding over the same thing. "When my life is through . . . then I shall tell them I remember you." Again, one doesn't have to take this literally: "You's" and "baby's" come and go, but the emotion in the sobbing is genuine if you listen to the subtext, which is the same in all Mercer's songs. "Isn't this a goddamn beautiful tune?" is what they're saying so passionately. "Can you hear what I hear? Please love it as much as I do."

Mercer was a man of more than one Rosebud, and if the Victrola in the parlor was his first true love, a second comes through almost as strongly. Without a doubt, what he liked best about Hollywood was that to get there and back you had to take a train: the only form of transportation ever devised capable of breaking a man's heart. Mercer seems to have dreamed about locomotives before he ever took one, and he remained a lifelong addict. "I took a trip on the train," he wrote for Jimmy Van Heusen, "and I thought about you." But I'll bet what he really thought about was more trains—not cardboard choo-choos leaving for Chattanooga and Alabam', whisking babies hither and yon, but real ones, blowing lonesome whistles across trestles on the way out of Philadelphia. Trains were worlds unto themselves, everywhere and nowhere, with parlors and pantries, uppers and lowers, chugging along together to a solid beat; and they were full of America and its talk, like rolling dictionaries of slang. No wonder Mercer's lyrics traveled so well. They were all written in the *lingo de club car,* not to mention of mothers whispering to infants and Pullman porters cajoling drunks into upper berths. "Time to hit the road."

So Mercer must have felt that things were truly winding down when both the songs and the trains seemed to stop running in the midfifties. But his mild bitterness about this did not consume him, as it did so many of his colleagues, or consign him to his memories. He revised his slang every year, popping in a "switcheroonie" in the fifties and using verbs like "bug" and "split" in the sixties and seventies. He kept going. As that great song with Carmichael says, "You can tell 'em I'll be there." This was a determined man, and while there was still a tune left out there unattended by an English lyric, he'd sing tenor or countertenor, and forget he'd ever heard of jazz if he had to, just to be there, giving his all. As the years went by, he laid words on top of French tunes such as "Autumn Leaves" and "When the World Was Young" and a swell German one called "Summer Wind" and a little something by Rimsky-Korsakov ("Song of India"). He did the best he could with Henry Mancini's maudlin "Moon River" and better than that with "Days of Wine and Roses," winning Oscars for both in a by-now-empty field. If he had slowed down, it wasn't because his creative powers were failing.

Even his one big disappointment was of a kind to keep a man trying. He couldn't seem to buy a hit show on Broadway, with the half exception of *L'il Abner.* Mercer's songs were private worlds, complete unto themselves, and they never seemed comfortable as parts of plays. So for all the ingenuity he poured into shows like *Texas Li'l Darlin',* *Saratoga,* and *Foxy,* he achieved only one Broadway standard, "Come Rain or Come Shine" (music: Arlen), from *St. Louis Woman*. Ah, well. He didn't much care for that mode of song-plugging anyhow, as he explained to us at the Y that night. Someone might steal your ideas while you dawdled through tryouts and cast changes. Still, if you had a good story for him . . .

Meanwhile, offstage, he kept on going around, like the whirling dervish he wrote about, doing people "real good turns" in the private sector. He secretly paid off his father's Depression-related real estate debts, only to have the press get hold of the story, which a cynic might say was the best of all possible outcomes. He cofounded the Songwriters Hall of Fame, apparently to cheer up an old friend called Abe Olman, who had found life a touch stale after co-writing the hit "Oh Johnny, Oh Johnny, Oh!" in 1917. And he did more small acts of kindness than he ever wanted people to know about.

In my mind, his last days will always be entwined with Alec Wilder. One late-summer evening in 1975, when Johnny Mercer was ill, I remember Alec mentioning in passing that he couldn't for the life of him remember that song that neutralized John's drunken rages. Not that it mattered anymore. When I next heard from Wilder, he said, "Did you hear that John died?"

A stroke, a tumor, life support—Johnny loathed and avoided hospitals, so there's no reason to hang around one now, and even less reason to end his story there. After dying on June 25, 1976, Johnny resumed official residence in Savannah, where his body now lies alongside his wife's and parents' in Bonaventure Cemetery, of which it is said locally that it is almost as good to be dead there as alive anywhere else. Typically, his grave does not have pride of place, which belongs by protocol to his father's first wife. His is the next one over and bears the simple legend "And the Angels Sing." Ginger's headstone says "You Must Have Been a Beautiful Baby." Amen and amen.

Whatever ambiguity Brigadier General Weedon Mercer may have left behind has been long since cleared up. Johnny owns the town now, with a boulevard and a theater named after him and with his own personal sign in the cemetery pointing to his grave. And maybe he has brought Savannah some good luck in return by helping to inspire John Berendt's evocative book *Midnight in the Garden of Good and Evil*, which has filled the town with the kind of tourists who don't want to change anything, a rare and valuable breed.

But one can't imagine Johnny staying put year round. Johnny may have been an Episcopalian choirboy once upon a time, but his spirit was always pure pantheist and can still be found in woods and streams and blossom-covered lanes—not to mention railroad depots, late-night saloons, and any town in America that has a funny name. All you have to do is whistle. Or, if you can still find one, hop a train going anywhere, and listen.

Part Five

Survival on Broadway—
The Curtain That Won't Stay Down

# Frank Loesser's
# Great New York Musical

FRANK LOESSER

$S$imply in terms of keeping up with the Joneses—the Romes and the Parises—both world wars were quite good for New York. At the end of World War I, New York emerged fully armed as a great world city, as if it had been rehearsing and designing sets all along, and here it was, complete with its own Left Bank (Greenwich Village) and Rue de Rivoli (Fifth Avenue) and London's West End (Broadway), only with lights.

But then suddenly at the end of the real world war, New York was the *only* great world city. But it wasn't quite the same New York, and two musicals tell the story. *On the Town,* by the team of Comden and Green and Leonard Bernstein, is about New York as seen from the outside by its first postwar tourists, the U.S. military. Every time you turned around in 1945, the fleet seemed to be in town and fracturing New Yorkers' most venerable rule by actually looking up at the buildings. (Did they think they were in Kansas City?)

Naturally, Broadway was on the tour. But to get there you had to wade through, or bypass, the district called Hell's Kitchen, where a quite different New York was in the works. *West Side Story* is all about that world, and as always with this city, it is full of strangers, but their foreign accents have changed and they dance to a very different drummer. And as the Jets and Sharks act out their blood feud, it's hard to believe that just a few years and blocks away, the Algonquin wits zinged each other with one-liners and left it at that. So it was perhaps appropriate that the scores to both these guidebooks were written by Bernstein, a New Yorker with a deep feel for the city but with a Carnegie Hall accent and point of view, capable of turning out brand-new folk songs without a trace of Tin Pan Alley about them.

However, there was still life in the old Alley. It was trickling out of Hollywood and taking up full residence in the Brill Building. It was less like an alley now and more like the United Nations building, with Alexander Borodin's music being placed in Baghdad for the show *Kismet,* and the Austrian Fritz Loewe contributing scores set in Paris, London, and Scotland. Or, as Cole Porter put it, "We open in Venice." And we next play Bali Hai and the palace in Siam.

Amid this smorgasbord of styles and places, the Alley struck in 1950 with its most authentic and welcome gift: nothing less than the great *New York* musical and the most brilliant evocation ever of the city where the songs and shows and so many of the writers came from. It dawned on me, as I reach for my pencil, that the last act of *Guys and Dolls* is still being written at this very moment, because right outside my window the streets of Manhattan are undergoing a transformation that will permanently move the setting of this glorious story beyond the reach of living memory. Thus, I decided to write this last-minute salute to a part of the New York imagination that would never be imagined quite so well again. Unless we somehow get lucky.

Walt Disney, meet Damon Runyon: It's a New Yorker's worst nightmare. So ever since the Disney company announced its plans to renovate the *Guys and Dolls* country, aka Times Square, old-timers have had visions of theme parks full of wax figures dialing imaginary bookies, while Harry the Horse quietly turns into Horace Horsecollar, Louie the Lip splits into Huey, Dewey, and Louie, and Mindy's Bar and Grill changes its name to Minnie's Ice Cream Emporium. No Smoking Anywhere, of course.

Say it ain't so, Nathan. And so far, it ain't . . . quite. But the Disney people seem bent on making the formerly seedy Times Square area wholesome, a shining suburb on the hill, full of empty space and clean air. A Runyon character might experience difficulty breathing in such an atmosphere. If he were still around, that is. Luckily for Disney, most of Runyon's originals left town years ago, sometime between the death of the nickel phone call and the arrival of offtrack betting. No doubt Harry the Horse is now on the Internet, wondering why Big Louie insists on the Mac, while Bennie Southgate mows the lawn in his Bermuda shorts. Meanwhile, their old hunting ground had become an urban wasteland like any other, where telephones dangled from broken hooks and first-night audiences showed up in blue jeans, the way they do it in Moscow.

So maybe the best Disney could do was clean it up and start over. No doubt, the dirt will be back. Either way, history doesn't care, because by good chance the old place has been preserved forever in maybe the most authentic folk-musical we have. As we've seen, you could move Rodgers and Hammerstein's *State Fair* from Iowa to Oklahoma, or the South Pacific or the Austrian Tirol, and it would still be the same old place: Broadway, in the Scarsdale years.

But in the same period, a couple of real New York guys had put their heads together and managed to replicate this time and place with pitch-perfect fidelity, down to the last pari-mutuel ticket floating in the gutter outside Sardi's. And they locked it into a script so evocative that *Guys and Dolls* may also be our most cast-proof musical. Give it to any group of actors you like, from Englishmen to inner city African Americans to surfing high school students from Malibu, they'll all wind up reminding you of New Yawk.

And the aforementioned two guys accomplished all this in spite of Damon Runyon. All that Mr. Runyon of Florida and Colorado actually did was take one strand of New York speech—the occasionally eloquent pedantry of self-taught street guys on their best behavior—and reduce it to a formula as easy to imitate as Jimmy Cagney reciting Ernest Hemingway.

So Frank Loesser kept Runyon's three-page plot and his characters' names and wrote some songs in his own language, and Abe Burrows wrote some dialogue in *his* own language around the songs, and Loesser wrote some more songs around the dialogue, and Presto!—Times Square as it was and always will be. "Sidown, you're rockin' the boat," "I got the horse right here"—the phrases come straight off the street, as if the actors had just rushed them into the theater, as they do in "Waiting for Lefty."

Only more so, because they are set to equally red-hot, street-smart tunes, which is where the genius comes in. Ask anyone what he remembers best about the show and it's a probable, twelve to seven, he'll shoot back with a song title or phrase: "Take back your mink/To from whence it came," "It's a cinch that the bum/is under the thumb/of some little broad."

Once upon a time, New Yorkers really did talk like that, and a few still do, but Henry and Julia Loesser most decidedly had not raised their little boy Frank to do so. What he was supposed to talk was German, and the songs he was supposed to write, between symphonies, were presumably German lieder. The Loessers were Prussian immigrants fresh off the boat and for all of their high-minded lives they carried a torch, a blowtorch in fact, for high culture.

So Frank, one of nature's lowbrows, had his work cut out for him from the cradle. Since his old man was a well-known classical piano teacher, Frank's wayward genius warned him to avoid piano lessons at all costs— although he apparently could play the instrument anyhow, by instinct. And since his mother was a snob at large, he naturally took to talking like a Dead End kid or stage-gangster, apprenticing himself to the culture that came in through the window, the music of the street, as thoroughly as a Juilliard student learning his Bach and Mozart.

Yet Frank also loved his parents, and at the age of sixteen would wander the streets desolately himself after his father suddenly up and died. Although Henry is best remembered for the screaming rages that terrorized his students, and although Julia would remain, according to her granddaughter, Susan, cold and unapproachable to the end of her days, young Frank emerged from this menacing household bubbling with confidence, as if he'd just had the happiest childhood in history. So the Loessers presumably loved each other, whatever they thought of the rest of us, and they especially loved Frank, whose preternatural charm and good humor show up even in his baby photos and would serve him as a talisman against malice all his life. No one could ever stay mad at Frank for long, either as a child or as an adult.

Which is just as well, because he grew up to be a Loesser himself, in an upside-down sort of way, with a ferocious, perfectionist temper just like his daddy's. Eyewitnesses swear that they saw both his feet leave the ground together midtantrum. And on one famous occasion, he actually slugged the singer Isabel Bigley for messing up at a rehearsal. But his rage was so theatrical and kind of funny, and over so quickly, that it left no serious trace on anyone. (Except on Frank Sinatra, who never forgave Loesser for telling him how to play Nathan Detroit. The nerve of some people.)

The other thing Frank got from his family was a sufficiently thick skin to survive on Broadway, in Hollywood, or in Hell itself. The Loessers flung criticism around like cream pies in a silent comedy, and even after Frank became rich and fairly famous, his half-brother, Arthur, would write a lordly put-down of all pop music as being ephemeral "merchandise" which was rammed "down the ears of an abject public." (He admitted that his brother, Frank, did it quite well—but so what?)

Arthur Loesser had by then become Cleveland's arbiter of taste, and his condescension borders on the comical, not to say the maddening. Yet the two men apparently rejoiced in each other's company. And icy old Julia stayed close too, in the curious family style of loving the man and hating his music. "Baby, It's Cold Outside" simply doesn't sound like an art song, even in German, and neither does "Bloop Bleep," Frank's meditation on leaky faucets. By the end, Frank's royalties had swept Julia up from genteel poverty to the top of the hog, but neither she nor Arthur could ever face the possibility that the author of "Bloop Bleep" might be the real musical genius of the family and themselves the stooges and straight men in his life story.

Frank seems to have had trouble facing it himself. When he first edged into songwriting in the early thirties, it was strictly as a lyricist, not a tune guy. By then the Depression was raging and no form of making money was to be sneezed at, even by the Loessers, who hit bottom right after Henry's death in 1926. So Frank wrote some material for vaudeville and such while his mother waited for him to find a real profession. As Richard *"Damn Yankees"* Adler describes him a few years later, this should not have been a problem, even in the worst of times, since he was also a "skilled astronomer, a master carpenter and cabinet maker, a terrific cartoonist." So why go on with a career his family despised?

Well, astronomy didn't pay that well, and there wasn't much call for cabinets, and one song led to another . . . until thirty years had gone by in a twinkling, with his mother still waiting for him to find a profession. By the time Frank hit Hollywood in 1937, his new partner, Hoagy Carmichael, would find him "so packed with ideas, he was overloaded." But they were still ideas for words only. It took another five years or so for anyone to find out that Loesser could write tunes too.

So he settled for being the best or second best lyricist in Hollywood in the late thirties and early forties, depending on how you rate Johnny Mercer. As with Mercer, his double gift gave him an almost unfair advantage in the race for hits, because his words were not just clever but musical. They made the tunes they went with sound their absolute best. Songs like Burton Lane's "The Lady's in Love with You," Victor Schertzinger's "Sand in My Shoes," and almost everything he wrote with Jimmy McHugh— "Let's Get Lost" and "Say It (Over and Over Again)"—are good songs that sound like great ones because of Loesser's touch.

"Don't get a clever rhymer," he said to Jule Styne, after the two of them had together written "I Don't Want to Walk Without You" and gone back to their separate studios. When a genius gives advice, he's usually talking about himself and it's a sure sign of a Loesser song that afterward you can't be absolutely sure whether it rhymed or not. A Loesser lyric is a poem that you forget is a poem because there's so much else going on. Not even Mercer could sound so natural while being so literary. "I've got spurs that jingle jangle jingle." Who else on Tin Pan Alley ever wrote a song about his spurs or packed so much music into a verbal phrase?

The other thing the Hollywood years revealed was that Loesser didn't turn his ears off when he crossed the Hudson. He continued to pick up phrases from all over, including places he'd never been. "Small Fry" (music: Carmichael) is so all-American that people assume it must be one of Mercer's, and "Murder, He Says" (music: McHugh) remains the best guide we have to the slang the kids were using in World War II. And then there's "I get the rumble seat ride," which conveys not just the sound of middle-American life, but the whole texture of it. "When there's a company weekend/I get the couch in the hall" (McHugh again). As a boy, Loesser had somehow managed to get thrown out of both school and college, but this was obviously because they couldn't keep up with him; no one could teach as fast and as well as he could learn on his own.

Finally, his gift of melody came squirming out, not cocky like everything else about him, but as a last resort. In 1941, America needed a patriotic song right away to match the suddenness of Pearl Harbor. In no time, lyricist Loesser found just the phrase he wanted, "Praise the Lord and Pass the Ammunition." A real chaplain had said it, never guessing it was just what the nation needed: something jaunty but not irreverent, as if to say, "We're a God-fearing nation, but we're not pantywaists, by golly."

The only trouble was that no one could come up with a tune fast enough that caught this mood as well as Frank's own dummy version did, so out it came at last, a rollicking hymn that perfectly launched Tin Pan Alley's war effort, with a wink at God and a growl of determination and a subtext that said "This war is going to be a riot."

But one song does not a great songwriter make, and Loesser's next wartime classic, "They're Either Too Young or Too Old," would find him back safe and sound in the studio system, writing words to Arthur Schwartz's tune. And so it might have continued if it hadn't been for the war itself and its manic demand for entertainment. In the fall of 1942, Frank decided at his own whim to become a private in the U.S. Army—perhaps the only private ever to have all his uniforms tailored.

He was eventually stationed by a prescient War Department in a hotel just off Times Square, where his only duty was to manufacture entertainment on the double, any way he knew how. This meant that if he thought up a lyric, he had better provide his own tune, and stand by to sing it too, in a voice he once compared to that of an auctioneer, and in an accent somewhere to the right of William Bendix. Thus, under the lash of military discipline (he was once reprimanded for sleeping when he should have been meeting the general), his knack for matching the tune to the circumstance surfaced once again and earned him the title of "the GIs' own songwriter." "What do you do in the infantry? You march, you march, you march" captures the essence of war, namely, the drudgery and grumbling; the song makes your feet hurt just to listen to it. So the brass rejected it and the infantry marched to it anyway.

Loesser's own war doesn't sound that drudging—three suites at the Navarro Hotel is a long ways from a pup tent or a foxhole—but he'd already known for several bad years in Hollywood what it was like to dine on a can of beans for two, so now he captured the stoicism and frustration of the real grunts to their total satisfaction. "Ain't I never gonna get a girl in my arms?" was his other big army hit, and the tune self-mockingly whines to set the precise mood. The U.S. was winning the war, and that was great, of course, but it wasn't happening quickly enough for the singer to get started with the fräuleins and mademoiselles, and he was having a high old time feeling sorry for himself about this.

Clearly, Loesser's songs now belonged in stage musicals, where the music helped the story, or was the story. However, he returned to Hollywood, where the songs had nothing to do with the story, but were instead dotted around like comfort stations among the clichés. The big difference now was that the dam had broken. Frank wrote some tunes himself, including the gorgeous standard "Spring Will Be a Little Late This Year" and the semistandard "I Wish I Didn't Love You So."

And by the late forties, when television ended the party and Hollywood had kicked most of its songwriters out, or at least off the payroll, half of ASCAP was milling up and down Broadway looking for work. Frank found himself back on the Broadway job line with the likes of Ralph Blane and Burton Lane and Sammy Fain, watching the aristocrats Berlin, Rodgers, and Porter sweep by in their limos.

For once, though, luck was a lady to Frank. He agreed to write the lyrics for the kind of show that usually closes after one horrible night in Philadelphia—a musical based on the Victorian farce Charley's Aunt. At the late minute, the composer Harold Arlen's house burned down and Frank was asked to write music as well as words for this dog. He seized the moment, dashing off some Englishy-sounding songs (as he would later write Danishy-sounding ones for the film Hans Christian Andersen) that, with the strenuous help of Ray Bolger, made Where's Charley? the surprise hit of the Golden Age of Musicals.

Broadway success comes fast or not at all. With one show behind him, Frank was on a collision course with immortality. He'd proved he could write all the types of songs you need for a musical, from ballads ("Once in Love with Amy") to comedy ("Make a Miracle") to bits of business. His neo-Californian soul ached for New York, and these were the two chief prerequisites for the masterpiece he was about to write. All he needed was a fellow spirit to help with the libretto, and this he already had, though it took him a minute to realize it, and a couple of more minutes to nail his man down.

Frank first met Abe Burrows at a party in 1943, where Abe, as was his wont, was making up and singing a funny song called "I'm Strolling Down Memory Lane Without a Single Thing to Remember." Frank liked it so much he wrote it down, which was a good thing, because Burrows claims in his book *Honest, Abe,* the next day, he, the composer, had forgotten the song completely.

It was friendship at first sight, and it rapidly ripened at the omnipresent pianos of the period, where the two self-taught musicians took turns improvising new songs, or improvising them together, until it was hard to tell who wrote what. But one that they definitely did concoct together suggests they'd started work on *Guys and Dolls* long before they knew it. "Leave us face it/we're in love" could have been inspired by either Nathan Detroit or Miss Adelaide. "Leave us not blush with no shame/if people bandage our name." By George, they'd got it. Even before they needed it.

Abe Burrows was a New Yorker through and through, born and raised in, respectively, Manhattan, the Bronx, and Brooklyn (like many New Yorkers, he found Queens unnecessary), but not exactly in the streets. The Burrows family was as respectable as you can be on a shoestring, and Abe's own earliest ambition was to be a Latin teacher. But the streets crept in, and Burrows grew up sounding, in his own words, "the way Jersey City residents think Brooklynites talk and the way Brooklynites think people from Jersey City talk." Which, if you split the difference between the two locations, lands you somewhere near Times Square.

Abe's second ambition had been to be a businessman like the only successful adults he knew, but once again the Depression took over, drastically downsizing Wall Street and reducing Abe to selling all he had: his wit. A customer where he worked thought he was funny, introduced him to a gag-writer, and away he went.

By the time Frank Loesser met Abe, he was the head writer of the immortal radio program that began with the words "Hello, this is Duffy's

Tavern, where the elite meet to eat—Archie the manager speakin', Duffy ain't here . . . oh hello Duffy," which is vintage Burrows right there, half-Virgil, half-Brooklyn. You can't write good slang if you don't have a poet's heart and a solid beat, and it's no accident that one of Burrows's throw-away lines of dialogue for *G&D*—"the oldest established permanent float-ing crap game in New York"—sounded like a song to Loesser the moment he heard it.

In his five years at Duffy's Tavern, Abe blazed whole new trails in bad English. Characters like Clifton Finnegan, Clancy the cop, and Two Top Gruskin did not require that a person stand on ceremony, and before his time there was up, Burrows even received a diploma in bad English from the master himself, Mr. Runyon, who wrote him a note praising the show's dialogue and admitting that his own was a fake.

After the war, Abe performed solo for a few years in cabarets, radio, and TV, for which he did a show called *Breakfast with Burrows* that aired at nine P.M. ("I sleep late"), which produced yet more songs and song ti-tles in the Loesser-Burrows vein, which now ran straight through both of them. After *G&D*, Frank would write an homage to their partnership in the form of a song in *The Most Happy Fella* called "Likewise, I'm Sure," which was actually one of Miss Duffy's taglines, but could have been writ-ten by either one of them. As Pogo might have put it, they had met two-headed Gruskin—and he was them.

So when they at last put their heads together for *G&D*, their heads didn't have far to go. And it's nice to imagine the moment of recognition "You?" "Yes. You too?" and then firing lines at each other, like jazzmen ex-changing riffs, competing and collaborating in one breath and hitting the gong again and again. "Marry the man today and train him/sub-sequently," "You'll know at a glance/by the two pair of pants," "What's playin' at the Roxy?" "What's inna *Daily News*?" There should be a picture of this mo-mentous cataclysm in the National Gallery.

"They were just a couple of mugs," Abe's son Jimmy says fondly, and it's a tribute to how thoroughly Loesser had willed himself into this role that Jimmy assumed he had worked his way up from the gutter, not down to it. "If you heard his voice in the next room," says lyricist Richard Adler, sharpening the point, "you'd swear he was a street-corner bookie," except that Loesser's version came with both words and music. "And just a minute boys/I got the feedbox noise," "The name is Epitaph/he wins it by a half"—even the horse players in the audience must have relaxed as this song rang out, starting *Guys and Dolls* on its run to infinity. This was clearly a show in which a person could repose his confidence without fear of being sold a bill of goods by parties ignorant whereof they spoke.

But *Guys and Dolls* is more than just the sum of its great lines. It is also a superb piece of theatrical construction, with a great opening and a dandy close and maybe the best first-act curtain in musical history: Sky Masterson has just sung the loveliest song in the show, "My Time of Day," and won the girl, when the mission house door flings open and the gamblers fly out in all directions, pursued by a red-faced Lieutenant Brannigan.

The show is also one of the minute number of musicals without a single weak tune. So these were the respective directions the two men would take off in afterward: Burrows into construction work as a play doctor and director, and Loesser into ever more ambitious tunesmanship. When you're born to do a particular masterpiece, you're not going to do anything else quite so well, but neither would rest on his laurels. (Loesser could barely sit still.) Burrows's fingerprints can be found all over the Broadway history of the fifties, while Loesser's scores for *The Most Happy Fella* and *Greenwillow* show him out of the closet all the way, as a serious composer by even his family's standards.

Having proved these points, the two mugs joined forces one more time for the admirable show *How to Succeed in Business Without Really Trying,* giving Abe a chance to thumb his nose at the career he never had, and Loesser to celebrate one he did have—because it goes without saying that he was a crackerjack businessman too, in his spare nanoseconds. As the founder and proprietor of Frank Music Corp. music publishers, he was, among other things, "a better copyright lawyer than the lawyers who worked for him" (Adler), not to mention, no doubt, a better typist than his secretary and a better accountant than the computer. Loesser's weakness, if you can call it that, was too much talent and too many ideas. He spent a frustrating five years after *How To* concocting elaborate plots for musicals that went nowhere. Maybe they were just *too* clever, or maybe luck had decided to get back on the shelf and blow on some other guy's dice for a change. More to the point, the Age of Aquarius was just around the corner and Frank liked nothing about it, starting with its music. So when the five years or so were up, he quit, at least for a while, absentmindedly closing an era on the way out. In the catalogue of revivals, *How to Succeed in Business* now figures to be the last of the great post–World War II musicals born of the Depression, war, and jazz, and everything since simply has to be called something else.

So, as fan magazines say, what was he really like? Exactly the same as you thought he was. His peculiar family kept him from ever getting seriously stuck on himself, and the first and last word everyone I talked to used about him was not "brilliant" but "nice"—nice to everyone, that is, not just to cronies but to such unpromising groups as strangers, lawyers, and other people's children. Jimmy Burrows, who knew him from infancy (and who, incidentally, would grow up to direct the splendid TV equivalent of *Duffy's Tavern,* to wit, *Cheers*), even manages to glow over the telephone as he speaks of Frank.

But the best of all character references comes from that sternest of judges, one of Loesser's children. Susan's loving, sparkling book, *A Most Remarkable Fella,* hides no warts, neither his nor anyone else's. She reveals that her father had a terrifying temper, at least to a child, and that when he turned it on her for the first time, swear words and all, "It was annihilation. . . . I felt sure I was being blown to bits." His perfectionism was scary too, albeit exhilarating, because his appreciation was as extravagant as his rage, and everyone wanted a piece of it. But his disappointment could be towering too, and it took him much too long to realize that his laid-back son, John, had a right *not* to be a genius if he didn't want to be. Also, Loesser smoked too much.

And there the warts end, to be drowned in the howls of laughter one imagines echoing through the Loesser household whenever Frank was around, or whenever one of his letters arrived from someplace else. Better than nice, he was funny, and unlike most pros, he took at least as much trouble entertaining his family as he did the paying customers, with a stream of cartoons, comic verses, and thoughtful gifts. The man was alive every minute of his life, expending enough energy to light up a baseball stadium or small city, not to mention a living room.

Perhaps it was too much. There are hints in Susan's book that Loesser's gregarious vitality simply overwhelmed his first marriage, to her mother, Lynn. Many of Susan's early memories take place in a daze of Hollywood parties and a wash of alcohol, which he burned up like so much fuel for his high-combustion brain. He could even start his workday with a predawn dry martini, like a Rabelaisian giant downing a barrel of mead before battle. (Susan denies this, but my source is good enough to suggest that maybe, sometimes, anyway, a man tends to get the legends that suit him.)

Loesser's wife Lynn, being merely human, seems to have fallen apart somewhat trying to keep up, and became known, inevitably, as "the evil of the two Loessers." No one in that set escaped without a wisecrack, and this one followed poor Lynn, who had once been the life of the party, to the grave and beyond.

But nobody, including Lynn, seems to have gotten really angry at Frank when the marriage finally broke up and he married, instead, the genial young singer Jo Sullivan from the cast of *The Most Happy Fella*. His talisman still worked, because as usual he behaved as decently as circumstances allowed—but also because, if you got angry, you might miss the next joke.

In the end, Susan holds only one thing against her father, and that is the maniacal smoking that eventually killed him in 1969, the year his beloved New York Mets won the World Series. (To repeat, he was interested in everything.) And even on this she can imagine him giving her an argument, in a loud voice in her head. "It was my life, kid." Dramatically speaking, this ghost has a point. Frank wasn't about to write rock and roll, and one can't imagine him hanging around as a museum piece, writing oldies for the old folk. He'd had a perfect life of its kind—why spoil it with a sour old age? He'd accomplished his main mission here on earth, which was obviously to write *Guys and Dolls*. That show, and the world it celebrates, will be around long after George Steinbrenner has turned Times Square into a skating rink and moved it to Englewood, New Jersey, with Donald Duck in hot pursuit.

Frank Loesser, as his daughter stresses, wrote entirely for the moment, not for immortality. And the odds can go on forever against your ever seeing this particular parlay occur more than once in a person's lifetime. After that, quick curtain, and out.

# Gershwin's Last Heir:
# Burton Lane

BURTON LANE

*A*nd then there were none.

Of the handful of musical geniuses who lit up the smog of Hollywood in the golden thirties and the off-pink haze over Broadway in the plutonium forties and fifties, Burton Lane was the last to leave this planet in January 1997, turning off the lights as he left.

Not that the composer of *Finian's Rainbow* and *On a Clear Day You Can See Forever,* and a peck of fine individual songs to boot, had ever seemed like the end of anything to his friends. When I last heard him a couple of years before he died, he was pounding the piano as vigorously as ever and singing, if anything, slightly better. Lane had been the youngest member of the club for so long that youthfulness seemed part of his character. But technically speaking, he was indeed the last of the great theater writers in the jazz song mode, and one of the least known. For reasons of temperament as much as history, Lane has apparently been consigned forever to the limbo between the immortals and the trivia questions—where, the evidence suggests, you can live a lot longer and a bit happier than the neighbors both upstairs and down. Some artists have obscurity thrust upon them, early and often, but Lane won his mild variety of it fair and square by going to Hollywood before he was famous on Broadway, and as Warren and several others proved, you can't get here from there: No one ever made a name writing anything in Hollywood, and if his great friend Harry Warren couldn't dent the public awareness with his record of forty-four songs on the Hit Parade, there was no point bothering it with less.

And besides, Burton wasn't the type to bother. It was a good life out there, and he was quite content to jog his way through the thirties, raising the occasional divot by day, in the eternal songwriter's golf game, and playing the best party piano in the county by night. There were worse ways to pass the Great Depression. Lane had taken the precaution of hitting town with a masterpiece, "Everything I Have Is Yours," written, I believe, before he was twenty-one, so he had a wobbly sort of tenure out there and was free to indulge his occasional hobby of rising to challenges, even if he had to invent them himself.

For instance, Burton set himself right away the task of writing "the perfect" Fred Astaire song just in case he should ever need one. Eighteen years later, Fred danced on the ceiling to this very song in *Royal Wedding*: "You're All the World to Me." (Talk about being upstaged; no one has ever heard the song to this day.) And later, at studio request this time, he would also write the perfect Bob Hope song, to round out the great trilogy, "Thanks for the Memory" (music: Ralph Rainger), "Two Sleepy People" (music: Hoagy Carmichael), and Lane's entry, "The Lady's in Love with You," which sounds more like Bob Hope than Bob Hope did, but is typically the least known of the three.

Another challenge Lane seized upon or created was a chance to work his patron's name into a song, and this he did with a bang. The only line of lyric he ever wrote for himself must be one of the best-known in Tin Pan Alley history—"I like a Gershwin tune," from "How About You." Gershwin was his biggest challenge, so naturally Lane wrote him into his best song. Yet thereby hangs not just a tale, but a whole biography.

"You play just like my son George." I've already told this story in relation to Gershwin, and George hardly needs another story. So imagine this time how it must have felt to a kid who'd been practicing and fooling around at a summer hotel piano when he heard a Russian lady say these words. For perhaps a split second Burton Levy, as he was then called, must have wondered "Who's George?" before doing a double take that lasted the rest of his life.

Mama Gershwin didn't talk like that to just anybody. So it is fair to assume that Burton in his teens was already better than good. As a veteran at sixteen now, he'd long since made the crucial discovery that his mistakes at the piano were more interesting than his right notes. But if his mistakes were anything near as interesting as George Gershwin's (to repeat, Mama's compliments didn't grow on trees), he might need to hire a Brink's truck just to transport them to the publisher, and his future suddenly lay serene before him. The only question that remained was whether to take his golden egg upmarket to the investment house of Carnegie Hall or down to the ATMs of Tin Pan Alley, two opposite worlds less than five minutes apart on the subway. Either way, his first stop had to be the Gershwin townhouse on West One Hundred-third Street, where by chance "my son George" was wrestling with the same problem, dashing off orchestrations for his Concerto in F with one hand and great middle-period songs like "Soon" and "How Long Has This Been Going On?" with the other.

For the next two years or so, Burton apprenticed, or more precisely listened, under this divided soul, the rough equivalent of receiving private revolution lessons from Lenin in the years 1915 through 1917. Not that Gershwin ever made that kind of difference on the classical scene, which was one big revolution already—another bomb-thrower here or there couldn't blow it any higher; still, his effect on the American popular song was positively seismic. And Burton Lane was there, sitting at the master's pedals, the last, truest heir to the family fortune.

To make doubly sure that his new protégé knew exactly what he wanted, Chairman George set the kid up with an appointment to meet

Walter Damrosch of the New York Philharmonic. If Lane had a symphony up his sleeve, now was the time to roll it out. But Burton had already made the same choice as Irving Berlin to avoid technical instruction: He didn't know where the music came from, and he didn't want to know—although fifty years later he still wasn't sure that this was the right decision. Anyhow, all the trains were running downtown that year, and Burton had the fever, the thing that "It Don't Mean a Thing" if it ain't got, and all that rolled out were more and more songs, a half-century's worth if you count the unpublished ones he kept writing after the bell sounded and the tide turned against him. Yet to the end, you can still find a potential classical composer in there someplace who announces his fleeting presence in the middle of songs with harmonic notions just too rare and sly for one hearing, which is usually the only hearing that songs can ever count on. So there's much snobbish pleasure to be had discovering all the Lane songs that were simply too good to be standards, like "Something Sort of Grand-ish," which may be the best, and is certainly the least-known, song from *Finian's Rainbow.* Lane's instinctive sophistication did him no harm at all in 1930s Hollywood, because that was the decade when sophistication went public. But it did him no particular good after World War II because sophistication was now *out* all over America—look where it got you. And then there was TV, which had already robbed the studios of enough mad money to pay for new songs on spec. The musical class system had returned to stay, with the good songs heading henceforth to Broadway and the rest heading in the general direction of "The Doggie in the Window."

So Burton Lane rounded up, or was rounded up by, a fellow member of the Manhattan diaspora named Yip Harburg, and together they batted out *Finian's Rainbow* while they were still in California. Not surprisingly the result was a very New York show. Although Harburg loved the idea of Ireland, his lyrics never really got out of the harbor, or all that far from McSorley's Wonderful Saloon either. This suited Broadway fine in its postwar phase of rediscovering the outside world only to find that, once you got past the funny phrases and costumes, it was just like the good old U.S.A. And the show passed the other more serious post–Rodgers and Hammerstein test of perfectly matching the melodies to the scenes, so that the tune sounds as if the scene had written *it*. This was quite an achievement for a Hollywood trainee who'd been raised on the unspoken division of labor out there, whereby you just shut up and write your nice songs and leave the rest to us. On Broadway, contrariwise, the more you could do for yourself the better, from picking the project and finding a like-minded producer whose casting of it would not be too ridiculous, to placing the songs and protecting them just by hanging around rehearsals and making a pest of yourself. Like Frank Loesser, that prince of pests.

Just to recite the requirements is to picture Yip Harburg, a charming but persistent fellow, who had actually gotten his nickname from his terrier-like qualities, and who had employed them to squeeze in a successful business career just in time for the Crash in 1929 and a new career in songwriting. Now Yip was back on his home ground and one imagines him fairly exploding onto Broadway. Anything MGM could do musically he could do better on his own, and just as he had helped his old friend Harold Arlen to write his most successful show, *Bloomer Girl,* he now helped his other friend Burton Lane to write his, leaving him even more stranded afterward.

In a more reasonable world, *Finian* would have constituted a flying start, but immediately afterward, Lane went back and stood on line with all the other composers to compete for an ever-shrinking number of theaters. It was as if the dream factory of Hollywood had been replaced overnight by a small cottage industry that kept losing cottages because the same real estate costs that were squeezing the Brooklyn Dodgers and New York Giants out of the city were driving up theater rents beyond endurance. In those same 1950s, John Osborne called the British royals a gold tooth in a mouthful of decay, but he could have said it even more accurately about the Great White Way, which only became even a gold tooth as long as the curtain was up on the latest million-dollar investment. Between epiphanies, it reverted to a small number of shabby buildings set among future massage parlors—or, from another angle, a handful of clean theaters overlooking fleabag streets.

So Burton needed the right partner more than ever, and Harburg's obsession with politics, which had been an inconvenience to Arlen but not a fatal one, tied Burton in knots. It seems that those years in Hollywood had accentuated a tendency in Burton to sit on the tracks and wait for someone, Mama Gershwin or Louis B. Mayer, to tap him on the shoulder and tell him what to do next. And since good partners were hard to find and Yip was still right there, Burton wasted valuable prime time before giving up on him, and even more time looking for Mr. Right in the next generation. In the forty-plus years remaining to him, he would in fact find only one—and it would be magic, like the village of Brigadoon, for five minutes or so.

Alan Jay Lerner was perfect while he lasted, incredibly venturesome with a rich kid's knack for getting what he wanted. He had virtually begun his career with the hit show *Brigadoon,* and with an Oscar for screenwriting the movie *An American in Paris,* before proceeding to the daunting task of rewriting George Bernard Shaw and reimagining his great play *Pygmalion* into the great un-American musical *My Fair Lady.* The only catch was, of course, that for most of his firecracker prime, he had been tied to Fritz Loewe. Burton would only get Lerner for one perfect screen score—*Royal Wedding,* which exploded with pent-up talent in such gems as "Too Late Now" and "I Left My Hat in Haiti"—and one sublime Broadway musical featuring a batch of songs so vivacious and inventive that they seemed to announce the high noon of a career and certainly not the twilight. It is typical of Lane that he was at once passive enough to wait a Rip Van Winkle–like twenty-eight years between stage appearances and sharp enough to be at his absolute best. "What Did I Have That I Don't Have," "Come Back to Me," and most particularly the title song of the show, "On a Clear Day," may be his most adventurous ever. Unlike certain rock composers, who seem stunned by the first musical phrase they come to and repeat it with mounting excitement until the tape runs out, Lane gave us a lot of tune each time. In fact, the A section of "On a Clear Day" seems itself like a mere suggestion, a launching pad from which he and his co-pilot, Alan Jay Lerner, take off to the wild blue yonder in a series of breathtaking maneuvers, as if they expect to stay up there forever.

But forever proved even shorter than usual, Broadway time, and within the next year or so, all of the old songwriters had been grounded and an era had ended, just like that, like a record spinning to a close. It was the mid-sixties by then and the noise outside the theater couldn't be kept out much longer. Shows like *Grease, Tommy,* and, God help us, *Jesus Christ Superstar* were more like it, not because the public demanded it—the average theatergoer was still as square as ever, and any revival of anything was warmly welcomed—but in response to supply-side imperatives. The creative spirits of any era will always want to express their own world and their own moment in time, and starting with the midsixties, this became hard to do if you weren't young. The peace movement and the civil rights marches, combined with all the phrases and attitudes of the hippie revolt and the free speech movement and the drug culture, flung down a barrier between the generations that reached from coast to coast like our own Great Wall of China. By chance, I was present on a night when even Yip Harburg found his visa being rejected, although I'm not sure he ever realized it.

Since the hippies simply loved the word "political" and applied it to everything from brushing your teeth to refusing to brush your teeth, Yip assumed that they were fellow spirits and going his way. So, in a spirit of gemütlich solidarity, worthy of the Popular Front in the 1930s, he threw a party to welcome Dan Berrigan, the Jesuit peacenik, home from a short stretch at the aptly named Danbury State Prison. And the generational battle lines were drawn immediately with a cartoon sharpness and sublime unconsciousness. On the one side, in straight chairs, sat old Yip and his Old Left friends, who could have passed collectively for a meeting of a Garment Workers local, and on the other, crouched or sprawled on the floor, Dan and his Hippies for Jesus, wondering no doubt what the hell they were doing here with all these old people. The session kicked off with a few condescending words from the trendy lawyer William Kunstler, who talked to the old-timers as if they were pale-faced middle-class types in need of reassurance ("I don't blame you for feeling scared"), and ended on the high and low note of the evening, when our host got up and sang his own masterpiece "Brother, Can You Spare a Dime?" with wattles fluttering and Adam's apple going up and down like a grain elevator. "Once in khaki suits, gee, we looked swell. . . ." I myself would have gladly slogged "through hell," as the song says, for this man, but from a cool corner of my eye I noted some of Dan's disciples actually still chattering and even tittering among themselves. And I thought, Never trust a song over thirty minutes old, I suppose. Now if someone had just grabbed a guitar and started riffing on Danbury Dan in the Danbury Can, well, all right.

But the old songs were the worst thing they could be just then, inauthentic and unspontaneous and definitely on the wrong side of the Great Wall. Any new jazz songs that made it now would have to follow the famous advice of Gertrude Stein to Ernest Hemingway—"Do it over," and "Make it new." Lane's *On a Clear Day* and Loesser's *How to Succeed* were perfect shows about fifties themes, psychiatry and office work, that were no longer in the worldview or on the national screen. Yet mysteriously another, even older, theme showed up around then and did just fine. The plot of *Cabaret* had actually run on Broadway in the 1950s without music and under a different name. But the young team of Kander and Ebb had made it new, musically speaking, by plugging in its nostalgia and making it jump and live for at least fifty years, especially as accompanied by the staccato and erotic irony of Bob Fosse's choreography.

Being, and staying, "with it" does not necessarily require constant changes, maybe just one or two in a lifetime. But Burton had missed the big one and watched its ship sail away.

So Mr. Van Winkle returned to his couch and slept right through the Age of Aquarius, woke up long enough to try one more musical with Lerner (*Carmelina* in 1977), only to realize that the jig seemed to be up with Lerner as well. Even before *On a Clear Day*, Alan Jay had proved much too slow and erratic for the fussy Richard Rodgers, but now, under the rumored influence of certain drugs, he was almost too much for the patient Lane. Talking a few years later with the last Mrs. Lerner, I found her presuming that Burton must have been an awful man—until, that is, she met him. So obviously, bad blood had begun to flow on both sides before they quit.

Burton returned to his piano and waited for posterity to come to its senses, while meanwhile "Who do you like for mayor next time?" was what you were most likely to hear if you called up the Lanes. Lynn Lane took a particularly ferocious interest in Upper West Side politics, but when I last saw Burton at a meeting some years back, his dreamy smile suggested he might possibly be humming under his breath. Happy the man with a good tune in his head, especially a tune that might be a hit in the next century or so.

And this time, Lane's limited times at bat (compared with Berlin's and Porter's) may have cost him a piece of his rightful glory. In a prolonged burst of muddleheadedness the sages at the Kennedy Center managed to overlook him to the end, which was plain embarrassing, like the Oscar that Cary Grant didn't get. Not that it ever seemed to bother Burton. If it took even a pinch of self-promotion to attract that kind of attention,

Burton couldn't be bothered with it. By show biz standards, the man had a serious showing-off disorder, a most un-Gershwinian ego deficiency brought about, he explained, by that unsung specimen, a "stage father." Repeated doses of the line "You must listen to my son play" had sent Burton into permanent reverse early in life, and as I know from experience, he could waste whole interviews talking about other people.

Although he seemed, like a sports announcer might say, very tall for a songwriter, he even looked self-effacing in a distinguished sort of way—so much so that Louis B. Mayer went to his grave convinced that his ace composer was actually Judy Garland's rehearsal pianist. If ever a man was handed an innocent chance to shine, Burton's discovery of Garland should have been it. Judy was still a mere Gumm sister when he spotted her, one childish voice out of three, although admittedly the dominant one from the get-go. But Lane was so sure of her greatness and of his own judgment that he marched the tot round to MGM himself and insisted she be auditioned—not the act of a milquetoast. Yet when it came to taking a bow for himself, he got stuck.

So you can imagine how many bows he took for his own work. As far as Burton was concerned, no award or applause for past achievements could provide anything like the kick of putting on a new show or even just playing a new tune for a friend, of which I believe he had enough to fill at least an off-Broadway theater. But his friends weren't the kind of hustlers who would help him get back in the game. I don't believe he really liked such people. And perhaps the game itself had lost some of its flavor. He kept writing songs because that's what songwriters do.

Whatever an artist may think he thinks, his heart decides at some point whether he really wants to stay in the swim that much or is content just to be remembered. And all I can say is that Burton was remembered and seemed happy about it. One time I found him bristling because he was having trouble getting paid for a commercial that was using "How About You," but it was a major commercial so he had cause, and he wasn't bristling that hard.

"I hear music/Mighty fine music." If you had to reduce Lane's oeuvre to one song for the space capsule, how about this? The opening is a solemn tease, deadpan music that might go anywhere—and then it magically springs to life, and for a moment you feel as if you've moved into an actual music box with melody coming from everywhere. This was Burton Lane's regular neighborhood, and its physical counterpart was, as nature intended, the Upper West Side, which provided the real-life doors and windows through which the music streamed. All the inspiration Burton ever needed could be found someplace between Riverside Drive, next to which he once played Ping-Pong with Oscar Levant and the piano with George Gershwin, and Central Park West, on which he lived and worked nonstop for his last forty years or so. If the great modern jazz songs began life on the Lower East Side, they wasted no time moving to more spacious quarters, many of them in the upper left corner of the city, where Richard Rodgers was born and raised, and George Gershwin of Brooklyn held court: the uptown school of American music of which Burton Lane was for years the dean, crown jewel, and Grand Old Man in residence.

The last amiable proof that he must have been doing something good on this planet, Burton Lane was one of those blessed souls who look better as they age. Just a few minutes of conversation usually revealed his secret. As soon as the talk turned to music, the man lit up like a stained-glass window. And if you could maneuver him toward the piano stool, by, say, dropping a hat, you could watch the years slide away and, on a clear day, maybe even see Mama Gershwin, that somewhat different fairy godmother standing just behind him. Anything might happen at the piano, which served Lane over the years as best friend, cash cow, and fountain of youth. There is no love like that of a composer for his instrument; Hemingway and his typewriter, Salk and his test tube, and Hershey and his chocolate bar all finish far down the track.

"I Love a Piano," wrote the great Irving Berlin, and he could barely play the damn thing. When you played as elegantly as Burton Lane did, you had the makings of a grand passion to which no earthly honor could add much of anything. In a profession in which depression seems to expand in ratio to success (e.g., Berlin, Rodgers, and Arlen), Lane struck a salubrious balance: enough success, a major talent, a happy man.

Or at least he was the last time I saw him, because he was doing a two-man concert with the indispensable Michael Feinstein. This metamorphosed into some excellent tapes that will undoubtedly soon become collector's items. And, as I say, Lane sounded better than ever.

# Cy Coleman and the Future

CY COLEMAN

*T*his book is lightly suffused throughout by the presence of Cy Coleman, whom I met toward the start of the project and who died, to my shock and sorrow, just as I began to wind it down. In between, I would see enough of him—laughing his gleeful chuckle and, above all, always working on a new show—to get a sense of the writing life as it is and has been for living memory. These guys were *always* working on new shows. The great songs began life as by-products, although they might wind up living forever while main products—the new shows themselves—probably would not.

So why not just skip the show and write songs for their own sake? Because the biology of the business seems to insist on shows. Around the time I met Cy, I had (unknowingly) said my last goodbye to Burton Lane, and had already sensed the frustration of a showman without a show, trying to write songs in a vacuum without something to hang them on or put them in. In contrast to Lane, Cy Coleman presented the bustle and optimism of a man at work. He didn't just have to think up new songs, he also had to bring down curtains and introduce characters. And the hits would come—or, if not, maybe the show itself would be a big hit and cover for them.

Cy Coleman was of special interest to me because he had apparently kept the faith with the old songs and gotten away with it. He was of interest also to Walter Isaacson at *Time* magazine because he had just scored the old-fashioned, Richard Rodgers–style double of two hit shows on Broadway at the same time. So *Time* asked me to write about Cy.

Fortunately, Coleman lived just down the street, a mere two Hamptons away as the gossip flies, and quite close enough to go from a journalism subject to a friend in no time flat. He was a comfortable man. Some musicians may be inarticulate, but songwriters work with words, and usually like to talk, and they know how to do it.

We dived right in. In the interest of my book—*Time* could wait I wanted to know whether a form of music like the jazz song could still be said to be alive if nobody wrote it anymore. I can't remember who were that particular year's hot contemporary concert artists, but whoever they were, where were their matching songwriters? If a young modern-day writer suddenly wants to write like Gershwin, what does he do next? How does the machinery work these days?

Back in those days, Cy said, you knew you'd written a hit and were on your way "when Tony Bennett made the record." But, he supposed, starting off today he would have to establish his own record company and make his own records (maybe even playing the piano himself—I can't hear him singing). And, by the way, to hell with the sound synthesizers, he added, which he considered the great Satan and the enemy of all human creation. "I would always write music," he added so decisively that I can still hear him.

And what kind of music would he "always write"? I didn't have to ask, but did anyway. It seems he had fallen in lifelong love with the music that came out of the radio in the late 1930s and early 1940s, and that was the sort of thing he still wrote: great old radio songs. Although, as he said, one never knows how they will come out. For example, when the great Brazilian stylist Antonia Carlos Jobim wrote "The Girl from Ipanema," he was convinced that he was writing regular American jazz. Cy said the main thing was to avoid imitations ("pastiche is for kids"), write what comes naturally, and hope some of the year's fresh air will sneak in and blow the dust off.

His master strategy for somehow staying both hip and out of date became clear to me a few days later when I visited his Manhattan office on Fifty-seventh Street and realized that the occupant had taken full advantage of our greatest modern convenience: the freedom to live in the tense of one's choice, if not in several of them. At first glance, his office was the model of an old-show biz shop, spilling over with playbills and fading photographs, plus an upright piano and a rolltop desk big enough to hold an escaped convict.

Yet Cy himself did not seem like an anachronism or a museum keeper. Although it was then too soon for most people to own computers, I'm sure he later snapped one up as fast as you can say George Gershwin (who always bought the latest of everything). And even then, Cy's musty rolltop probably contained at least one possible show script set in the twenty-fifth century.

In fact, of his two hit shows running just then, one, *City of Angels,* was set in a futuristic Los Angeles, and contained a streamlined score written with an up-to-the-minute lyricist, David Zippel, of the Richard Rodgers family. The other, *The Will Rogers Follies,* was set comfortably back in the 1920s and '30s, with my old friends Betty Comden and Adolph Green on the lyrics.

In order to find new things in himself and maybe find new song ideas in the script, Cy told me that he liked to work with new lyricists each time out. And he volunteered two examples of songs dictated by the needs and limitations of particular productions and helped into life by a like-minded words person.

His show *Wildcat* required a signature song for Lucille Ball, who had begun her career as a chorus girl, but had since developed incipient stage fright at the prospect of singing in front of living people. So Cy ordered up from his subconscious a song for everywoman, or at least for everycelebrity. He came up with "Hey Look Me Over," a brassy but simple barroom ballad that even Minnie Mouse could belt out, or seem to belt out, right through to its triumphal ending. "So, look out world—here I come!" Take that, you amateurs!

Similarly, *Little Me* needed a showstopper for yet another television casualty, Sid Caesar, a comedian not famous for his singing. For him, Cy dashed off a bathtub waltz called "Real Live Girl," which practically sings itself and barely even needs a real live singer. And once again, one imagines the real-life ambience of the great songs, the influence of performers like Sophie Tucker and Bob Hope and Frank Sinatra on their histories.

In both of Cy's examples, the words seem to understand the tune like a perfect marriage. It figures, because the partnership between Cy and his fellow Bronxite Carolyn Leigh was artistically if not humanly perfect. Besides (or because of) being brilliant, Carolyn Leigh seems to have been a (thoroughly justified) perfectionist. She demanded the same from her writing partner in what may have struck the so-far single Cy as a shrill married sort of voice. Apparently, she brought out the screamer in him, too—along with some of his best, jazziest work. Like Irving Berlin, Cy was never happier than when chopping up his rhythms and injecting a surprise kick to them. And Leigh could ride his choppiest beats like a bronco buster in such typical numbers as "Witchcraft" and "I've Got Your Number." Carolyn even insisted on writing a lyric for one of Cy's more demanding warm-up finger exercises. "The Best Is Yet to Come" became a hit when Frank Sinatra made the record, although Cy said it couldn't be done right up until the point when it was.

However fruitful, such a comic-strip professional marriage could not endure. Perhaps no writing partnership ever should come that close to a marriage. Cy could be excessively complimentary about Carolyn, although their rows were not just audible, they were actually legendary, so I didn't need to pry and could just imagine. As Cy elsewhere described the act of composition, it sounded almost mystical and, hence, solitary. So, to return from his efforts and find someone waiting with a rolling pin—and find himself raging back—may have ultimately been just too much.

To picture Cy in memory is to remember him smiling. His natural means of expression was the chortle, not the insult, the celebration rather than the postmortem. His last partner, Ira Gasman, even went so far as to say that songs came from him "like gurgles from a baby."

Not that there was anything infantile about Cy. But he had found a locus of pure joy in music dating back to the days when his carpenter father used to nail the piano shut to get a little peace around there. Luckily, "as a carpenter's son, I knew how to un-nail it." And the family milkman, hearing the same sounds, declared that whoever was making them was a genius, which led somehow or another (who knows how grown-ups arrived at these things?) to lessons and a spell as a child prodigy with a special gift for Beethoven. Years later, Jule Styne, another prodigy, would say to him at ASCAP meetings, "You and I are the only real pianists here." And Cy never stopped playing the classics, but gave excellent mixed concerts right to the end.

As a teenaged maestro in World War II, he found immediate work entertaining the troops, who seldom requested Beethoven. Thus, he stayed in touch with radio, until his musical bones hardened. And his first big hit afterward strikes a note of iron resolve. "Why Try to Change Me Now?" could be a declaration of musical intent, although the actual words were written by Joseph A. McCarthy.

Nevertheless, the world *would* try to change him, as it changes everybody. So my second question at our first meeting concerned this issue: How in the world had he managed to keep out "the music in the air" all this time while letting in any fresh air at all?

"Selective deafness," he said quickly, with his biggest smile, as if there really were no way to change him now. Rock and roll had come and mostly gone, in all its mutations, and *nouvelle* folk music, and then New Age, or dentists' music, until at last melody itself seemed to be on the run from rap and heavy machinery. Cy Coleman still found all he needed by listening to the classical radio stations and to jazz in all *its* permutations. When these weren't available, he tuned in to the orchestra playing in his own head, which he could strike up when the going got dull over cocktails or dinner. I don't know if I ever talked to him at such a moment, but if so, the Coleman grin covered every possibility in the wide world. He carried it off perfectly.

Meanwhile, back at the office. Cy didn't leave Ms. Leigh (or hadn't been left by her) for just some nobody. His next partner, Dorothy Fields, was a step up from practically everyone. Sublimely peaceable, she'd withstood the thunderbolts of Jerome Kern, and even coaxed an all-American score from Transylvanian Sigmund Romberg. (*Up in Central Park* must be the best musical never revived, and its big hit "Close as Pages in a Book" the best song never played.)

Blessedly, Fields had one more great show in her arsenal, and it would turn out to be Cy Coleman's greatest claim on the future. Listening to *Sweet Charity* today—with its great bordello numbers, "Big Spender" and "If My Friends Could See Me Now"—it's hard to believe that the words came from one of Broadway's great ladies on her next-to-last assignment. Before Dorothy died, the pair did manage one more quickie, the unpromising and unsuccessful *Seesaw,* thus ending a professional marriage made in heaven (like all of Dorothy Fields's marriages—which is not to say that they lasted, just that they were heavenly).

Working with Dorothy Fields must have seemed as close to graduation as it gets in this field. From then on, Cy was the old master, and a gracious one he was, enjoying both the role and the work, which kept coming in bushel baskets. I remember that he was particularly tickled at having won (on his scorecard anyhow) an exchange of insults in the London press with Andrew Lloyd Webber. He also expressed a lordly disapproval of Bob Fosse for building a recent show out of old songs instead of commissioning some new ones. (He and Fosse still owed each other plenty for *Sweet Charity,* so there were no real hard feelings.) Above all, Cy found time in those later mellow years to make a most serene and satisfactory marriage to a most unshrewish young lady. She was tactful enough to tell me that she read my *Time* piece on Cy at the right moment, and so she accepted a date. And she made me feel like Cupid every time we met.

As noted, Cy was kept young and busy by the endless small chores of the theater, punctuated by the flow of downright rebirths and do-overs as new shows blew into town to play musical chairs (or musical theaters) with old ones. And the old-timers returned too, like Harold Prince or the late George Abbott, gliding in as if on pink clouds, as good as new with each revival.

Although there are fashions on Broadway, as everywhere, they are not binding. Every show is its own small world, free to set up its own styles or to borrow one from the ever-present past. Kander and Ebb's *Chicago* is a splendid rendering of the American twenties, and so is Jerry Herman's *Mack & Mabel,* but they are completely different interpretations. And who would ever try to typecast Stephen Sondheim, a man of a thousand styles?

To answer my first question, the jazz song still lives on Broadway: on stage, in the wings, or on somebody's drawing board. It's always changing, as if to reassert that it's still alive, but its very roots are never more than just one or two degrees away from Irving or Cole themselves. And though Burton Lane and Ann Ronell are no longer around to "see" George Gershwin on his daily rounds, he lives on in the musicians' heads and on the boards of Broadway.

Cy Coleman gave me a sense of this undying brotherhood of song. I was amazed, though I shouldn't have been, to realize that he must have been seventy-six years old at our last meeting. His age made no difference in his plans or his life. If he grew old in one decade, he could always move into another one and keep right on going. And if you heard him play, say, George Gershwin, it was not an old man playing old music, but an immortal taking a dip in the fountain of youth.

Until further notice, these songs live and breathe on Broadway, as well as on the mini-Broadways of the cabaret circuit. Together these two live venues replicate two former musical workshops: the Vaudeville tour and the speakeasy. For the speakeasy effect, nowadays you have to imagine the illegal part, with the sirens and the Keystone Kops, but that very real tingle is still very much available. One night, the fine entertainer Baby Jane Dexter said, "I feel as though something very exciting is going to happen tonight." And I felt it too. Mary Cleeve Haran was, as I recall, about to interpret Irving Berlin in the twenties as he had never been interpreted before.

And I understood why the English won't leave Shakespeare alone, why the Austrians fiddle with Mozart. Not that I'm making great claims to artistic purity, only placing these songs in the American story and in the girders of our cities, the memory of our railroads and our Ford V-8's. At one important moment in history, these songs represented America to the world, and they represented us well. As Hoagy Carmichael said to me in 1947 at the London Stage Door, "You and me got to be good ambassadors for America, son," and he certainly was, along with the rest of the musical diplomatic corps represented in this book.

As noted earlier, George Gershwin said, "My place is America and my time is now." That still goes. And if Cy throws in a medley of his own music, you needn't adjust your watch or your calendar. These songs are here to stay.

# Coda: Three More Majors
# (for Good Measure)

ARTHUR SCHWARTZ

By its nature, any book on this subject will try to become an encyclopedia, if you let it. So just to prove this isn't, I'll end with some loose ends—three representative names from the top of the class, each of whom is a byword to fans but rings only the most distant of bells, if any, with the Unwashed. (The word is not pejorative. I am myself unwashed in many areas, including the latest rock music, and indeed the exact significance of the word "rock" by now—I am unwashed and unbowed.) Although millions of people have heard the song "Makin' Whoopee" and perhaps seen the film *The Band Wagon,* the authors' names have not been indelibly attached to either of them. Walter Donaldson and Arthur Schwartz remain head-scratchers. "Hmm, the name sounds familiar. Give me a clue." The drive to amnesia is mighty strong, and even Vincent Youmans, whose name seems close to unforgettable, remains shrouded in fog. " 'No, No, Nanette'? 'Tea for Two'? 'The Curse of the Bambino'?" There is an underlying financial connection. Harry Frazee, the iniquitous chap who sold Babe Ruth from the Red Sox to the Yankees, is said to have used the proceeds of the sale to fund *No, No, Nanette,* and it is by this thread that the composer Vincent Youmans's name recognition now hangs.

So where did Walter Donaldson, Arthur Schwartz, and Vincent Youmans—and all the other near misses—go wrong? Walter Donaldson had actually gotten off to a fine start by being a protégé of Irving Berlin as World War I ended and Prohibition opened up a brand-new market for saloon songs. In fact, Donaldson seemed the closest thing to an heir apparent to the very throne of Tin Pan Alley. Admittedly, that was while people still thought of Irving as mortal, and before all the other heirs had checked in. But so long as the Alley remained in New York, Donaldson at least reigned supreme in their speakeasies and on what might be called lowercase Broadway—the several hundred theaters that did not run operettas like *Naughty Marietta,* or anything like it. But songs like "My Buddy," "My Blue Heaven," and "Yes Sir, That's My Baby" sold an awful lot of sheet music with Donaldson's name on it, and physically speaking the man was quite a familiar figure around town, especially if you fancied the racetrack. And in the later twenties, he would establish perhaps his best claim on immortality with the songs that became the repertoire of Ruth Etting. (She's the saloon singer with the sad, sad story told so well in the great Doris Day movie *Love Me or Leave Me.* As long as that film remains in stock, so does Donaldson.)

But then came sound, and Tin Pan Alley moved to Hollywood, where Walter gradually evolved into just another studio writer. MGM gave him one last chance to shine by making a Busby Berkeley spectacular out of his Broadway show *Makin' Whoopee,* to which Donaldson added the standard "My Baby Just Cares for Me." And he made the most of smaller openings too, with the Broadway style barn burner "You" and the song that Cary Grant mauled unforgettably, "Did I Remember?" But on the whole, Walter Donaldson was just another misplaced New Yorker.

Hollywood was simply not his kind of town, or any kind of town at all, and one imagines his personal map of it consisting of a few good racetracks connected by some trolley tracks and various watering places or safe houses where he might find some other Gotham exiles. In those same years, his own map would change too, from that of a sensitive, almost ethereal young poet to a middle-aged voluptuary along the lines of Sydney Greenstreet. Johnny Mercer, who met him halfway through the thirties, found him wonderful company and still brimming with talent. But he had lost his place in line to the latest carpetbaggers. And since the studio paid you whether you worked or not, Donaldson preferred playing the horses to playing studio politics. He wasn't fixated on personal immortality, and so he didn't quite get it, although his daughter, Ellen, who barely had time to meet him (she was seven years old when he died, but remembers him as a warm and loving man), seems to be ambitious enough for two and keeps his name in the well-earned running.

Arthur Schwartz also has a relative, the super-disc-jockey and old friend of mine Jonathan Schwartz, who has also served his old man well by keeping *all* the boats afloat, Arthur's very much among them, and letting them speak for themselves. "Dancing in the Dark," "Alone Together," "You and the Night and the Music"—there is a classic quality to Schwartz's best tunes that separates them from the crowd and seems to qualify him for his own statue and his own book. "Something to Remember You By" is a song my grandmother used to sing, and that one, along with her other favorites, Berlin's "What'll I Do" and Romberg's "When I Grow Too Old to Dream," form their own little timeless repertoire in my head dating back to the Garden of Infancy, when all the songs were young.

Of Arthur Schwartz as much as anyone, it could be said that in any less crowded time and place, he would surely have been deemed a grand master, but that in any such normal circumstances, he might not have become a songwriter at all—certainly not if his father, Solomon, had had anything to say about it. I have seldom heard of such implacable opposition to anything as Solomon's was to music. He went to the root of the matter by forbidding all music instruction in the home. And after that Daddy Schwartz insisted that Arthur become a real lawyer (like himself) rather than a piano-playing graduate student. Arthur set a songwriter's record with four years of actual legal practice.

But the music in the air prevailed. There was simply so much demand for more of it and so many young men (and even a few women) looking for ways to provide it that they finally outnumbered Solomon. A kid with a head full of melodies was money in the bank, and Sol had made the fatal mistake of not getting his kid out of town immediately. Worse, he let him go to Columbia University, where three great, hungry lyricists—Hart, Hammerstein, and Howard Dietz—prowled the halls of learning in search of musical kids like Schwartz (since there just wasn't enough of Richard Rodgers to go around).

Probably, Arthur didn't need all that much temptation. In his quiet way, he was as willful as his old man—but the mix of talent and opportunity gave him the most useful of gifts in a sticky situation: early success. Arthur had actually already written a standard as a camp counselor with Larry Hart, of all unlikely camp counselors. But Hart's lyric for it was so unstandardlike and, in fact, so summer-camp-like ("I Love to Lie Awake in Bed," for Pete's sake) that Arthur retired it to the back of his head for better times, which were just around the corner.

It is typical of the King Midas–like hot streak that was about to pass through Schwartz that his next partner, the third man in the Columbia triumvirate, Howard Dietz, would quickly turn that same tune into the ever-popular "I Guess I'll Have to Change My Plan." Arthur had found the best possible partner for him. And to make things even better, the one-two punch of talking pictures and the financial depression that had reduced the Great White Way to off-Broadway size made it just right for this year's crop of geniuses—that is, if they already knew all the angles. Like Dietz and like Schwartz, they needed at least a valise full of unforgettable tunes ready to go. The (East) Coast was clear, because at least half the A-list writers had gone to Hollywood, while at the same time the local streets still swarmed with song-and-dance refugees from the closed vaudeville houses, who hadn't gone west yet themselves. So the young men joined forces in the kind of graduate school revue one now associates with the *Harvard Lampoon,* called *The Band Wagon,* and it took Broadway by storm in 1931. Besides packing enough hit songs to guarantee success in any era, it starred, for the last time on any stage or in any form, the great brother-and-sister team of Fred and Adele Astaire, as much a big-ticket item then as it would be now.

Even the audiences were just right for them then, because they were too hip for the movies but hell-bent on escape. In Schwartz and Dietz's golden years that followed, roughly 1931–36, all the businessmen were tired—or in the polite phrase, "between jobs"—and were in no mood for the emotional travails of a *Show Boat* or the integrated musical in general. Gags, gals, and tunes you could whistle on the way out and take home in sheets were more like it. And the hit shows from the freshmen class bore names like Harold Arlen's *Life Begins at 8:40*, Vernon Duke's *Ziegfeld Follies of 1934* (and also *of 1936*), and Schwartz's own *Flying Colors*.

And it wasn't just the freshmen at play, lowering the tone and bond rating of Broadway. Some of the best people also catered to the short attention spans of those straitened years. Irving Berlin scored with a great one called *As Thousands Cheer,* and the world's oldest sophomore, Cole Porter, whipped off *Red, Hot and Blue!* starring Ethel Merman, Jimmy Durante, and Broadway's hottest young hoofer, Bob Hope. Next stop, Hollywood, for all concerned: 1936 would witness the greatest emigration of musical talent since the outbreak of sound almost a decade earlier and, incidentally, see the end of Arthur's one and only real run of luck.

The arrival of Cole Porter that same year would symbolize the end of Schwartz's winning streak. For some time now Howard Dietz had doubled as publicity director for MGM, inventing both the company lion and the fancy motto, *Ars Gratia Artis,* as a sort of hobby supporting a hobby; but the stakes had never been so high before, and the dabbling days were done. By 1936, it was no longer enough to mail in one's work. Louis B. Mayer had to *see* you working.

That year, MGM signed up Cole Porter for the most money ever paid to any composer to do anything, and you can't make such a rich omelet without breaking a few eggs like Schwartz and Dietz. So Arthur was on his own. To make a long story short, he never again captured the same magic with anyone else, or even with Dietz himself when they rejoined forces a few years later. Instead, he used his all-around intelligence to become a successful film producer and, during World War II and afterward, to develop a rare knack for writing funny songs, the secret of which, he claimed, was to start with the most romantic tune he could think of.

Sometimes I can hear it and sometimes I can't. "What do they do on a rainy night in Rio?" could be romantic, I guess. "They're either too young or too old" merely sounds kind of wistful, and "Rhode Island is famous for you" is too well hidden behind its whimsical wall of words. "Pencils come from Pennsylvania." Oh my.

But why, hearing what he heard, didn't he turn his romantic themes to love songs anymore? Perhaps he was prescient. A TV set cannot whisper "I love you" the way a radio can. With the box, one is aware of technicians in between. With radio, it was just Frank Sinatra (or Peggy Lee) and you. Besides which, the baby boom had just started and a large part of the audience wanted to know the price of "The Doggie in the Window" more than how much some grown-up singer out there loved them.

But just before the standards stopped coming altogether, Hollywood made up for at least some of its damages by reviving Schwartz's lucky title "The Band Wagon," and placing it in a movie that expertly celebrated the six glorious years in which Schwartz and Dietz poured out hits as if there were no tomorrow—as indeed there wasn't on that scale. For the occasion, Fred Astaire himself was on hand, appropriately older and wiser. "I'll go my way by myself," he sang, now that he'd lost Adele for sure, and Ginger too; Fred was ready to take his old bandwagon on its last ride. Schwartz and Dietz also rose to the occasion, as if it were still routine to do so, with one of those anthem songs built to last forever. Like Berlin's "There's No Business Like Show Business" or Cole Porter's "Another Opening Another Show," so too Schwartz and Dietz's "That's Entertainment" will probably stick around in some kind of digitalized form as long as MGM's ghost has anything to say about it and listeners can still carry a tune, or still want to.

So perhaps not quite the immortality that Arthur Schwartz deserved, but his musical legacy is solid, and can still make you laugh, or fall in love, as the case may be. Which is more than can be said about most dead lawyers, including, rest his soul, Solomon Schwartz. As I give Arthur's work one last hum-through, I am struck by the fact that while he obviously could write good songs with anyone, they only sounded like genuine Schwartz songs if they had genuine Dietz lyrics. And the rapport cut both ways. Dietz was a firm believer that how the words sounded was more important than what they meant.

For a similar attitude among composers, one turns to Vincent Youmans, the ultimate lothario of lyrics, who never stopped playing the field among wordmen, partly, like Cy Coleman, to find something new in himself but mainly to find hits—and perhaps because nobody else wanted to work with him more than once.

The saintly Oscar Hammerstein even went so far as to call Youmans the only man he didn't like. But that was probably, in Gatsby's words, "just personal." The usual problem was Vincent's work habits, which didn't go into effect until the last speakeasy in New York had closed, at which point he'd totter home and start strumming chords and whistling tunes and calling for lyrics as if they were another drink. As his last partner, Ed Eliscu, told me, "It helped if you'd been napping at his place waiting for developments."

As it was, perhaps his most famous song was rounded off by a partner who'd already gone home and had to hear the chords over the telephone. "Oh, tea for two," said Irving Caesar, I assume sarcastically, "and me for you, et cetera, et cetera," and call me in the morning for the real lyric. All he needed right at that moment was a dummy, a beat to hang his real words on.

What is also both typical and strange is that the resulting song, dummy lyrics and all, would end up expressing the 1920s—1925 to be exact—so perfectly because, according to Eliscu, Youmans got everything wrong in real life, from the wrong clothes and haircut to the wrong things to say for every occasion—from which one might deduce that either he or Eliscu was slightly displaced. Conversely, my next interlocutor, Margaret Whiting, met Youmans as a child in Hollywood and thought he looked like the most glamorous thing she'd ever seen even in that community. And in the 1920s, the newspaper gossip rated him one-two with George Gershwin as "the most eligible." Scott Fitzgerald also used Youmans's persona in one of his novels.

Larchmont, where Youmans grew up, was a million miles from Tin Pan Alley, which may explain why he seemed so glamorous and out of synch. The Youmanses could fairly be described as a rich WASP family on their way down, just at the point where things start to degenerate. Vincent's father had already succumbed all too zestfully to the glamour of the White Way, not to mention its chorus girls and what are now called adult beverages.

So his stern, but blessedly musical mother seems to have taken the cartoon-WASP course of keeping the old man home, high and dry, but then not talking to him. And she adopted the rare child-raising technique of buying a pair of grand pianos for her son and daughter to serve as babysitter and tutor. Vincent spent his early years listening to more music than dialogue and learning how to express his feelings and to hide them on the keyboard. So perhaps it's not surprising that he wrote the tune for his impossibly happy hit "Hallelujah!" while still a teenager serving a hitch in the navy and relishing his freedom.

Soon after which, Zelda Fitzgerald claimed, he pretty much took over New York, in the early 1920s pouring out the songs that you heard everywhere, or at least everywhere Zelda went. Youmans was spurred by desire to keep up not just with the times but with George Gershwin, his virtual twin in life and a pacesetter, or mechanical rabbit, to a whole generation. "So the son of a bitch thought of it," he'd say after each Gershwin tune. But through the whole decade he kept up nicely with George, writing some great songs in the new bluesy, jazz mode, such as "Time on My Hands" and "More Than You Know," and then actually beating him to a gorgeous slice of the new Latin American territory with the swinging samba "The Carioca," and the best tango ever penned by a gringo, "Orchids in the Moonlight." "That's a lot of song," a friend of mine who is a singing pianist herself claimed as she formed the chords. And it's a good thing, because with the great score of *Flying Down to Rio,* which contains these gems, Youmans stopped. Not quite literally, because he still tried to write. But a double dose of alcohol and TB seem to have affected his judgment, and he thought he should advance in the classical front now and write a ballet—in short, still keep up with the Gershwins, who were currently taking time off to write an opera. Perhaps, as with Donaldson, the Hollywood assembly line had also taken away some of the fun. "Don't you wish it was still 1927?" he wrote to his friendly enemy, but Gershwin was always too busy to look back. And George was still setting the pace on his deathbed in 1937.

Gershwin's death may have taken whatever wind was left out of Vincent's sails, and although Youmans would remain a name to contend with until his own death in 1946, there was an expiration date on him now. As if to make doubly sure, he had actually turned down an offer to make a film out of his life, on the grounds that he wasn't good enough.

Ed Eliscu was right: The man was truly a raging misfit in show business. (Not good enough? The guy must be nuts.) Still, it's always a good time to revive *No, No, Nanette,* which remains incurably young and fresh, or to play Frank Sinatra's version of "Without a Song" and hear two great musical intelligences jamming along the lane together for all eternity.

"Those whom the gods love die young," said the Greeks, although fate had a funny way of proving it to Youmans. But at least his short career has kept his music forever young. It has also left him with the highest batting average—or ratio of hits to misses—in the business. So it's a pleasure to rediscover him and get a sense of how his music exploded into the 1920s, matching the brilliance of the Lower East Side with the best of the Silk Stocking district.

I have already paid tribute to the black and Jewish contributions to these songs, but there was a third, sturdy stream proceeding from the British Isles and emanating in the stomps and reels of the hill country and the tavern singing of New England. "Songs that smile," as the advertisers would call it: "There Is a Tavern in the Town," "Turkey in the Straw," "Too Many Rings Around Rosie." Vincent Youmans, the eternal American misfit, forms a link with the nineteenth-century American songbook, and his rivalry with Gershwin would carry their same sound to the 1950s. To someone like Scott Fitzgerald, Youmans was a classmate who could introduce him to the new thing that was happening. And for anyone unfamiliar with this music, he remains a charming and irresistible starting point.

# Some Names That
# (Almost) Got Away

For years I have lulled myself to sleep conjuring names of songwriters who have written two standards or more. What follows is the product of this labor—nothing definitive about it. It's a list of occasional or full-time swingers from the top of my head on this particular day. Other heads and other days would no doubt yield other lists. Since it usually takes two to make a songwriter, I have appended (in parentheses) the names of lyricists where they seem part of a whole.

RICHARD ADLER AND JERRY ROSS: "Hey There," "Whatever Lola Wants." In a heroic span of just two or three years, this team—who apparently wrote words and music interchangeably—worked in the shadow of Mr. Ross's medical death sentence to finish two classical musicals, *The Pajama Game* and *Damn Yankees*. Mr. Ross died at the age of twenty-nine.

MILTON AGER (Jack Yellen): "I'm Nobody's Baby," "Ain't She Sweet?" "Hard-Hearted Hannah."

FRED AHLERT (Roy Turk): "I'll Get By," "Mean to Me," "Walkin' My Baby Back Home."

HARRY AKST: "Am I Blue," "Dinah," "Baby Face."

LOUIS ALTER: "Do You Know What It Means to Miss New Orleans," "You Turned the Tables on Me," "Manhattan Serenade." Alter studied at the

Boston Conservatory, and was always more a swinging musician than a song-writer proper.

HARRY BARRIS: "Wrap Your Troubles in Dreams," "I Surrender, Dear," "Mississippi Mud." One of the Rhythm Boys, with Bing Crosby and Al Rinker, who probably deserve credits too.

EUBIE BLAKE (Noble Sissle): "I'm Just Wild About Harry," "Memories of You." A long-lived black pianist-entertainer, Blake's a transitional figure who wrote shows called *Shuffle Along, Chocolate Dandies,* and *Blackbirds of 1930*— "Look at me, I'm black" titles that lived on, like occasional blackface itself, right up till World War II. Eubie triumphantly outlived both trends.

RUBE BLOOM: "Day In, Day Out," "Fools Rush In," "Don't Worry 'Bout Me." Bloom was a great jazz pianist and a modest man. "I didn't know that Ruby wrote songs too," said Ellen Donaldson. Yes, indeed. And not just any songs: great ones.

JERRY BOCK: "Too Close for Comfort," "She Loves Me," and a lot of fine songs from *Fiorello!* and *Fiddler on the Roof* that don't quite count.

BROOKS BOWMAN: "East of the Sun (West of the Moon)." Here I break my own (two-standard) rule, but with a note from teacher. Brooks wrote the above classic for Princeton's Triangle Club, signed up with Warner Bros., and promptly died in a car crash after a Princeton-Yale game. I'm willing to put my money where Warners once did, betting on this man's enormous promise. But for tragedy, there had to be more music (and at least one more standard).

SHELTON BROOKS: "Some of These Days," "Darktown Strutters' Ball." See Duke Ellington chapter.

NACIO HERB BROWN (Arthur Freed): *Singin' in the Rain* in toto. Also, "You Stepped out of a Dream." See Hollywood chapter.

JOE BURKE: "Moon Over Miami," "Tiptoe Through the Tulips," "Shoe Shine Boy."

SAUL CHAPLIN: "Please Be Kind," "Until the Real Thing Comes Along."

CON CONRAD: "Margie," "Barney Google," "The Continental." The titles perfectly illustrate the difference between vaudeville, where Conrad began, and movies, where he won his Oscar.

J. FRED COOTS: "You Go to My Head," "For All We Know," "Santa Claus Is Comin' to Town." A gentleman about town and a habitué of the New York Athletic Club. By chance, we shared the same doctor, though years apart. In his final days, he once asked our doctor if he could possibly hurry up, and the doc answered, "I'm dancing as fast as I can." To which J. Fred replied, "Well, I'm dancing with tears in my eyes," thus going down in a volley of song titles.

MATT DENNIS (Tom Adair): "Let's Get Away from It All," "Everything Happens to Me," "Angel Eyes." A protégé of Tommy Dorsey, Dennis was still playing the clubs some fifty years later.

GENE DEPAUL: "I'll Remember April," "Teach Me Tonight," "You Don't Know What Love Is." A latecomer, DePaul began with wartime novelties like "Mr. Five by Five" and "Milkman, Keep Those Bottles Quiet," before going on to the above postmodern beauties.

WALTER DONALDSON: "My Blue Heaven," "Yes Sir, That's My Baby," "Love Me or Leave Me," "Those Little White Lies," and "My Baby Just Cares for Me." See the Coda for more on Donaldson.

VERNON DUKE: "April in Paris," "Autumn in New York," "Taking a Chance on Love." See Gershwin chapter.

SAMMY FAIN: "That Old Feeling," "I'll Be Seeing You," "Secret Love." Not only his name sounds like Tin Pan Alley, so does his work, which is schmaltzy, prolific, versatile—everything but major. In fact, Sammy flopped badly on Broadway, though he could write his own ticket in Hollywood.

FRED FISHER: "Chicago (That Toddling Town)," "Peg o' My Heart," "Your Feet's Too Big."

JOHNNY GREEN: "Body and Soul," "I Cover the Waterfront," "I Wanna Be Loved." A rich kid classically trained, he had graduated from Horace Mann and Harvard by the age of twenty with a major in economics, yet Green wrote with as much soul and gut emotion as anyone on the street. After a meteoric career, he continued to serve music for several years as the musical director at MGM and conductor of the studio orchestra.

MARÍA GREVER: "What a Difference a Day Made," "Magic Is the Moonlight." Ms. Grever was a Mexican, Americanized after the fact by Stanley Adams and I can still hear the Mexican street bands in the background.

RAY HENDERSON: "Bye Bye Blackbird," "The Birth of the Blues," "The Best Things in Life Are Free" (Lew Brown and Buddy DeSylva). The third title is a tough choice because Henderson was one of the great prolifics, and it's hard to turn off the faucet. "Button Up Your Overcoat," "Alabamy Bound," "Life Is Just a Bowl of Cherries." Is this all really the same guy? Yet for all his variety, Alec Wilder's book does not even pay Henderson the compliment of a put-down; it does not mention him once. To an aesthete maturing in the 1920s, Henderson must have personified commercialism. But the pop song is an impure form, and commercialism by itself need not be fatal.

ARTHUR JOHNSTON (Johnny Burke): "Pennies from Heaven," "Just One More Chance," "Moon Song." One of Irving Berlin's brilliant musical secre-taries. Johnston's "Moon Song" is a sublime composition for jazz piano.

ISHAM JONES: "It Had to Be You," "I'll See You in My Dreams," "On the Alamo." A Midwestern coal miner with a Welsh gift of harmony, Jones led one of the great "sweet" bands, which somehow metamorphosed into Woody Her-man's Herd, a postmodern swing band and a joy of my youth.

JERRY LIVINGSTON (not to be confused with Jay "Mona Lisa" "Que Sera, Sera" Livingston): "Blue and Sentimental," "It's the Talk of the Town," and "Under a Blanket of Blue," which opens with the most exquisite series of chords since "Prelude to a Kiss."

MATTY MALNECK: "Goody Goody," "I'm Through with Love," "Stairway to the Stars." A violinist and arranger for Paul Whiteman, and hence an early friend of Crosby and Mercer, which placed him at the heart of a movement-within-a-movement, where he thrived.

GERALD MARKS: "All of Me," "Is It True What They Say About Dixie?"

HUGH MARTIN (Ralph Blane): "Buckle Down, Winsocki," "The Girl Next Door," "Have Yourself a Merry Little Christmas," one of the few defensible Christmas pop songs.

JIMMY McHUGH: "I Can't Give You Anything but Love, Baby," "Don't Blame Me," "A Lovely Way to Spend an Evening." "Professional" is the one word his partner Dorothy Fields used to describe McHugh, and I daresay her succes-sors Frank Loesser and Harold Adamson would have nodded. The son of a plumber, boy Jimmy became what the Brits call a "dogsbody" at the Boston Opera House, improvising on the arias in his spare time and later becoming with Ms. Fields the first writers for Duke Ellington at the Cotton Club, then with Adamson the first writers for Sinatra at the movies. My McHugh kick comes from guessing how the bridge will jump. He's a resourceful chap, and I somehow have a hunch his old man was a good plumber too.

KERRY MILLS: "Meet Me in St. Louis," "At a Georgia Camp Meeting," which is played in old movies but never sung because the old tune celebrates the great black contribution to American minstrels while its words inevitably sound patronizing. Interracial laughter was still up the road.

JIMMY MONACO: "You Made Me Love You," "I've Got a Pocketful of Dreams," "I'm Making Believe." Born in Italy, Monaco wrote the first of these way back in 1912, and had to wait a generation for Harry James and Judy Garland to catch up. Luckily, he had the time, and was still writing hits at Paramount thirty years later.

RAY NOBLE: "The Very Thought of You," "I Hadn't Anyone till You," "Cherokee." An Englishman who "got" the Yank sound perfectly while playing a Brit twit on-screen and radio. He led an all-star band originally handpicked by Glenn Miller before Glenn got a band of his own.

RALPH RAINGER (Leo Robin): "Thanks for the Memory," "Love in Bloom," "June in January." See Hollywood chapter.

HARRY REVEL (Mack Gordon): "Did You Ever See a Dream Walking?" "Stay As Sweet As You Are," "Goodnight, My Love." Another Brit, Revel may hold the record for most songs published that *weren't* standards. He was always good, but seldom memorable.

HARRY RUBY AND BERT KALMAR: See the movie *Three Little Words.*

VICTOR SCHERTZINGER: "I Remember You," "Sand in My Shoes," "Tangerine." A violin prodigy from Pennsylvania who evolved into a movie-producer-cum-songwriter and was still evolving when he died at age fifty-one before his last film, *The Fleet's In,* premiered and introduced two of the above standards to the outside world.

ARTHUR SCHWARTZ: "Alone Together," "You and the Night and the Music," "Louisiana Hayride." See Coda, which discusses Schwartz.

STEPHEN SONDHEIM: "Comedy Tonight," "Everybody Ought to Have a Maid," "Send in the Clowns." Sondheim loves the old songs, and I wish he would write more of them.

SAM STEPT: "All My Life," "That's My Weakness Now," "Please Don't Talk About Me When I'm Gone." Stept also joined another native of Odessa, Lew Brown, and one American, George Tobias, to write the great home-front anthem of World War II, "Don't Sit Under the Apple Tree (with Anyone Else but Me)."

AXEL STORDAHL AND PAUL WESTON: "I Should Care," "Day by Day." Young Frank Sinatra's favorite arranger, Stordahl, and Jo Stafford's husband, the bandleader Weston, dashed these off to see how the other half lived. Too bad they didn't do it more often.

JULE STYNE: "I Don't Want to Walk Without You," "Time After Time," "The Party's Over." The only writer to master the stage completely *after* he'd been a star writer for films, Styne was so prolific sitting at the piano that Sondheim would tell him to back up: Jule had just played through a whole new tune without noticing. By all accounts, Jule was the nicest guy in the business, and one of the few men to finish a show while simultaneously on dialysis *and* handicapping the horses.

KAY SWIFT: "Can't We Be Friends?" "Fine and Dandy." George Gershwin's legendary girlfriend ("There goes the future Kay Swift!") and musical soul mate. Odds are that the two never would have married, but would still be friends.

BOBBY TROUP: "Daddy," "(Get Your Kicks on) Route 66." Troup wrote the former, a hymn to the profit system, while still at the Wharton School of business, but his own best years were unselfishly devoted to helping rehabilitate his wife Julie London from addiction problems and to making her incomparable records of standards as good as they could get. On the other hand, the only kick I could find on Route 66 came from imitating Ezio Pinza at the top of my lungs on what was, back when Troup wrote about it, the loneliest road in Christendom.

ALBERT (GUMM) VON TILZER: "I'll Be with You in Apple Blossom Time," "Oh, by Jingo," "I Used to Love You, but It's All Over Now." His older brother, music publisher Harry (Gumm) von Tilzer, was the famous one, but Albert was the swinger—partly thanks to the Odessan genius Lew Brown, who divined the mythic hold of apples on the American soul and the latent swing in catchwords like "gosh" and "dolly," and indeed "by jingo." I believe the Gumm brothers were related to the Gumm sisters, i.e., to Judy Garland.

FATS WALLER (Andy Razaf): "Ain't Misbehavin'," "Honeysuckle Rose," although I prefer his jazz vamps like "Alligator Crawl" and "The Minor Drag."

Misbehaving was exactly what Fats did, jiving behind the teacher's back and swinging into a Bach cantata for appearances. As a kid in charge of the record player, I found Waller my best compromise with the highbrows who came calling. Fats knew their language—good music—and he spoke to the devil in every man.

MABEL WAYNE: "Ramona," "It Happened in Monterey," "In a Little Spanish Town." Born in Brooklyn, she had private music lessons in Switzerland and became a singer, pianist, and dancer in vaudeville. Clearly, like many women, Ms. Wayne deserves to be much better known.

SPENCER WILLIAMS: "I Ain't Got Nobody," "Basin Street Blues." Along with many black jazz musicians, Williams "made it" in Europe between the wars, writing and adapting jazz classics for Josephine Baker at the Folies-Bergère in Paris, where he was probably more celebrated than Henry Ford and Calvin Coolidge put together.

HARRY WOODS: "When the Red, Red Robin Comes Bob, Bob, Bobbin' Along," "Try a Little Tenderness," "What a Little Moonlight Can Do." Famous for his ferocious temper and his artificial hand, legend has it that someone once saw Woods pounding some poor chap with the latter and said, "So that's the guy that wrote about *tenderness*?"

ALLIE WRUBEL: "Zip-a-Dee-Doo-Dah," "Music, Maestro, Please," "Gone with the Wind." As with the part of Scarlett O'Hara, there was much competition for the use of the famous book title for a song. Mr. Wrubel's excellent entry won, and his son was one of the celebrators at a copyright party I attended more than fifty years later. Once again, the standards had been good to children and grandchildren yet unborn.

VINCENT YOUMANS: "I Want to Be Happy," "Sometimes I'm Happy," "Hallelujah," "Great Day." Could anyone *really* be that happy? See the Coda for more on Youmans.

VICTOR YOUNG: "Stella by Starlight," "Street of Dreams," "I Don't Stand a Ghost of a Chance with You." One more violin prodigy and later a great arranger for Paramount and others, and one of the most musically sophisticated composers ever to embrace this particular form. Incidentally, Young's "Street of Dreams" was allegedly Manhattan's Fifty-second Street, where the jazz jumped and the drugs flowed and the dreams, while they lasted, were the best ever dreamed in America.

# INDEX